Cambridge Studies in Social Anthropology

General Editor: Jack Goody

66

THE MAKING OF THE BASQUE NATION

For other titles in this series, turn to page 264.

The making of the Basque nation

MARIANNE HEIBERG
Norwegian Institute of International Affairs

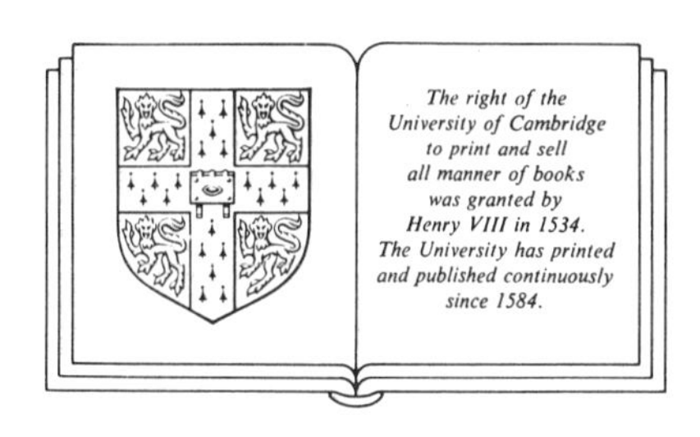

CAMBRIDGE UNIVERSITY PRESS
Cambridge
New York   New Rochelle
Melbourne   Sydney

Published by the Press Syndicate of the University of Cambridge
The Pitt Building, Trumpington Street, Cambridge CB2 1RP
32 East 57th Street, New York, NY 10022, USA
10 Stamford Road, Oakleigh, Melbourne 3166, Australia

First published 1989

Printed in Great Britain at the University Press, Cambridge

British Library cataloguing in publication data

Heiberg, Marrianne
The making of the Basque nation. –
(Cambridge studies in social anthropology).
1. Spain. Basque Provinces. Nationalist
movements, to 1987
I. Title
322.4′2′09466

Library of Congress cataloguing in publication data

Heiberg, Marianne.
The making of the Basque nation.
(Cambridge studies in social anthropology; 66)
Bibliography.
Includes index.
1. Basques – History. 2. Nationalism – Spain –
País Vasco. I. Title. II. Series: Cambridge studies in
anthropology; no. 66)
GN549.B3H45 1989 946′.6 88-23753

ISBN 0 521 36103 6

UP

For Nicolas

Contents

Maps

Preface

A nation is a community of people who consider themselves to be a nation (Seton-Watson: 1977). To create a nation involves a dramatic substitution of diversity with uniformity. People who felt themselves to be culturally distinct and distant must be transformed into a community bound by cultural affinity and solidarity. An array of divergent traditional loyalties must be ruptured, reshuffled and redefined in order to fuse neatly around the boundaries of this community. This monograph is a study of Basque nationalism and the means by which this complex, often violent, political phenomenon created the Basque nation.

To understand Basque nationalism I initially attempted to concentrate on only one manifestation of it – in the first instance, the Basque language schools (*ikastolas*), in the second, nationalism in a specific village. The intention was to use a small-scale study as a means by which to view the Basque movement as a whole. However, this narrow approach yielded a narrow, partial picture. The critical aspect of Basque nationalism remained obscure. This aspect was that Basque nationalism has transformed the culturally diverse human raw material upon which it operated into a national entity. It has endowed this entity with new collective representations and with claims to political rights, most of which are currently recognized by the Spanish state. The more I learned about Basque nationalism the more I became aware that it involved a closed system of belief that produced wide-ranging processes of ideological and political organization, mobilization and legitimation. It was the nature of those beliefs and of the processes generated by their logic that I wanted to understand. In consequence, I felt forced to adopt a telescopic, rather than microscopic approach to my subject.

Although I have regularly visited the Basque country since 1969, my main research was based on two periods of fieldwork. The initial period took place in the summer of 1971 when I lived in a village near San Sebastian. The purpose of this field trip was to collect information for a postgraduate dissertation. In addition to the valuable material assembled at this time, I gained enduring personal contacts that were to prove crucial for the success of my second period of fieldwork.

I returned to the Basque country in February 1975 and remained until September 1976. While the Basque country during 1971 was relatively peaceful, during my second period in the field the Basque country was convulsed by a level of violence unparalleled in the post-civil war era. The period corresponded roughly to the two years surrounding the death of General Francisco Franco in November 1975. During these two years in the Basque country more than 140 people died through political violence. Many thousands of people were arrested for politically motivated offences and there was convincing evidence that a large portion of these were subjected to torture. This violence was a constant part of my fieldwork and had serious effects on the manner in which my research was conducted.

My research proceeded on three levels. First, I cautiously expanded my contacts with urban nationalists in Bilbao and San Sebastian in order to build the networks required to operate with some mobility inside Basque political circles. Because of the bitter polarization between Basque nationalist and non-nationalist groups, the possibilities of maintaining close contacts with individuals on both sides of this political cleavage were few. The boundary between the two political camps was like a semi-permeable membrane. Free movement from the nationalist camp to the non-nationalist one was permitted. Free movement the other way around was very difficult indeed. Therefore, I chose to work almost exclusively with Basque nationalists during the first part of my field research and work with non-nationalists only towards the end of my field period. Eventually leaders and supporters from all Basque political groups were interviewed – many in depth – and detailed biographies of numerous political and cultural activists were obtained. Second, I carried out a study of the village of Elgeta, where I lived for most of the nineteen months spent in the field. Members of the family with whom I lived were among the leading activists in village affairs and helped introduce me to the more covert aspects of village life. Third, background material on various historical, economic, linguistic and demographic aspects of the Basque country was collected from a range of sources. These included official publications, newspapers, archives and interviews with Basque historians, agronomists, economists and so forth.

I am aware that for the anthropologist the incorporation of historic materials is often a risky affair. Lacking both the appropriate training and time to do primary research, the anthropologist is thrown back onto secondary sources. In this context any endeavour to understand Basque history seemed particularly risky. The Basque political world was sharply polarized into opposing camps – the nationalist and non-nationalist. Each possessed a distinct interpretation of Basque history used to underwrite and justify current political attitudes and positions. Moreover, much of Basque historical research has been conducted with this explicitly political aim in mind. Historical discussions among Basques were usually highly emotional affairs. In rough, general terms the two versions of Basque history can be summarized as follows:

(1) Because of their unique language and culture, the Basques have always been a people apart; a nationality which has struggled over the centuries to defend its political autonomy and, thereby, its cultural heritage. This constant resistance in order to survive culturally can best be seen in the Basques' staunch defence of their *fueros*, Basque traditional rights which had their core in custom – in the fabric of traditional society. The various Basque regions were themselves autonomous with each region enjoying an autonomous political apparatus. The alliances and political links between these regions and especially between the Basque region as a whole and Castile were voluntary pacts entered into by juridically sovereign and equal partners. These pacts were seen as dissolvable because sovereignty, although partially delegated, was never surrendered. Internally, Basque society was an egalitarian one even though sharp economic differences were recognized. It was free from rigid social stratification and permanent class differences. The political system – a sort of 'peasant democracy' – ensured real political participation for all Basques. Moreover, this equality was explicitly emphasized in the *fuero* which extended the status of nobility to all Basques. The dynamic behind Basque history can best be understood in terms of the continual drive of the Basques to maintain both their autonomy and their egalitarian mode of life.

(2) In the context of the slow emergence and development of Spain as a politically unified entity, the Basque country, given certain economic peculiarities, was as integrated into this wider political entity as the other regions of Spain. The Basque *fueros*, similar to the *fueros* of other regions, were by no means Basque primordial rights which, among other things, guaranteed Basque liberties. They were concessions from the kings of Castile. Basque society was strictly stratified with control of both economic and political power in the hands of small élites. Due to changing circumstances, these various élites (urban, rural, local, provincial, etc.) pursued a strategy of complex and shifting alliances in order to defend their vested interests which at times brought them into conflict and at times into collusion both in regard to each other and to the Madrid political centre.

In spite of their apparent irreconcilability, I believe that these two images refer to different aspects of Basque history and that both are partially valid. I shall suggest that inside the Basque country two opposed but overlapping social orders have existed side by side since the Middle Ages – the one urban, Hispanicized, complex, prosperous and powerful and the other, encompassing the vast majority of the population, rural, *Euskaldun* (Basque-speaking), relatively impoverished and largely impotent to affect events in the wider world. In the Basques' own view this basic cultural opposition is conceived in terms of *kaletarak* (those from the street, i.e. urban dwellers) and *baserritarak* (those from the farmsteads). The coexistence of discrete urban and rural cultures has deep historical roots in the Basque country. The nationalist version of Basque history looks primarily to rural society where the ideas of social equality and cultural distinctiveness have been deeply embedded. In the non-nationalist version the motor of Basque history resides in the urban centres.

Modern Basque society has been shaped by the intricate, fluctuating relationship between these two traditionally antagonistic orders. The Basque nation has been shaped by their merger.

Rather than give a general overview of Basque history, the historical material presented here will attempt to delineate certain specific historical themes that become critical with the emergence of Basque nationalism. These are: (1) the historical relationship between the Basque country and the rest of Spain; (2) the nature and evolution of the foral regime, the Basque traditional political system; (3) the emergence and development of the Basque bourgeoisie; (4) the social and economic evolution of the rural areas and (5) the process of industrialization.

Many people have contributed to the making of this book. In the Basque country I am particularly indebted to Javier Corcuera, Yolanda Iturbe, Gotzone Echebarria and José Gorriti who shared with me their abundant knowledge of Basque life and who have become enduring friends. I should also like to express my gratitude to Xavier Amuriza, Julio Caro Baroja, Dionysio Blanco, Jon Lopategui, Abel Muniategui and Juan San Martin for their constant support and intelligent counsel. My debt to the people of Elgeta, who tolerated my presence during a very difficult period, can never be repaid. In particular, the family of Don Marcelo Basauri, the family of Don Modesto Elcoro and the *cuadrilla* of Patxi Basauri made my stay in the village a deeply rewarding experience.

There is an original debt of gratitude to Dr Peter Loizos who generously nurtured my initial interest in nationalism and under whose aegis I first began to think seriously about the subject. I gratefully acknowledge the kindness of Professor Julian Pitt-Rivers whose unfailing efforts on my behalf made it possible for me to carry out research and whose valuable insights into the Mediterranean and the Basques helped guide my research.

My main intellectual debt, however, is to Professor Ernest Gellner whose work is basic to my understanding of nationalism and who year after year patiently supervised the preparation of my doctoral thesis upon which this book is based.

Finally I wish to thank Manu Escudero.

Financial support for the field research upon which this thesis is based was provided by the Social Science Research Council, London.

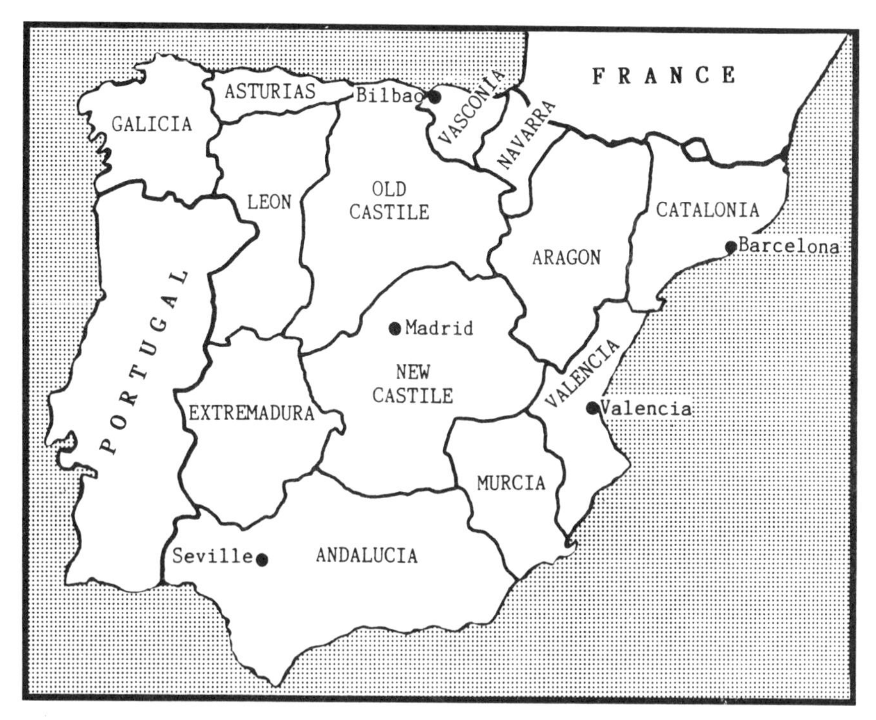

Map 1 The historical regions of Spain

Introduction: empire and the emergence of Spain

Spain, or rather, 'the Spains in their pluralistic unity' (Vicens Vives, 1970:32), was born out of the Reconquista (718–1611). She arose from an unstable alliance of independent Christian kingdoms stretching in a line from Galicia to Catalonia pushing southward against the Islamic invaders. The initial unifying idea behind Spain was that of Christian opposition to the Muslim threat. Unlike Navarra, Leon, Aragon and Catalonia, Castile was a product of the Reconquista. She had no prior separate political existence. Castile was part of the repopulated areas and her dominant classes consisted of Basques, Cantabrians, Aragonese and so forth. In short, Castile was an amalgam of the peripheral ethnic and regional groups over which Castile in turn attempted to assert authority.

Neither the Catholic kings (1469–1516) nor their descendants, the Habsburgs (1516–1700) tried to force a unified royal administration upon the Iberian peninsula. The Basque provinces, Navarra, Catalonia and Aragon maintained distinct legal codes (*fueros*) and autonomous political institutions. This disparate political arrangement was institutionalized in the *Pacto Monárquico* which granted formal recognition to and respect for the autonomy of the different regions under the Castillian Crown. Moreover, the Spanish regions were regarded as having a contractual rather than subordinate position to the central, royal authority.

Whereas Spain's political institutions gave substantial guarantees for regional autonomy, the degree of autonomy the regions actually exercised has been frequently exaggerated. Here the role of Spain's empire must be mentioned. Imperial expansion generated considerable social and political integration in Spain. It imposed a type of organic solidarity.

A critical element in the imperial endeavour which was of benefit to all Spain's regions was military control over the seas and colonies. This requirement demanded the mobilization of human and material resources well beyond the capacity of any single region. The Spanish state in general and Madrid in particular owed their prestige and coherence as a political framework and centre to their ability to fulfil this requirement. But, as importantly, each region in Spain had different, specialized imperial ambitions. The Basque country was oriented toward the Americas. Castile looked toward North Africa, America and the centre of Europe. Aragon and Catalonia turned toward the Mediterranean. However, the realization of these specialized overseas ambitions and interests required cooperation and social integration between the regions. Thus, the requirements and benefits of empire forged an extensive urban and administrative network throughout Spain that linked the country socially, economically and politically.

When Spain began to lose control over the mechanisms of imperial power – for example, naval supremacy – and, thereby, lose control over her composite empire, the bases of Spanish unity – and prosperity – were also eroded. The need for a more explicit administrative unification to replace this organic solidarity became acutely apparent. However, a more formal, stable unity was only possible if Spain's diverse regions were able to perceive their specific economic interests in terms of metropolitan Spain herself. A successful political centralization was dependent on the pre-condition of some form of Spanish internal economic unity. It was to this goal – political centralization and the formation of an internal market – that the Bourbons in the eighteenth century and, more energetically, the liberals in the nineteenth addressed themselves. The fact that a satisfactory economic and political alternative had not emerged to substitute for empire when it finally collapsed in 1898 lay close to the heart of what was to become Spain's intractable regional problem.

But the obstacles to modern state formation in Spain were formidable. They were not just confined to the temptation to allow the enormous spoils derived from empire to delay an inevitable confrontation with political realities. An obdurate obstacle to change lay in the nature of the imperial state itself.

Imperial Spain was Counter-Reformation Spain; and the wealth of the colonies disappeared into opulent churches and the support of swollen bureacracies. Catholic dogma and the entire massive structure of the Church had been reanimated and extended. Whereas, in Reformation Europe the state had been trimmed down through reform or revolution, in Spain the 'Renaissance State' with its ever multiplying and increasingly parasitic bureaucracy remained largely intact (H. R. Trevor-Roper, 1956:78–79). Indeed the sale of official office and bureaucratic posting was a major source of state revenue. These officials produced little, being dependent upon those who did, whom they exploited and regulated until the producers of wealth emigrated.

Bourbon reforms and state centralization

The accession in 1700 of the Bourbon dynasty to the Spanish throne marked the beginnings of a serious attempt to overhaul the Spanish state and society.

Spain was fragmented. Lacking any overall political control, each region, religious order and social sector was locked in a continual process of confrontation as specific interests were pursued and the idea of a general interest remained non-existent. Economic development was plagued by a massive waste of resources. Two-thirds of all land was held by the nobility and Church in entail and mortmain and a large part of the active male population (30 per cent according to the 1797 census) was employed in unproductive activities (Carr, 1966:39). Moreover, aristocratic privilege and local autonomies combined to create a motley taxation system which left the state economically anaemic. Arguably, in a society where political and economic attitudes disregarded and scorned the vocation of wealth production and industry and emphasized the values of heroism, luck and prestige, economic development simply was not a possibility.

The reform-minded ministers and civil servants assembled by the Bourbon monarchy were the architects of a political vision and social programme which would form the inheritance of nineteenth-century liberalism. As Raymond Carr has pointed out (1966:62), uniform centralization was the administrative precondition of all other reforms. Philip V (1700–46) managed to abolish the special privileges and local *fueros* of most of Spain's regions – including Catalonia – between 1706 and 1714. However, the *fueros* of the Basque country and Navarra, which had given much-needed support to Bourbon claims during the Spanish War of Succession, remained intact and constituted the major challenge to administrative unity.

Spanish 'Enlightenment' reached its peak during the reign of Charles III (1759–85). Inspired by notions of utility and felicity and appalled by the chronic poverty of much of the countryside, Bourbon bureaucrats proposed a series of radical agrarian, Church and education reforms which were crucial for their centralizing mission (and which in 1931 had still to be carried out) (Carr, 1966:62). According to the theory, these reforms were to provide proof that the national welfare could best be served by strengthening the power of the Crown and the central state (Clissold, 1969:96).

However, Bourbon attempts at enlightened reform and state centralization failed dismally. It was a failure that marked the end of Spain's *ancien régime*. Some of the reasons lay inside the regime itself. The over-staffed and paper-loving administrative apparatus was incapable of effective, concerted action of any kind. The increasing power of the Crown degenerated into an increasing dependency on the calibre of the king's ministers (Clissold, 1969:96). The weakness of enlightened despotism became personified in Godoy, the extremely unpopular and resented prime minister of Carlos IV (1788–1808). Godoy accumulated more personal political power than any other Spanish political figure with the possible exception of General Franco.

Just as importantly, Castile's striving to exert her hegemony over the

Spanish periphery coincided with the stagnation of the Castilian economy and the renewed prosperity of the peripheral areas. Succession of the Bourbon dynasty had led to a reinforcement of commercial links between Spain and Europe and helped a 'take-off' in both Basque and Catalan commerce (Laborda Martin, 1978:137). But Spain's mercantile empire was contingent on her ability to maintain political control over her American colonies and military control over the seas. The independence movements in the Americas, disastrous war with England (1796–1802) and Napoleon's invasion of the Iberian peninsula effectively defeated Spain's commercial aspirations. Although all Spain's regions suffered the economic consequences, Castile was the least able to respond. The Castilian wool trade, the backbone of her economy, crumbled. Castile had no other commodities which she could profitably feed to overseas markets.

In contrast to Madrid, the periphery at the end of the eighteenth century was experiencing rapid demographic growth, rising wages and forced commercial and industrial modernization. The tensions resulting from peripheral economic vitality and Castilian sluggishness would lie near the heart of the Catalan 'question' and the Basque 'problem'.

However, the Bourbon regime's problems were not confined solely to economic ones. The fatal flaws were political.

The War of Independence and the failure of liberalism

The reign of Carlos IV and Godoy had been disgraced by its foreign adventures, the loss of the American market, the subsequent economic depression and ministerial dictatorship. Napoleon's drive into Spain offered the opportunity for its overthrow. In 1808, the year of the Spanish uprising against the French invaders, the initial struggle was concerned with liberating Spain from Godoy rather than from Napoleon's troops (Vicens Vives, 1970:122). Under the force of popular pressure Carlos IV abdicated and Napoleon set about imposing an efficient administration, a liberal constitution (the Constitution of Bayonne) and a new king, Joseph I.

The popular reaction came on 2 May 1808. The revolution of *dos de mayo* had two motives. The obvious one was to oust the French in the name of Spanish sovereignty. But the revolution also provided the means by which the monarchy could be reoriented and restricted so as to prevent a reoccurrence of the despotic excesses of the past (Vicens Vives, 1970:122). With the state apparatus in chaos and the traditional ruling classes attempting to accommodate the French, the prime movers of the rebellion were the lower classes who made their first dramatic entry onto the Spanish political scene and frightened Spain's established orders as much as they did Murat. Moreover, new types of men – military officials with political ambitions, financial speculators, intellectuals, local gentry and rhetoricians – quickly assumed leadership and power.

One product of the situation in 1808 was the emergence of regionalism as a political factor. The Spain of the War of Independence was a type of federal republic (Carr, 1966:91). Resistance was organized – to the extent that it was organized at all – by provincial *juntas* (assemblies) which functioned as sovereign states and often displayed as much hostility toward each other as they did to the French. But the leaders of the *juntas* were not separatists; they aimed at reform and social renovation and, thus, saw the need to reestablish some sort of centralized order. A Supreme Central *Junta* was organized and the reformers convened a constituent *cortes* (parliament) in Cadiz. The result of their deliberations was the Constitution of 1812 which attempted to transform and modernize Spain's entire political structure.

The War of Independence created an opportune moment for far-reaching change. W. C. Atkinson has argued (1960:263) that the *de facto* vacancy of the throne and the total collapse of traditional society made new concepts of national unity possible. The Constitution of 1812 affirmed that national sovereignty was to reside in the people rather than the King and a division of powers between parliament and Crown was imposed. Proportional representation, a complex version of universal suffrage and a uniform tax structure were proposed. Moreover, the constitution aimed at the elimination of special feudal and regional jurisdictions, abolition of internal customs lines and the disentailment of the common lands. Although Catholicism was reaffirmed as the state religion, the Holy Office was suppressed. Liberty, equality and property were the new God-given, natural rights. It was to become the classic nineteenth-century liberal constitution.

But Spanish liberalism failed majestically. The central vision of liberalism was the construction of a political and economic framework for a modern bourgeois society. Politically, it sought constitutional unity as a means of transferring power away from the realms of sectoral and regional privilege into the hands of Spain's middle classes. Economically, liberalism insisted upon the establishment of absolute individual property rights as a means of stimulating production and creating a viable internal market. Influenced by the 'ideas and armies of the French Revolution' (Carr, 1966:79), the main ideological assumption underlying these considerations was the idea of national sovereignty, of Spanish nationalism.

Liberalism did achieve certain partial successes. A uniform educational system was established and fiscal and administrative uniformity imposed. Limited social welfare legislation was enacted and Spain received the rudiments of a national communication system of roads and railways.

Although liberals saw their reformist tasks as both socially liberating and economically urgent for the national welfare, the concrete effects of liberalism were not as selfless and patriotic. Gerald Brenan has commented (1969: 109) that liberalism handed the Spanish peasantry over to a new class of exploitative landlords. 'Liberalism... united to a swarm of lawyers, tradesmen and petty capitalists anxious to enrich themselves by cultivating land, brought this about. This is the class that since 1843 has held political power in Spain – a middle class enriched not by trade or industry but by ownership of land...' Certainly the major goals of liberalism – such as an agrarian reform and the consolidation of Spanish nationhood – were never achieved.

Among the more basic reasons for the fiasco of Spanish liberalism was that the centrepiece of a bourgeois revolution – an increasingly influential national middle class based in industry and modern commerce who possessed certain attitudes to life and politics – did not exist. This type of bourgeoisie only developed in Catalonia and the Basque country. The lack of capital, entrepreneurial skills and technology made the emergence of a solid Spanish – as opposed to local or regional – middle class impossible.

These same factors severely restricted the creation of an internal market. However, an additional, major barrier lay in the agrarian problem. Without agrarian reform the majority of Spaniards simply could not be brought into a market economy. Peasants had to be transformed into consumers in a modern sense. And agrarian reform required a political power and unity the liberals lacked.

Although liberalism strengthened and broadened the functions of the Spanish state, it could never overcome the fragmented nature of Spanish society. The idea of a cohesive Spanish nationalism crumbled upon a new form of intrusive state aimed at protecting shifting conglomerations of local vested interest groups. With the empire lost, this state, centred in economically stagnant Castile, was no longer viewed as a source of economic benefit or as an essential requirement for the country's more dynamic peripheries. This failure of Spanish nationalism to provide Madrid with a moral authority and Spanish citizens with an overarching and binding political identity was the background upon which Basque nationalism grew.

At the end of the nineteenth century when the two most tenacious illustrations of Spanish fragmentation made their first serious bid for separate national status, the Spanish state was incoherent and dislocated. Unlike London, Paris or even Berlin, Madrid was unable to transform the people over which it governed into Spaniards. The core problem was not, paraphrasing Eugen Weber, of turning peasants into Spaniards, although this too was a serious matter. Madrid was unable to endow the identity of 'Spaniard' with advantages and a dignity that outweighted the identity of 'Basque' or 'Catalan'.

Modern Spain – the Spain, still devastated by the War of Independence, that arose with the first liberal constitution of 1812 – was born politically defective and divided. During the last 170 years or so there have been two Spains as partly different polarities have succeeded each other. First, the absolutist and constitutional gave way to the arch-conservative and progressive which was finally replaced by the rightist and leftist (Farias, 1975: 19). Until very recently, Spain has lacked a political centre and consensus that would have provided a stabilizing buffer for the violent competition between the two antagonistic blocks into which the country was divided. Throughout the nineteenth century various versions of liberalism clashed with the vestiges of dynastic absolutism for control over an unstable political order. The country was shattered by revolts, civil wars, and dozens of *pronunciamientos* (military uprisings) by disaffected generals who felt they could run Spain better than unscrupulous, inept politicians. Typically the first act of Fernando VII upon his return to Spain in 1814 as a constitutional monarch was to abolish the constitution, reestablish the *fueros* and restore pure absolutism.

PART 1

From plurality to Basque ethnic solidarity

1

The Basques in history

The two regions that developed the most aggressive and confident nationalist movements in Spain – the Basque country and Catalonia – had many features in common which set them apart from the rest of Iberia. Both enjoyed a relatively prosperous agricultural base characterized by medium-sized landholdings, security of tenure, polyculture, dispersed residential patterns and an inheritance system that transmitted the rural farmstead intact to only one heir. Both were in direct geographical contact with Europe and developed powerful mercantile classes which were enthusiastic recipients of European technical and ideological innovations. Finally, during the nineteenth century both experienced an industrial take-off. In Catalonia and the Basque country industrialization was managed by a native industrial bourgeoisie and generated a politically militant proletariat of mixed regional origins. Despite these similarities, however, Basque and Catalan nationalism are very different political creatures.

The Basque country – or Euskalherria – runs along the Bay of Biscay. It extends from Bayonne in the northeast to just west of Bilbao and, straddling both sides of the Pyrenees, cuts inland some 200 km. This hilly, luxuriant region, whose densely green appearance belies an infertile soil, is composed of seven provinces: Guipúzcoa (*Gipuzkoa*), Vizcaya (*Bizkaia*), Alava (*Araba*), Soule (*Zuberoa*), Basse-Navarre (*Baxanabarra*) and Labourd (*Lapurdi*).[1] Covering slightly more than 20,000 km^2, the region contains 2,376,134 inhabitants (1974 census) of which about 90% live in the Spanish Basque country and the remainder in France. Divided politically between two states, Euskalherria is divided geographically by two massive mountain ranges. The Pyrenees separate the French Basques from their Spanish counterparts. The Cantabrian cuts Guipúzcoa and Vizcaya off from Navarra and Alava as well as from the rest of Spain. The Basque country has no sharp physical boundaries. Alava and southern Navarra have the climate and landscape of the Castilian meseta into which they smoothly merge.

Theories and arguments concerning the origins of the Basques and how the Basques can be defined in cultural terms as an exclusive and separate group are numerous. The origins of Euskera, the Basque language, remain

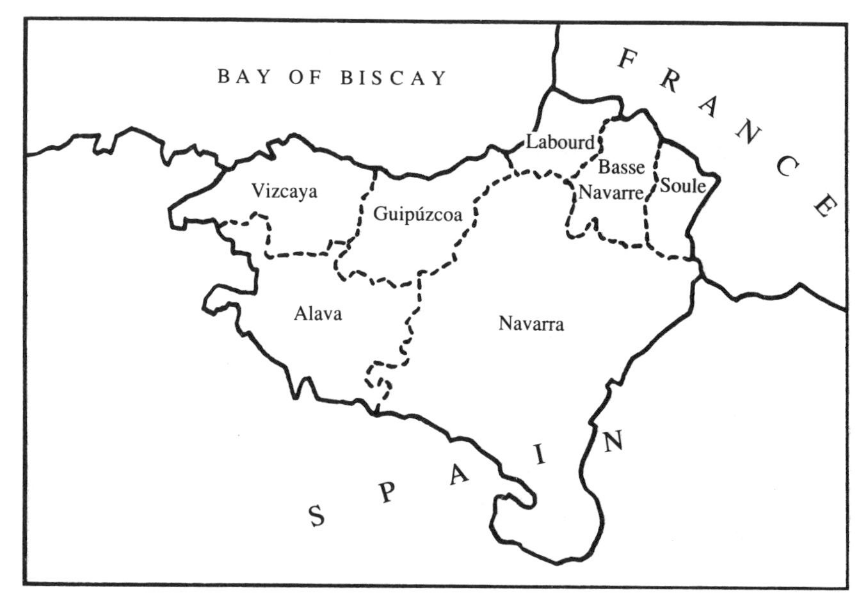

Map 2 Euskalherria

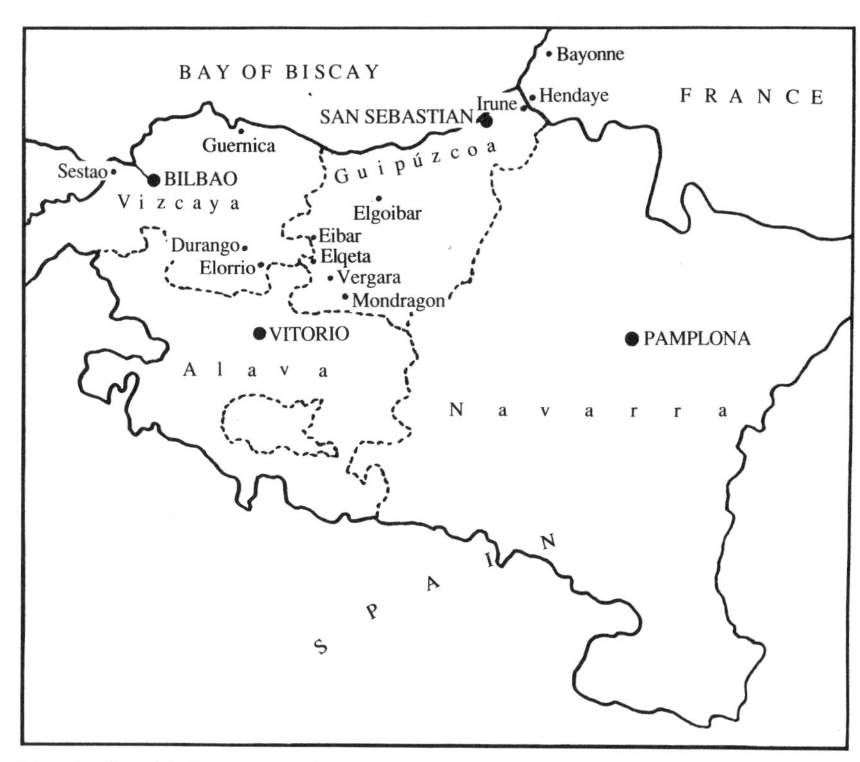

Map 3 Spanish Basque provinces

unknown and firm correlations between Euskera and other known languages have still to be demonstrated. In 1825 the Abbot Diharce de Bidassouet argued that Euskera was the original language of the Creation and, therefore, the only language spoken before the Tower of Babel.[2] Manuel de Larramendi, who in the eighteenth century compiled the first Basque dictionary, claimed more modestly that Euskera was one of the seventy-five languages that emerged after the Tower of Babel (cited in R. Gallop, 1948:10).

More recently linguists have shown structural similarities between Euskera and some of the Hamitosemitic languages of North Africa, especially Berber and various languages of the Caucasus mountains in Georgia. In the early 1970s several Soviet linguists reaffirmed linguistic kinship between Georgians and the Basques. Some, for example Alexei Mandeleyev and Alexander Kiknadze, suggest that the Basques may have originally come from Georgia from which they migrated around 1500 BC. This theory conflicts with earlier ones such as those of Collignon (1894) and Aranzadi (1905). The former, examining Basque recruits to the French army, argued that the Basques were the descendants of an autochthonous Pyrenean race modified by the successive invasions of the Iberian peninsula. Aranzadi, on the other hand, suggested that the Basques were a local variant of a wider family of south-west European peoples.

Physical anthropologists, also attracted to Basque peculiarities, have shown that the Basques have a higher incidence of RH – and blood group O and much lower incidence of blood group B than any other European population (Goti Iturriago, 1962:39–65) although considerable variations seem to exist between the French and Spanish Basques on all these indicators.[3] Regardless of academic speculation, most Basques view themselves proudly as Europe's oldest and, they claim, purest surviving race.

Basques regard themselves as forming a single cultural unit cemented by a distinctive race and language. Especially in the rural countryside dotted by *baserriak* – the Basque farmsteads – the architecture, forms of dress, modes of agricultural exploitation and, of course, the language spoken are in marked contrast to the surrounding non-Basque areas of France and Spain. However, since early historical times Basque society has been a complex one. Stanley Payne (1974:47–48) states: 'Historically the Basques are, without doubt, an amalgam of various primitive ethnic groups of the western Pyrenees: their unity based in language and culture... they spoke an ample variety of tribal dialects of Euskera which in some cases were mutually unintelligible...'

Whatever linguistic and cultural unity existed among the Basques was, however, irreversibly disrupted by the process of urbanization which was initiated in the twelfth century. For political and commercial reasons the kings of Navarra and later Castile founded numerous mercantile and administrative centres in the Basque region. Located along the pilgrimage route to Santiago de Compostela or articulating landlocked Castile to the sea, these new towns were often populated by a high proportion of non-Basques. Towns with Castilian names of Villafranca and Salvatierra are as much an historical part of Basque geography as villages called Ormaiztegi and Egiarreta.

As these towns were created, however, so was the tension and conflict between Basque rural areas and the urban centres. While the language of the countryside was Euskera, the political and cultural language of the towns was Spanish, French or Latin. In short, from very early times the Basque country has been populated by two culturally differentiated, but inextricably linked, types of people each operating in a different economic, political and social context. The agriculturalists of the rural areas were largely undifferentiated in terms of economic activities and probably egalitarian in outlook, while those in the urban centres were characterized by specialization and social hierarchies.

Integration of Basque territories into Castile and the foral regime

The earliest accounts of political organization among the Basques are those of the Greek and Roman geographers, especially Strabo (born c.63 BC) and Ptolemy (born second century AD). They described four different tribes who spoke various dialects of Euskera and all of which enjoyed a reputation for ferocity, brutality and paganism. Mainly pastoralists, these tribes gradually expanded toward the east, the area of western Aragon, and during the sixth century there was considerable migration of one tribe, the Vascones, over the Pyrenees into the region of southwestern France later referred to as Gascuña (the name derived from the Roman word, *gascón*, meaning Basque). Political organization appears to have centred on obscure lineage heads.

The Roman administrative centre was established in Pamplona and relations between the Romans, who were never very numerous, and these various Basque tribes were in general amicable. The notion of Roman imperial sovereignty was accepted in exchange for Roman disinterest in this remote, mountainous territory. Moreover, Roman civilization was totally confined to the cities. Basque culture in the countryside was little affected.

With the collapse of Roman supremacy came successive onslaughts of Germanic peoples through the passes of the western Pyrenees which Vicens Vives (1970:50) has described as 'the eternal route of Europe's great racial contributions to Hispania'. Most important were the Visigoths. Although the Visigoths were to occupy Pamplona, they never managed to gain a real foothold in the Basque country. The Visigothic period, however, witnessed the first significant intrusions of Christianity into the pagan north. Converted to Catholicism in 589, the Visigothic state delegated a key role to the Church in mediating between the increasingly isolated Gothic oligarchy and the surrounding peoples (Vicens Vives, 1970:25–27).

The early political evolution of the Basque country is intimately linked to its role as a frontier area. The history of the Basque country as a definable and distinct political territory began with the Muslim invasion of the Hispanic peninsula and that long push of Christian retaliation – the Reconquest. Vicens Vives (1970:32), describing this historical period, writes:

> At that moment the Spains, in their pluralistic unity, were born. Along a line from Galicia to Catalonia ... they were like great rocks jutting up out of the waters, bearing witness to the Islamic tide – these enclaves of Christians began their career in history.

Like the Goths before them, Muslim infiltration into the north-western reaches of the peninsula was limited. In 732 al-Andalus forces entered Pamplona on their way to do unsuccessful battle with the Frankish empire across the Pyrenees. Directly or indirectly Pamplona was under Muslim rule for the remainder of the eighth century. In the Basque region three nuclei of Christian faith existed: one in Pamplona itself, another in Alava, and the most famous for its intellectual brilliance in Leyre to the east of Pamplona. These centres provided focal points in the struggle to maintain independence from Muslim supremacy.

In the southern part of Navarra an autonomous principality was formed under the ruling dynasty of Banu Quasi, descendants of a local Gothic noble. Converted to Islam in 714 and allied to the al-Andalus of Cordoba, representatives of this dynasty governed in Pamplona until the end of the eighth century. Through a complex series of political manoeuvres, assassinations and armed confrontations, rule by the Banu Quasi was overthrown by Navarrese loyal to the Franks who in short order were overthrown by Iñigo Aritza, a Vascon by birth and Christian by faith, who at the beginning of the ninth century founded the independent principality of Pamplona later to become the Kingdom of Navarra. One century later this principality had expanded to cover a large part of the Basque country. Navarra, then the dominant power in Christian Spain, was to be at the spearhead of the Reconquest.

Navarra[4]

Federico de Zabala (1971:103–13) argues that with the disintegration of the Roman empire and its unifying mantle, the Vascones evolved an increasingly complex and stable political organization in order to respond to the perpetual threats posed by the wars with the Visigoths, Franks and Muslims. The social organization of the Basques, Zabala continues, was based on clans divided into lineages with each level of organization headed by a *buruzagi* or *aide nagusia* (lit. superior kinsman). The *buruzagiak* (plural-ak.) were responsible for the defence of lineage property and territory. Because of its inherent instability, Zabala suggests this form of organization was insufficient to compete with the powerful, disciplined armies of the enemy. With the Visigoths and Muslims providing the models, an indisputable military organization became regarded as essential in order to consolidate and direct the attack against the successive waves of invaders. Unlike the Asturian monarchy which consisted of the remnants of the Visigothic aristocracy imposed upon the local population, the Navarrese monarchy evolved from the Basque social structure at a particular historical moment because of an external danger and the influence of a new culture. From the little information that exists, Iñigo Aritza would appear to have been a lineage chief with considerable military skills. However, his authority and, therefore, the boundaries of the Principality of Pamplona, seem initially to have been recognized only by the Vascon clans.

The Church played a decisive role in the consolidation of the new monarchy. While militarily Navarra was trapped between the Muslim empire to the south and the Frankish to the north, culturally this geographical encirclement placed Navarra in a privileged position. The numerous monasteries in the region had become a refuge for Hispanic Christendom while simultaneously they became increasingly inspired by and active transmitters of the intellectual innovations of the Carolingian renaissance and later the Cluniac reforms. The Church gave enthusiastic support to this new Christian state in return for considerable influence over it. As a result the Navarrese monarchy adopted 'modern' notions concerning political organization, administrative and commercial techniques, and military technology as well as religious policies (Payne, 1974:53). In the process Navarra was transformed into the most advanced of the Hispanic Christian states.

It was Sancho Garcés III, the Great (999–1035) who brought Navarra to her pinnacle of power and territorial expansion and made Navarra into what the historian Sanchez Albornoz has called 'the grandmother of today's Spain'. With the collapse of the Caliphate in Cordoba, Navarra expanded eastward into the former Arab domains of Aragon, Sobrarbe and Ribagorza stopping only at the boundaries of the Catalan territories. In the same year as he ascended to the throne, Sancho Garcés III, whose mother was of the royal family of León, married the daughter of the Count of Castile. The Count, upon his death in 1007, left a seven-year-old son as his only heir. Sancho was duly appointed 'protector' of Castile. When his young nephew was assassinated in 1028, Sancho incorporated Castile into the Kingdom of Navarra. Sancho also occupied the eastern part of the Kingdom of León. When León declared war on Navarra, Sancho made a triumphal entry into

León. With his kingdom stretching from León to the frontiers of Catalonia, Sancho declared himself 'King of all the Spains'.

Because of the prestige gleaned from his victories against the Muslims and his territorial aggrandizement, Sancho III was also granted the loyalty of and accepted as sovereign by the various *buruzagiak* (lineage heads) in Alava, Guipúzcoa and Vizcaya as well as by *buruzagiak* in many Basque areas on the French side of the Pyrenees (Zabala, 1971: 119). Hence, not only was all of Christian Spain, with the exception of Catalonia, united under the Navarrese Crown, but most of the Basque-speaking regions were consolidated – for the first and only time in their history – under one political jurisdiction.

However, the empire forged by Sancho III, the Great, did not survive his death in 1035. Viewing Navarra as his personal patrimony, Sancho's testament fragmented the Kingdom of Navarra into its component territories and distributed them between his four sons. In the process two new kingdoms – those of Castile and Aragon – were formed. The new monarchs of Castile and Aragon, younger brothers of the heir to the Navarrese Crown, immediately rejected Navarrese sovereignty. Enclosed by Aragon and Castile, and thus denied the possibility of further territorial expansion, Navarra from the eleventh century onward entered a period of isolation and rapid territorial dismemberment. Weakened by civil war and economic disasters, Navarra, reduced to its present boundaries, became caught in the war between Castile and France. She was invaded by Castile in 1512 and finally annexed to the unified Spanish Crown by Fernando V. French Navarra remained an independent kingdom until 1620. However, the Catholic kings did not exercise significant direct power in Navarra. Organized as a viceroyalty, Navarra retained its own independent constitution, court and *fueros* until 1842.

Alava

While Navarra constituted a discrete political territory from the ninth century onwards, the formation of the remaining three Spanish Basque provinces is less precise. Alava is first mentioned in the eighth century. During the eighth and the early part of the ninth century, the Asturian monarchy seems to have exercised a tenuous hold over Alava. Perhaps due to its position as a political hinterland caught between the emerging Christian states, the countryside of Alava contained numerous fortifications under the control of local nobles whose main function was initially military, but who later developed into an hereditary landed aristocracy. Alava, either as a whole or in parts, oscillated between the orbits of Castilian and Navarrese control and was incorporated at various times into both monarchies.

The central political structure of Alava was an assembly known as the *Cofradia de Arriaga*. The first documents concerning this *Cofradia* date from 1285, but the *Cofradia de Arriaga* probably was of earlier origin (Zabala, 1977a:141). Alava as a political unit could be defined as the territory over which the *Cofradia* held traditional jurisdiction. The *Cofradia* consisted of representatives from the various social sectors of Alava society – the clergy, nobility and small landholding peasantry. The *collazos*, a type of landless peasantry, were excluded from participation. The *Cofradia* regulated all of Alava's political and economic affairs and held the function of final arbitrator over property rights. No one could found a village or town (*villa*) without a grant of land from the *Cofradia* of Arriaga.

However, by a process begun in the latter part of the 1100s, the authority of the *Cofradia* of Arriaga was gradually eroded until it finally disappeared in 1332. In spite of the restrictions imposed by the *Cofradia*, the kings of Navarra and later Castile founded numerous *villas* in Alava principally for military reasons. The most important of these was Vitoria, which was to become the capital of Alava. The towns were situated in the *llanada* (open land) of Alava and were strategically placed to control movement to and from Castile. Vitoria, established by Sancho, the Wise of Navarra, in 1181, was invaded and conquered by Alfonso VIII of Castile in 1200 in an attempt to open direct, protected routes to Guipúzcoa and the coast and to fence off Navarra. Unlike the open countryside governed by the *Cofradia*, these walled *villas* were under royal jurisdiction. Closed in by the lands of the *Cofradia* of Arriaga and usually populated by people who owned no land in Alava and, therefore, no rights to representation in the *Cofradia*, these new *villas* posed a frontal threat to the authority of the *Cofradia*.

Duality of political power soon developed into economic and political confrontation. The *villas* needed access to pastures, agricultural and mountain lands. As the *Cofradias* were compelled to cede additional territory to the *villas*, the areas under royal jurisdiction expanded (Zabala, 1971b:143; Caro Baroja, 1974:31–50). The struggle between the *Cofradia* of Arriaga and the *villas* was finally resolved in 1331 with the dissolution of the *Cofradia* and the voluntary integration of Alava and Castile. A key force behind this decision, which was taken by the *Cofradia* itself, was the Alava nobility. With Alava part of Castile, the Alava nobility gained the same economic and political privileges as their illustrious, powerful and prestigious Castilian aristocratic counterparts.

Vizcaya

Like Alava, during the early ninth century Vizcaya was associated with the Asturian monarchy, as association that was ruptured by the successful rebellion of the Vizcayans in 870. Although its exact origins are unknown, a seigniorial form of political organization had emerged in Vizcaya by the eleventh century. With his functions limited to political leadership and military protection, the *señor* of Vizcaya was elected by the local notables and initially the position was not inheritable nor did it imply dominical rights. Once inside the orbit of the monarchy of Navarra, the *señorio* (seigniory) of Vizcaya became inheritable even though the rights of the *señor* remained restricted. The first known *señor* of Vizcaya was Iñigo Lopéz who was elected during the reign of Sancho, the Great, and was a Navarrese courtier and probably Vizcayan by birth. While Iñigo Lopéz served at various times the monarchs of both Navarra and Castile, his second son, Lope, gave his allegiance to the Castilian king in return for which he was rewarded the Castilian feud of Haro. Adopting the family name, Lopéz de Haro, Lope's descendants maintained the position of lords of Vizcaya for the better part of three centuries. Indeed the house of Lopéz de Haro became one of the most powerful of the Castilian noble families (Payne, 1974:56). The connections between the *señores* of Vizcaya and the kings of Castile were consolidated through marital alliances. In 1379 the titulary of the *señorio* fell to the wife of the Castilian king, Enrique II, who united the title of *Señor* of Vizcaya to that of the King of Castile. Although Vizcaya and Castile acknowledged the same monarch, however, Vizcaya was not incorporated into Castile. It preserved its independent status and constitutionally was regarded as a separate territory. Vizcaya was not constitutionally integrated into the Spanish state until 1876 after the Carlist defeat in the Second Carlist War.

Guipúzcoa

Guipúzcoa, the only Basque province surrounded on all sides by other Basque regions, is the smallest of the Spanish provinces and the last to adopt its present boundaries. Although little is known about Guipúzcoa before the eleventh century, early documents describe the province as divided into politically autonomous valleys and rural districts with political authority vested in local lineage heads (Caro Baroja, 1971:89). Quite possibly a wider political organization with consultative functions existed in the form of a general assembly of lineage heads. Incorporated into Navarra during the reign of Sancho, the Great, Guipúzcoa remained under Navarrese sovereignty for some 200 years. The authority of the king was represented by an appointed *señor*, a position that was not inheritable. The last of the Navarrese monarchs to rule Guipúzcoa was Sancho, the Wise, who founded San Sebastian in a last attempt to curb Castilian expansion into Navarrese territory. However, for reasons and by means that are still debated, Alfonso III, king of Castile, peacefully annexed Guipúzcoa in 1200. Some historians have argued that the inhabitants of Guipúzcoa and in particular the coastal fishermen much preferred the liberal character of the Castilian monarchy to the increasing feudal tendencies existing in Navarra (Payne, 1974:54). Although the Castilian monarchy took over the military and judicial functions formerly exercised by the kings of Navarra, the traditional legal and political institutions of the province remained untouched.

In summary, then, unlike Catalonia, the Basque country has never formed a single political entity except for the brief period when it was brought under the personal rule of the king of Navarra. With the exception of Navarra all of the peninsular Basque country was associated in one form or other with Castile already by the year 1200. Guipúzcoa, probably by voluntary treaty, was a province of Castile. Alava had been invaded. The *señores* of Vizcaya were close allies of the Castilian monarchy. In fact it was the *Señor* of Vizcaya in the service of the Castilian king who invaded Alava in 1181. All the Basque territories, however, retained autonomous political systems and constitutional frameworks until the nineteenth century.

Basque fueros and the foral regime

The political systems of the various Basque territories were regulated by *fueros*. The *fueros* were collections of local laws and customs together with special economic and political immunities underwritten by the kings of Castile (and later Spain) in return for political allegiance to the monarchy. Although the *fueros* of the different Basque areas showed many similarities, particularly in domestic law, one effect of the *fueros* was to establish each Basque area as a little world of its own. Unlike the Catalan *fueros*, the Basque *fueros* never institutionalized a wider Basque unity.

The *fueros* provided the foundation of Basque economic and political life from the thirteenth and fourteenth centuries when they were first codified until the mid-nineteenth century when the *fueros* were revoked by decree of the Madrid government. The ordinances of the *fueros* covered nearly every aspect of Basque life from marriage and dowry to inheritance and political participation. As a symbol of Basque autonomy and traditions, the reinstatement of *fueros* has always constituted a major nationalist demand.

Fueros were not, however, a unique attribute of the Basque country nor of Spain in general. This system of local laws was a common feature throughout medieval Europe. In Spain the newly installed Bourbon dynasty, in its campaign to unify the rebellious country constitutionally, suppressed the *fueros* of all the regions in Spain between 1706 and 1714 except for those of the Basque provinces and Navarra which had supported the Bourbon claims during the War of Succession.

The Basque *fueros* evolved over the centuries through a constant process of modification. Many Basques view the *fueros* as derived directly from the structure of Basque traditional society. Elias de Tejada (1963:37) states, for example, 'the *fueros* were first custom and later law. As such they were a popular creation.' Alfonso X, the Wise (1257–75), defined a *fuero* as 'something in which two things are combined, practice and custom. Both must enter into a *fuero* for it to be binding.' When the *fueros* are referred to in official documents, the phrase, '*fueros, buenos usos y costumbres*' (*fueros*, good practices and customs) is nearly always used.

However, the relationship between the Basque social structure and the *fueros* is obscure since little is known about either prior to documentary evidence which first dates from the Middle Ages. Although the distinction is not explicitly made in the *fueros* themselves, in broad lines the *fueros* consisted of two types of laws: those covering private, domestic law, e.g. rules concerning transmission of homestead, dowry, domestic economic relations, and those concerned with public law, i.e. rules covering political and economic relations in the non-domestic sphere. Whereas the first type of law was arguably derived from social practice, the evolution of 'public' law followed a different course.

The concession of *fueros*, which were written in low Latin or Spanish, has to be viewed in the context of (1) the strategic position of the Basque country and (2) the need of the Castilian monarchy to impose public order in the Basque territories.

In the fourteenth and fifteenth centuries the Basque country was the part of Spain's northern frontier that was most vulnerable to military incursions from France. Spain lacked the resources to station a full army in the area permanently and the Basque region was sparsely populated. To solve this defence problem, *fueros* which gave important fiscal privileges – such as exemption from all state taxation – were granted by the Castilian monarchy in order to stimulate rapid population growth. *Fueros* were also extended to exempt all residents of the Basque territories from military conscription. In return the Basques pledged to defend their own territory. Such a resistance bought the time needed to bring the state army into position if the French onslaught were especially severe (Greenwood, 1977:91).

But the military vulnerability of the Basque area was further aggravated by the state of constant civil war which embroiled the entire Basque country during the fourteenth and fifteenth centuries, but which was fought only in the interests of the *parientes mayores*. The *parientes mayores* were heads of powerful families who through marriage and control over land built up large clientalist followings in their fierce competition for political prestige. In this competition the *parientes mayores* were frequently tempted to look to France for potential allies. The wars between the *parientes mayores*, called the *luchas de bandos* (fights of the bands) represented a serious security risk for the state. They also created a general economic impoverishment among the Basque peasantry and chronic social disorder. The kings of Castile attempted to diminish the power of these belligerent notables through the *fueros*. During most of the fourteenth and fifteenth centuries the majority of ordinances added to the *fueros* were aimed at the warlords and brigands who operated under their protection. They comprised penal legislation concerning collective security.[5] These foral innovations were introduced through the initiatives of the king and his functionaries in the Basque region and were backed by important sectors of the Basque population. The grants of collective nobility, which will be discussed shortly, must also be viewed in this context.

Furthermore, in all four Basque provinces the division which existed between the *villas* (urban centres) and the surrounding rural hinterland (*tierra llana*) was clearly reflected in the *fueros*. The *villas* were under an administrative and political framework dependent on direct royal jurisdiction as distinct from the countryside dependent on the jurisdiction of the provincial *Juntas Generales* (General Assemblies). As mentioned previously, the *villas* were established largely for strategic reasons. They were granted generous economic and political immunities in their charters of enfranchisement (*Carta Pueblas*) in order to promote rapid population growth. Politically closed off from the surrounding countryside, the *villas* have been depicted as 'a type of small republic, an autonomous island inside a primitive governmental district' (Monreal, 1977:359).

The Basque foral regime was founded on three essential elements, the *Junta General*, *el pase foral* (the foral pass) and the *corregidor*, the king's representative to each of the provinces.

The provincial *Juntas Generales* were the political and administrative bodies at the apex of the traditional Basque political system which had its roots in municipal councils. Formally the flow of political authority and representation stemmed from the local assemblies up to the provincial one. This system did ensure a notable degree of popular political participation although the organization of the *Juntas Generales* and forms of representation differed in each Basque territory. The equivalent in Navarra, which was organized as a viceroyalty, was the *Cortes* (court) composed of representatives of the nobility and clergy and headed by an hereditary viceroy.

The different Basque provinces were politically articulated into the Castilian monarchy and state administration mainly through two institutions – the *corregidor* and the *pase foral*. The first functioned to affirm and impose the king's authority and the second to limit it.

The *corregidor*, an administrative element characteristic of medieval Spain (Payne, 1974:60), was the king's principal agent in the Basque country. The first *corregidor*, Gonzalo Moro, was appointed in 1394 in response to petitions from Guipúzcoa and Vizcaya requesting assistance to help control the warring nobility, the *parientes mayores*. Initially appointed for a three-year term, the functions of the *corregidor* were extensive. He presided over the *juntas* to ensure that no agreements contrary to the interests of the Crown were made. All modifications of the *fueros* required the sanction of the *corregidor*. Moreover, he exercised far-reaching judicial and administrative functions, especially concerning fiscal matters, and played an important role in overseeing the equity of the foral institutions.

The *pase foral* was conceded by the Crown of Castile to Alava in 1417, Vizcaya in 1452 and to Guipúzcoa in 1473 and guaranteed the autonomy of the foral constitution. Zabala (1977a:148) defines the *pase foral* as the mechanism by which it became impermissible to apply or execute any law or decree of the king or the tribunals without previous approval of the provincial foral authorities.[6]

Because of the contradictory effects of these two institutions, the degree of political autonomy the Basque country actually enjoyed is difficult to establish. Certainly the foral regime provided guarantees of liberty and protection from arbitrary rule which were possibly unique in Spain. The Basques were exempt from the use of torture, arbitrary arrest and obligatory service in the king's army. Formally the relation between the Basque foral regimes and the Castilian Crown was a contractual one. The contractual element, at least with reference to Vizcaya, was underlined by the ceremonial obligation of each new king of Castile, who was also *señor* of Vizcaya, to confirm and swear fidelity to the *fueros* under the venerable oak tree at Guernica.

However, in the eighteenth and nineteenth centuries, when the foral regime came under attack both from within the Basque provinces and from Madrid, it was the special fiscal immunities conferred by the *fueros* which provided the core of contention. Two principal immunities were of crucial importance to the prosperity of the region and to the development of the Basque commercial bourgeoisie. These were (1) exemption from state-imposed taxation and (2) exemption from Spanish customs duties, i.e. internal customs lines. Most of the constant conflict and disputes surrounding the *fueros* were concerned with these two issues. With some very minor exceptions, the Spanish Crown had no right to levy taxes or impose tributes of any sort inside the Basque country. The few attempts of the Crown to do so were met with immediate and violent reaction. The collection of taxes and the administration of provincial budgets were in the hands of the Basque provincial authorities solely.

Internal customs lines were even more crucial to the Basque economy. The *fueros* established the Basque region as a duty-free zone and merchandise and foodstuffs could be freely imported into and exported from the area. Guipúzcoa and Vizcaya were separated from both Navarra and Castile by customs barriers and tariff duties were payable on goods only when they entered these latter areas.

To understand the vital importance of internal customs lines and the nature of the foral regime and pre-industrial Basque society in general, the evolution of the Basque social structure and, in particular, the specific development of the Basque urban bourgeoisie and rural élites must be examined.

The evolution of the Basque bourgeoisie

The Basque country enjoys three major economic resources which have profoundly patterned its entire economic and social history. These are: (1) its abundant and readily available reserves of iron and lumber, the basis for the Basque iron and steel industry, as well as shipbuilding; (2) natural, protected harbours in the Bay of Biscay, and (3) an advantageous geographical setting. The Basque country was a cross-roads between two important economic areas – England and Flanders to the north and the recently liberated Castilian meseta rich in wool and grain in the south (Monreal, 1977:358). These resources were economically capitalized mainly by the urban centres (*villas*) which were dedicated to commerce, administrative and military activities and small artisan industries. The urban centres linked wool and grain exporting Castile to her external markets.

Against these advantages of which the *villas* have been beneficiaries, the Basque rural countryside, with the exception of southern Navarra and Alava, has been burdened with a steep, arduous terrain and infertile soil in addition to chronic overpopulation. The poverty and high demographic density of the rural areas, together with the Basque inheritance system which transmits the *baserria* (Basque farmstead) intact to only one heir, has impelled a contant flow of people into the towns which in turn has increased the Basque economy's dependency upon commerce and small industry. Moreover, Guipúzcoa and Vizcaya have been (as they still are) deficient in cereal production. In response to urban opportunities and rural limitations, these two provinces have traditionally exported Basque goods and people abroad and acted as commercial brokers between Castile and Europe (and later the New World) in return for importing foodstuffs and other items. The foral regime and especially exemption from Spanish customs duties were the linchpins of this entire economic enterprise.

The Basque language, Euskera, lacks the descriptive terminology for a social class structure. The terms designating political and social hierarchy or nobility are all derived from Castilian. The closest word in Euskera is *jaun* which originally meant a person who held a seigniory or fief in a given territory. Already by the sixteenth century, however, the term *jaun* had been expanded to connote a generalized term of respect more or less equivalent to the Spanish word *don* or *señor*.[7]

In spite of the lack of descriptive terminology, however, medieval Basque society was stratified. The *parientes mayores* were the heads of the richest and most powerful families although their economic strength was slight compared to the great Castilian families. Their incomes derived from landholdings, iron foundries and maritime trade. Moreover, the *parientes mayores* commanded extensive rights of private jurisdiction and commendation over tenants, monopoly over public offices, patronage of churches and the right to levy taxes and collect tithes (*diezmos*) (Pinedo, 1974:35).

Below the *parientes mayores* were a wide range of minor nobility, *hidalgos*, most of whom were tied by links either of kinship, affinity and/or clientalist relationships to the *parientes*. The next social stratum was occupied by an heterogeneous group with no claims to noble status and consisted of *laboradores censuarios* (yeomen) who paid a yearly tribute in return for certain rights. Beneath these were the *collazos*, of whom little is known, although they appear to have been permanently tied to the land of a particular noble and, in Alava, *siervos rurales*, serfs whose legal position has been described as slavery (Pinedo, 1974:35).

The Church enjoyed little autonomous power. Unlike the Castilian clergy, the Basque clergy had no independent rights to collect tithes. Instead, the tithes of the faithful were raked in by the nobles under whose patronage the Church operated. Although closely linked to the upper aristocracy, especially in Vizcaya and Guipúzcoa, the clergy in the Basque country have traditionally been more alienated from the formal political apparatus than in other parts of the Hispanic peninsula. Priests (and, according to the *fuero*, certain 'relatives' of the clergy) were excluded from political office and the omnipotent Inquisition was partly curbed (Payne, 1974:85).

Cloistered in enclaves within this rural, medieval society, was an emerging mercantile class resident in the *villas*. Whereas the *parientes mayores* had some commercial interests, conversely, the urban merchants invested part of their profits into land.

The crisis of 1300–70 affected most of Europe and brought war, famine and plague. The situation of the Basque nobility became precarious as income from agricultural sources declined precipitously. The *parientes mayores* responded by increasing their demands on the peasantry (Pinedo, 1974:43–50). The system of tributes was expanded and made more severe. Throughout the fourteenth century the power of the Basque aristocracy grew dramatically as did the conflicts between them. The rural aristocracy dedicated to a predatory struggle for honour and prestige embroiled the entire region in civil war. The rivalries between the families of specific *parientes mayores* generated a process of alliance formation which accelerated until the *parientes mayores* were divided into two bitterly opposed groups, or *bandos*. The western part of the Basque country was split between the *oñacinos* and *gambinos* while in Navarra on the other side of the Cantabrian the pro-French *agramonteses* were pitted against the pro-Castilian *beamonteses*.

Although peasant resistance to the *parientes mayores* lacked cohesion, the peasantry found potent allies in other sectors of Basque society whose interests were prejudiced by the constant belligerency of the aristocracy. Merchants required regularity and security of transport and roads and they opposed the arbitrary tributes extracted by the *parientes*. The clergy sought an alternative to their economic dependency on noble patronage (Albaladejo, 1975: 110). The general offensive against the *parientes mayores* commenced in 1457 and was led by the *hermandades* (brotherhoods), composed of *labradores censuarios* (yeomen), urban merchants and parts of the lower aristocracy with the close support of the unified Spanish monarchy under Enrique IV of Castile (Pinedo, 1974: 54). In the campaign to establish peace and order the power of the aristocracy was swiftly curtailed by new foral regulations which denied the aristocracy both political vote and voice.

The sixteenth century, imbued with a strong anti-*señorial* spirit, witnessed the decline of the *parientes mayores*, the consolidation of an assertive monarchy under the Catholic kings, the emergence of municipal power, a general economic expansion and a dramatic demographic increase. Particularly in Guipúzcoa and Vizcaya, the lower classes experienced political and economic emancipation. These two provinces became socially the most liberated and politically the most egalitarian area of Spain (Payne, 1974: 62). The previous domination of the upper aristocracy was not replaced by new relations of large landowners and tenant farmers as in Castile. Rather a new small landholding peasantry began to emerge (Pinedo, 1977: 137).[8] Julio Caro Baroja (1971: 222) argues that from the end of the Middle Ages the social and legal foundations of a servile class had by and large been suppressed. The recently granted rights to carry arms, hunt and fish and the use of land and forest by the municipalities were features of a new social structure. Especially important was the rise of municipal power spearheaded by the *villas* and *hermandades* and backed by royal approval. In addition to forest and grazing lands, many iron foundries also fell under municipal ownership.

The culminating legal achievement of the sixteenth century was the extension of the status of nobility, *hidalguía*, to all native residents of Vizcaya in 1526 and Guipúzcoa in 1610.[9] Basque universal nobility – a key notion in Basque nationalist doctrine in which it is regarded as a primordial attribute of all Basques – should be viewed in relation to two factors. First, as Stanley Payne has pointed out (1974: 63), in the traditional Spanish system this device was the only means by which relative equality before the law could be assured. The *Hermandad* of Guipúzcoa had agitated for universal nobility since the end of the fourteenth century as a means to create a judicial barrier against the excesses of the aristocracy (Otazu y Llana, 1973:115). Second, the legal status of *hidalguía* facilitated emigration from the persistently overpopulated rural areas and aided a mass exodus of excess population. In the context of the opportunities offered by the Reconquest and the opening of the Americas to exploration and exploitation, noble status was an essential first step for achieving military or administrative position.

Indeed, a critical factor in understanding why relations between the Castilian monarchy and the Basque foral authorities tended to collaboration rather than confrontation (at least until the early 1800s) was the role of Basques in the state administration. At least from the reign of Carlos I (1516–59), the first Habsburg king, and especially notable during the reign of Felipe V (1700–46), the first Bourbon monarch, Basques exercised an important role in the royal administration in which they formed a definable, compact group. Along with the priesthood, commerce and military service, administrative service provided the successors of the *parientes mayores* – usually in the line of younger sons – their means of survival. Basques, all of whom were equipped with noble status, staffed the state administration, not only in the Spanish capital, but in the Americas, Flanders and the Austrian Empire. To a large extent their incomes were dependent on maintaining royal favour and, thus, the position and influence of Basques at court had important political and economic repercussions inside the Basque country. These state officials exerted a powerful influence over their counterparts – to whom they were frequently related by kinship – inside the Basque foral regime.

Additionally, as Julio Caro Baroja has shown (1974:55), in contrast to the customary nationalist image of the Basque ill at ease when speaking Spanish, a language which he never comes to dominate, from the sixteenth to the nineteenth century a large portion of Spain's important essayists, publicists, teachers of Spanish calligraphy as well as the clerks and notaries who amply and profitably served the central administration were Basques.

Simultaneously, the mercantile classes resident in the Basque coastal towns and Vitoria acquired increasing economic predominance. As exporters of semi-finished iron products, ships and Castilian wool, their markets were dramatically broadened by the opening of the Americas. Already by the late sixteenth century families enriched by their stay in or trade with the New World began to form a powerful class whose impact was especially visible in Bilbao. Within the Basque country this new class began to supplant the old aristocracy economically. In contrast to the court-oriented aristocracy who dominated the foral administration, the Basque mercantile elite – who were linked by marriage to important French and English commercial families – were more interested in the price of iron or the quality of ships than in the fashionable affairs of the Madrid court (Baroja, 1971:210).

The prosperous Hispanicized urban centres presented a stark contrast to the austere life offered by the *Euskaldun* (Basque-speaking) rural areas. Julio Caro Baroja writes (1974: 27) 'Already by the sixteenth century in the Basque country the *villas* were modern, the clothes worn by the urbanites were modern. Bilbao had been rebuilt after a fire and the problems presented by its economy and industry were also modern.' However, until industrialization there were only three large urban centres in the Basque country: Bilbao, San Sebastian and Victoria. Principally commercial centres, these towns imported, exported, consumed but produced very little. Nor did these towns absorb much of the constant flow of rural emigrants. It was the smaller *villas* in the interior – Mondragon, Placencia, Eibar, and so forth – that absorbed the disinherited sons and daughters of the *baserriak* and in which a large artisan class developed.

Merchants and state officials were the heirs to the benefits of the sixteenth century. The losers were the lower nobility whose incomes, based on fixed land rents, collapsed with the steep increases in prices and salaries (Pinedo, 1974:59).

In the seventeenth century a new rural élite was consolidated in the Basque provinces as in the rest of Spain (Pinedo, 1974:59). These rural notables consisted of merchants who had invested a large portion of their acquired wealth into land, recently enriched peasants and the occasional returned Basque state official. Although the economic foundation of this élite was land, supplemented by ownership of iron foundries and mills, only in a very few cases was this wealth originally derived from landownership. Few families had accumulated their fortunes before the onslaught of Spain's imperial endeavours. Within a few generations through strategically contracted marriages – often between the mercantile élite and the descendants of the old aristocracy – and successive inheritance, much land in the Basque country again became concentrated into a few hands. Moreover, Otazu y Llana (1973:329) has shown how this new aristocracy, both urban and rural, were intimately linked through kinship and affinity and were largely resistant to penetration from other classes.

Although the mercantile classes, industrialists and professionals were to become the main carriers of the liberal creed, they were not its initiators. In the eighteenth century liberalism was a doctrine adopted mainly by the upper ranks of Basque rural landowners and the urban bourgeoisie who also owned or desired to own land. This group were ardent speculators in foodstuffs and had benefited greatly from increased prices especially after 1760. They were eager to place more land into circulation – in particular the ample reserves of municipally owned land – in order to decrease land prices and hopefully increase profitability of agricultural production. Advocates of disentailment also included the still emerging rural bourgeoisie composed mainly of those peasants who, during the slack periods of the agricultural cycle, dedicated themselves to small businesses – mills, metalworks, etc. – and with the accumulated profits were also anxious to acquire land.

The main agency for the diffusion of the ideas of the Enlightenment and liberalism into the Basque country was the Real Sociedad Bascongada de Amigos del País (Vicens Vives, 1970:117), the Royal Basque Society of Friends of the Country, founded by the Basque aristocracy in Azcoitia in 1764. This society provided the reformist, Carlos III (1759–88), with the model for the subsequent establishment of similar societies throughout Spain. Faithful to the idea that extensive reforms were required to raise the technical level and economic profitability of Basque agriculture and commerce, the main attentions of the Basque society were oriented toward the modernization of agriculture and the Basque metallurgical industry, the two main pillars of Basque aristocratic income.

Unlike its languid and stagnant Castilian and Andalusian counterparts, the Basque aristocracy has traditionally displayed an exceptional vigour and industry. In many respects the Basque élite – both urban and rural – were, along with the Catalans, the most culturally advanced social sector in Spain. Urbane and cosmopolitan in outlook, they were quick to adopt the technical advances emanating from other European countries. Many sent their children to French and English universities and the Academy of Vergara, founded in 1767, was the first secular school established in Spain. This social sector also gave the entrepreneurial inspiration to the Caracas Company, a Basque controlled trading concern largely responsible for developing Venezuela.

In terms of identity this sector often described itself as the most 'Spanish' in Spain. Its members regarded themselves as the direct descendants of those, 'uncontaminated by either Jewish or Moorish blood', who had reconquered Spain from the infidels and restored civilization and Christianity to the country. Although many were familiar with Euskera, Spanish was their preferred language both domestically and publically.

While the period up to the late eighteenth century saw the consolidation and ascendancy of a new Basque aristocracy and commercial bourgeoisie, the economic and political fate of the Basque peasantry was not so illustrious.

The decline of the *parientes mayores*, economic expansion and legal changes paved the way for many tenant farmers to purchase land. By 1704 in Vizcaya and Guipúzcoa some 50% of the peasantry owned some land. The remaining 50% were tenant farmers or, very infrequently, landless labourers working the land of the *jauntxoak* (rural notables) many of whom were resident in the nearby *villas*. These small landholdings were characterized by low technological level, weak capitalization, a labour force limited to the resident domestic group and self-sufficiency. Animal husbandry –

basically cows and sheep – was combined with the cultivation of wheat, corn, turnips, apples and chestnuts. Mountain lands provided abundant pastures as well as lime, timber and firewood. Deficiencies in household self-sufficiency were compensated for by monetary incomes supplied by the production of charcoal and activities related to the metallurgical industry.

The system of transmission of the *baserria* intact to a sole heir gave a certain stability to the system. To a considerable extent excess population was forced from the land and *minifundia* prevented. The *baserria* was seen as indivisible and unalienable. Simultaneously, the land was marketable. That which remained immutable was the name of the *baserria*, not the farmstead itself. Land in the Basque provinces has always been extremely fragmented. For the heir in the case of smallholders the uni-transmission of the farmstead regularly created serious economic problems. The inheritor was under an obligation to compensate both male and female disinherited siblings with dowries (*dotes*) and legitimate portions (*legítimas*). Although usually paid in cash or other forms of liquid household reserves, in those frequent cases in which such reserves did not exist, one alternative was the fragmentation of the farmstead.

Most *baserritarak* (peasants) were in debt. Any sudden increased demand on household reserves – dowry for a daughter, purchase of land, new taxes or a bad harvest and the subsequent purchase of foodstuffs – would often force the peasant to take out a loan, usually from the local *jauntxo*. If the harvests were adequate and surplus goods sold or extra income was produced by occasional employment, the debt could be repaid. In the opposite case, a spiral of indebtedness was initiated and the peasant had no other recourse than the sale of land or the farmstead itself. After 1770 this pattern of indebtedness leading to the sale of land became increasingly common (Pinedo, 1974:266). Because of increased dependency on markets, indebtedness, demographic pressures and periodic agricultural slumps, the proportion of tenant farmers grew markedly. Whereas in 1704 around 50% of the peasantry was smallholders, by 1810 less than a third owned land.

While economically the position of the Basque peasantry was progressively eroded, politically the peasantry as well as artisans experienced successive attempts to restrict and finally eliminate their participation in the centres of political decision-making. The initial movement, following the defeat of the *parientes mayores* roughly stretching throughout the sixteenth century, was to open the *Juntas* (provincial assemblies) and local councils established by the foral regime to popular representation. The *fueros* formalized the obligation of all *vecinos* (those with legal residence in a given *vecindad*; lit. neighbourhood) to attend the sessions of the local councils in which problems were discussed and resolved.[10]

But this movement was shortlived. The new rural élite, supported by their increasing economic potency and influential contacts in the state administration, began to force through restrictive stipulations for political participation. In 1526, the same year in which noble status was extended to all *Vizcaínos*, the Ordinance of Azpeita which regulated municipal elections in Guipúzcoa established a property requirement as a qualification to be elected as *alcalde* (mayor) of the municipal council.

The principal means through which the peasantry was disenfranchised was the introduction of specific property qualifications called *millares*. On the provincial level literacy in Spanish became an additional requirement. Differentials in wealth increasingly determined differential access to political power. Otazu y Llana has suggested (1973:358) that the accelerating restrictions placed upon political participation were largely due to the formation and consolidation of local élites who progressively monopolized access to the political apparatus.

For example, in the Ordinances of Renteria of 1606 it was established that all high public officials needed the equivalent of 100,000 maravedis in immovable goods. For less important posts 50,000 maravedis was sufficient. In Elgoibar, Guipúzcoa, only those *vecinos* who commanded immovable goods to the value of 500 ducados were eligible for the franchise or to be candidates for office. In Azpeitia, Guipúzcoa, at the end of the fifteenth century out of a total population of approximately 3,000, 300 or 10% were *concejantes* (i.e. could participate in the municipal assembly). At the end of the eighteenth century in Azpeitia with a population of over 5,000 inhabitants, only some forty to fifty individuals fulfilled the *millarista* (property) requirements enabling them to participate in the local assemblies (Otazu y Llana, 1973:358). In Gordejuela, Vizcaya, the Ordinances of 1548 established that although election was by universal suffrage – defined as all heads of households – only those who were literate in Spanish were eligible for election. In 1671 universal suffrage was suppressed. The *alcalde* was to be elected by the *regidores*, a type of alderman. The *regidores* in turn would directly appoint their own successors and all public officials had to be *millaristas* which in this case meant 400 ducados of immovable property in addition to literacy, the status of *vecindad* and proven nobility.[11]

Although the exact terms varied from locality to locality, the general mechanism of exclusion in both Vizcaya and Guipúzcoa was similar: property qualifications and literacy. Although many peasants had a rudimentary understanding of Spanish, the ability to read and write the language was limited to the educated ranks of the Basque élite. Thus, Spanish became an instrument wielded by the Hispanicized Basque notables to exclude and control the Basque-speaking '*turbulento aldenaje*' (tumultuous peasantry).

Whereas the process of political elimination of the peasantry and artisans from local level politics was a drawn out affair, on the provincial level the process was completed rapidly. The *Junta General* of Guipúzcoa in 1529 and the *Junta General* of Guernica in 1612 approved measures making literacy in Spanish an essential requirement for all elected delegates to the *Juntas*. Finally, with the augmenting power of the *Diputaciones*, the permanent executive bodies elected by the *Juntas*, the Basque notables – and in particular a few families such as the Idiaquez in Guipúzcoa – gained a crowning control over the entire foral political apparatus.

In short then, as Pinedo has stated (1974:356), 'The *Juntas* represented democracy between the notables who controlled the administration and political power both on a local and provincial level.' Manuel de Larramendi, a Jesuit priest and defender of the notion of Basque egalitarianism, which shall be considered shortly, writing at the considerably earlier date of 1756, condemned the *junteros* (members of the *Juntas Generales*) for the betrayal of the original meaning of the *junta* and for the conversion of these assemblies into 'a government of aristocrats...'

Partly because of their alienation from political institutions, peasant and artisan dissent was channeled into extra-legal forms. From the seventeenth century onwards the Basque country was the scene of frequent, frenzied popular uprisings called *matxinadas* (a term derived from the Basque word, *matxin*, meaning villager or peasant).[12] Indeed armed confrontations accelerated up to the end of the nineteenth century when the Basque peasantry suffered its final defeat.

Basque egalitarianism

In spite of the development and reinforcement of unequal political and economic relations which are so evident in Basque history, the notion of Basque egalitarianism has had a long and respectable ideological history. Perhaps ironically, the maximum diffusion of this ideology coincided with the development of an aggressive and expansive Basque bourgeoisie. In many respects it has been used by the Basque peasantry and petty bourgeoisie as a language to protest the growing ascendancy of the Basque élites. For example, in the Salt Uprising of 1631 when the Basque provincial authorities acquiesced in the imposition of a tax on salt by the state government in violation of the *fueros*, the women of the insurgents were reported to have cried that now their husbands and sons would be *alcaldes*. All people are equal and it is not right that some eat chicken while others must eat sardines! It would be difficult to imagine a similar incident taking place in other regions of Spain. Historically the language of equality – as distinct from the language of virtue – never formed part of the Spanish political or cultural vocabulary until quite recently. But in the Basque region the stratified *is* has always been strongly censured by the egalitarian *ought*.

Basque notions of equality must be viewed, however, within the general Spanish context. Until the late eighteenth century Spain was obsessed with concepts of honour, purity of blood and prestige. Among other things, these concepts gave rise to complicated legal codes, an entire literary tradition as well as the Inquisition. Moreover, the content of these concepts and their principal defenders changed in accordance with Spain's changing social structure and underlying social assumptions and needs (Pitt-Rivers, 1961, 1965, 1977; Caro Baroja, 1965). To a significant degree, Basque notions of egalitarianism and universal nobility are a regional variant of Spanish notions of honour and can only be adequately analysed within this wider framework.

Certainly the early Basque essayists on Basque universal nobility, such as Zaldibia and Lope de Isasti who wrote in the sixteenth and early seventeenth centuries equated Basque nobility with the purity of Basque blood 'unmixed with that of foreign peoples'. Lope de Isasti, however, added another element into the ideology of Basque nobility which was to become a major theme in later writings on the subject. Since all Basques are *hidalgos de sangre* (noble by blood), Isasti reasoned, they could never lose their nobility by manual work or poverty. As Caro Baroja has indicated (1971:217), the relationship between manual labour and noble status and/or honour has been radically distinct in the Basque country in comparison to the rest of Spain. In a largely peasant society in which everyone was of noble birth,[13] no occupation (except a few exercised by foreigners) was regarded as despicable or defiling. In Castile and Andalucia, on the other hand, manual labour was seen as degrading – an activity confined to those of lowly origins. Precedence was granted only to those who pursued the loftier professions. The poor might claim virtue, but they were never entitled to prestige. This negative value placed on the role of work has never formed part of Basque popular ideology.

Prior to the advent of Basque nationalism, the ideology of Basque universal nobility and noble equality was given its most complete expression by Manuel de Larramendi, A Jesuit priest, in his *Corografía de Guipúzcoa*, written in 1754.[14] Many of the ideas expounded by Larramendi reappeared with a vengeance in writings of the Basque nationalists. Larramendi's conception of Basque universal nobility was also connected to notions of purity of blood; but he went much further. A keen observer of his period which coincided with the deterioration of the economic and political position of the peasantry, Larramendi was the ideologue of the small landholder and tenant farmer. Nobility was an attribute of the land and those who worked it. The traditional *baserritar* cultivating the land and governed by the rural values of austerity, social harmony and egalitarianism in social relations was, for Larramendi, the original Basque in a state of grace. It was this state of grace and virtue that had been shattered by the cities and their easy, luxurious lifestyle. From this decadent, outside world came all inequalities. Larramendi assailed the urban bourgeoisie, the rural *jauntxoak* resident in the *villas* and the *indianos* (Basques who had returned from the Americas) as the sources of this evil. Although Larramendi distinguished wealth from nobility, 'all are equally noble of blood, be they great or small, rich or poor, of one occupation or another, labourers or liberals...', he nonetheless questioned the true nobility of the *parientes mayores* and their successors to Basque élite status. They were rich and powerful and the rich and powerful, to Larramendi, were morally tarnished. Using Pitt-Rivers' terminology, the Basque élite's claim for honour as virtue was rejected and, therefore, its claim for honour as precedence was dismissed as simple arrogance. While the social struggle in Spain – and among the Basque traditional élites – centred around the notion, *valer mas – valer menos* (to be of more worth – to be of less worth), generally in the Basque country this struggle has used the term, *valer iqual*, or in Euskera, *berdin-berdin* (equal-equal). Economic inequalities were not disputed. Social inequalities were.

Unfortunately not enough is known about the nature of social life on the local level during this period to evaluate the assertion of rural social egalitarianism. However, I shall try to show in Part 2 dealing with the village of Elgeta, that egalitarianism is a firmly held value among Basques today and affects all aspects of social behaviour. Moreover, current peasant attitudes strongly echo Larramendi's distrust and resentment of urban life and culture.

One crucial aspect of Basque universal nobility must be mentioned here. While Basque nobility ideologically affirmed the equality of neighbours, it also functioned effectively to exclude outsiders. This needs to be emphasized because a slightly different version of this concept lies at the very heart of modern Basque nationalism. In the overpopulated rural areas dependent on limited, fixed resources Basque nobility became the foundation of legislation designed to regulate settlement and residence in the *vecindades*. The *Junta General* of Cestona declared in 1527 that 'no one who is not of noble status can be admitted to the villages of this province of Guipúzcoa – neither as a *vecino* nor can they be domiciled in them'. Some ordinances went even further. For example, one ordinance stated, 'Those who are not noble and cannot demonstrate their nobility will be expelled from the province' (quoted in Otazu y Llana, 1973:115). Moreover, many cases have been reported of Bilbao merchants using this legal mechanism to eliminate competitors. Unlike similar legislation in the rest of the peninsula aimed solely at the Jews, Basque law cut off immigration by Castilians and French and in the process hermetically sealed off the Basque countryside from non-Basque and non-aristocratic infiltration.

2

The foundations of the modern Basque country

The crisis of the foral regime

The modern Basque country – like Spain herself – emerged deeply divided. It was created out of the abolition of the foral regime. Foral abolition meant the political defeat of the rural notables and the further alienation of the peasantry. It also meant the final ascendancy of the expanding urban centres.

The loss of Spain's traditional overseas markets and the political changes and physical destruction caused by the War of Independence resulted in an acute crisis also in the Basque country. Typically the agricultural and urban sectors sought diametrically opposed solutions for their ailments. In the Basque country the Hispanicized urban and *euskaldun* (Basque-speaking) rural modes of life were conceived of as antagonistic social orders. The interests of the one could only be served at the expense of the other. Compromise was neither contemplated nor sought. The tensions produced erupted twice into civil war and after the final rural defeat resulted in the abolition of the foral regime in 1876.

After 1795 trade with the Americas had almost ceased. With the collapse of foreign commerce, the Basque bourgeoisie looked to the potential of a Spanish market and specifically the potential of a modernized Basque metallurgical industry in such a market for its economic salvation. However, such an economic change required radical political surgery.

Three aspects of the foral regime exercised a stranglehold over the possibilities of industrial growth. (1) The foral regime upheld rural society and the privileged position of the rural notables within it. When in conflict, rural interests were almost inevitably protected to the detriment of urban ones. (2) The main resources of the Basque country, lumber and, more importantly, iron ore were municipal rather than private property. Moreover, the Vizcayan provincial *Junta* prevented the export of iron ore. (3) Internal customs lines established the Basque country as a duty-free zone. Hence, Basque industry was cut off from the Spanish market while simultaneously subjected to an unrestricted inflow of competing industrial goods from abroad.

Liberalism which sought the disentailment of common lands together with political and economic uniformity was an obvious political creed for the Basque urban bourgeoisie. Thus the centralizing tendencies of the various Madrid governments combined with the aspirations of the Basque urbanites to attack frontally the traditional Basque political system based on *fueros*.

Not surprisingly, the political attitude adopted by the rural notables was belligerently anti-liberal. Although their economic power had been weakened, the notables' control over the provincial political apparatus had been maintained.[1] Their political advantage depended on the maintenance of the old order. Here the issue of internal customs lines was crucial.

The Spanish state – like the Basque bourgeoisie – required the development of a Spanish national market. In contrast, the rural notables and the peasantry were fiercely opposed to integration into a national market. Such a move would mean the free import of Castilian cereals and livestock which would increase competition and further decrease prices. Imposition of Spanish customs duties would also result in a dramatic increase in taxation on rural consumption. In addition the sale of the common lands, which had intensified throughout the early nineteenth century due to liberal disentailment legislation, had already undercut a crucial buttress of the Basque peasant economy.

The Church had its own reasons for alarm. Fearing liberal intentions to subordinate it as a political, economic and educational institution, the Church consolidated its support for the *jauntxoak* and the peasantry in their foral cause. Hence, in the Basque countryside an anti-liberal alliance was formed which lasted throughout the nineteenth century. It united rural notables, peasantry and clergy under the slogan of 'God and *Fueros*!'

The rural defeat: the Carlist Wars and the abolition of the foral regime

Carlism is a complicated affair and cannot be readily reduced to a straightforward struggle between urban and rural interests. Nor can it be viewed, as many Basque nationalist historians have attempted to do, as an embryonic nationalist struggle. Instead Carlism should be placed in the context of the confrontation between two opposing social orders inside Spain and the economic, social and political visions used to legitimize these orders. In an important sense, neither Spanish liberalism nor Carlism were founded on a unified, coherent ideology. Roughly stated, liberalism provided justification for those diverse social sectors which had economically benefited from the eighteenth century and stood to become the political victors of the nineteenth. Carlism was one reaction of an amalgam of social groups and ideological tendencies which perceived themselves as victims.

Carlism, the creed enthusiastically championed by the Basque rural population, implied a conception of state formation entirely opposed to that embodied by liberalism. Divine right monarchy and Catholic supremacy were combined with the protection of traditional social order and local autonomies. The result was an absolutist, but decentralized state. Carlism as a whole was a populist movement, anti-patrician in sentiment in spite of its emphasis on monarchy. For its peasant supporters Carlism meant the defence of *fueros*. And *fueros* above all meant a defence of common lands and protection from state taxes.

The liberals condemned the Carlists and all those who supported the *fueros* in general as proposing a return to the seventeenth century. Dismissed as primitive and romantic, Carlism was regarded as part of the general reaction in Europe against the ideas of the French Revolution (Garcia Venero, 1969: 165).

Significantly, the Carlist Wars were Basque civil wars. The liberal, anti-*fuero*, urban centres were pitted against the Carlist, pro-*fuero* rural areas. All Basque cities, including Pamplona in the heartland of Carlist territory, remained liberal strongholds throughout.

The First Carlist War broke out in 1833 and was effectively ended in 1839 with the signing of the Treaty of Vergara. Nominally the Carlist uprising involved a conflict over succession to the Spanish throne. The champions of Don Carlos, brother of the deceased king, Ferdinand VII, allied against the defenders of Isabel II, the unanticipated daughter of the late king and the wife of his old age, Maria Cristina of Naples. Its massive peasant support – and the guerrilla tactics employed – gave Carlism its military potency.[2] The rural nature of Carlism made it difficult to defeat. Conversely it made success for the Carlist forces impossible (Carr, 1966; Brenan, 1969; Oyarzun, 1965). The Spanish army was unable to penetrate the Carlists' rural strongholds. The Carlists were incapable of leaving them.

However, there were two strands to Carlism – its grass-roots appeal and its overbearing ideological pretensions. The military stalemate was broken by the Carlists' political ambitions. The Carlist leadership, based in Navarra, insisted upon taking Madrid. For these doctrinaire Carlists, control of Madrid was central to their main goal. The real meaning of Navarrese, or rather ideological, Carlism was not the protection of *fueros*, the cause that galvanized the peasantry, but the religious reunification of Spain. To the Navarrese, Carlism meant a dogmatic, ideologically unified mode of thinking in which heretical blemishes would be cleansed under the auspices of an invigorated and renewed Inquisition.

Carlism lost much of its popular support when the peasantry began to feel the full economic burden of the war and a settlement which would guarantee the Basque *fueros* became imminent. The Treaty of Vergara offered this guarantee and peace was made possible. The Navarrese could never accept the treaty. Hence, the political division between Guipúzcoa and Vizcaya on one hand and Navarra and, to a lesser extent, Alava on the other was underlined and confirmed. This division would reemerge repeatedly over the course of the years.

In spite of assurances given at Vergara, after the First Carlist War the *fueros* were rapidly eroded. The Law of 1839 which confirmed the Treaty of Vergara stated: 'The *Fueros* of the Basque provinces and Navarra are reaffirmed unless they are prejudicial to the constitutional unity of the monarchy.' While the formal structure of the provincial foral apparatus remained largely intact, foral continuity was more apparent than real. Obligatory military service was introduced. Navarra was transformed from a viceroyalty into a foral province. All legislative and executive powers were transferred from the provincial *Juntas* to the Spanish parliament and government. In 1833 a royal decree had restructured the Spanish state into forty-nine administratively uniform provinces. In 1841 the customs lines were definitively removed to the coast.

The Carlist cause erupted once again into war in 1872 when Spain had a federal constitution which, had it ever been implemented, would have converted the Basque provinces into part of a federal state. The chronic instability and renewed anti-clericalism of the First Republic had given Carlism, centred again in Navarra, another opportunity to try to impose itself on Spain. Except for the major cities, during the Second Carlist War the majority of Basque territory was under a type of Carlist state. With the second Carlist defeat in 1876 a new Spanish law upheld the *fueros* of Navarra which had been negotiated in 1841; but the *fueros* of Vizcaya, Guipúzcoa and Alava were abolished.

Very importantly, however, the Basque urban liberals were dedicated to preserving within the new system of Spanish constitutional unity the one aspect of the foral regime which had been of considerable importance to their interests; fiscal autonomy. In 1878 the Spanish parliament approved a special fiscal and administrative regime – the *conciertos económicos* – for the Basque provinces. Essentially the *conciertos económicos* enabled the Basque provinces to negotiate their own taxes with Madrid and pay a fixed sum into the Madrid treasury. The quotas agreed upon, which were significantly inferior to the taxes paid out by other Spanish provinces, were to be raised in whatever manner the Basque provincial governments deemed suitable.

Industrialization, 1876–1900

Basque industrialization began with the definitive unification of the customs lines along the Spanish national frontiers in 1841. Until 1900 industrialization was largely confined to the areas surrounding Bilbao and, to a lesser extent, specific urban centres in Guipúzcoa. Navarra and Alava remained mainly rural until the 1950s. The heart of Basque industrial potential lay in the supremely rich deposits of high quality iron ore located in the mines near Bilbao.[3]

Under the foral regime the mines were municipal property and rights of usufruct were available to all municipal residents. Thus, the mines were characterized by a proliferation of extractions, low technological investment and limited production and profitability (Pinedo, 1977: 149). After 1825 many mines fell into private ownership, but their exploitation was severely restricted by under-capitalization and foral legislation. In 1863 foral taxation of ore, which had almost prevented its sale outside the province, was reduced and in 1868 a new mining law permitted the export of ore (Fusi, 1975: 17). As a result, from 1863 to 1871 extraction of ore rose from 70,720 to 402,142 tons.[4] However, only after the abolition of the foral regime in 1876, did production of iron ore pass 1 million tons per annum. At this point the industrial take-off of Bilbao commenced in earnest.

The new mining law also opened the way for foreign, especially British, investment. Foreign interests eventually controlled some 50% of the Basque mining industry. Basque and foreign capital combined to increase extraction of ore by more that 1000% between 1876 and 1900.[5] By the end of the century Spain was producing 21.5% of the world's annual output of iron ore and most of this ore was extracted around Bilbao (Payne, 1974: 106). Because of the lack of a Spanish market for ore, the commercial links between Bilbao and England, and Bilbao's easy access to the sea, 90% of all production was exported. Between 60% and 70% of this went to Great Britain. The massive export of iron ore was to be the motor for the entire process of Basque industrialization. In return for ore, Bilbao imported British capital and British coke which was cheaper and of higher calorific content than Spanish coal. Both these commodities were used to modernize the metallurgical industry.

The profits made by the mining industry were impressive. Pablo de Alzola, a Basque economist of the period, estimated that the profits obtained between 1878 and 1907 by local Basque capital came to 542,7 million pesetas (approximately £18,600,000)[6] (cited in Fusi, 1975: 22).

After 1900 and in particular after 1910 the mining sector declined significantly due to ore depletion. However, the expansion of Basque industry continued unabated. Because of the export of ore and the capital thus accumulated, the Bilbao port had been modernized to become one of the largest and busiest in Europe. Aided by readily available supplies of Basque timber and iron, Bilbao became a major centre for shipbuilding.

The mobilization of financial resources in Bilbao was expedited by the growth of Basque banking. Whereas in 1870 only one bank (the Banco de Bilbao founded in 1858) was functioning, by 1907 five major banks had been established and total local banking reserves had grown by almost 1000% (Fusi, 1975: 22). This capital, mostly accumulated in the mining sector, was used to develop the mainstay of the Basque industrial economy – the Basque iron and steel industry.

The metallurgical industry was concentrated along the left bank of the Nervion River and utilized the pre-existent infrastructure of railroads[7] and port facilities built up for the export of ore. The core of this industry was Altos Hornos de Vizcaya along with five or six other major concerns. Although initially sluggish and technologically backward, an invigorating infusion of capital and Bessemer's discovery of a simplified process of steel production had dramatic effects. Production of iron and steel ingot increased from 55,818 tons in 1886 to 208,000 tons in 1901 (Alzola y Mirondo, 1902: 81).

In the wake of the expansion of Basque heavy industry a proliferation of small, subsidiary industrial enterprises mushroomed. In Guipúzcoa the profusion of these artisanal family run and owned concerns was less dramatic, but similar. Characterized by low productivity and poor quality production, these concerns were dependent either directly or indirectly on the steel and shipping industries and formed the economic base of the emerging Basque middle classes.

By 1900 45% of Spain's merchant fleet, nearly all her production of iron and steel and 30% of Spain's investment capital were in Basque hands. Within a brief span of twenty years Basque – or more specifically, Bilbao – industrialists and bankers had become the single most powerful financial interest group in Spain (Carr, 1966: 435). This prodigious economic energy was a creation of liberalism and the abolition of the foral regime.

Basque industrialization received ample suppport from government policies. The *conciertos económicos* provided an extremely advantageous fiscal arrangement. Proportionately the Basque provinces enjoyed a significantly lower level of taxation than the rest of Spain even inspite of a 50% increase in Basque fiscal quotas in 1887. Moreover, in Vizcaya direct taxation on property and industry was minimal. Instead taxes were raised indirectly through taxation on consumption. Basque industrial expansion was further encouraged by solid walls of protectionism.

Even though many new technological processes had been incorporated into the steel plants constructed after 1876, nonetheless the general technological level of the industry remained well below European standards. Basque industry – especially the smaller, artisanal industries – was a high-cost industry, uncompetitive in the international market and only 'modern' in relation to the rest of Spain. Protective tariff barriers were essential. Spanish governments responded to Basque and Catalan pressure by erecting the highest tariff barriers in Europe. On average tariffs equalled 40% of the official value of the product and covered, among other items, the entire shipbuilding industry, everything connected to mining and metallurgy and railroad construction (Garcia Venero, 1969: 366). Because the Spanish market was underdeveloped, the government also extended generous subsidies to the Basque steel and, especially, shipping industries.

The social transformation

Basque heavy industry developed with great speed and so did the two new social classes it created – the Basque industrial élite and the non-Basque urban proletariat.

All writers on the process of Basque industrialization agree that from 1880 onwards the Vizcayan economy demonstrated an accelerating tendency toward monopoly capitalism (Fusi, 1975; Solozabal, 1975; Portilla, 1977; Corcuera, 1979; Beltza, 1976, 1978). Portilla has argued (1977: 88) that in comparison to the textile industry upon which Catalan industrial wealth was based, steel industries lend themselves to capital concentration because of their high initial capital requirements and proportionately low salary costs. In any case a new, tightly knit industrial oligarchy, descendants of sectors of the former Basque commercial and landed élites, quickly gained control over most of Basque heavy industry and banking. Linked by marriage, this oligarchy centred on five families. The most important was the Ybarra family, the major stockholders of the Banco de Bilbao and Altos Hornos de Vizcaya (the largest iron and steel company). The other families were the Martinez de las Rivas family, owners of San Francisco and Astilleros de Nervion, the Chavarri and Gandarias families, owners of La Vizcaya and the Sota y Llano family, owners of Astilleros Euskalduna and the Sota y Aznar Shipping. Together these families controlled over 50% of the metallurgical industry and most of Basque shipping. The capital they accumulated provided the foundation for Basque banking. Portilla has stated (Doctoral thesis: 683) that in 1896 the three biggest Basque concerns, La Vizcaya, San Francisco and Altos Hornos de Bilbao, produced 77% of Spain's output of iron ingot.

The monopolistic tendencies were exacerbated by Spanish protectionist policies which permitted the major Basque steel concerns to control a large part of the national market. As Fusi has suggested (1975: 31) the price of iron and steel in Spain was not determined by market forces, but by the needs of Altos Hornos de Vizcaya. This was especially prejudicial to the interests of small-scale producers. For instance, in 1897 through monopoly pricing practices, the price of iron was doubled and many such small producers went bankrupt.

By 1893 the Basque oligarchy had consolidated not only its economic power, but its political position within Vizcaya as well. Through electoral corruption and clientelism the Bilbao economic élite, adherents of centralizing liberalism and later conservatism, exercised a firm rule over the Vizcaya *Diputacion* (provincial government) and the Bilbao *ayuntamiento* (city council). During the 1891 elections to the Cortes, votes were purchased on a massive scale and economic force became the major determinant of election results for the next twenty-five years. Benigno and José Chavarri became the heads of the political machine operated by the Basque industrialists. One or the other of the brothers was elected without interruption as deputies from 1893 to 1916. The Gandarias and Ybarra families also consistently provided deputies to the Cortes during the same period. This group of industrialists came to be popularly known as *la Piña*. Their official title was Unión Liberal.

However, social changes were most dramatically visible in the lower ranks of Basque society. The intense rhythm of industrialization demanded an ever-growing pool of cheap, unskilled labour greatly in excess of that which could be provided by Bilbao, Vizcaya or even the Basque country as a whole. Hence, a vast inflow of non-Basque immigrants from the impoverished, rural regions of Spain was pulled into the industrializing areas. From 1876 to 1900 the population of Bilbao almost tripled and Vizcaya became the most densely populated province in Spain. At the turn of the century less than 20% of Bilbao's population had actually been born in the city and close to half were non-Basques by origin. Notably, around one-third of Bilbao's immigrants were recruited from the rural parts of the Basque country.

A study by the Basque historian, Javier Corcuera (1979), shows that the Basque and non-Basque residents of Bilbao demonstrated significant differences in occupation. Two aspects of these differences have a direct bearing on the emergence of Basque nationalism.

First, whereas only about a third of Basques born in Vizcaya were employed as industrial workers, more than half of the non-Basque immigrants were part of the urban proletariat. In absolute numbers the industrial class in Bilbao consisted in its majority of non-Basques. But these figures obscure the full extent of the separation by type of employment of Basques and non-Basques. While the Basques frequently worked in the smaller, more personalized factories, the non-Basque workers were concentrated in the steel works and the mines. For example, of the 13,000 workers employed in the mines in 1910, only around 3,000 were Basques by origin.

Second, in Spain employment opportunities and the prestige assigned to various occupations traditionally have differed from region to region. In the industrializing Basque provinces prestige and economic opportunity were linked to the private sector rather than to public service. Few ambitious Basques found the poorly paid jobs in provincial or local administration alluring. Hence, although the majority of the non-Basque population was placed among the lowest ranks of the economic ladder, non-Basques also dominated the public administration of Bilbao and indeed they occupied

70 % of all posts. That the public apparatus in Bilbao was under the political sway of the Basque economic élite and under the administrative control of non-Basques was viewed as an ominous political collusion by those sectors of the population which were to fill the nationalist ranks.

In this context it is important to note that, unlike Catalonia, what one could call, for lack of a better term, 'an autonomous middle-class culture' never developed in the Basque country. The vast majority of both the Basques and non-Basques of Bilbao in 1900 had only a minimal education, if that. There was no Basque university, theatre or experimentation in architecture and the arts (Carr, 1966: 436). Although European influences were enthusiastically absorbed in Barcelona, in contrast Bilbao remained proletarian in appearance and proletarian or semi-rural in attitudes. Bilbao's population of shopkeepers, traders, artisans, clerks and manual workers was diluted only by the illustrious Basque economic aristocracy housed in opulent palaces well removed from the rest of the city.

The demographic crush and the intense pace of an uncontrolled industrialization placed intolerable strains upon the social fabric of Bilbao. For the middle sectors of Bilbao the whole nature of social life deteriorated rapidly. The problems of inflation (especially in food prices), urban congestion, crime and the lack of adequate public services shattered what had previously been a relatively stable community. The old city centre became hemmed in by the proliferation of shanty towns and heavily polluting factories. Physical and social deterioration was particularly acute during the period 1891 to 1896 in which heavy immigration coincided with an economic recession and a long series of lethal epidemics due largely to Bilbao's fetid water supply. Bilbao's mortality rates in 1894 reached 45.1 per 1,000 annually, the highest mortality rate recorded in Europe. The index for London in 1894 was 19.4, for Nancy 35.3 and for Madrid 41.4 per 1,000 (Echevarria, 1894: 171, cited in Solozabal, 1975: 55–56). Moreover, the Basque petty bourgeoisie in particular experienced a sharp economic decline. As numerous small artisan enterprises went bankrupt, many formerly independent skilled workers were forced into the ranks of the industrial proletariat.

While social and economic grievances were accumulating among Basques, simultaneously resentment and rancour were increasing among the immigrant workers in the mines. Wages did not become a major issue of workers' protest until 1898.[8] But, the working and living conditions of the miners in particular were grim, brutal and oppressive. Echevarria (1894: 20) described the situation with awe:

> What is happening to the proletariat in Bilbao is truly incredible. The way in which hundreds of *desgracidos* live can't be believed until it is seen. Cruelly oppressed by usury, they are heaped together in rooms in which 6, 8 and 10 or more of both sexes sleep joined in a horrible moral and hygienic confusion.

The lack of basic hygiene, widespread malnutrition and overwork combined with Bilbao's damp, rainy climate made disease among the working class reach proportions which were considered alarming even for Bilbao. Particularly despised was the system of company barracks and canteens located alongside the mines and set up initially by the mine owners in order to provide some form of housing and board for the miners. The system was quickly made obligatory. Miners were forced to buy foodstuffs and other needed items on credit from the canteens at inflated prices and to reside in the dirty, ill-ventilated barracks in which one bed was frequently shared by four workers sleeping in shifts. After deductions for rent, canteen bills and time lost due to rain, many miners ended the month with little or nothing paid in wages and frequently in debt.

The first branch of the Partido Obrero Socialista Español, the PSOE, and the first workers' organizations (which later became incorporated into the Unión General de Trabajadores, the UGT) were founded among the Bilbao miners in 1890. Propelled by the deepening anger at living conditions and partly organized by the socialists, a violent, bitterly fought general strike – the first in Spain – paralyzed the iron mines and industrial belt in May the same year. The strike was supported by some 30,000 workers. The provincial governor resigned and was replaced by a military governor who declared martial law. Over the next twenty years the industrial area of Bilbao and especially the mines were the scene of thirty partial strikes and five general strikes most of which became violent (Fusi, 1975: 88–94).

The socialists gained their first real mass support among the Bilbao miners. Bilbao, described by the writer, Ramiro de Maeztu, as 'the Mecca of socialism', became the most militant centre for the advocacy and export of socialism in Spain.

One important aspect of these strikes should be noted. The strikes, directed against the managers and proprietors of the mining and iron industries who were almost exclusively Basque, were led by Spanish socialist organizers and Spanish workers were their most exuberant and turbulent followers. In other words, vertically, the opposition of interests in these strikes corresponded to ethnic divisions. Because few Basques lent support to these strikes, many immigrants viewed the Basques in general as an exploiting, privileged class, a view often reflected in the socialist literature.

Spanish working-class militancy was paralleled by the growth of Basque middle-class bewilderment and hostility. In 1893 *La Lucha de Clases* (The Class Struggle), the socialists' newspaper, and *Bizkaitarra* (The Vizcayan), the magazine of an embryonic group of Vizcayan nationalists, appeared for sale on the streets of Bilbao almost simultaneously.

3

History as myth*

Three features of the nineteenth century formed the critical background to Basque nationalism. The first two were instrumental for the development of Basque nationalism in the first place. The third factor helps explain why it emerged specifically in Bilbao in the 1890s.

First and foremost, Spanish nationalism was a failed nationalism. It was incapable of overriding local and regional loyalties. Because of the economic and political failures of nineteenth-century reforms, an economically stagnant and politically corrupt and unstable centre was unable either to inspire or control Spain's more vigorous peripheries. Moreover, the creation of a national market came late and in any case was insufficient. Secondly, the Basque country had never been a 'regular' part of Spain in the same sense as Extremadura or Andalucia. It enjoyed a foral regime and, therefore, economic and administrative autonomy considerably longer than other Spanish regions. Also, parts of the Basque country were characterized by a culture markedly different from other Iberian cultures. This 'fact' of political and cultural differentiation provided the raw material which Basque nationalism drew upon to construct its ideology. Thirdly, although Basque industrialization helped merge the interests of important sectors of Basque society and the financial and political apparatus of the state, in Bilbao industrialization generated extremely high social costs and created two new and powerful social classes, the Basque oligarchy and the non-Basque proletariat. In contrast Navarra and Alava remained rural and in Guipúzcoa industrialization was confined mainly to small-scale producers.

Basque nationalism first emerged in Bilbao – the Basque industrial heartland – during the last quarter of the nineteenth century. This period was one of severe social crisis during which the traditional Basque country, governed by local political institutions and dedicated to commercial and agricultural enterprise, was superseded by a new Basque society founded on a unified Spanish constitution and heavy industry. In a sense Basque

* The English versions of cited texts are my translations. The spelling of various Basque words, e.g. Jaun-Goikua, varies in this text because it varies in the original.

nationalism was a political reaction to two compelling integrative forces. One was state centralization imposed from Madrid. The other was Basque industrialization imposed from within. However, the feature that sets Basque nationalism apart from other European ethnic movements is that its principal attack was not centred on Madrid, the political centre. The main concern of Basque nationalism was with the new social and economic relationships inside the modernizing Basque country.

Notably, Basque nationalism evolved out of Vizcayan nationalism. Its early ideologues and followers referred to themselves as *Bizkainos* (people from Vizcaya) and not Basques. The first nationalist magazine was called *Bizkaitarra* (The Vizcayan) and initially the movement was widely known as *bizkaitarrismo*. Although bedecked with the symbols of Basque rural culture and language, Basque nationalism was an ideology constructed by urbanites whose major concern was with the problems of industrializing Bilbao and not with the Basque country as a whole. Only with the spread of industrialization to other Basque areas at a later date did Basque nationalism lose its bias toward Vizcaya and become a wider 'Basque' doctrine.

The nationalist ideology: a Basque paradise lost

The cultural prelude

The vast majority of Basque peasants perceived the nineteenth century as a period of economic, political and cultural humiliation and regarded their *euskaldun* rural roots as a prime barrier preventing integration into urban prosperity. Indeed, when Basque nationalism made its first appearance in Bilbao, the Basque language, Euskera, had been virtually extinct in the city from the beginning of the nineteenth century and was rapidly receding throughout the Spanish Basque country. Basque urban politics and business were conducted in Spanish. Reliable figures concerning the disappearance of Euskera are non-existent. However, the rough estimates available put the total number of Basque speakers in the Spanish Basque country during the mid-1800s at around 4–600,000 which represented from 55% to 84% of the population. By the nineteenth century, Euskera had largely died out in Alava, the southern part of Navarra and the language was used as the vernacular only by the *baserritarak* (peasantry) in Vizcaya, Guipúzcoa and in the Pyrenean valleys of Navarra as well as by the coastal fishermen.[1]

The number of Basque speakers declined rapidly after the Second Carlist War when primary schools were established throughout the Basque country. These schools provided instruction in Spanish exclusively. Thus, the rise of literacy and the regression of Euskera became parallel processes. In general the Spanish language unrelentingly radiated out from the pathways and nodal points of long-distance communication. The retreat of Euskera was most notable in those areas which had direct geographical links with major national roads, administrative and commercial centres and industrial complexes with their large immigrant populations. The only exception was the Catholic Church which perforce frequently used Euskera to communicate to the faithful.

As importantly, Euskera was stigmatized as the language of the stables, the language of unsophisticated rustics in contrast to Spanish, the language of refinement, culture, education and urban success. And the stigma on Euskera deepened as the cities gained in prestige.

The vulnerability of Euskera was partly due to its lack of literary production. The language was mainly an oral one. Although the first book written in Euskera was published in 1545,[2] by the start of the nineteenth century only a total of 111 publications had been issued in the language (Payne, 1974: 168). Most of these publications were obscure religious tracts and pamphlets. Moreover, the lack of magazines and newspapers in Euskera at the end of the nineteenth century meant that the increasingly educated masses read only in Spanish.

It is doubtful that the preservation of Euskera was notably helped by the various attempts at the turn of the twentieth century to purify the language and give it a distinct orthography. Euskera was purged by nationalist linguists of the letters *c*, *ç*, *ch*, *f*, *h*, *g*, *v*, *w* and *ll* which were deemed alien influences as were many words in common use that had been imported. Thus, although the naval industry had been of supreme importance in Basque economic history, in Azkue's standard Basque dictionary the works for galleon, pirate, shipbuilder, etc. are absent (Caro Baroja, 1974: 88). But endeavours at linguistic purification were only part of a surge of Basque romantic literature originating from the cities – and usually written in Spanish for an Hispanicized urban audience – which lauded the peasantry as the paragon of liberty, moral purity and true Basque values. The *renacimiento euskerista* contained many of the cultural symbols and moral oppositions which later were given a ferocious political content by Basque nationalism.

Antonio de Treuba, Joseph Augustin Chaho, Yparraguirre, Arturo Campion and Resurreción Maria de Azcue were among the leading figures in this literary movement. The majority of these writers came from Carlist or Integrist[3] political backgrounds and had their sentiments and literary visions firmly fixed in pre-industrial Basque society. Intellectually – both inside and outside the Basque country – they were eclipsed by the three important Basque members of the famous literary generation of 1898, Ramiro de Maeztu, Miguel Unamuno and Pio Baroja, all of whom achieved international recognition and none of whom had patience with the rural nostalgia or political posturing of the *renacimiento euskerista*.

Two themes especially were stressed in the *renacimiento*. One was the image of the ideal, harmonious and moral nature of Basque traditional life in opposition to the contaminated misery of industrialized society. The second concerned the epic struggle of the Basques in defence of their liberties and unique cultural heritage in the face of foreign usurpers.

Voyage en Navarre by the French Basque, Chaho, in which he gives his personal description of the First Carlist War, contains many of the pre-nationalist elements which characterized this romantic tradition. The Basque is depicted as a type of natural man, inheritor of a glorious, legendary country governed by *fueros* and inherent Basque democracy derived from original liberty. This heroic image is placed in bitter juxtaposition to authoritarian, degenerate Castile inhabited by 'a people without name'. For Chaho, the Carlist War was a war of national reaffirmation and, thus, part of a long tradition.

In the writings of Campion the opposition between the Basque and Spanish is also fundamental. This opposition is viewed both in terms of the virtues of the Pyrenean north versus the degeneration of the centralizing south and in terms of social forces inside the Basque country. The individualistic Basques are set in contrast to the cosmopolitan nomadism of the 'bastardized Celts, decadent Latins and corrupted Moors who try to poison our souls with the grotesque ideals of envious slaves' ('La Personalidad Euskara', 1901). The 'universal socialization', impiety and promiscuity of the immigrant, according to Campion, presented the major peril for the Basque race. The language was of special importance since Campion regarded Euskera as the heart of the Basque people, support of the race and transmitter of the culture. 'Euskera', he wrote, 'is retiring to the mountains in order to die closer to heaven' ('El Baskuenze', 1901). Its demise spelt the final death-blow to all that was truly Basque and, therefore, preservation of the language had to be the first duty of all true Basques.

During the last quarter of the century various, often short-lived, cultural associations which sought to study, conserve and promulgate the Basque language and culture were founded. The journals published by these associations – *Revista de las Provincias Euskaras*, *Euskal Erria*, *Euskara*, etc. – blended culture and politics in an ill-defined, diffused way. Although liberalism and centralism were attacked and the loss of the *fueros* mourned, few of the Basque intellectuals who published in these journals questioned the inherent unity of Spain. Even Campion, the leading cultural figure in the nationalist movement, saw the Basque country as an integral part of the Spanish monarchy and was only a lukewarm political supporter of the nationalist creed.

For example, in 1880 Campion helped to organize a Basque cultural week complete with grand displays of bonfires, bell ringing, *txistularis* (players of the *txistu*, a Basque flute) together with a special mass with the sermon in Euskera. The parades that started the week were headed by massive Spanish flags, a gesture which today would provoke riots.

The use of literature to serve a clear nationalist political message began with the inauguration in 1895 of *Vizcay'tik Bizkai'ra*, an operetta by Azcue which received tremendous popular acclaim.[4] The operetta deals with the destruction of Basque traditional society by industrialization and the central state which combined to create electoral corruption financed by money from the mines. The operetta ends with the election – in spite of all odds – of the 'Basque' candidate who loves his people and their customs and is untainted by contact with the established political and economic power centres.

However, as a whole the *renacimiento euskerista* was limited to small intellectual circles and had little social impact. But it marked the cultural overture to Basque nationalism. Rural culture gave Basque urbanite intellectuals a model for a utopian past which stood in noble relief to the bleakness generated by industrialization and 'foreigners'. Basque nationalism was to be the instrument by which this paradise lost would be restored.

Basques and anti-Basques: the ideology of Sabino de Arana-Goiri

At the heart of the nationalists' vision of their cause lies the ideology of Sabino de Arana-Goiri, the founder of Basque nationalism as a discrete political doctrine and its most revered ideologue. A lawyer by profession, Arana was born in Bilbao and came from an ardent Carlist family. His father was a prosperous constructor of river barges who had come close to bankruptcy because of his financial support for the Carlist cause. Personally introspective and physically frail, Arana inherited from his Carlist family an adherence to religious fundamentalism and a total aversion to modern, liberal Spain.

Arana became a Basque nationalist while studying in Catalonia where he lived for almost six years.[5] Although it provided an inspirational model Catalanism and Arana's conception of Basque nationalism had little in common. Catalanism saw itself as a modernizing movement and its arguments rested on the special intellectual achievements, administrative requirements and economic interests of modern Catalonia. It sought to restructure the cumbersome, corrupt and unresponsive apparatus of the Spanish state with something more suited to the needs of an industrializing society. Catalanism was not separatist. The unity of Spain was never really an issue.

In contrast, Arana held a visceral dislike of capitalist industrialization and modern Bilbao society in particular. He perceived Vizcaya, or Bizkaia, according to Arana's orthography – to be in an advanced state of moral, political and ethnic decay. He laid the blame on Spain. To Arana, Vizcaya was 'mangled by the foreign fury and dying, but not dead which would have been preferable; rather humiliated, trampled and mocked by that weak and miserable nation, Spain' ('El discurso de Larazabal', 1893). Social injustice and class conflict – like the disruptive, violent process of industrialization itself – were non-Basque, foreign imports. The only solution for Vizcaya lay in a complete separation and isolation from all things Spanish.

Condemnation of industrialization led to an exaltation of traditional society. The authentic Vizcaya was the *euskaldun* (Basque-speaking), egalitarian, rural Vizcaya governed by *fueros* and locked in bitter battle with the *villas* and especially Bilbao. 'If Bizkaya were poor and only had fields and livestock, then, we would be patriots and happy' ('Caridad!', C.W., p. 441). This was a Vizcaya about which Arana, born in Bilbao during the height of mining and industrial wealth, had little knowledge.

Like most *Bilbaínos*, Sabino de Arana was ignorant of Euskera. The first stage of his career was dedicated to studying the language. Although he never became fluent, Arana published *Gramática Elemental del Euskera Bizkaino* in 1888. However, Arana's real interests were political. The first public statement of his political orientation came in 1892 with the publication of a small pamphlet, *Bizcaya por su independencia.* Following in the footsteps of the *renacimiento euskerista*, Arana describes four battles – of dubious historical authenticity – in which he proves that Vizcaya had always fought to preserve her liberty and sovereignty against Spanish encroachment and that she had always emerged victorious. But now debased by luxury and effeminacy, Arana warned, Vizcaya had opened her floodgates to the invaders.

Arana's nationalism had one central function – the struggle against the *maketo*[6] invasion. For not only were the Basques already corrupted by *españolista* tendencies – liberalism, 'that son of Satan', for example – but more importantly, the Basques were under a monumental frontal attack inside the Basque country. The *maketos*, the nationalists' derogatory label for Spanish immigrants, were 'by nature immoral and impious' ('Efectos de la invasion', Collected Works, p. 1329) and these perverted qualities were contagious. Thus, the *maketos* were subverters of Basque values, invidious disrupters of religious and social order and in essence anti-Basque.

Unlike most nationalist movements which principally emphasize the relationship between a dominant political centre and a subordinate, culturally differentiated periphery, Basque nationalism confronted social relationships and developments inside Vizcaya. Its chief targets were the two main protagonists of Basque industrialization – first and foremost, the militant, non-Basque working class, adherents of centralizing socialism and secondarily, the small, powerful Basque industrial oligarchy, advocates of centralizing liberalism.

Arana's ideology was essentially a symbolic one. The overt historical and cultural arguments upon which it was constructed were less important than the covert political functions these arguments were meant to serve. His ideology can be broken down into two interrelated sets of symbols. One set was composed of the elements of Euskera, religion, Basque customs and Basque character. These four elements defined the Basque mode of being in opposition to the Spanish one. This set of symbols functioned to differentiate and articulate one sector of urban society defined as 'Basque' in order to exclude other sectors defined as 'anti-Basque'. These symbols, derived from Basque pre-industrial society, were destined to provide moral legitimacy to a struggle for economic and political precedence inside the Basque country – an *internal nationalism*.

The second set consisted of the elements of Basque history, *fueros* and original sovereignty. These symbols served to separate the Basque country as a whole from the process of state unification and centralization and, therefore, provided the legitimacy for an *external nationalism* directed toward Madrid.

Standing over these two sets of symbols and linking them together was Arana's supreme symbol – the Basque race. The linchpin of his ideology, his concept of race, had both internal and external functions. On the one hand the Basque race was a totally exclusive and totally moral category. Ascription was determined by birth and continued inclusion by moral action. Race was a God-given condition that could never be achieved. Integration was impossible. It could, however, be readily lost. On the other hand, historic races, like the Basques, had a natural right to self-government. They were the *sine qua non* of nations. The overriding feature of Arana's stress on race was a concern about political loyalties. Political loyalty was seen in terms of the moral duties of the race. It did not mean the defence of the Basque language, Catholicism, customs or notions derived from Basque history. Political loyalty in Arana's ideology meant an adherence to the covert political functions – the cohesion and mobilization of one group and the exclusion of other groups – symbolized by the elements which structured his arguments. Political action of a very specific nature was inextricably interwoven with the general moral prescriptions governing continued membership in an exclusive moral community. These points become clearer when Arana's ideology is examined in more detail.

There is little evidence that Sabino de Arana was particularly familiar with the German and French 'scientific' literature on nationalism and race then in vogue in Europe. His proof came from God, not science. For Arana, a group of families with a common origin formed a race. Like the families of which it was composed, a race was 'the moral union of individuals born from the same trunk, who maintain among themselves relations elaborated by blood through time' ('La Patria', C.W., p. 1762). A race gave the *raison d'être* for a *patria* – or nation.

> The patriarchal family, that is to say, the *patria* is the union of individuals of an historic race for whom time has formed customs and language and on whose behalf history has created a patrimony of liberties which all generations (of that race) have the perfect right to enjoy. ('La Patria', C.W., p. 1762)

In the same manner in which an individual could not belong to two families – or change families – so he could not belong to two races or *patrias*. Race and nation were founded on the immutable decision of blood and biological kinship. A Basque could never be Spanish and a Spaniard could never be Basque. These were permanently mutually exclusive categories.

Since race was a matter of blood, the stamp of a member of a race was to be found in the surname. A Basque was a person with Basque surnames – a proof of Basque descent even though he spoke only Spanish. Conversely, a Spaniard was someone with a Spanish surname, even though he spoke only Euskera. A Sanchez would always be Spanish. A Zubizarreta always Basque. For Arana and the Basque nationalists in general surnames took on an overwhelming importance. Indeed, they were often the only reasonable guarantee of racial ascription to be found among the otherwise thoroughly Hispanicized urban Basques.

Since the race was the foundation of the *patria*, the protection of the race was a key aim of patriotism. Unlike many of his European contemporaries, Arana did not regard territoriality as an essential or constant feature of the *patria*. Arana argued that the *patria* could not be measured by the metre – that is by the territory it occupied: 'the *patria* is measured by race, history, laws, customs, character and language...our Euskeria would still be Euskeria...even if it were moved to an island in the Pacific' ('Vulgaridades', C.W., p. 426). Ultimately territory was important only to the extent that it functioned to differentiate spatially, isolate geographically and, thus, protect the race.

Similarly – in spite of Arana's efforts to study and preserve Euskera – he did not regard the language as important in itself. 'What is the national language, considered by itself, except a simple sign by which members of a nation communicate their ideas and emotions? If it is repressed and replaced by another, the nation will continue exactly as before' ('Efectos de la invasión', C.W., p. 1327). To some extent this view reflects the fact that few of the early nationalists spoke Euskera. Therefore the language could not be used as an essential attribute of the nation.

For Arana, Euskera provided a vehicle for the virtues of the race. 'Euskera cannot be considered merely as a beautiful language, worthy of being cultivated in literature: it is the support of our race and the buttress of the religiosity and morality of our people' ('Epílogo', C.W., p. 432); 'the preservation of our language is a great help for also preserving religiosity and morality in our country' ('Qué caridad!', C.W., p. 297). Although Euskera expressed the Basque mode of morality, the language had to be subordinated to the race. A language, if lost, could always be regained; but a race, once lost, was lost forever. For the first nationalists the principal value of Euskera was its ability to differentiate Basques from Latin Spain and place a barrier of linguistic incomprehension between Basques and their enemies.

> If we had to choose between a Bizkaya populated by *maketos* who spoke only Euskera and a Bizkaya populated by bizkainos who spoke only Spanish, without doubt we could select the latter... Bizkainos are as obliged to speak their national language as they are not to teach it to the *maketos* or Spaniards. Speaking one language or another is not important. Rather the difference between languages is the means of preserving us from the contagion of Spaniards and avoiding the mixing of the two races. If our invaders learnt Euskera, we would have to abandon it, carefully storing away its grammar and dictionary, and dedicate ourselves to speaking Russian, Norwegian or some other language unknown to them.
>
> ('Errores Catalanistas', C.W., p. 404)

The main role of Euskera, then, was a part of the defensive armament to be employed against foreign infiltrators.

Arana regarded the Basque race also as a moral category. Basque morality had its source in religion and was made manifest through the Basque character and traditional customs. For Arana, the supremacy of Roman Catholicism was essential for sacred and, hence, moral order upon which all social order ultimately rested. A prime mover behind Arana's ideology was the belief that only through nationalism could the Catholic faith be adequately defended. 'My patriotism is not founded in human motives, nor is it directed toward material ends: my patriotism is founded, and each day more, in my love of God and the end in Him which I seek is to lead to God my brothers of the race: my great family, the Basque *pueblo*' ('Tres Cartas', C.W., p. 2073).

According to Arana, the decline of Basque religious sentiment and the loss of Basque independence were simultaneous processes. They had a common origin – the illicit intrusion of liberal, anti-clerical Spain. 'Bizcaya, dependent on Spain, cannot go toward God. It cannot be Catholic in practice' ('No Rezan con nostros', C.W., p. 418). Spain was anti-Basque and anti-Christ. The proof of the inherently atheist nature of modern Spain was abundant. Liberals, free-thinkers and Masons, 'the cult of Lucifer', had undercut the unity, purity and discipline of the faith. In Spain, superstition masqueraded as faith and fanaticism as piety.

However, Arana's conception of the unity and universality of Catholicism was also subordinate to his nationalist political message. The universality of Catholicism was only applicable on the abstract level of the Pope in Rome. Arana denied unity on the practical level. As Italians did not pray with Spaniards and Spaniards did not pray with non-Spaniards, so too Basques should not pray with non-Basques. And religion was basically a spiritual matter of faith in and communication with God. Arana severely lambasted the Catholic charity of San Vicente de Paul for aiding immigrant families.

to favourize the inroads of the *maketos* is to foment immorality in our land: because it is clear that the customs of our *Pueblo* have notably degenerated in this period due without doubt to the dreadful invasion of *maketos* who bring blasphemy and immorality with them. ('Qué caridad!', C.W., p. 296)

Moreover, the Spanish Catholic Church was a foreign element in the Basque religious community. The swell of irreligion could only be halted by isolation from the *maketo* defilers and the Spanish Catholic Church.

Arana's religious beliefs were condensed into his notion of *Jaungoikua*, a critical emblem of the nationalist doctrine. The Basque word for 'God' or, literally, 'Lord on high', *Jaungoikua*, was the fountain of all sacred and wordly authority inside the Basque country. But implicitly, *Jaungoikua* was an exclusive God. He was the God of the Basques and, as such, provided an autonomous framework for religion.

Arana's stress on morality was further elaborated in his description of the Basque character and traditional customs. Again the opposition between the moral Basque and immoral Spaniard was the fundamental issue. 'The Basque is intelligent, noble and masculine; the Spaniard inexpressive, sullen and effeminate. The Basque is capable of handling all types of work; the Spaniard inept even at the most simple tasks. The Basque is a learner, born to be his own master. The Spaniard never learns and is born to be servile. The Basque is generous even to his enemies. The Spaniard is avaricious even towards his brothers. The Basque character degenerates with foreign intermingling. The Spanish need a foreign invasion from time to time in order to civilize them' ('Qué somos?', C.W., p. 627).

This same pattern of moral opposition was also valid for Basque and Spanish customs. Whereas Basque dances are infused with a pristine joy, glory and dignity, 'at a Spanish dance, if you don't feel nauseated at the unchaste, disgusting and cynical embrace of the two sexes, the credit goes to the robustness of your stomach. But decide afterwards if you have enjoyed the spectacle or rather if it has caused loathing and sadness' ('Qué somos?', C.W., p. 627). As final proof of the degenerate and degenerating nature of the Spaniard, 'according to statistics, 95% of the crimes in Bizkaya are perpetrated by Spanish hands, and Hispanicized Bizkainos are responsible for four of the remaining five per cent' ('Qué somos?', C.W., p. 628).

In short, Arana's conception of Euskera, religion and Basque customs and character provided symbols of exclusion and moral differentiation which yielded ethnically and ethically separated groupings inside the Basque country. The boundary thus created was both a political and a moral one. In nationalist ideology the Spanish immigrant proletariat – like all things Spanish or Hispanicized – was not only excluded from 'Basque' and, hence, 'national' status; it was also ejected from the moral universe.

Similarly, but operating on a different level, Arana's conception of Basque history and *fueros* was directed toward differentiating and separating the

Basque country from the rest of Spain. While Catalonia was a mere region, according to Arana, Vizcaya was by history an independent nation conquered by Spain in 1839 when the Basque provinces were integrated into the constitutional unity of Spain. 'The Catalans and Bizkainos do not have the same enemy. The enemy of Catalonia is the central power of the nation to which she naturally belongs, Castilla ... the enemy of Bizkaya is the foreign nation which has made her into a vassal' ('Errores Catalanistas', C.W., p. 405).

In Arana's interpretation of Basque history his idea of Basque original sovereignty played a pivotal role. Original sovereignty was an innate attribute of Basques and conferred an eternal right to and drive for independence. The Basques had never been drawn into the domain of the foreign power nor been subjects of a personal ruler. Political authority was symbolized by the egalitarian *boina*, the Basque beret, and 'the *boina* (at least the Bizkayan) and the Crown are in essence incompatible' ('Ilusiones Carlistas', C.W., p. 294). Political process was symbolized by the oak tree at Guernica under which popularly elected representatives assembled to legislate and Spanish kings swore fidelity to the customary rights and independence of the Basques.

Original sovereignty was intimately tied to original nobility, *hidalguía originaria*. The latter, like the former, was an inalienable part of the Basque condition. For Arana, the grants of collective nobility were a public acknowledgement of Basque original nobility, independence, purity of blood and, on the local level, Basque egalitarianism. The Basques, 'in foreign lands [Spain] were all noble; in their own country they were simply citizens all of whom had equal rights' ('Polémica doctrinal', C.W., p. 1177).

Arana argued that the Basque *fueros* were a product of a noble, independent people and as such represented the only legitimate Basque system of political organization. They were the 'national legal codes of the *Pueblo Vasko*'. Whereas the *fueros* of Catalonia and Aragon, for example, were privileges and exemptions conceded by the Spanish central authority: 'The institution which is called *Fueros Vasko–Nabarros* are not privileges: they are the laws of free *pueblos* with original liberty; they are freely created by the people for the people without interference from any foreign power' ('Polémica doctrinal', C.W., p. 1143).

Consistent with this view, the relation between the Basque provinces or states, as Arana referred to them, and Castile was one of voluntary alliances between equal, politically independent nations. Partial authority had been delegated to Madrid, but never sovereignty. Such alliances were eminently dissolvable.

From this Arana drew a major political conclusion. In other regions of the Spanish state demands for the reinstatement of *fueros* were consistent with demands for autonomy. But, if Euskeria embraced autonomy, it would embrace its own death sentence. A race that sacrificed even part of its sovereignty sacrificed its right to survive. Demands for Basque *fueros* could only mean one thing, separatism – the reestablishment of a totally independent state.

Arana expanded his view of *fueros* into what he called *Lagi-zara* (lit. = ancient law) which, along with *Jaungoikua* (God), formed the second pillar of the nationalist emblem. For Arana, *Lagi-zara* contained four aspects: (1) *fueros*, the national legal code; (2) the race, the essence of Basqueness; (3) customs and traditions, part of the differential elements of Basque nationality, and (4) Euskera, the national language ('La pureza de raza', C.W., p. 545).

Arana summed up his nationalist ideology in the overarching slogan, 'Jaungoikua eta Lagi-Zara' (God and Old Laws), a slogan usually referred to by its anagram, JEL. In this slogan morality – defined mainly in opposition to things Spanish – was inextricably fused to an exclusive, separatist political loyalty. The moral gave spiritual value to the political. For the nationalists, JEL expressed a crystalline synthesis of their political vision and social cause.

Moreover – and this is fundamental for understanding the socio-political nature and logic of Basque nationalism both past and present – adherence to the prescriptions of JEL was made into the real defining point of a Basque in contrast to the anti-Basque. These prescriptions were the political functions of differentiation and exclusion on both the internal and external level symbolized by the elements – Euskera, race, *fueros*, etc. – which were contained in the slogan JEL. In nationalist ideology and politics it was not sufficient to be Basque in terms of surnames, language or religion. One had to be a 'good' Basque. Ultimately Basque racial ascription was not determined by descent. For Basque nationalism, when applied to Bilbao, to have its desired effects, Arana had to make race a politically operative category – not a static matter of once and for all biological inclusion or exclusion. Basque status was granted solely to those who faithfully and publicly adhered to the political behaviour implicit in the slogan 'Jaungoikua eta Lagi-Zara'. In short, a real Basque could only be a Basque nationalist.

Thus, nationalism perceived the modern world as morally divided into Basques defined as those who adhered to the dictates of JEL and anti-Basques defined as those who were the negation of JEL. The two sides were viewed in terms of a series of oppositions. The Basque represented tradition, pre-capitalist society, egalitarianism and democracy, peace and social order, Catholicism and spiritual rectitude. The anti-Basque represented modernization, industrial society, hierarchies and authoritarianism, violence and disruption, anti-clericalism and spiritual corruption. The former was the foundation of moral life and was under grave threat. The latter was immoral and contagious. The Basque was, therefore, under obligation to defend the nation from this contagion. To do so the Basque had to become an *abertzale* (patriot) and, thus, would be granted the status of the insider, of the 'national'. The anti-Basque was an *españolista* and, therefore, had to be rejected as an outsider, a 'non-national'. The justification for nationalism came from nature. Nationalism was a defence of the sacred, natural order of things.

This ideology was directly transformed into an emotive and powerful political strategy which would eventually gain the nationalists an unquestioned political and economic hegemony inside the Basque country. However, this ideology also corresponded, albeit obliquely, to deep-seated pre-existent cultural structures upon which social ordering within Basque traditional society had been achieved. These structures were under attack by the process of Basque industrialization. While nationalism was successfully applied in a fierce competition over political and economic resources inside the Basque region, it also reflected a profoundly real cultural conflict and crisis.

The politics of JEL

Because of the nature of its ideological underpinnings, Basque nationalism was non-ecumenical. It was a total, demanding ideal that did not admit a plurality of political visions. Alternative options were not only politically unacceptable; they were morally unacceptable.

> For us, Vizcayan nationalists, it is the same if councillors, deputies and senators are socialists, liberal monarchists, republicans, Catholic Carlists or integrists, or platonic autonomists... All of them (and that includes in practice so called Catholics) are enemies of *Jaun-Goikua*; all of them are enemies of *Lagi-zara*.
>
> ('Las pasadas elecciones', C.W., p. 1288)

Arana's immediate political targets were the socialists supported by the miners and the workers in the iron foundries and the liberals representing the Basque economic élite.

Arana was aware of the severe social problems generated by industrialization. 'All of us know that today the poor are inhumanly exploited and treated like animals by the industrialists, merchants and mine owners' ('Las pasadas elecciones', C.W., p. 1289). However, socialism was anti-Christ, anti-Basque and unnecessary.

> Don't they see that having overthrown bourgeois domination, with socialism *los euskerianos* [Basques] still remain subjugated to *maketo* domination... ? Give up socialist ideas which are anti-Christian and anti-Basque. For justice and equality to be realized in Vizcayan society, it is not necessary to resort to socialism... These sacred ideals are indelibly engraved in the history of our race, in the doctrine of our fathers, in the nationalist banner. ('Las pasadas elecciones', C.W., p. 1290)

The most damning feature of socialism was its foreignness. Imported into the Basque country by immigrant workers, socialism was nurtured by Spanish envy and greed for Basque wealth. It was an excuse for indolence and the antithesis of the Basque spirit and tradition. 'What can we say about socialism? It is advocated by three or four *maketos*, sons of a country which has never known liberty nor equality nor fraternity nor economic equilibrium. Socialism is a system radically opposed to our ancient and wise laws...' ('Glorias y fiestas bastardas', C.W., p. 275).

The social problems affecting workers could only be solved through nationalism which aimed to reestablish the natural and perfect social harmony of an independent Basque state. Moreover, socialist propaganda to the contrary, Basque and Spanish workers were not allies sharing the same interests. Their interests were opposed and in competition. The Spanish invasion meant fewer jobs and lower wages. It meant Basque emigration.

The *baseritar* (peasant) who comes down to the city, to the quarry, to the mines, to the workshop comes down pursued by necessity and seeks work in order to live. He finds a plague of Chinamen who eat in name only because they work in name only. The *baseritar* will have to accept their ridiculous wages and, therefore, will have to eat like them – although not work like them – in name only.

('Los chinos en Euskeria', C.W., p. 1781)

Arana thought it incomprehensible that even one Basque worker could join the socialist ranks. Bourgeois oppression was terrible; but so was foreign oppression. Consequently, he argued for the formation of a labour union consisting of Basque workers only.

And if there are still suspicions and fear that there are differences between the bourgeoisie and proletariat, between capitalists and workers inside the nationalist party, why do the Basque workers not unite, separating themselves and completely excluding the *maketos* in order to combat the despotic bourgeois oppression against which they so justly complain? ('Las pasadas elecciones', C.W., p. 1290)

However, Arana never envisioned an independent working-class organization. Despite economic exploitation, the tragic plight of the workers was largely a result of their lack of discipline and their inclinations toward gaming, drinking and other frivolities. The bourgeoisie had grossly abused its power. But its appropriate role, 'the high and noble mission which God entrusted' ('De allá y de acá', C.W., p. 2153), was to provide leadership, education and protection for the working class.

But if industrialization was responsible for bringing in the massive waves of Spaniards who threatened Basque spiritual traditions, then the root fault was clearly in those responsible for industrialization. The enemy was not only the Spanish *maketos*; it was also the Basque *maketófilos*, those Basques whose economic and political activities favoured immigration. For Arana, the major Basque industrialists, 'who have no other talents or virtues than ore and ingot,' and whose political position was maintained through electoral corruption, were the source of all 'the immorality, blasphemy, crime, free-thought, socialism, anarchism ... that is corrupting the Vizcayan soul' ('Caridad!', C.W., p. 441). The Basque industrialists had corroded the Basque sense of identity. Their liberalism was a sin against both *Jaungoikua* and *Lagi-Zara*. Their role was another replay in the endless conflict between the *euskaldun* (Basque-speaking) Vizcaya of peasant democracy and nobility and Hispanicized Bilbao, 'the focus from which radiates all the pestilence which is killing Bizkaya' ('El caciquismo', C.W., p. 1346).[7] Because of their behaviour which Arana regarded as treasonable, the important Basque industrialists were morally disenfranchised and placed firmly into the anti-Basque camp. Although Arana never used the term, his nationalism was a populist doctrine.

> The only party that detests with all its soul the lilies of their coat of arms and the gold in their coffers is the nationalist ... It is the only party which does not have any aristocrats or big capitalists among its initiates. It is capable tomorrow of converting all capital into guns in order to obtain freedom for the aspiring nation; of expelling all remnants of ancient and renowned aristocracies and of establishing such an equality between its citizens so as to contradict so-called natural and necessary class differences. ('Educación moderna', C.W., p. 446)

The Basque state

Larronde (1977: 151) has pointed out that Arana did not project the demands of Basque nationalism for a separate state onto the international level. The Hague Conference of 1898 which proclaimed the right of self-determination for national minorities was by and large ignored by the Basques. The Basque state was viewed more as a state of mind. It was the same as Basque patriotism. Arana was more concerned with the nature of patriotism than the nature of the state.

> The integrity of the Bizkayan Patria does not consist in the integrity of its territory, but in the integrity of its emblem *Jaun-goikua eta Lagi-zarra*. A Bizkaya located in these mountains but deprived of one of the characters of this emblem is no longer Bizkaya. Conversely, one square metre in whatever part of the world where families faithful to this emblem live, that is Bizkaya. ('Areitz orbelak', C.W., p. 614)

Patriotism was not an option, a matter for choice. It was a moral obligation as binding as obligations between kin and as sacred as the obligation toward God.

> Ideologically speaking, God comes before Patria; but in practice here in Bizkaya, to love God it is necessary to be a patriot, and to be a patriot it is necessary to love God. This *eta* [and] in our emblem is what many Bizkainos do not want to understand. The liberals say that to be a patriot one does not have to be Catholic; and the Catholics feel that in order to serve God one does not have to be a patriot. These (Bizkainos)

cannot be judged as members of Bizkayan society. In effect, they ought to belong to *maketo* society. ('Areitz orbelak', C.W., p. 615)

Thus, it was not cultural markers that determined nationality, it was the attribute of patriotism or unquestioned public fidelity to one political goal. But the fundamental drive behind patriotism and patriotic behaviour was not toward the creation of an independent state. Patriotism was an end in itself. In the nationalist ideology independence, like Euskera, Basque folklore, etc., was a symbolic element of differentiation, exclusion and preference. If Basque nationalism is seen primarily as a movement for political independence, then the whole nature of the movement, its internal disputes and the apparent contradictory changes of ideological direction become thoroughly bewildering. As will be discussed in following chapters, Arana in 1902 declared himself in favour of autonomy rather than independence and several nationalist parties which have advocated independence have nonetheless been branded as *españolista* and anti-Basque.

At its core Basque nationalism is not a dispute concerning territory. It is a struggle for power within a territory.

However, Arana also had a more concrete conception of a future independent Basque state based on his interpretation of Basque history. Since the Basques as a whole had never formed a unified state and since the various Basque territories had formerly existed as independent states, the new Basque state was to be a confederation comprised of the four Spanish Basque provinces and the three French ones. The foundation of this state was to be unity of race to the extent possible, and Catholic unity. Notably, this confederation was to be based on voluntary alliances between the political units and equality of rights and obligations within the confederation. Each member state retained its independence and, hence, the absolute right of succession. The confederation would unite its members solely in terms of the social order, upon which Arana did not elaborate, and international relations. This new Basque state would be a perfect state in which all social tensions and contradictions would be resolved by definition.

In 1901 Arana coined the term, Euzkadi,[8] to describe this independent Basque confederation. Arana had always been uncomfortable with the traditional Basque words for the Basque country and indeed for Basque. Euskalherria means 'the country of the people who speak Euskera' and Euskaldun, 'possessor of Euskera'. Technically speaking, therefore, most of the early nationalists would not have qualified as proper residents of the Basque country nor in fact as Basques at all. Arana solved the problem by taking the stem, *euzko*, which according to him, meant the Basque race, and adding the suffix -di, which meant locality. Thus Euzkadi was designed to mean 'the place of the Basque race'.

4

From the illuminated few to the Basque moral community

Let us join under the same flag, found purely Basque societies, write Basque newspapers, open Basque schools and even Basque charitable institutions. That everything seen by our eyes, spoken by our mouths, written by our hands, thought by our intelligences and felt by our hearts be Basque.

(Sabino de Arana, 'Regeneración', *El Correo Vasco*, 11 June 1899, C. W., p. 1674)

Arana's was the message of nation-building. But the message also had to be heeded, understood and acted upon by large numbers of disparate, often incompatible, individuals. And in the Basque country the task of nation-building was not straightforward. With industrialization the cleavage between town and country had deepened and become more truculent. In Bilbao new social sectors advocating different versions of centralizing ideologies had been propelled into prominence. The social configuration had become more complex and less coherent. In short, as raw material for nation-building, the residents of the Basque country were divided by culture, divergent economic and political aspirations and history. They had never shared a common identity. The job of the early urban nationalists was invention, not regeneration.

The nucleus of the nation: the origins of the Partido Nacionalista Vasco (PNV)

The inauspicious beginnings from which the Basque nation eventually emerged can be traced to the Euskaldun Batzokija (The Basque Society), a political/recreational club founded in 1894 by Sabino de Arana and his followers.

Faithful to Arana's primitive nationalism, the organization of the Euskaldun Batzokija mirrored the model of organization the early nationalists sought for Vizcaya. The expressed aim of the club was to 'establish close ties of unity and friendship between the *vecinos* of (Bilbao) and its surroundings who profess the doctrines contained in the Bizcayan Emblem, *Jaun-Goikua eta Lagi-Zara*'. Strictly confessional, the Batzokija was open only to those of proven Basque descent and closed off from contact with parties and persons who were anti-Catholic or *españolista*. Four aspects in particular are illustrative of more fundamental features of the Basque movement.

First, the statutes of the Batzokija established the principle that access to political power was dependent on degree of racial purity. The statutes defined three categories of members: original members, adopted members and supporter members. This gradation was based on the numbers of Basque surnames which demonstrated purity of descent. For instance, supporter members 'have among their first four surnames at least two that are Basque and among the rest some *erdérico* [Spanish] surnames inherited from a grandfather born in foreign territory'. Only original members were eligible for election to official posts and had full rights to vote and voice in all Batzokija matters.

Second, inside the Batzokija life was strictly 'Basque'. Spanish books, magazines, music, games and discussion of Spanish political themes were prohibited. The members were sealed off from a non-Basque nationalist world and their social vision compressed inward.

Third, of the 110 articles which comprised the statutes, all those which pertained to doctrinal orthodoxy – the cornerstones of nationalist ideology – were 'absolutely irrevocable'. Nationalist doctrine was above discussion and change. To ensure that the doctrinal dictates of the statutes were obeyed, a *Calificador* functioned as a type of theological censor. In addition, the *Calificador* determined which books were permitted in the library and the Basqueness of the surnames of applicants. Sabino de Arana was both president of the Batzokija and *Calificador*.

Finally, the statutes of the Batzokija placed tight reins upon the accumulation of personal power within the club. The statutes proposed a system in which access to official position would circulate evenly among all original members. The candidates for election to office were randomly chosen by lottery among those eligible. No office-holder could succeed himself in office and new officers were elected annually. In practice, a dispersal of authority never occurred. Within four months of its foundation, seven members had been expelled because of 'a conspiracy against the attributions of the office of president' (quoted in J. Corcuera, 1979).

The maximum number of members of the Batzokija never surpassed 130. The sociological composition of these early nationalists is indicative of the social base upon which radical nationalist sentiment rested until the civil war in 1936. Like so many other similar movements, these early nationalists were young. The average age of the *bazkides* (members of the Batzokija) was between twenty-six and twenty-eight years. Roughly one-half were not of voting age which was then twenty-five. Moreover, the club's members were principally from the middle sections of pre-industrial Bilbao. They were urban artisans, clerks, salesmen, professionals. Many of them formed part of Bilbao's mercantile traditions. In short, the *bazkides* represented that sector of Basque society which had been pushed to the periphery by the main industrial thrust.

The Euskaldun Batzokija had an eventful, but brief, existence. To all intents and purposes it was dissolved in 1895. Arana had entered into litigation with a Bilbao liberal. Upon losing the case, Arana was sentenced to one month and eleven days in prison.[1] More importantly, however, the foundation of the Batzokija coincided with the Cuban secessionist rebellion in 1895. In response the Madrid government decreed all separatist ideas and activities illegal. Although directed mainly at Cuba, this decree served for the closure of the Batzokija, along with its magazine, *Bizkaitarra*, and charges against all 110 members.

The closure of the Batzokija provided the impetus for a change of tactics and the Euskaldun Batzokija quickly reemerged under the new name, Partido Nacionalista Vasco (PNV), currently the ruling political party in the Basque country.

However, if the PNV had rigidly adhered to the political line of its main theorist and initial membership, Basque nationalism may well have remained confined to a group of Basque urban romantics with only limited political leverage.

The first fusion: radicals and moderates

The year 1898 was to be the turning point for Basque nationalism. The Spanish political morass had become worse with the assassination of Spain's prime minister, Cánovas, in 1887 and war with the USA. The devastating loss of Cuba in 1898 was a calamity of such magnitude that the viability of Spain as a modern state was placed in question (S. Payne, 1974: 128). Political 'regeneration', the search for radical political alternatives, and a patriotic exaltation of Spain were the dominant themes in an atmosphere that also injected renewed vigour into Spain's regionalisms.

Arana and his followers viewed Spain's many afflictions with a certain pleasure. Indeed, they publically praised Spain's adversaries. But the reaction of other sectors of Bilbao society was not so self-assured. The attitudes of Bilbao's industrial middle classes were to prove critical.

Although it was interpreted differently by different sectors of the population, foralism[2] was an article of faith in the Basque country similar to protectionism in Catalonia. The major aim of foralism was to preserve the fiscal and administrative autonomy of the Basque provinces. Its chief defenders were the Basque liberals.

The Partido Liberal Fuerista was founded in 1876, the year of foral abolition. In Bilbao this party was known as the Sociedad Euskalerría, its members as *euskalerriakos*. The party dominated the Basque provincial governments and exerted constant pressure on Madrid for some sort of foral restoration. The vast majority of the party membership was recruited from the ranks of the non-monopolistic Basque middle financial and industrial bourgeoisie although their unofficial spokesman was Ramon de la Sota y Llano, one of the most important Basque industrialists.[3]

Like their Catalan counterparts, the *euskalerriakos* sought to rescue the Basque country from the Spanish political débâcle. These liberals viewed a devolved government, protected from the intrusions of an inept and corrupt Madrid government, as a crucial element for the modernization of the Basque country. However, due to the consolidation of control of the Basque oligarchy over the main provincial political institutions, the *euskalerriakos* began to suffer serious electoral defeats. By 1897 they had been reduced to a small organization in Bilbao.

Staunchly religious and increasingly anti-Spain, the *euskalerriakos* were slowly pushing toward a nationalist, rather than a foralist, position.

There is little indication that the *euskalerriakos*, headed by Soto y Llano, found Arana's primitive, strident nationalism any more attractive than Arana found the *euskalerriakos*. To Arana the foral liberals had the souls of traders, the corrupting fever of industry, and espoused merely another version of Spanish regionalism that sought to distort and confuse Vizcaya. As mentioned before, Bilbao – composed of a Basque oligarchy, Spanish proletariat, recently urbanized Basque peasants and a pre-industrial petty bourgeoisie – lacked a politically sophisticated, commanding and 'autonomous' middle class similar to that in Catalonia. It could be argued that an alternative, more moderate and pragmatic formulation of the nationalist cause simply was not feasible. Certainly, the *euskalerriakos* had tried. In the popular mind nationalism was coupled to the charisma and crusade of Arana.

In 1898 for the first time the PNV seriously contemplated participating in the electoral process which previously had been condemned by Arana as 'this sad spectacle that shows the moral decadence of the nation of Bizcaya' ('Anuncio', C. W., p. 362). The PNV presented two candidates (Sabino de Arana in Bilbao and Angel Zabala in Guernica) for the provincial elections of that year. Despite their many misgivings, the *euskalerriakos* gave outspoken support to the PNV and Arana's candidature. Arana was duly elected as deputy to the Vizcayan provincial government.[4] The *euskalerriakos* entered into the ranks of 'the followers of JEL'. The event marked the birth of the PNV as a modern political party.

This fusion of the political skills and modern economic thinking of the middle bourgeoisie to the nationalist fervour of the petty bourgeoisie gave the PNV a hybrid, in many respects contradictory, ideology. It also gave strength and the capacity to capture mass support. But the coexistence of the

Basque petty and middle bourgeoisie was never to be harmonious. The conflicts and tensions – often violent – generated by this fusion were to characterize the Basque movement from then on. On one side the ultra-Catholic, fiercely anti-Spanish, intransigent nationalists defined a political line whose main aim was the establishment of an independent, religious Basque state. They excluded absolutely any alliances with Spanish political parties. (The modern equivalent of this line can be found in the parties and groups that circulate within the orbit of ETA.) On the other, the moderate, reform-minded nationalists, economically dependent on Spanish markets and protectionism, aimed at wresting an advantageous autonomy statute for the Basque country. To achieve their autonomist aspiration, the moderates were willing at propitious moments to ally with Spanish parties in accordance with political common sense.

Regardless of their differences concerning the desired relationship with Madrid, however, both streams were united in their goal inside the Basque country. For differing reasons, both had been pushed to the periphery of Basque economic and political life by the main protagonists of Basque industrialization. Arana's ideology of moral differentiation and disenfranchisement was to be the powerful and coherent instrument by which these dispossessed social sectors would establish political hegemony.

Sabino de Arana died of Addison's disease in 1903. He was thirty-eight years old. While maintaining his vision of the authentic Euzkadi as a Basque Arcadia, a major new element had entered his ideology. In part this ideological change reflected the Basque middle bourgeoisie's moderating influence over Arana's thinking. In part it reflected the PNV's growing need for money. The construction of the party's infrastructure and its propaganda campaigns were expensive endeavours. Tellingly, Arana and several of the early nationalists had become ardent investors in the Bilbao stock market (J. Corcuera, 1979). In short, Arana slowly embraced industrialization. Whereas industrialization was the source of spiritual indifference and fanaticism, the destroyer of nature and the corrupter of moral beauty, it was also a product of the Basque race. Bilbao was simultaneously the focus of a contagious virus and an example of 'the energy of our race'. Nationalism would no longer demand the dismantling of industrialization. The new Basque society was an irreversible fact. The chore of Basque nationalism was to administer and control it. Industry would be forced to conform to the spiritual and egalitarian strictures of Basque tradition. It would become 'Basque'.

In the last few months of his life, Arana went through an '*españolista* evolution', the causes and sincerity of which provoked intense debate within the nationalist ranks. On 22 June 1902, while Arana was in prison, an article called 'Grave y Transcendental' appeared in *La Patria*, the official organ of the PNV, apparently with prior consent from Arana. The article reported the rumour that Arana had accepted the unity of the Spanish state and felt that nationalism should cease to be separatist. Some weeks later Arana replied to a journalist that the purpose of nationalism should be to seek 'the most radical autonomy possible within the unity of the Spanish state – an autonomy adapted to the Basque character and modern needs' (*La Gazeta del Norte*, June 1902).[5]

The increasing electoral importance of the PNV together with the power vacuum that existed after Arana's death gave stimulus to the fratricidal rivalries, separations and brief reunifications between the intransigents and moderates inside the PNV as both attempted to achieve control over the party. In terms of ideology, political action and initiatives the PNV was effectively divided. Serious splits affected the party in 1910, 1921 and during the Second Republic. Characteristically the party published two magazines, *La Patria* (*Aberri*) and *Euskalduna*. The former expressed the views of those – usually young and from the petty bourgeoisie – who insisted on strict adherence to Arana's radical, separatist nationalism. The latter was the organ of the ex-*euskalerriakos* who portrayed the PNV as a party of legality, law and order, interested mainly in an advantageous autonomy statute.

The effects of these bitter internal struggles could have reduced the PNV to shambles. However, quite the reverse was the case. On the one hand the intransigents – who always formed the majority – captured an increasing hold over the ideological apparatus of the party. *La Patria*, defender of ideological orthodoxy, became the official voice of nationalism.[6] In public meetings and demonstrations radical nationalism took pride of place. On the other hand the entrepreneurial skills of the moderates ensured them control over the party's political structure. Indeed the main weakness of the intransigents within the PNV lay in their failure and incapacity to participate fully in elections which they invariably condemned as fraudulent. Almost all of the PNV's municipal councillors and provincial deputies were members of the moderate block. These elected representatives in turn formed a powerful pressure group inside the party.

This duality – the separation of political power in the hands of the middle bourgeoisie from ideological power under control of the petty bourgeoisie – has been a constant feature of Basque nationalism. As a result the ideological statements of the PNV have rarely corresponded to the party's actual political platform. This contradiction, although a source of constant political instability, has provided the bulwark for a wide-ranging popular support. The pragmatic Basque nationalist middle bourgeoisie and the intransigent Basque nationalist petty bourgeoisie are united because of a shared ideological belief and purpose. Both groups adhere to the dictates of *abertzalismo* (patriotism) – the political function essential for the consolidation of an exclusive national community. Underneath this ideological cohesion the relationship between the two, although viewed as competitive, is symbiotic. The moderates enable Basque nationalism to act in a coordinated political manner. The intransigents ensure that nationalism can consolidate and reproduce itself as a social and ideological movement. Thus, this duality enables the PNV to weld together divergent, at times antagonistic, sectors of Basque society. The two blocks serve and pursue different, but complementary political functions and strategies. Because Basque nationalism as a whole contains a range of different, at times opposing, political responses, it can survive and even thrive under conditions where overt political action is permitted and under conditions where it is not. Discrepancies on all levels are absorbed by the ambiguities of the symbolic nature of the nationalist ideology itself.

The second fusion: the urban and rural[7]

In the cities nationalism was basically, although by no means entirely, a particular type of political strategy. The urban nationalists were by language and lifestyle more akin to other urban Spanish citizens than to their rural Basque counterparts. The symbols of Basque culture were displayed – to a large extent theatrically – as badges of a new political identity and exclusivity. However, it can be shown that in the rural areas which were rapidly being drawn into the industrial process, the symbols of Basque culture had a different meaning, and culture in a structural sense was a fundamental determinant for the emergence and consolidation of nationalist sentiment. Stated schematically, nationalism for many urbanites implied the creation of an ethnic identity. For the peasantry it came to mean a reaffirmation of underlying cultural norms.

Rural Basques were latecomers to nationalism. The urban nationalists simply assumed that the rural stress of their ideology would receive an automatic welcome from the Basque peasantry. Yet a major obstacle to nationalist infiltration into the rural areas lay in the nationalist ideology itself. The nationalist image of the peasant as a noble savage was an improvement over the more common image in which the peasant was simply a savage. But the image of the *baserritar*, the Basque peasant, as the moral and free repository of Basque traditions was designed to mobilize an urban political following and weld it together by a heightened sense of ethnic differentiation and mission. It was entirely irrelevant to rural conditions and concerns. Indicatively, despite its insistence on Euskera as the national language of Euzkadi and despite the peasantry's inability by and large to speak any other language, the PNV did not propose a public regime of bilingualism until 1914. In the countryside nationalism – together with other forms of party politics – was often scorned as an occupation of urbanites and other privileged groups. It was treated with suspicion or apathy by a peasantry whose traditional resentment of the cities and the intrusions of their representatives had been exacerbated since 1876.

Eugen Weber's (1976) description of the French peasantry up to the First World War is also pertinent for the Basque peasantry. In general the Basque peasant was unable to write or indeed often understand Spanish and was only marginally integrated into a monetary economy. Before the building of roads and the serious onset of trade in the early twentieth century, each peasant community existed largely as a world unto itself.

In electoral terms, peasant participation had two conspicuous and related features. The first was a high level of abstentionism. Depending on the specific election, from one-third to over a half of peasants eligible to vote never voted at all. Secondly, of those peasants who did vote, their vote was solidly, and usually reluctantly, behind the candidates supported by the rural notables, the *jauntxoak*. The vast majority of Basque peasants were tenants on the farms of Carlist landowners. With spiritual sanctions from the clergy, the *jauntxoak* utilized their economic hold over the peasantry to bar competitors from gaining a popular foothold. Peasants who showed signs of political defection were threatened with eviction, immediate repayment of debts and so forth. The provincial elections in Guipúzcoa of 1905 are illustrative. In the district of Azpeitia, in the heart of rural Guipúzcoa, a full 99.66% of the votes went to the Carlist candidate. The rate of abstention was 47%. In Zumaya, a rural coastal district, the situation was similar. The candidate of the rural notables received 99.2% of votes cast and 56% of voters abstained (figures taken from Cillán Apalategi, 1975b: 289–93).[8]

The PNV made substantial efforts at rural expansion. Assisted by an impressive, if ineffective, propaganda campaign the *jelkides* (followers of JEL), often sporting neat peasant jackets over their urban attire, organized public meetings throughout the countryside. Normally these meetings took the form of banquets – commensality is an indispensable requirement of all Basque political activity – and were attended by members of the local, rural intelligentsia (the doctor, pharmacist, priest) and some wealthier smallholding peasants. Sometimes these meetings would result in the creation of a *batzoki* (a local PNV branch). But the nationalist message was rarely listened to by the wider rural community.

However, this situation gradually changed. Spanish neutrality during the First World War brought considerable prosperity to the Basque country. This prosperity was particularly noticeable in the countryside on the margins of the industrializing zones. New roads and schools were built, mass literacy was introduced and cash, rather than payment in kind, became the primary medium of economic transactions. Very importantly, many peasants, enriched by increased agricultural prices and lucrative supplementary jobs in industry, found themselves in a position to become small landholders and, thereby, break their reliance on the local notables.

Critical for the spread of nationalism was the emergence of new occupations in the countryside. Shop owners, traders, teachers, barkeepers and local industrial artisans not only helped to articulate town and country, but also acted as carriers of urban political ideologies, in particular, nationalism.

Although the *baserritar* (peasant) stereotype continued to be lauded as the antithesis of the socialist agitator (Elorza, 1976: 484), the PNV slowly became aware of the extent of the agrarian problem and began to advocate the purchase of land by the peasantry as the means to their economic and political emancipation. Several political parties had expressed the need for agrarian reform; but the PNV took decisive action. The Basque Nationalist Party established a whole series of schemes – insurance policies, legal and technical aid, credit facilities, etc. – which were of direct benefit to the peasantry especially with respect to land purchase. From 1917 to 1936 the number of peasant landholders increased dramatically, a trend for which the 'social program' of the PNV was given ample credit.

Nationalism's expansion into the rural areas was further aided by the cultural renaissance, sparked off by nationalist activity. Although a more detailed discussion will follow some of the implications of this cultural movement should be mentioned.

Industrialization was not viewed by the peasantry as posing any special economic threat. On the contrary, it offered those peasants affected by it economic opportunity and political enfranchisement. However, among rural Basques at its periphery, the process of industrialization produced serious cultural disruption. In Basque pre-industrial society the town and country functioned economically and politically independently of each other to the extent possible. However, industrialization forced a rapid economic as well as cultural integration of the rural hinterland into the orbit of the urban centres. Spanish, literacy, skill in manoeuvring in official bureaucracies, a minimal formal education, knowledge of legal procedures and knowledge of the subtle rules of accepted urban behaviour became essential requirements for operating successfully in the modernizing rural areas. Whereas the economic and educational improvement of the peasantry had cleared the way, it was the cultural movement that furnished an urban political élite with a language which transcended, if only symbolically, the urban-rural cleavage and consolidated a rural following for nationalism. As Eugen Weber has observed, patriotism is learned at different rates by different people. In the Basque countryside patriotism was pulled in the wake of industrial expansion. By the election of 1931, which marked the inauguration of the Second Republic, the nationalists were the principal force in rural Guipúzcoa and Vizcaya. The Basque peasantry who lived on the periphery of the rapidly expanding industrial areas had become the unwavering pillar of nationalist support.

Infrastructure of the national community

Arana's symbolic ideology, underwriting the political functions of ethnic consolidation and solidarity, provided the foundation upon which the diverse social sectors of nationalism rested. However, it was the institutional infrastructure, gradually erected by nationalism over the first three decades of the twentieth century, that furnished this foundation with strength and durability. This infrastructure created the framework for an ethnically differentiated, exclusive society inside the Basque country essential for the final transformation of nationalism's fellow travellers into a self-contained national community.

The first and most important of these institutions was the Partido Nacionalista Vasco itself.

Partly reflecting its view of traditional Basque political organization, the PNV was conceived as a federation of community nationalist clubs, called *batzokis*. The *batzoki* was the main unit of the party and the focal point for all nationalist activities. Coordination of the *batzokis* occurred on a provincial and 'national' level. All the *batzokis* of a province elected delegates to the provincial *buru-batzar* (council) and in turn each provincial *buru-batzar* was federated into the central organism of the party, Euzkadi-Buru-Batzar. A *batzoki* was opened in San Sebastian in 1904, in Vitoria, the capital of Alava, in 1907 and finally in Pamplona, Navarra in 1909. By 1910 all the important towns and cities of Vizcaya and Guipúzcoa had local branches of the PNV, although the influence of nationalism in Navarra and Alava was to remain negligible outside the capital cities.[9] Moreover, nationalism rapidly spread among the large Basque diaspora in the Americas. Basque clubs were inaugurated in Mexico, Argentina, the Philippines, Cuba, Uruguay and New York.[10] The first full general assembly of the PNV was held in 1911. During this assembly the four provincial councils – Bizkai-Buru-Batzar, Gipuzko-Buru-Batzar, Araba-Buru-Batzar and Naparra-Buru-Batzar – were elected.

In 1901 Euzko-Gaztedia (EG, Basque Youth) was formed as the youth branch of the PNV. One aspect of EG should be noted. Composed mainly of students, EG showed a certain openness toward the grave problems of Bilbao's working class. Directing himself to EG members, 'the beautiful and noble youth of the patriotic party', Arana wrote in alarm, 'beware of falling, beware of abandoning nationalism in order to become socialists; beware of denying Christ, your God, and Euzkadi, your country' ('Alerta', *La Patria*, 9 March 1902, C. W., p. 2168). Despite Arana's admonitions, EG provided some important converts to socialism. The most notable was Tomás Meabe, founder of the youth branch of the PSOE, from 1903 editor of *La Lucha de Clases* and one of the most articulate Basque advocates of the socialist cause.[11]

Mendigoitzale Bazkuna (Mountaineering Association), founded in 1908 by members of the Basque Youth, was also to play a crucial role in the Basque movement. Initially dedicated to Sunday excursions in the Basque mountains, the Mendigoitzaleak (mountaineers) became the shock troops of radical nationalism during the Second Republic (Larronde, 1977: 323). During the civil war and the repression that followed, the Mendigoitzale Bazkuna formed the core of the Basque militias and later organized the Basque resistance and the clandestine flow of Basque exiles across the French–Spanish Pyrenean border.

The nationalist labour union, Solidaridad de Obreros Vascos (Solidarity of Basque Workers) or SOV, was established in 1911.[12]

Deepening social tensions – marked by periodic violent strikes resulting in the imposition of martial law – forced the PNV to recognize the need to extend into the working class. The leadership of the SOV was strongly influenced by the Church and several of its main leaders were priests. Beltza states (1978: 180) that the SOV was 'Christian, patriotic and accepted the bourgeoisie as brothers in race and as the producers of wealth which was then distributed to the workers'. Although the main task of the SOV was, 'to emancipate the Basque working class from socialist tutelage', the SOV viewed its role as a struggle on two flanks. Father Policarpo de Larrañaga, one of SOV's originators, wrote, '1912 was a real test for the Solidaridad because it had to fight on two, apparently antithetic, fronts both of which were complementary in destroying Basque workers. One side socialism ... and on the other, furiously centralist and anti-Basque monopoly capitalism' (*Contribución a la historia obrera de euskalherria*, 1977, p. 37, cited by Beltza, 1978: 231).

However, the SOV mainly steered away from politics and confined itself, in accordance with its statutes, 'to achieve the maximum welfare for Basque workers via efficient practical instruction which cultivates their intelligences and educates their will, to lead them to the most faithful and zealous fulfilment of their duties as workers and as Basques'.

Like the PNV and Euzko-Gaztedia, membership in the SOV was restricted to 'Basques' only – the definition was more political than genealogical – a restriction which markedly limited its appeal in a region in which the vast majority of industrial workers were of immigrant origins. Most of its members were recruited from the ranks of white-collar employees and the workers in small industrial workshops. The only major factory in which the SOV was significant was the Euskalduna shipyards owned by Ramon de la Sota y Llano. Regardless, the SOV gave the PNV a type of working-class base that was to become of increasing significance.

Of major importance for the growth of the PNV was the conversion of large numbers of the lower clergy, previously adherents of Carlism, to the nationalist doctrine. Stanley Payne has suggested (1974: 138) that the nationalist sympathies of the clergy were due to the links between religion and local life which were closer in the Basque country than in other parts of Spain. Certainly this was a contributory factor. But additionally, the clergy along with the rural notables had been defeated by the Carlist wars. Support for nationalism was also support for the supremacy of the Church and, thus, an attack on modern secular Basque society which had undercut both the political power and the prestige of the clergy. In any case, with the pulpit as platform the clergy made powerful apologists for nationalism especially in the rural areas.

Of critical importance was the foundation of Jaungoiko-zale Bazkuna (The Association of Enthusiasts of God) in 1912 by a group of Basque priests. The precursor of the *ikastola* (Basque language schools) movement, this association aimed at giving a Christian education in Euskera. The *ikastolas* not only became an essential carrier of the nationalist creed to successive generations, but eventually provided the nationalist community with its own educational system.

A central institution for the consolidation of nationalism in the rural areas was the establishment, during the Second Republic, of the Eusko Nekazarien Bazkuna (Basque Agricultural Association) which was dedicated to the 'social, moral and economic improvement' of the peasantry and which was linked to the local *batzokis*.

With regard to long-term organizational effects, the creation of the Emakume Abertzale Batza (EAB, Association of the Patriotic Women) was one of the nationalists' more significant achievements. The inspiration was borrowed from Ireland, specifically the role of Irish women and the women's organization, *Cumann namBan*, in the Easter Rebellion of 1916. Hitherto women in the Basque movement had been largely confined to the image of the noble and pure Basque Mother (Elorza, 1978:388). However, the PNV realized that the role of women could be decisive. On one level women could offer support of powerful propaganda value for the actions of men through public demonstrations, organization of nationalist meetings, promotion of Basque culture, collection of funds for patriotic causes and so on. As the EAB expressed it, 'Now the [male] patriots are not alone in their struggle; their wives, mothers, daughters and sisters walk by their side and with them suffer and with them rejoice' (EAB document 1922, from compilation of Bursain, 1978:461). On a more basic level, however, women functioned as transmission belts for the nationalist ideology inside the domestic sphere. Women in their roles inside the family (and by extension inside schools) formed the first offensive for the formation and mobilization of new generations of nationalist youth, 'the preparation of future patriots' (EAB text). Although the Emakune Abertzale Batza was dissolved during the Primo de Rivera dictatorship, it was quickly reorganized in 1931 and by 1936 consisted of approximately 28,000 active and well-disciplined militants.

The institutions listed above were complemented by a host of other institutions which ranged from publishing houses to financial organizations. Their net effect was to create a parallel society in which the *abertzale*, the true Basque, could operate in most spheres of public life closed off from the outside, anti-Basque world.

The rise of the moderates: Basque parliamentary nationalism, 1914–23

The golden age of Basque bourgeois nationalist activities and aspirations began and ended with the First World War.

On the ideological level the war was seen as the 'war of the nationalities' and, thus, gave a sense of international respectability to the Basque nationalists. Woodrow Wilson's proposals for a geopolitical reform of Europe provided the final seal of approval for the nationalists' mission.

As importantly, Spanish neutrality in the war had immensely profitable consequences for the Basque country. Vicens Vives has written (1972:681), 'A waterfall of gold irrigated agriculture and industry, liberating Spain from her debts contracted during the 19th century… ' Basque capitalism was one of the main beneficiaries. From 1915 to 1918 Basque banking profits doubled and by 1919 had tripled. In the Basque iron and steel industry the value of production tripled between 1914 and 1916 (Elorza, 1978: 235–36). But the most spectacular benefits of all accrued to the Basque naval industry both in its capacity of maritime transport and shipbuilding. The principal protagonist and symbol of this prodigious economic growth was Ramon de la Sota y Llano, founder of Sota y Aznar Shipping and unofficial spokesman of the PNV moderates.

This massive industrial growth had direct repercussions on Basque nationalism. More than ever, the Basque economy was linked irreversibly into Spain. But simultaneously the stubborn ineptitude of Madrid governments continued to preclude completely an efficient state framework which could adequately protect far-flung Basque interests. Consolidating the trend begun in 1902, in 1917 moderate Basque nationalism officially declared itself to be regionalist. All separatist rhetoric was forcefully and publicly repudiated. Obviously, for the nationalist intransigents this was treason. For them even a decentralized unitary Spain represented an act of gross violence against the Basque soul and nation.

The PNV's electoral strength grew steadily from 1908 onward. In 1915 the PNV sent deputies and senators to the Madrid Cortes for the first time. In the municipal elections of 1917 the nationalists gained a majority in the provincial assembly in Vizcaya and completely dominated the Bilbao *ayuntamiento* (municipal council). But the crowning glory came in 1918.

In the parliamentary elections of 1918 a series of factors rebounded overwhelmingly in the nationalists' favour. Spain had been plunged into another period of grave political crisis which at times threatened to erupt into civil war. In addition the inspirational effects of the Russian Revolution, low salaries and galloping inflation brought renewed workers' militancy. In August 1917 Spain was paralysed by the most extensive and violent general strike she had experienced. Moreover, the military also showed disturbing signs of rebellion against the incessant corruption, favouritism, incompetence and instability of the Madrid government. In Catalonia and the Basque provinces as well as in regions such as Extremadura, Galicia and Murcia, there was general enthusiasm for regional autonomies. Inside the Basque country prosperity flourished and the non-nationalist right was bitterly divided despite its fear of the socialist hordes.

Responding to all these factors, Basque nationalism presented itself as a regionalist party aimed at the protection of law and order as well as Basque prosperity. It captured seven out of the twenty Basque parliamentary seats and obtained representatives in every Basque province except Alava. Of the six seats in Vizcaya, five went to the nationalists and only one was retained by the socialists. The vision of a restructured 'Spain of the nationalities' within a Europe of the nationalities lay before the euphoric nationalists.

As usual the nationalist intransigents refused to participate in these elections on the grounds that patriots should not elect representatives to foreign parliaments.

However, the moderates' position was severly undercut by circumstances over which the party had little control. First, the Basque economy began to suffer the effects of peace in Europe. Industrial contraction led to rapid increases in unemployment, bankruptcies and social conflict which in turn was reflected in ever more severe levels of violence. Next to Barcelona, Bilbao was the most politically violent city in Spain. The moderates had shown themselves clearly unable to maintain either law and order or Basque prosperity. The intransigents' reiteration of visceral attacks on the socialists, *maketos*, and the Basque oligarchs, combined with heavy doses of populism again received a sympathetic hearing.

Second, the political atmosphere was marked by acid tensions as governmental attempts to dampen workers' militancy degenerated into widespread repression. The Basque nationalists had achieved their electoral victories by attracting part of the conservative electoral constituency. Under the stress of workers' militancy on one hand and the government counter-offensive on the other, Basque society polarized. The former conservative defectors returned to the conservative flock.

Finally, and most devastatingly, the much heralded negotiations for Basque autonomy ended abruptly in total failure. In 1919 an inter-parliamentary commission had been set up to prepare a Catalan autonomy statute. Also a subcommission was to prepare recommendations for Basque autonomy. Because of intense opposition from left-wing radical Catalans, the whole project fell through. Moreover, the Navarrese delegate to the Basque subcommission firmly rejected the commission's recommendations.[13] In any case, overwhelmed with larger events – the spectre of war in Morocco – Madrid began to lose all interest in regional autonomies. The whole thrust of the moderate nationalists' tactics in Madrid had come to nothing.

In the provincial and parliamentary elections of 1919 the nationalists' electoral base disintegrated. In the provincial elections the nationalists lost Vizcaya. In the parliamentary elections they lost four of their seven deputies and retained only three out of their five seats in Vizcaya. By 1923 the nationalist electoral presence had been more or less eliminated.

The rise of the radicals: rural culture as nationalist ritual

Reversing the pattern of most European nationalist movements, in the Basque country political nationalism preceded the emergence of a cultural nationalism. Previously I have said that Basque nationalism has always been a political alliance between two symbiotic blocks. The moderates, representative of Basque industrial modernization, have been the pragmatists adept at political manipulation. The radicals, products of Basque pre-industrial traditions, were the defenders of doctrinal purity, the definers and guardians of the ethnic boundaries.

Historically the moderates dominated Basque nationalism during those periods when Spain enjoyed a version of a democratic regime and party politics were the coordinates of political life. The radicals have come into their own during the periods of dictatorship.

By the onset of the Primo de Rivera dictatorship (1923–30) although much of the organizational infrastructure for the nationalist community had been laid, these organizations still lacked the ability and solidity to mobilize and generate cohesion on a decisive scale. The individuals integrated into these organizations were faithful, but still few. The electoral results of the preceding democratic period indicated the shaky basis upon which nationalism still rested. Arguably, the moderates' preoccupation with parliamentary politics had led them to neglect the full organizational possibilities offered by the nationalist ideology. With the imposition of dictatorship in September 1923, the main activities of nationalism perforce were transferred into the ideological, cultural and social realms.

In these realms the radical nationalists, who were the direct descendants of the primitive Sabino de Arana and who had no parliamentary preoccupations, were infinitely enthusiastic. For the radicals the main job – the only worthwhile job – was the 'renationalization of Euzkadi': 'that is to say,

Basque nationalism will not have triumphed until the hegemony of the patriotic characteristics of the Basque nation has been achieved...' ('In defence of doctrinal policy', *Aberi*, 22 Dec. 1917).

Importantly, by 1923 these energetic and young militants enjoyed almost total control over the organizations which most lent themselves to mass mobilization and the diffusion of nationalist ideology. These organizations were those dedicated to music, Basque popular festivals, Euskera and the theatre. Primo de Rivera had prohibited political nationalism; but cultural nationalism was tolerated and under the dictator it flourished.

Promoted mainly by nationalist youth, the decade of the 1920s witnessed a grandiose explosion of Basque cultural activities. Basque musical, theatrical and dance groups proliferated throughout the Basque provinces. Performances which amassed well over 500 dancers and musicians were frequent. Journals devoted to the scholarly study of Basque culture and language (for example, *Eusko-Folklore* and *Euzko-Deya*) were published. A new generation of Basque writers and landscape and portrait painters gained prominence. The Basque schools, the *ikastolas*, offering for the first time instruction in Euskera or, more frequently, Euskera and Spanish, opened.

Unlike the Catalan movement which in the main presented Catalan culture as modern and part of a wider European tradition, the Basque movement looked backward and was heavily oriented toward rural folklore. To a certain extent this helped remove the stigma attached to traditional culture. Euskera, which had been regarded as the language of an uncultured peasantry, now became the language promoted and lauded, although not necessarily spoken, by an urban cultural vanguard.

The movement revived rural culture mainly as a vehicle for the urban nationalist ideology. Cultural performances inevitably contained clear political messages. Theatre works such as *Alma Vasca* (The Basque Soul) stressed the need to return to rural values and isolation in order to defend the nobility of the Basque race. Basque dances were often accompanied by the political message describing the purity and virility of these dances in comparison to 'imported customs and among them the perniciousness of the immoral "*agarrao*" dances' (Gudari, *Por la libertad vasca*, p. 211, quoted in Elorza, 1978: 386). (*Agarrao* are those dances which require two partners to be in close physical contact.) In short, with some notable exceptions, the cultural movement saw rural culture mainly in terms of its potential to yield symbols of moral and cultural differentiation. It aimed at instilling a sense of nationalist, rather than cultural, identity. Its basic theme was not so much the 'Basque' as the conflict between the 'Basque' and the 'anti-Basque'. Along with offering a means to transmit nationalist ideology, the cultural movement also functioned to mobilize large numbers of people and generate interaction between them.

The *mendigoitzaleak* (Basque mountaineers) were an important element in the cultural movement. Because of their physical mobility and because they tended to attract the most militant nationalists into their ranks, under the Primo de Rivera dictatorship the *mendigoitzaleak* often operated as political organizers and coordinators of cultural nationalism. In the villages visited during their mountaineering excursions, the *mendigoitzaleak* promoted Basque dances, Basque history, Euskera, and sought converts to the nationalist cause especially among rural youth. The cultural movement represented a mass invitation to nationalism. It fomented grass-roots participation. People were encouraged not only to watch cultural events, but to learn Basque dances, form musical groups or, at any rate, help organize cultural events in their local communities. Although the inspiration behind the movement came from the big cities, the frequent mass performances of singers, dancers, *bertsolaris* (spontaneous oral poets) and so forth were perceived as popular, local productions. Usually under the direction of the local youth, whole communities would be mobilized as spectators, organizers and/or participants. The event itself would occasion considerable communal pride as outsiders in general and urban notables in particular flocked to assess the quality of the performances and the liveliness of the atmosphere. These frequent mass events and the organizational activities surrounding them resulted in growing personal interaction among the increasing numbers involved. Slowly the nationalists became friends or friends of friends.

By the dawn of the Second Republic the Basque nationalist community had been forged. It defined itself in reference to the nationalist ideology and in opposition to other political and social forces inside the Basque country. Despite internal dissensions, it saw itself as one great family tied by blood, culture, shared interests and destiny. It had its own theatre, clergy, press, schools (the *ikastolas*), women's organizations, labour organizations, youth groups, academics' and farmers' associations. Its culture and identity were continually reaffirmed in the cultural movement. It obeyed discrete social and moral codes determined by the prescriptions of JEL. Membership was transmitted from parents to children. For the nationalists, the Basque nationalist community was the moral centre of the Basque country. It was the *pueblo vasco* and, therefore, it possessed exclusive claim to national legitimacy. A large proportion of its members were young people who had been socialized into nationalism during the Primo de Rivera era. During the Second Republic the Basque nationalist community would enter into its political adulthood.

Sabino de Arana constructed the ideology of Basque nationalism. In turn the social logic and mobilizing power of his nationalist doctrine created a discrete Basque nation. Once created – once this ideology had been adopted as the collective ritual and collective representations of a group – the Basque nation became a political fact.

5

The moral community and its enemies

For the patriot who wishes to affirm his nationality, all anti-Basques are enemies, although dressed in the sandals of the *rojo* proletariat or wrapped in the prestige of capital. He who confesses to Christ is the same as he who adores Lenin.

('Gudari', 'Nacionalismo y cuestión social', *Jagi-Jagi*, 11 March 1933)

The counter-attack

In most of Spain the political spectrum has been, broadly speaking, bi-polar: right-wing forces have confronted left-wing forces. In the Basque country since the 1890s, the alignment has been triangular. Basque nationalism has had two traditional adversaries: the liberal/conservatives, supported by the Basque oligarchy, and the socialists, supported mainly by immigrant workers.

While Basque nationalism has reserved its most bitter diatribes for the socialists, the reverse has also been true. Vizcayan exclusiveness was held to be the direct opposite of the socialist ideal of universal humanitarianism. Basque socialist propaganda was almost obsessed with the theme. The socialist leader, Carretero, declared, 'We socialists have always fought against the nationalism of Arana because we consider it inhuman, insular, poor in conception and spirit, founded in an unjust hatred toward the rest of Spaniards and because it is entirely uncivilized and reactionary' (cited in Solozabal, 1975: 188).

Although Spanish socialists were frequently ambivalent and contradictory in their view of nationalist movements, their usual judgements – shaped by Marxist orthodoxy – were negative. Nationalism was 'an aggressive isolation', 'a form of collective egotism, an agglomeration of the worst individual instincts' (*La Lucha de Clases*, 16 July 1898). Striving for an 'irrational' division of mankind, nationalism was the means by which bourgeois privilege was achieved, maintained and transmitted. The *patria* – that 'brutal conception', in the words of Tomás Meabe – was at its core 'war and protectionism... the two building stones of bourgeois patriotism. Without an army and tariff barriers the bourgeois fatherland would drown, carrying all its glories to hell' (*La Lucha de Clases*, 9 July 1898).

Whereas nationalism had little to recommend it in general, *bizkaitarrismo* (Vizcayan nationalism) was regarded as a particular malevolent manifestation of the doctrine. For Miguel de Unamuno, who was linked to, although not active in, the socialist cause, the cornerstone of the Basque movement was not separatism, but *antimaketismo*. 'It is above all else an hostile explosion against the Spaniard, the *maketo*, who lives and works here in Bilbao' (Unamuno, 'El antimaquetismo', *El Heraldo de Madrid*, 18 Sept. 1898, cited in Fusi, 1975: p. 199).[1] And for Unamuno and the socialists *antimaketismo* was simply a total hostility towards the working class and a contempt for the poor. Because nationalism denied the class struggle, its chief function was as a weapon of the dominant class.

> The nationalist party is composed of upper and petty bourgeoisie and the intelligentsia (*gente de escritorio*). The ideal which nationalists of comfortable position pursue is not unknown: to be the only ones who rule the destiny of this region of Spain. The others – the small industrialists, merchants and the employees in the mines, shipyards, banks, etc. etc. – their objective is, for some, business, and, for others, good jobs.
> (*La Lucha de Clases*, 1903, cited in Solozabal, 1975: 220fn.)

The socialists often depicted the nationalism of the Basque bourgeoisie as a manoeuvre to divert and divide those they exploited with notions of race, nationality, *fueros* and other 'non-scientific' irrelevances.[2] It was more than mere coincidence, they argued, that in the only two regions of Spain with strong working-class movements, Catalonia and Vizcaya, indivisible capitalism had raised the separatist banner.

The socialist attack also emphasized the clerical nature of Basque nationalism. The triumph of nationalism, it was claimed, would signify a Basque country 'asphyxiated under the weight of religious orders'.

According to the socialists, a distinct Basque nationality just did not exist. It had no basis in history or race. The Basque provinces had always formed part – and a privileged part, certainly not a colonized and oppressed one – of the Spanish nation. Nor did the socialists accept arguments concerning Euskera, that 'tuberculous invalid' (*La Lucha de Clases*, 5 Oct. 1901). Few people spoke Euskera and fewer still read or wrote it. Moreover, its parting was a sign of progress. The language not only separated Basque from Spanish speakers, it also separated Basque from Basque because of dialectical differences which made mutual comprehension often impossible. Reflecting socialist attitudes, Unamuno in a speech in 1901 on the death on Euskera argued that Bilbao speaking *vascuence* (Basque) was a contradiction in terms. Scientifically it could be demonstrated that Euskera was not adaptable to modern thought. The modern Basque soul could only be freed if it was pried loose from the narrow mould of the Basque language.

However, in pace with nationalist political gains, the socialist rejection of Basque nationalism did not remain so self-confident. After 1901 the socialists began to organize meetings and publish articles in Euskera (Larronde, 1977:

246). But more significantly, implicit concessions to nationalist sentiment began to permeate socialist propaganda. Tomás Meabe, one of the more implacable anti-nationalists, wrote in 1902: 'In the good sense of the idea we are as patriotic as the rest; we love our country and desire its welfare, prosperity and peace, all things which the other patriotism – the one of war and 'national honour' – destroys.' ('Qué es la Patria?', *La Lucha de Clases*, 30 Aug. 1902)

As Elorza has pointed out (1974: p. 104), this evolution toward an accommodation with Basque sentiment is very pronounced in Unamuno. Basque nationalism, he argued, was also a movement of social protest and, as such, merited close study and a certain collaboration. Moreover, Unamuno attempted to reconcile 'the spirit of the Basque', which he saw as a differentiated entity, with socialism.

Cannot socialism be translated into the Basque spirit? I do not mean into *vascuence*, not at all, but into the Basque spirit. That most of (socialism's) first apostles and propagandists neither were from here nor know of this spirit has damaged the cause of socialism in Vasconia. A doctrine, regardless of its universality, can be made fruitful only by injecting local sentiments into it.

('Socialismo y localismo', *La Lucha de Clases*, 28 Apr. 1906)

Basque nationalism and Basque socialism grew in opposition out of the same social ferment. They grew with roughly similar speed and maintained a political parity until the civil war. Throughout, nationalism remained unyielding in its repudiation of socialism. However, the socialist onslaught slowly became disorientated as bits and pieces of nationalist premises were imperceptibly absorbed into socialist thinking. Initially Basque nationalism was viewed as a phenomenon to be combated wholeheartedly. Eventually it became a 'problem' which the socialists could neither struggle against, collaborate with nor understand.

The initial liberal/conservative reaction was also uncompromisingly adverse. On the occasion of Arana's electoral triumph in 1898, the liberals dismissed the nationalist leader as 'a degenerate spirit who hates the nation' and 'a hysteric' (Fusi, 1975: 197). The liberals regarded the PNV as obsessively religious, anti-liberal and divorced from mainstream 'regenerationist' political reality. Liberal alarm grew with the increasing nationalist presence which began to threaten liberal–conservative supremacy. From 1903 to 1913 the nationalists captured from a quarter to a third of the seats in the Bilbao city council. Although the confrontation and hostility between the liberals and the nationalists was sincere, the two had a common political enemy – the socialists. An overriding feature of the relationship between the PNV and the main right-wing parties – both in the pre-war and post-Franco periods – can be described as one of ideological opposition and tactical collaboration.

Like the socialist and liberal reaction, the first government reaction was openly hostile and the PNV was subject to harsh, although intermittent, repression until 1902. However, a major change in attitude occurred with the conservative Maura government (1907–9). Maura sought to develop a strong system of local government which he believed would help end the endemic electoral corruption of Spain's 'tribal chieftains', the *caciques*, and provide a framework for a solution to the Catalan problem (Carr, 1966: 479). Maura needed to enlist Basque as well as Catalan nationalists in his project of conservative decentralization (Payne, 1974: 141–42). To a certain extent, Maura and the moderate Basque nationalists were ideal partners. Both wished to break the electoral monopoly of local political élites while simultaneously containing working-class militancy. In pursuit of this policy the Maura government in 1907 and again in 1909 appointed Basque nationalists to the office of mayor of Bilbao. Paradoxically, by giving the PNV official recognition, this injection of government support helped to push the nationalist message to areas outside Bilbao.

One final point: while political acceptance for Basque nationalism was not so readily forthcoming from other Madrid governments, Basque economic demands inevitably received a sympathetic hearing.[3] Renegotiations of the *conciertos económicos* were invariably concluded on favourable terms. For example, in 1913 the government agreed to extend the fiscal privileges of the Basque naval industry to profits earned outside the Basque region (Beltza, 1974: 150).

The triangular nature of Basque politics has been a major factor in explaining the peculiar course of political events in the region. It has also complicated all attempts, both from within the Basque country and from Madrid, to deal successfully with the Basque question. Basque reactions to the crucial events of the Second Republic well illustrate the point.

The quest for autonomy

One issue dominated Basque politics during the period 1931–36, negotiation of a Basque autonomy statute. The Catalans achieved home rule in 1932. Basque aspirations were not met until 1936. The triangular nature of Basque politics was a fundamental reason for the delay.

The PNV had emerged vigorously into the Second Republic under the leadership of another youthful lawyer from Bilbao, José Antonio Aguirre (1903–60). Like Arana, Aguirre came from a middle-class Carlist family and had received a Jesuit education. Unlike Arana, Aguirre was moderate, urbane and spoke Euskera.

The impact of nationalism upon the political scene was immediate and impressive. The full range of nationalist organizations clandestinely nurtured under the Primo de Rivera dictatorship were formally instituted and revelled in their massive support. By the end of 1930 the PNV had opened some 200 local *batzokis* in Guipúzcoa alone. The streets of Basque villages and cities witnessed prodigious displays of Basque athletic demonstrations, religious events and cultural activities with aggressively nationalist overtones. Endless noisy and colourful parades of nationalist youth, dance groups, choral associations, *nekazariak* (peasanats), *emakumeak* (women) and the *mendigo-itzaleak* (members of the Basque Mountaineering Association) gave evidence of the ample contours of the nationalist community. The PNV had reemerged in splendid strength and stood in rigorous isolation.

Despite the Republic's dedication to the creation of a Spain based on regional autonomies (Fusi, 1979: 144), the PNV had not participated in the formation of the Second Republic. In its newspaper, *Euzkadi*, the PNV had stated that a change of regime *per se* was of little importance (Payne, 1974: 168). The nationalists' only concern was autonomy. Moreover, the PNV was highly suspicious of the anti-clerical, radical nature of the socialists and various republican parties and, thus, refused to join the anti-monarchic opposition.[4] At the crucial meeting in San Sebastian in August 1930 when a diverse grouping of opposition parties drew up the guidelines for the future democratic regime (the Pacto de San Sebastian), the PNV was not invited. The Pacto de San Sebastian specifically promised an autonomy statute for Catalonia. Basque claims were not mentioned.

The republicans viewed the PNV's religiosity and stress on ethnic distinctiveness as excessive and, indeed, repugnant. The nationalists' respect for democratic principles was also doubted. Moreover, while general Spanish opinion of the Catalans was admiring and deferential, as Fusi has pointed out (1979: 55), Spanish opinion of the Basque was conditioned by the image of the Carlist Wars. The Basque country was identified with Carlist absolutism and theocratic obscurantism. In literature the Basques were frequently portrayed as either wildly romantic, somewhat puerile, adventurers or witless bureaucrats.

However, the main barrier to a Basque statute lay in the utter lack of consensus within the Basque country rather than in any fundamental reluctance on the part of Madrid. There was little, if any, agreement among the three main blocks of Basque politics – the right, the left and the nationalists – as to the desired future of the Basque country, and none of the three blocks possessed sufficient political weight to impose its own solution. Simultaneously, the differences separating the three precluded stable alliances on any issue.

The three blocks were distinguishable by the nature of their social base. The various right-wing, monarchist parties gained their main support from the industrialists and rural notables in Vizcaya and Guipúzcoa and the peasantry outside of urban influence in Navarra and Alava. The socialists were firmly rooted in the immigrant proletariat and sectors of the Basque working class (for example, in Eibar) and their allies, the republicans, represented the anti-clerical sectors of the lower middle class.[5] Finally, the nationalists drew their support from the intermediate social sectors in the two industrial provinces. (See Cillán Apalategui, 1975 for electoral evidence, and Fusi, 1979.)

But more importantly, as Fusi has argued (1979: 61), the three main forces were separated by quite distinct and frequently antagonistic visions concerning the geographical, historical, cultural and political character of the Basque country. Whereas the nationalists insisted on the term Euzkadi to designate an historic Basque fatherland which incorporated the four Spanish provinces and the three French ones, the other two forces used the terms Vasconia, Vascongadas, Euskalherria or País Vasco, terms which did not define the Basque area as a culturally uniform or ethnically differentiated region nor extend necessarily to include Navarra or the French Basque area. In short, neither the Basque right nor left accepted the concept of a Basque nation. For its part, the left adhered to a political tradition in which the principles of liberalism, modern democratic rights, the subordination of Church to state and regional autonomies within the unity of Spain provided the basic political vocabulary. In contrast, the nationalists, while sharing the left's republicanism, were averse to liberalism, insisted on the supremacy of Church over state and rejected any notion of an overarching Spanish nation however autonomously defined. Finally, the right shared the nationalists' concern about Catholicism, the maintenance of public order and rejection of liberalism; but for the most part they were ardent defenders of monarchy and the integrity of Spain both as nation and state.

Two additional factors exacerbated the drawn-out and bitter struggle over Basque home rule. First, the Basque nationalists on the one hand and the Basque socialists and republicans on the other were locked into intense competition in order to gain control over and derive the main credit from the autonomy process. Second, the autonomy negotiations corresponded to a period of escalating political instability, marked by numerous local and state elections which occasioned major shifts of political power. Hence, the calculations of the Basque political parties concerning their relative power inside the Basque country and the relative power commanded by their allies in Madrid were frequently dramatically upset.

Additionally, in its single-minded pursuit of Basque autonomy, the PNV was often pushed violently off balance when issues of a different order swept over the horizon. The October Revolution of 1934 provided a telling example.

The newly formed Confederación Española de Derechas Autónomas (CEDA, Spanish Confederation of the Autonomous Right), the most important party in the parliament elected in 1933, had declared itself totally hostile to all regional autonomies. In protest, on 12 June 1934 the Basque nationalist deputies marched out of the Madrid parliament in order to galvanize their resources and supporters in a frontal attack on the government from the streets and political institutions of the Basque country. In this campaign the nationalists were supported, although for different motives, by the Basque left. The left used the campaign to defend its conception of the Republic against a government which it feared was monarchist in sympathies.

Basque popular agitation, which reached spectacular proportions, was counterbalanced by fines, arrests of mayors and town councillors, suspension of *ayuntamientos* and litigation. By September some 1,500 Basque mayors and town councillors had been fined, detained or put on trial (Payne, 1974: 200). Government repression forced the PNV into a staunchly anti-rightist and separatist position, to the great delight of the nationalist intransigents. The PNV tried to warn the government, in the words of Telesforo de Monzón, a PNV deputy, that 'When all Basques demand more than autonomy, then you will want to give us a little autonomy. But by then it might be too late as it was in Cuba.' The government's reply was unequivocal. 'Faced with regionalism, understanding. Faced with separatism, executions in the public square!' (quoted in Payne, 1974: 208).

Locked into battle with the right, which the PNV now censured as the root of all Basque problems, the party was desperately wrong-footed when the left issued the call for revolutionary insurrection in October 1934.

The immediate cause was a reshuffle of the Spanish cabinet in which members of the CEDA, regarded by the left as proto-fascist, entered government for the first time. The socialists in particular were convinced that the event signalled an attempt to institute fascism in Spain.

In Catalonia a Catalan Republic was proclaimed which ended embarrassingly a day later when the Catalan government surrendered to the Spanish army. More seriously, the mining region of Asturias erupted in a rebellion which cost over 4,000 casualties and took the Spanish army, reinforced by African battalions, two weeks to crush. Next to Asturias, the Basque region was the other part of Spain in which the October Revolution had its most serious consequences. The socialist trade union, the UGT, along with the anarchists, communists and, less actively, the nationalist trade union (the STV) declared a general strike on 4 October. The strike was total in most of the Basque industrialized areas. In San Sebastian, Eibar, Mondragon and the industrial belt around Bilbao, revolutionary workers' committees, backed by workers' militias, effectively took over power. Barricades and street battles brought most of these areas to a standstill. A state of emergency was proclaimed. The uprising was eventually quelled by military intervention.

The October Revolution underlined the essential dilemma in the PNV's position. Most nationalists experienced the revolution as days of pure terror. The PNV – estranged from both the right and the left – declared strict

Table 1 *Election results 1936*

	Alliance of the right	PNV	Popular Front
Alava	24,701	8,958	9,521
Guipúzcoa	45,153	50,108	41,193
Navarra	111,442	14,799	34,987
Vizcaya (prov.)	24,726	36,013	10,424
Bilbao	30,274	43,548	69,684
Total	236,296	153,426	165,809

Table 2 *Distribution of parliamentary seats*

	Alliance of the right	PNV	Popular Front
Alava	1		1
Guipúzcoa		4	2
Navarra	7		
Vizcaya (prov.)	1	3	
Bilbao		2	4
Total	9	9	7

neutrality and abstention from all involvement. This declaration satisfied no one. The left condemned the PNV as cohorts of fascism and repression. The right accused the PNV of collaboration with the left and complicity in the revolution. In the subsequent government repression, nationalist centres were closed and nationalist leaders detained. The ex-Minister Calvo Sotelo summed up the right-wing reaction in a speech, delivered in San Sebastian in November, with the celebrated phrase, 'Preferiría una España roja a una España rota!' (I would prefer a red Spain to a broken Spain).

The 1936 elections were a plebiscite between two totally hostile and incompatible political options. The PNV as usual was trapped in the middle between the right which was pro-Catholic, but Spanish nationalist, and the left which was pro-autonomy, but anti-Catholic. As the electoral campaign developed the PNV became the main target of the political invective of both the Popular Front and the right-wing Alliance. The Popular Front taunted the PNV for the clerical, reactionary and racial nature of its politics and accused the party of complicity in the previous conservative government (Fusi, 1979: 129). The right-wing Alliance campaigned on the slogan, 'Contra la revolución y sus cómplices' (Against the revolution and its accomplices). And the PNV was thrust into the same camp as the ravagers of convents and Leninist hordes.

The 1936 election results can be seen in Table 1.

In terms of electoral support the three blocks of Basque politics had emerged roughly equal.

True to its election promises, the parliament, dominated by the Popular Front, approved a statute of Basque autonomy on 1 October 1936. On 7 October under the venerable oak at Guernica, José Antonino Aguirre, president of the PNV, was sworn in as president and minister of defence of the Provisional Government of Euzkadi.[6] The occasion was marred by stringent security measures which prevented a multitudinous affirmation of national veneration and a small demonstration of nationalist intransigents who chanted boisterously, 'Statute, no! Independence, yes!' The statute of 1936 covered Alava, Guipúzcoa and Vizcaya. But by then the exact terms of the statute were largely irrelevant. Euzkadi had already been dismembered and cut off from the rest of Spain by civil war.

Civil war

The reactions of the PNV to the military uprising of 18 July 1936 underlined the multifarious social base and, at points, contradictory nature of the ideology upon which the party rested. Some months previously secret meetings were allegedly held between certain PNV leaders and the right requesting arms 'to form Basque militias which would function as soon as a communist revolution, which we assume is approaching, explodes' (quoted in Payne, 1974: 220–21). A few days before the uprising two PNV deputies, Irujo and Lasarte, declared that the PNV would support the Republic in case of a military intervention. On the night before the military rebellion, the Euzkadi-Buru-Batzar (the PNV executive) retracted these assurances of automatic PNV loyalty.

On the day of the uprising the first section of the PNV to react was Napar-Buru-Batzar (the PNV executive in Navarra) which declared its opposition to the government 'responsible for religious persecutions'. Navarra was the only area in Spain to produce an immediate, spontaneous uprising in favour of Franco. Volunteers, 42,000 in number and called the *Requetés*, financed by the Carlists, were recruited mainly from the peasantry and organized into militias in defence of 'God and His Church, King and *Fueros*!' By 22 July, eight columns of *Requetés* had entered Guipúzcoa from the south and east. Many *Requetés* marched under the slogan, 'Death to Euzkadi!'

In Alava on 19 July the military garrison at Vitoria rose in support of General Franco. The initial response of the PNV in Alava was to declare neutrality and offer no resistance to the new authorities. This neutrality was changed reluctantly to support for 'the military movement'. Also on 19 July the PNV in Guipúzcoa and Vizcaya, much to the surprise of the ecclesiastical authorities and Spanish conservatives in general, officially affirmed its loyalty to the besieged Republic.

Given the struggle between the citizens and fascism, between the Republic and monarchy, the principles of the PNV lead unavoidably to the side of the citizens and the Republic which is congruent with the democratic regime that was particular to our people during centuries of freedom.

(Declaration, Bizkai-Buru-Batzar, 19 July 1936)

However, the unstinting support extended by moderate nationalist leaders, such as Aguirre and Irujo, to the republican cause throughout the war did not necessarily correspond to the attitudes of most PNV members. Aguirre later admitted that one-third of Basques were in favour of the Republic, one-third were opposed and one-third were neutral. Sabino de Arana's brother, Luis de Arana, now over seventy, probably gave a more accurate reflection of nationalist attitudes.

The Basque Nationalist Party in JEL lives only for Euzkadi and if this government and regime is bad for Euzkadi, a fascist, military government would be worse. Therefore, the PNV is obliged to maintain order at all costs because we live in our house, in our fatherland, in our Vizcaya and our duty is to conserve it.

(quoted in Garcia Venero, 1969: 574)

Arana argued that Basque nationalists should struggle against any invasion of 'Vizcaya and her sisters in race, but never should a nationalist soldier carry the struggle across the boundaries of our fatherland, Euzkadi' (quoted in Garcia Venero, 1969: 575).

The 'maintenance of order' not only pitted the PNV against the insurgent military, it also placed the PNV in confrontation with revolutionary groups of workers who took to the streets in Vizcaya and Guipúzcoa armed with whatever was available. The revolutionary activities of these groups were limited to executions of right-wing sympathizers and priests and the destruction of churches. The Basque country was the only area of the Republic in which no revolutionary changes were forced through. No nationalizations or collectivizations of land or industry occurred. This was in large part due to Basque nationalism which also fought to preserve 'Christian civilization'.

Although in the industrialized areas the PNV were numerically inferior to the Popular Front, from early on Basque nationalists took political control over the war effort. The Popular Front was fragmented and its constituent parts incapable of sustained collaboration. Even though its military organization was frequently inadequate, the Basque government's social organization was impressive. As the PNV consolidated its power over the institutions of government, revolutionary executions and atrocities were successfully halted and respect for private property, including the crucial armament industries, imposed. The PNV was especially insistent that the heavy industry threatened by the national forces should not be sabotaged as demanded by the left and later ordered by the Republican government. Outside observers frequently commented that in Vizcaya one received the impression that there was no war. Order was total. Moreover, the Basque government quickly took on many of the functions of an independent state. It issued its own currency, established diplomatic links with several foreign countries and set up its own judiciary. In addition, the Euzko-Gudarostea, the Basque army, refused to accept central Republican authority.

For the national forces the Basque country was seen as an easy target. Basque iron ore and the armament industries made it a tempting one. Navarra and Alava sided with Franco's cause from the start. San Sebastian had surrendered without resistance on 13 September.

The weakness of the Basque military endeavour was due to a confluence of factors. Although the north-west of Spain had been cut off from the rest of Republican Spain by August 1936, there was no collaboration between the Basques, Asturias and Santander. And, as Hugh Thomas has pointed out (1965: 516), how could there be when the Basque provinces were conservative and Catholic while Asturias and Santander were led by communists and anarchists. Moreover, the Basque military effort was largely a homespun affair and lacked, with certain very notable exceptions, professional leadership. The Basque forces were not placed under a professional, integrated command until one month before their final surrender. As significantly, the Republican government gave little aid to the northern front which it considered less important than Madrid or the south (Thomas, 1965: 518). Furthermore, the socialists distrusted and the communists hated the whole Basque experiment. Consequently, the Basque forces were chronically short of artillery and aerial support. Finally the Basque nationalists pursued the war with ambivalence. Throughout the eleven months the war lasted in the Basque country various attempts were made by Basque nationalists, often without the approval of the main PNV leadership, to negotiate a separate peace treaty. The Carlists were approached on several occasions as were the Italians, once with the help of the Vatican, in order to arrange a surrender that would guarantee Basque autonomy.

Basque military strategy was purely defensive and centred on the 'Ring of Iron', a system of fortified trenches conceived as a Vizcayan Maginot Line, constructed around Bilbao. In April 1937 Mola's offensive on Bilbao began. The attacking force of some 40,000 men consisted of four brigades from Navarra, the 23rd of March Italian Division, Spanish legionnaires and Moroccan troops. The German Condor Division supplied air support (Beltza, 1974: 318). Under the concentrated onslaught the front lines to the east of Vizcaya collapsed. The Basque *gudaris* (soldiers) retreated to the 'Ring of Iron'. The actual attack on Bilbao was prepared by saturation aerial bombing on the towns of Durango and Guernica just outside Bilbao's main defences. The bombing of Guernica provoked an international uproar. General Franco denied all responsibility and replied officially to the protest, 'We have respected Guernica as we respect everything that is Spanish.'

On 12 July the 'Ring of Iron' was penetrated and five days later General Mola's troops entered Bilbao. On 1 July the new mayor of Bilbao, José Maria de Areilza, the Count of Motrico – later to become a leading democratic politician in the post-Franco period – declared in his inaugural speech:

Bilbao has not surrendered, but has been conquered by the army and militias with the sacrifice of many lives. Bilbao is a city redeemed by blood ... This horrible, evil nightmare called Euzkadi which was a result of socialism and Vizcayan imbecility has been defeated forever ... Vizcaya is again a piece of Spain through pure and simple military conquest.

With the fall of Bilbao many Basque battalions were moved west to help in the defence of Santander. In August Santander was also overwhelmed. For most Basques the civil war was over. The PNV negotiated a surrender of all Basque forces to the Italians. Aguirre's plan to transfer the *gudaris* (soldiers) to the Catalan front had been vetoed by the Republican government and found little favour within the PNV in any case. Shortly before the surrender on 25 August a small group of beleaguered Basque nationalists proclaimed the establishment of the 'Basque Independent Republic'. Nevertheless, with its heavy industry and armament factories still intact, nine months after its belated inception, Euzkadi had been overthrown by Franco's military crusade.[7]

6

'España, una, libre y grande'

The unity of Franco's Spain

Publicly the Basque nationalist community ceased to exist with the collapse of Euzkadi. The physical punishment of the Basques was to a certain extent restrained because Franco needed to retain the goodwill of Basque industrialists. But the *Caudillo* wanted to create what no other Spanish leader had managed – 'España, una, libre y grande' (Spain, united, free and great).

On the cultural level the unity of the Spanish nation was to be expressed and symbolized by the unity of Spanish culture and language. Franco regarded Basque culture, especially the language, as an excuse for and sign of separatism. Therefore, the regime unleashed a thorough campaign of cultural repression. The public use of Basque greetings, traditional garments, folklore, Basque names, publications and the teaching of Euskera were strictly forbidden. These prohibitions were backed by a formidable armoury of government decrees, of which the following represent only a small sample.

Orden 18–V–1938 (B.O. 21-V-38)
Norms concerning inscription in the civil register.
[There exist]... a large number of names which not only are expressed in a language distinct from official Castilian, but which imply a meaning contrary to the unity of the fatherland... The Spain of Franco will not tolerate aggressions against the unity of its language... It should be noted that the origin of these anomalies (in the register) is due to a morbid exacerbation of regionalist sentiment in some provinces... This is what occurs in the Vascongadas, for example, with the names Iñaki, Kepa, Koldobika and others which undeniably have separatist meaning.

Orden 16-V-1940 (B.O. 17-V-40)
It is the obligation of the public authorities to repress, to the extent possible, these practices (the public display of regional folk customs and 'native' languages) which help obscure the Spanish conscience and make it deviate from the pure national line by introducing in the customs of our people exotic elements which must be eliminated.

'España, una, libre y grande'

Orden 11-I-1945 (B.O. 24-I-45)
Designation of merchant ships.
All designations of ships which are not written in Castilian, the official language and symbol of the unity of the nation, are completely forbidden.

Whereas a certain reprieve from the full force of cultural repression could be found in the anonymity of the cities, in the *euskaldun* (Basque-speaking) rural areas official vigilance was more efficient. Obviously unable to repress the Basque language totally in the rural areas, the authorities concentrated on enforcing an array of petty and arbitrary restrictions. For instance, Basque peasants were frequently fined for using the Basque greetings, *agur* (good-bye), *egun on* (good-day), *kaixo* (hello) and so forth instead of their Spanish equivalents. Fines were also imposed for the wearing of *kaikus* (a type of woollen jacket) which in the cities, like Basque greetings, had often been used as a badge of nationalist identification, but in the countryside were a normal part of daily attire. In addition, the ecclesiastical authorities prohibited the common practice of permitting the sermon during mass to be given in Euskera.

On the political level Spanish unity was enforced by a highly centralized state which Franco described as 'a totalitarian instrument in the service of the fatherland', focused on Francisco Franco himself. Franco, the *Caudillo de España*, *Jefe del Estado* and *Generalísmo de los Ejercitos de la Nación*, was 'el representante supremo de la Nación; personifica la soberanía nacional, ejerce el poder supremo político y administrativo' (The Head of State is the supreme representative of the Nation, personification of national sovereignty; holder of supreme political and administrative power) (Leyes Fundamentales de Reino, Tit. II, Art. 6).

The ideological underpinning of this state was provided by its only political party. In April 1937 Franco fused the fascist Falange with the Carlists, '[who] have brought us the sacred trust of the Spanish tradition, tenaciously preserved, with its Catholic spirituality', to form the Falange Española Tradicionalista y de las Juntas de Ofensiva Nacional Sindicalista. This new party, better known as the Movimiento Nacional, was headed, not surprisingly, by General Franco.

Compliance with the new regime was ensured through a vast, byzantine administrative and military apparatus which stretched on the one hand from Franco as head of state through the Madrid-appointed provincial governors down to the local secretaries of the municipal councils and the local *jefes de movimiento*. On the other it ran from Franco as head of the armed forces through the provincial military governors to the local *guardia civiles* (in the rural areas), *policía armada* (in the cities), secret police and an extensive network of police informers. Under Franco very little authority was ever delegated to the lower ranks of this political structure. Decision-making in most realms was usually retained as the sole prerogative of Madrid. State control over the individual was further strengthened by a series of official documents testifying to good political behaviour, based on reports from the local authorities, which were required for an individual to obtain a passport, driver's licence, job in the public sector, etc. etc.

The economic transformation: Basque industrialization, 1940–75

Although under Franco the Basques were culturally and politically humiliated, economically they thrived.

Upon the 'liberation' of Bilbao in 1937, Franco declared Vizcaya and Guipúzcoa *provincias traidores* (traitorous provinces). His first act was to revoke the *conciertos económicos* – i.e. fiscal autonomy – of these two provinces. In a gesture of gratitude for their loyalty, both Alava and Navarra were permitted to retain fiscal autonomy.

However, by the end of the war Spain's shattered economy was left largely dependent on agriculture; 183 towns, including Madrid, Barcelona and Malaga, had been devastated; 75% of Spain's bridges were unusable. Production of cast iron and steel had slumped almost 50% in relation to 1929. The Spanish treasury was totally depleted. The revenue of the new regime had dropped to levels below that of 1900 (Gallo, 1973: 70–71). The reconstruction of Spain was gravely hampered by the commercial disruption of the Second World War. In addition Spain suffered from rampant corruption – as government officials conducted a profitable trade in materials and import licences – lack of raw materials, lack of foreign assistance, lack of trained staff and low morale (Payne, 1969: 55). Nevertheless, due partly to the international boycott imposed in 1946 and partly to its ideological preferences, the regime embarked on an ambitious policy of economic self-sufficiency.

The policy of autarchy provided an enormous opportunity for the Basque country. The mass destruction of industrial installations and infrastructure characteristic of the rest of Spain had not occurred in the Basque region, thanks mainly to the battalions of *gudaris* (soldiers) posted by the PNV to protect Basque heavy industry from left-wing sabotage. For the regime the protection of existing industry was of the utmost necessity. The protection of Spain's industrial sector meant the protection of Basque industry. This industrial base gave the Basque economy an overwhelming initial advantage which produced the second great boom of Basque industrial expansion. Since Spain was in need of almost everything and since the government insisted on the substitution of imports with home produced goods, all goods manufactured, regardless of how poor in quality or overpriced, had an ensured market. Individuals with access to capital turned immediately and profitably to manufacturing. Throughout Vizcaya and Guipúzcoa the building of small family-owned factories and industries proceeded at an enormous rate. The profitability of capital was reflected in the dividends paid out by the banks, which from 1943 through the 1950s averaged 11 % (Payne, 1969: 56).

However, the industries created were technologically primitive and depended on enormous pools of cheap labour. Basque manufactured goods were considered the most expensive and the poorest in quality in Europe. Although Spain had emerged from political isolation by the late 1940s, Basque industrialists – along with their counterparts in the rest of Spain – strongly resisted any free flow of goods, arguing that Spain's fragile industrial base would collapse overnight. The Basque industrial élite helped to procure a protectionist policy which allowed into Spain only those goods which were essential to industrial construction and which did not compete with Spanish products.

Because of government controls and inept planning in general, corruption, the substandard quality of most Spanish products (which therefore had a limited foreign market) and the need to import sizeable amounts of raw materials and capital goods, the state budget became grossly unbalanced. Printing new money was a standard solution. The price index from 1940 to 1959, reflecting inflationary pressures, grew close to 700 % (Payne, 1968: 62). Spain's currency was not convertible. By 1959 the country faced bankruptcy.

In response the government issued the Plan of Stabilization. The austerity measures introduced by this plan – extreme restrictions on credit, immediate recall of bank loans, devaluation of the peseta, etc. – acted as a hard brake on Basque industrial growth. However, after a period of difficult readjustment, Basque industry entered a more rational phase.

To solidify the gains made through the Plan of Stabilization, Spain adopted a series of four-year Plans of Economic and Social Development. Borrowing from the trend in regional planning in vogue in much of Europe, the plans attempted to create new industrial growth centres in agricultural areas in order to offset rapid rural depopulation. To achieve this, numerous 'poles of development', or growth poles, were established, all of which were outside the Basque provinces. Because of the scarcity of land and high labour costs in Vizcaya and Guipúzcoa and the already dense congestion of industrial plant, the development of new industries in this region was deemed ill-advised.

But the 'poles of development' were only one aspect of the Plans of Economic and Social Development. The plans also entailed a scheme to give tax and credit benefits to certain industrial sectors for modernization and expansion. These sectors were first and foremost iron and steel and shipbuilding, sectors heavily represented in the Basque provinces. Sectoral development aimed at modernization of existing plant, combined with high

Table 3 *Population growth 1955–75 (percentage)*

Alava	84.62
Guipúzcoa	61.87
Navarra	22.94
Vizcaya	76.29
Average Basque country	59.95

Source: Mendizabal, 1980: 368

but selective protectionist barriers of the Franco period, were ideally suited to Basque industry. Moreover, Basque heavy industry in particular benefited greatly from Madrid's generous export subsidies.

Another area of Franco's policies was also undeniably important to Basque industry. Denied rights to independent trade unions or free collective bargaining, the large numbers of workers that fed Basque industrial output remained generally compliant and cheap.

The expansion of the Spanish economy – the Basque economy included – ran at Japanese levels for most of the Franco period. By 1975 Spain had become the tenth most important industrial country in the world. In the Basque country this impressive economic growth was propelled by the traditional heavy industries in Vizcaya and an industrial take-off in Navarra and, especially, Alava, both provinces which had hitherto remained rural. While Spanish industrial expansion generated increased prosperity for large numbers of Spaniards, under Franco the Basques enjoyed the highest per capita income in Spain, averaging some 35% to 60% higher than the national norm.

The social transformation

This second great expansion of Basque industry generated the second great wave of Spanish immigration. During the period 1955 to 1975 the Basque country experienced the most rapid demographic growth in Spain with the exception of the province of Madrid. Whereas the population of Spain grew on average 23%, in the Basque country it expanded 60%.

The population explosion was most dramatic in the new industrial areas. Rentería in Guipúzcoa, for example, grew from 10,106 inhabitants in 1940 to 37,310 in 1973. Elgoibar, another industrial town in Guipúzcoa, went from 5,683 to over 13,000 inhabitants in the same period. In the province of Vizcaya, Durango increased from 8,251 to 22,354 (1970 census) and Ermua from 1,277 inhabitants to 14,563.

The reasons behind this mass immigration had not changed. Spain was still mainly rural and impoverished. Labour-short Basque industry offered employment and reasonable wages.

The rural exodus

The first influx of newcomers into the Basque cities, starting around 1940, were mainly *baserritarak*. Indeed the flight of rural Basques into the urban centres surged throughout the Franco period. By 1975 only some 10% of the active population were employed in agriculture and much less than 10% derived their income entirely from agricultural endeavours.

Although in the various urban centres rural Basques comprise from 25% to 50% of the immigrant population, this sector is never cited by Basque urbanites as constituting a distinct social category. However, rural Basques themselves generally find their position in the towns quite distinct from that of their urban counterparts. As discussed previously, in the Basque country the opposition between the *euskaldun baserritar* (Basque-speaking peasant) and *kaletar* (urbanite) is strong. Although irresistibly attractive in comparison to the drudgery of farm life, the *kale* (street) is also seen by the peasant as insecure, potentially hostile. The *kale* is often described as *kale gorria*, the red street. Here red, *gorria*, implies burnt, infertile and unprotected.

Many peasants regard their rural, *euskaldun* (Basque-speaking) background as a major barrier to urban success, augmenting the fundamental insecurity of town life, and as a source of constant embarrassment. Peasants often attempt to distance themselves from their Basque identity. Many *euskaldun* women insist that their children be spoken to only in Spanish. In one study (Nuñez, 1977: 86) 50% of Basque-speaking housewives in the capital cities, in comparison to only 33% in the rural areas, said they preferred their children to speak habitually in Euskera. Indeed from tastes in architecture and restaurants to clothing and leisure activities, rural Basques consistently display less enthusiasm for things defined as typically ‘Basque’. Therefore, one aspect of identity, among many, with which rural Basques have to contend is urban Basque ethnicity. The shifting and contradictory meaning of Basque identity is illustrated in the comments of Juan Luis, a young Basque whose family migrated to Bilbao in 1970.

assoc. of traits w/ parents

> We used to live in a *caserío* [farmstead] near Vergara (Guipúzcoa). My mother, who didn’t speak much Spanish, named me Juan Luis because she thought it more cultured. Basque names like Iñaki or whatever were looked down on... When I started school in Bilbao, those Basques – they usually came from nationalist families – with names like Joseba or Iñaki didn’t appear like Basques to me at all. They didn’t speak Euskera. They spoke Spanish like everyone else, but they wanted to be different from everyone else. They acted like *señoritos*. They were always telling

us we should learn Basque dances and spend our holidays in the *caseríos* because Franco was destroying Basque culture and the Basque *pueblo* had to fight back. They never *asked* me about Basque culture. They *told* me! They were Basques in Spanish and I was a Basque in Euskera. And I always felt that my way wasn't of any interest to them.

The political adjustment that many young rural migrants made to urban life consisted of the adoption of a radical nationalism in which the symbols of Basque identity were interpreted literally and turned unrelentingly against their Basque urbanite counterparts.

Non-Basque immigration

However, by 1951 significant numbers of workers were also being recruited from Old Castile, Léon and Asturias. By the late 1950s they began to arrive from regions further afield like Galicia and New Castile. Finally in the 1960s when immigration reached deluge proportions, new labour was drawn from distant Andalucia and Extremadura.

This new surge of immigration had a more far-reaching social impact than the pre-war one for three reasons. First, the number of immigrants was simply much greater. Second, unlike the first period in which industry and immigration were confined to a relatively few urban centres, now industrialization and, consequently, immigrants swept over most of the Basque region. Urban congestion and pollution, already characteristic of Bilbao, blighted each new industrial town, many of which were squeezed into narrow mountain valleys. Neither the state nor provincial authorities were willing to expend the public resources to support or regulate the swelling towns. Third, while the old industrial centres – like Bilbao and San Sebastian – had a long Hispanicized urban tradition, many of the new industrial centres – such as Mondragon, Durango, Ermua – grew up in the heart of the *euskaldun* rural hinterland. Currently the proportion of the resident population in the Basque country of immigrant origin is probably around 50 %.

By the mid-1960s the Basque reaction to the immigrants had turned fervently hostile. During my first field trip in 1972 *maketos* or *castellanos* were a constant topic of piercing complaint. People felt overwhelmed and said that they had become a minority in their own land. 'Our house is no longer our own!', they repeated. Although jobs remained in ample supply, many Basques saw the immigrants as usurpers of scarce employment. 'Han venido aquí para robar nuestro pan!' (they have come here to steal our bread) was a common expression that reflected widely held attitudes.

The immigrants were seen as carriers and representatives of Francoism and personified the oppressive state intent on destroying Basque life. The political values of the immigrants, it was claimed, were moulded by the

Francoist press and educational system which had taught them to despise all things Basque as unworthy and subversive. This resentment was fed by the fact that the hated 'Forces of Public Order' (i.e. the police) were entirely composed of non-Basques.[1] Immigrants were seen to treat Basque culture with contempt. Basques frequently tell stories in which a group of Basques speaking Euskera are disdainfully and loudly ridiculed by Spaniards exclaiming with great mirth, 'Habla en cristiano! Habla en cristiano!' ('Speak in Christian!' – a play on the word, *castellano*).

Basques often claim that they and the immigrants simply occupy two distinct socio-cultural worlds. The differences between them impede proper communication and mutual understanding. Underlying this stress on cultural divergence is also a sense of Basque superiority rarely admitted to publically, but often discussed privately. The immigrant is seen as arrogant, uncultured, untrustworthy and out only for himself, a scornful image reflected in numerous jokes and children's songs.

Many Basque priests have also fostered this view. The middle and lower clergy in Guipúzcoa in particular often voiced sombre suspicions about the anti-religious attitudes of the immigrants whom they saw as a moral threat to the community. During a Mass I attended in 1974 the priest claimed that the superior religiosity of Basques could be measured by the fact that Basques attended mass more faithfully. 'Look around you. Where are our immigrant brothers?', the priest intoned. 'They are geographically mobile and have become morally rootless.'

While the Basque reaction towards the immigrants tends to be antagonistic, the reaction of the Spanish immigrants towards their hosts was and is more ambivalent. Except for those active in political groups, immigrants are extremely unwilling to express their true opinions about Basques.[3] The immigrant sees his world as fragmented, powerless and dependent on a closed, self-sufficient Basque community in which most social benefits are held. The immigrant often sees his task in terms of reaching an individual accommodation with the Basque community which, he recognizes, bears his presence only with reluctance. Open, direct criticism of this community is not thought a practical proposition. Group action against it is not conceived as possible.

Several studies have shown that number is a critical determinant of the relationship between immigrants and Basques. Gaur (1970) suggests that the greater the proportion of immigrants to Basques, the more frequently immigrants express dissatisfaction at their ability to obtain jobs, housing and promotions. In the town of Elgoibar in which approximately 50% of the population is non-Basque, 16% of the immigrants felt they were in a *greatly* disadvantaged position in comparison to Basques. In Rentería, in which non-Basques are in a substantial majority, this figure had risen to 31%.

Except in the old industrial areas in which immigrant populations have lived for several generations, immigrants feel little sense of community. Immigrant neighbourhoods are fragmented by regional heterogeneity. Moreover, the families of more recent immigrants tend to be geographically dispersed. Siblings, parents and/or, less frequently, spouses have either remained in the village of origin or else migrated to other areas of Spain. Immigrants see their communities as *ad hoc* and transitory.

Most immigrants retain strong sentimental attachments to their place of origin, to which many return as often as possible. Within the confines of a specific regional group – say Galicians – this regional sentiment may be displayed, but usually with caution. Most immigrants realise that Basques can be sensitive about such displays of 'Spanishness'. One Andalucian worker who has lived in Azpeitia, Guipúzcoa, since 1967 remarked:

> I've heard the stories about 'Habla en cristiano' and I've seen it happen. But when I first worked in the factory I used to sing flamenco. But I saw that the boss didn't like it too much. 'Just another *maketo* singing *maketo* music', I heard him say one time. So I didn't sing anymore. Then I used to go with some friends – other Andalucians – to a bar owned by a *galego* [a person from Galicia]. And we started singing there. José, the owner, didn't like it either. He said if we sang like that *los de aquí* [those from here, i.e. Basques] wouldn't come to his bar.

Partly because of their lack of industrial qualifications and low level of general education, most immigrants enter on the lowest ranks of the Basque economic ladder. The large majority of the unskilled working class is now non-Basque in origin. Moreover, once employed the immigrants' opportunities for promotion are limited because the *patronos* and managers, by and large Basque, tend to give preference to Basque workers. The usual argument is that the *patron* is more familiar with the 'mentality' of the Basque worker, who is regarded as harder working, more serious, trustworthy and honest.

It is this strong feeling of discrimination that forms the core of the immigrants' resentment against the Basques and makes the need to find an accommodation with the Basque community appear imperative. The newly arrived immigrants, lacking networks of useful and conveniently placed relatives and friends, are exposed much more directly than their Basque counterparts to the inadequacies of the urban centres. Access to satisfactory housing, employment, promotions and social services is seen as difficult and dependent somewhere along the line on the mediation and goodwill of Basques.

This need to accommodate to the Basque community is often expressed in a desire to integrate – to claim Basque status and have this claim accepted by the Basques themselves. Both Basques and immigrants lament the lack of integration between the two groups. But there are few social mechanisms that encourage integration and several that militate against it.

Although it varies according to social class and specific area, communication between the Basque and immigrant populations tends to be minimal. The two groups tend to lead separate social lives which overlap only at the place of work. They are usually segregated through residential patterns – the Basques tending to live in the town centres and the immigrants in high-rise estates on the urban periphery. After working hours Basques and immigrants tend to frequent their own bars, places of recreation and shops.

Intermarriage, often described as highly desirable by immigrants, is frowned upon by Basques. Most Basques place a high value on the preservation of a Basque genealogy. One Basque lawyer, himself in search of a wife at the time, commented:

> The Basques are obsessed by their surnames. The more Basque surnames a person has, the prouder he is. Purity of ancestry is important even for those who are politically anti-Basque. When a person thinks about marrying, he also thinks about children and what he will transmit to them. You marry a Basque so that you can transmit undiluted Basqueness to your children. No one wants his child to be named, Koldobika Goikoetxea Perez.

When intermarriage does occur, the Basque is considered to have married 'down'. As one Basque woman said, 'Marrying a *maketo* here is like marrying a Jew in Majorca.'

Basques insist that one key to integration into and mobility within the Basque community lies in the language. Euskera, they claim, is the essence of the Basque mode of being. To learn it shows the immigrant's goodwill towards and support for the Basque community's wounded cultural condition. This is a view with which the majority of immigrants seem to agree. In one study a remarkable 78% of the immigrant workers questioned expressed a desire to have their children learn Euskera (Gaur, 1969: 205). In another study 56% of immigrants expressed the same wish (Gaur, 1971). Immigrants are as keenly aware that Euskera is an emblem of membership in the Basque community as they are of the fact that the majority of Basques are not themselves Basque-speakers. However, Euskera is a notoriously difficult language to learn properly. Only a very few have the linguistic skills, time and energy to manage it. In Guipúzcoa it is estimated that less than 4% of immigrants have some knowledge of Euskera (Gaur, 1971). In Vizcaya the percentage is probably less. The expressed wish of so many immigrants to learn Euskera can probably be more accurately interpreted as a desire to gain acceptance in the Basque community.

However, there is one, less testing, means by which an immigrant can become a full Basque. The immigrant can shift his total political allegiance onto the Basque community. In short, he can become a Basque nationalist. Faced with a deepening economic crisis and bleak futures, more and more young immigrants are choosing this option.

The fate of Euskera

Most Basques are convinced that, under Franco, Euskera faced extinction. The factors usually mentioned as detrimental to Euskera are: (1) Spanish cultural oppression in general which stigmatized Euskera and injected a sense of fear into many Basque-speakers; (2) Franco's official policy which prohibited the cultivation of Euskera; (3) the mass media which was exclusively in Spanish; (4) mass immigration of Spanish-speakers, and (5) the dwindling rural sector in which Basque culture and language were protected as an ongoing part of daily life.

That the incidence of Basque-speakers varies according to the degree of urbanization had been shown repeatedly. However, as noted previously, reliable statistics on Euskera are scarce. Recently a major study concerning Euskera has appeared (Siadeko, 1979) which, unfortunately, is weakened by methodical omissions as well as gross hyperbole. For instance, the study describes an *euskaldun* (Basque-speaking) couple who never spoke Euskera at home for forty years for fear of reprisals. The study comments: 'Much has been written about the Jewish ghettoes in Germany during the Nazi period. Although in different proportions and ways, here too this brutal cultural discrimination has been produced which has led many to be executed and at times in an even more brutal manner' (Siadeko, 1979: 53).

Nevertheless, the study provides one of the few new sources of statistical information concerning the language. It would be surprising indeed if the five factors listed have not had an extremely detrimental effect on Euskera. Therefore, from the study of Siadeko an unexpected result seems to emerge. Although the proportion of Basque-speakers in the Basque country has decreased, over the entire period of industrialization the absolute number of *euskaldunes* has held constant. This figure of 553,848 can be regarded as roughly similar to the 4–600,000 individuals estimated as Basque-speakers in the mid-nineteenth century. This conclusion also emerges from other figures provided by Nuñez (1977).

These figures seem to question one of the most widely and emotionally held beliefs in the Basque country today – that due to centralization and industrialization the Basque language has been decimated. On the contrary, despite its rural roots and lack of a developed literary tradition, Euskera seems to have survived these forces rather better than many similar languages in milder political climates, for example, Welsh and Gaelic.

However, over the past hundred years or so the quality of spoken Euskera has probably declined substantially. From 8% to 26% of those who say they are Basque-speakers are estimated to speak the language with difficulty (Gaur, 1969, 1971). Moreover, many of those who are fluent are unable to use the language when discussing a wide range of technical subjects. The high

Table 4 *Linguistic situation of Basque country, 1975*

Province	Population	Basque-speakers	Percentage
Alava	238,262	18,863	7.9
Vizcaya	1,152,394	174,366	15.1
Guipúzcoa	682,517	307,279	45.0
Navarra	483,867	53,340	11.0
Total	2,557,040	553,848	21.7

Source: Siadeko, 1979: 68

Table 5 *Basque-speakers in 1868 and 1970*

	Number of Basque-speakers	% of Basque-speakers in population
1868	391,000	54
1970	519,078	23

Source: Nuñez, 1977: 26 and 28

frequency of language switching is a striking characteristic of conversations between fluent Basque-speakers.

However, since 1960 – when the first *ikastolas* (schools in which Euskera is the language of instruction) opened in the postwar period – a slow but accelerating process of linguistic recuperation has been taking place. Whereas from 1940 to 1960 only 25 books in Euskera were published, by 1975 554 books in the language had appeared. The runaway bestsellers by far have been the Basque language course books. In addition, various newspapers, magazines and radio stations have appeared that cater exclusively to a Basque-speaking audience. Illustrative of this trend, 92% of phonograph records produced in 1975–76, as compared to a little over 33% in 1965–69, were in Euskera, reflecting the enormous upsurge of interest in Basque music (Siadeko, 1979: 196).

This increased interest in and use of Euskera has been particularly noticeable in schools. Whereas the three *ikastolas* which opened in 1960 had together only 60 pupils, the student population of the *ikastolas* in 1979 had reached almost 50,000 representing one-tenth of the entire school-age population. Moreover, during 1975–76 some 40,000 adults were attending Basque language classes either to learn the language, in the case of Spanish-speakers, or to learn to write it, in the case of Basque-speakers. Also 40% of Church-run private schools offer some instruction in Euskera.

In the Basque country Euskera today is highly valued as an 'integral element of the personality of the Basque people, a unifying bond between members of the Basque community and a cultural richness that must be conserved at all costs' (Siadeko, 1979). This view is shared by the vast majority of Basque-speakers and Spanish-speakers alike and has helped not only to halt the relative decline of Euskera, but to reverse it.

7

The moral community, from clandestinity to power

The radical nationalism of Sabino de Arana had its origins in the initial process of Basque industrialization. It was propelled by those social sectors who had become threatened by and trapped between the two main protagonists of Basque industrialization – the Basque financial oligarchy and the Spanish immigrant proletariat. Basque nationalism was a movement of vindication by those classes that had been pushed aside by Basque industrial history.

In many ways the Franco period was a variation on the same theme. Spreading industrialization transformed whole new sectors of Basque society into industrial producers. Although increasingly prosperous, these people lacked all political voice. They saw in the Franco regime and the new flood of Spanish immigrants the root causes of their political disenfranchisement.

During the postwar period nationalism was cherished in many families as a domestic tradition 'imbibed with the mother's milk'. But denied all possibility of cultural or political expression, the Basque nationalist community lay dormant. Its revival was gradual and coincided with the slow liberalization of the Franco regime from the mid-1950s onwards. The main agent responsible for its public awakening was, predictably, radical nationalism, this time carried by *Euzkadi 'ta Askatasuna* (ETA, Euzkadi and Liberty). The means used were, on the one hand, the engagement of growing numbers of the Basque population in direct, violent confrontation with the Franco regime and, on the other, the resurrection of nationalism's cultural infrastructure.

The clerical prelude

The role of the Catholic Church in the Basque country is essential to understanding the nature of ETA. A large proportion, if not the majority, of the more influential Basque militants of the 1960s and 1970s were recruited into radical nationalism directly from the seminaries and convents of the Catholic Church.

The Church saw Franco as an indispensable ally in its war against the creeping materialism that had already engulfed the spiritual resolve of much of the world outside Spain's frontiers. And for Franco good relations with the Church were a cornerstone of his regime. That the Catholic Church should be a university for a whole new generation of Basque nationalists and offer a powerful platform – albeit involuntarily – for resistance to the regime can be traced first and foremost to the contradictory nature of the Church in the Basque country. The Church had its roots in a population that was deeply religious and deeply resentful of the Franco regime. Its apex was positioned in the rarified heights of the power élite.

In the Basque country the priesthood tended to be drawn from two social sectors. A minority came from very conservative, often Carlist, middle-class urban families. Most of the Basque ecclesiastical authorities were recruited from this sector. However, the majority tended to come from the *euskaldun* rural areas; and they often represented the brightest and the most traditional section of rural youth.

Two factors in particular served to instil a sense of political militancy in a growing minority of seminarists and young priests. The fundamental factor was the collaboration of the Church with the cultural repression in the countryside. In general the Church viewed Euskera as an inferior language and equated it with separatism. Use of Euskera was strictly forbidden inside the seminaries and other Church institutions. Secondly, many priests regarded the humanitarian idealism which the Church taught and its total unwillingness to place the spiritual into a social context as a cynical contradiction.

Disenchantment with the political and cultural attitudes of the Church increased and many young priests left the Church as a result. But, critically, the Church offered what no other institution in Spain could provide – a sanctuary outside the jurisdiction of the law. Many priests felt that it was only under the protection of the Church that they could agitate for social and cultural change. From the late 1950s onwards the Church's institutions – spiritual exercises, pastoral services, religious conferences – and social organizations, such as Acción Católica, were used by priests to assemble people, in particular the young, in order to communicate the message of social commitment and nationalist aspiration. The priests' highly successful efforts were inadvertantly aided by the Church's propensity of banishing the more vocal clerical dissidents to the rural hinterland where they carefully moulded the resentments of the rural population into a nationalist shape.

The first open protest against the Church hierarchy came in 1960 when 339 priests from all four Basque provinces signed a petition denouncing the cultural oppression of the Basque people and the Church as an accomplice in this oppression. The petition was sent to the four Basque bishops and the Vatican. It provoked an uproar. In each province the Church levelled punishments on the signatories. Many were fined, had their licences revoked and, most counter-productively, were sent to rural outposts. In the seminaries the petition was damned as heresy. Consequently, the seminarists studied the document with a vengeance and the seminaries were transformed into a battleground of political controversy.

The confrontation between Church authorities and dissident priests quickly escalated. By 1965 priests had staged several demonstrations to the utter amazement of the general public and police alike. The priests demanded respect for civil rights and protested against the Church's support for the Franco regime. Also in 1965 public attention was captured by the arrest, for the first time, of a priest, Father Alberto Gabica, for subversion. Gabica had given a short sermon about oppression in the Basque country in which he had mentioned the torture of political prisoners. He was already well known for his open defence of the Basque cause and his talks to children during which the obligatory portrait of Franco was turned face to the wall.

As a result of Father Gabica and the growing militancy of the Basque clergy, in 1968 the Bishop of Bilbao converted a monastery in the city of Zamora, near the Portuguese border, into a prison for priests, the only such prison anywhere in the Catholic world. One year later, after innumerable clerical sit-ins, hunger strikes, demonstrations and seditious sermons, the prison at Zamora was filled to capacity.

Clerical militancy moulded and lent moral authority to Basque resentment. The monolithic image and moral certainty of the Church was shattered. Official Church condemnation was no longer a brake on the political activities of even profoundly religious Basques. Moreover, popular anger exerted constant pressure on the Church to protest at mass detentions, the use of torture and to give support to human rights and the imprisoned Basque priests. With seminaries closing down and churches emptying, the Church was slowly and reluctantly persuaded to confront the state and withdraw its automatic understanding from the political authorities.

By 1969 militant priests had been supplanted by Euzkadi 'ta Askatasuna (ETA) as the standard-bearers of the Basque cause. Many of the early ETA members had been converted to the nationalist cause by priests or indeed came straight from the seminaries. Their aim was Basque independence achieved through armed struggle.

The genesis of ETA – the rebirth of radical nationalism

Like the PNV before it, ETA represented a fusion between two different social strata. On one side were the young, middle-class intellectuals of *Ekin*. *Ekin* (meaning, to do) was a magazine founded in 1952 by a dozen or so students at the Jesuit University of Deusto in Bilbao. These intellectuals were either from Bilbao or San Sebastian, came from wealthy professional or industrial families and were, with very few exceptions, Spanish-speakers.

Their activities were limited to reading and discussing books by PNV writers – *La Historía de Euzkadi* by Padre Estella, Sabino de Arana, etc. – and publishing abstracts of these nationalist essays. In *Ekin* was the future leadership of ETA.

On the other side were the young activitists of the PNV's vastly reduced youth branch, Euzko Gastedi (EG). The members of EG tended to come from the smaller new industrial towns, were often Basque-speakers, had a vocational, rather than academic, training, and were anti-intellectual with little patience for theorizing of any kind. It was these people, in particular, who had been recruited to nationalism by priests. During the 1950s while *Ekin* organized study groups, EG members covered the walls and streets of the Basque country with political slogans and broadsheets. EG represented the militant base of ETA, a base over which the leadership would never manage to gain effective political control.

By 1956 the intellectuals of *Ekin* had entered Euzko Gastedi (EG) with the idea of rekindling nationalist militancy. Representatives were sent to the PNV in Paris in order to solicit recognition and support. Support was not forthcoming. To the PNV the new intellectual leaders of EG were '*communistas, fanfarrones y contrabandistas*' (communists, bullies and smugglers; cited in Ortzi, 1975: 279). For EG this refusal provided the final proof of the PNV's total inability to respond to the Franco regime. By 1959 all ties with the PNV were broken and ETA was founded in order to remobilize the Basque population into militant nationalism.

ETA's first military adventure occurred in 1961 when a group of ETA militants attempted unsuccessfully to derail a train carrying civil war veterans going to San Sebastian for a picnic. During the 1960s ETA's activities extended to bank raids and attacks on the symbols of Spanish domination: war memorials, railroads, radio transmitters and so forth. These actions – never as frequent as ETA publicists claimed – had an enormous impact. The regime was at first unsure as to how to deal publicly with ETA. Officially nationalism had ceased to exist. However, the police responded with an accelerating operation of massive repression. Constant road controls, arrests, house searches and the widespread use of torture became features of Basque life and Basque prisoners filled Spanish jails. For an increasing number of young people ETA came to represent the means by which to revolt both against Francoism and against a stagnant Basque society devoted to factories, churches, bars and little else.

The year 1968 was a pivotal one for ETA. The clandestine demonstrations, organized by ETA, celebrating *Aberri Eguna* (Basque national day) had erupted into riots as groups of demonstrators battled with the Spanish police. A few months later Txabi Echevarrieta, one of ETA's best known militants, was shot by a policeman and thus became the first of a long line of ETA martyrs.[1] Public protests and masses were conducted in his honour.

In revenge for Txabi's death, ETA assassinated the head of the political police in Guipúzcoa, Melitón Manzanas, well known for his use of torture during interrogations. The government responded by imposing a state of emergency in Vizcaya and Guipúzcoa. In the subsequent wave of repression hundreds of alleged ETA members were arrested. Those put on trial – often with little evidence and even less recourse to a proper defence – were inevitably given extremely long prison sentences or sentenced to death. Gun battles between ETA and the police became frequent.

Sixteen of those implicated in the death of Manzanas, among them two women and two priests, were finally brought before a military tribunal in Burgos in 1970. Many of the defendants clearly showed signs of torture. Their trial sparked off an avalanche of national and international protest. General strikes paralysed all activity in Guipúzcoa and Vizcaya. Universities were closed, the Palace of Justice in Madrid was occupied by dissident lawyers, violent demonstrations broke out in many Spanish cities, another state of emergency was declared in the Basque country and several foreign governments as well as the Vatican pleaded for clemency. The tribunal handed down 6 death sentences and more than 700 years of prison sentences. The army was placed on full alert for fear of a popular insurrection in the Basque country (Douglass, 1971: 147). The death sentences were eventually commuted to life imprisonment.

The Burgos trials erased much of the political apathy that had setted over the Basque country since the war. ETA had become a symbol of popular resistance to the Franco regime for nationalists and non-nationalists alike. Despite many private doubts, especially concerning its use of violence, ETA was above public censure. Open criticism of ETA was judged as open support for the regime.

In the early 1970s ETA's activities expanded to include the imposition of 'revolutionary taxation',[2] kidnappings and ever-increasing attacks on the police and suspected police informers. During 1975–76 ETA was responsible on average for one or two assassinations per week. ETA's supreme military achievement came in 1973 when 75 kilos of plastic explosives were detonated in a Madrid street killing Admiral Carrero Blanco, the ailing dictator's heir apparent.

However, ETA's activities were by no means confined solely to the military. A concept cherished by ETA – as it had been by previous intransigent nationalists – is the 'renationalization of Euskadi'. This concept became a key mobilizing force as radical nationalists strove to restore the Basque country to her full cultural personality. The resurgence of Basque literature, Basque singers, dancers, music and theatre escalated from the mid-sixties onward. But the crowning achievement was the *ikastola* movement, a movement aimed at providing education in the Basque language.

Ikastolas had been established by the PNV in the major industrial areas of

Vizcaya and Guipúzcoa during the Second Republic. Although strictly illegal during the initial Franco period, some *ikastolas* continued clandestinely under the guise of private classes given in private homes. In the beginning of the 1960s when most of the official restrictions on Euskera had eased, *ikastolas* reemerged usually as kindergartens. Throughout the 1960s and 1970s, following in the wake of the growth of nationalist sentiment, they spread to every industrialized and industrializing city, town and village in Vizcaya and Guipúzcoa. By 1976 some 195 *ikastolas* had been opened.

The desire to conserve Euskera and reverse its decline was held to be the one factor above all others responsible for the proliferation of the *ikastolas. Ikastolas* not only followed in the wake of industrialization, usually they were established in any given community as an explicit response to the influx of Spanish immigrants.

The social composition of the children in *ikastolas* reflects the social composition of the nationalist movement. In the twenty-seven *ikastolas* for which I have detailed information, the overriding majority of the children came from an urban middle or lower-middle-class background. Their parents were by and large skilled workers, self-employed tradesmen or merchants, small-scale industrialists and professionals. Almost no immigrant children attended the schools (except in Bilbao) nor did children from very wealthy backgrounds. In addition, few peasants sent their children to *ikastolas*. Rural families continued to view education in Euskera as detrimental to their children's future opportunities.

Usually the establishment of an *ikastola* in any given locality was a result of grass-roots initiatives. Those individuals whose nationalist sentiment remained intact during the Franco years tended to provide the bulk of the money and the children. The newly converted radical youth supplied the work required to organize the schools. These radical nationalists, heavily influenced by ETA, also tended to supply the school with teachers (*irakasleak*).

Until recently the *ikastolas* received no state funds of any sort and were frequently threatened with closure if the facilities offered fell below certain standards. Hence, fund-raising became a perpetual activity for all those connected to an *ikastola*. The greatest portion of money came from the parents themselves who paid a monthly tuition fee. But most importantly, fund-raising for the *ikastolas* became the major means through which the cultural revival, inspired by ETA, was disseminated. Displays of Basque sports as well as performances of Basque singers, dancers, musicians, theatre groups and *bertsolaris* (spontaneous oral poets) – carrying only thinly veiled political messages – became common affairs in every locality that had an *ikastola* to support. As support for the *ikastolas* was viewed as a duty of all Basques, so attendance at and help with the organization of these fund-raising cultural events also became a necessary gesture of Basque solidarity.

The establishment of an *ikastola* required people to actively confront the official bureaucracy which previously they had done their utmost to ignore. During the Franco period both the *ikastolas* and the cultural activities surrounding them occupied a status of ambiguous extra-legality. Although not strictly illegal, they were subject to a host of arbitrary prohibitions. The work involved in order to gain the appropriate authorizations was enormous. For instance, each person contracted to perform had to receive prior official approval. The text of each song sung had to be submitted to and approved by the official censor. Teachers employed at the schools had to assemble an array of documents testifying to their political credentials.

In short, the maintenance of an *ikastola* in a community required constant popular mobilization and vigilance. Because the *ikastolas* were linked into the full range of Basque cultural activities, they helped reintroduce the local population into nationalism.

Unlike the radical nationalism of the pre-war period which rested on a narrow sociological base, ETA managed to weld Basques and immigrants, nationalists and non-nationalists in a common struggle against a despised state.

From 1968 political strikes in support of ETA and nationalist demands in general became increasingly common. By 1975 deaths of ETA militants would almost automatically provoke strike action if not general strikes. Even strikes of a more economic nature would inevitably incorporate nationalist demands for Basque autonomy, recognition of Euskera and amnesty for Basque political prisoners. Notably a key force behind the organization of these strikes were the communist-led Workers Commissions (Comisiones Obreras) which were composed in their majority of immigrant workers. From the late 1960s onward the *ikastolas* – and indeed the entire cultural revival – also received enthusiastic support from many non-nationalists who also contributed money, time and effort on the *ikastolas*' behalf. Because of ETA's direct attacks on the Franco regime, anti-fascism and Basque nationalism were regarded as parallel, if not synonymous, ideologies.

During the main period of fieldwork which corresponded to the year preceding and the year following Franco's death in November 1975, Spain's political apparatus, centred for thirty-nine years on a personalized dictatorship, lost its exclusive control over power. Although various individuals and political groups claimed the right of succession, Franco had left no heir capable of ensuring the regime's continuity. As Spain's authoritarian institutions crumbled a proliferation of new political groups – one news magazine, *Cambio 16*, counted more than 200 of them in early 1976 – emerged, each proposing in one way or other to influence and benefit by the manner in which power would be restructured and distributed in post-Franco Spain.

In the Basque country two contradictory political processes gained spectacularly in intensity and scope. One process unified a whole range of groups; trade unions, neighbourhood associations, cultural bodies, political parties, student groups, professional organizations, etc.; and individuals opposed to Francoism joined to reiterate demands for democracy and Basque national rights. The campaign for amnesty for Basque political prisoners, for example, was initially organized by a small cross-section of the Basque nationalist and non-nationalist opposition. It began modestly when some 10,000 terrified demonstrators took to the streets of Bilbao on 18 January 1976. It quickly escalated into a constant series of hunger strikes, marches and public protests and demonstrations of all sorts. Some of these events mobilized up to 250,000 people. Similar campaigns were mounted on behalf of the legalization of the Basque flag (the *ikurriña*), the legalization of Euskera and Basque political parties and the implementation of Basque autonomy, to mention only some of the more notable popular campaigns. For all political parties – except those of the Spanish right – participation in these political events as well as support for the cultural events which invariably surrounded them were obligatory. These campaigns were transformed into impressive affirmations of Basque national solidarity as non-nationalists and nationalists converged by the tens of thousands to chant political slogans – usually in Euskera – applaud the inevitable illegal appearance of numerous *ikurriñas*, sing illegal Basque songs, like *Euzko gudariak gara* (We are Basque soldiers), cheer the return of noted Basque exiles, usually ETA members, and glare rancorously at the massed presence of the ominous and increasingly demoralized Spanish police.

Violence and bloodshed were frequent. To protest at the killing of demonstrators by police, general strikes which closed down all Basque industry, brought barricades to most roads and usually culminated in riots in San Sebastian and Bilbao became the standard response. Meanwhile, ETA intensified its attacks on the police, suspected police informers and Basque industrialists. Few political groups dared to criticize these assassinations. Those which very cautiously did, always hedged their criticism with stiff warnings to the government that ETA's violence would continue as long as the legitimate aspirations of the Basque people were not satisfied.

Thus, the residents of the Basque country presented an image of political consensus and joint national determination in its struggle against the eroded remnants of the Francoist regime. In relation to this regime most people in the Basque country had become impassioned Basque nationalists.

However, this period also witnessed an extreme polarization of all aspects of Basque public life and political activity. Political parties, artistic production, amnesty organizations, historical research, economic enterprises, schools, newspapers, public projects, popular festivals, publishing houses, etc. were forced into the mutually exclusive categories of *abertzale* (patriotic)/ *españolista*, nationalist/non-nationalist, Basque/anti-Basque. Through the insistent pressure of this polarization the boundaries demarcating the Basque nationalist community and its exclusive institutions became explicit, consolidated and impermeable. The construction of this boundary was a logical and desired outcome of Basque nationalist strategy.

The ideology of ETA

Inspired by the primitive Sabino de Arana, the initial ideology of ETA was taken directly from the traditional nationalist writers. However, ETA injected three modifications into the traditional nationalist view of the Basque past.

Relegating the concept of race to a minor position, ETA claimed the Basque language and Basque culture *in* Euskera as the supreme symbols of Basque identity, unity and right to independence. The essence of the Basque was the language, and the frontiers of Euskadi were those areas which at one time had been Basque-speaking. Whereas Arana saw the degeneration of the Basque nation in terms of the degeneration of the race, ETA saw it in terms of the linguistic genocide conducted by the forces of French and Spanish imperialism. The chief duty of the Basque patriot was no longer the protection of the race. It was the preservation of the language.[3]

ETA placed considerably more emphasis on the concept of territory than the PNV. Therefore, the French Basque provinces, or Euskadi Norte, took on major importance. 'Zaspiak bat' (the seven in one) became an ETA byword and demands for 'reunification' were an integral part of the ETA programme.

Because of the collaboration of the Church with the Franco regime, ETA was strictly a confessional. Catholicism was not seen as an inherent element of the Basque condition. If anything the Basques were formed by a pagan past and Basque moral virtue was embedded in Basque egalitarianism, an intrinsic part of the Basque mode of behaviour.

Among the original ETA leadership only a very few were Marxist and the rest shared one version or another of social humanitarianism. However, one factor above all others was instrumental in pushing ETA to the extreme left – the model of the revolutionary struggle of national liberation as exemplified by Cuba, Algeria and Vietnam. The relevance of this model to the Basque case was most clearly stated in the book *Vasconia*, published in 1962 by Frederico Krutwig. Krutwig, a self-taught Basque speaker of Spanish–German descent, first gained public attention when he declared to an astonished audience during the Basque World Congress in 1956 that guerrilla warfare was the only means of liberating Euzkadi.

Like Arana, Krutwig saw a fundamental opposition between Spain and the Basque country; but the terms of the opposition differed. According to Krutwig, Vasconia, which stretched from Perigord in France to Zaragosa, capital of the Spanish province of Zaragosa, arose as an independent Basque state with the fall of the Roman Empire. The defining element of this state lay in its language, Euskera, 'the mirror, repository and transmitter of Basque culture'. The important feature of language was that it moulded thought. Euskera was the motor which forced the Basque speaker to conserve his sense of brotherhood and egalitarianism. Euskera was the symbol of autonomy and fraternal liberty and Vasconia was an island of communitarian democracy in a sea of European feudalism. Krutwig rejected Arana's argument that the abolition of the foral regime by Spain marked the beginning of the Basques' existence as a Spanish colony. Instead he argued that the transformation had begun much earlier with the gradual penetration of Spanish and French capitalism which had drained Vasconia of her resources, introduced a regime of exploitation and produced the struggle between the oppressed and the oppressors. Spanish (or French) – the language of exploitation – was the fundamental cultural tool which subverted the Basques' will to resist.

In short, the social and national repression of the Basques stemmed from the same reality – colonial subjection. This reality meant that Basque nationalism belonged to the revolutionary nationalisms of the Third World. The anti-imperialist struggle for national liberation and the anti-capitalist struggle for socialism were the same. Using Algeria as his model, Krutwig mapped out the principles for the revolutionary war of Basque liberation. The 'colonialist model' gave ETA its ideological framework, military justification and social programme. Independence, armed struggle and socialism were adopted as a package deal.[4]

Two addenda filled out ETA's view of its cause. The first was the theory of the 'spiral of action-repression-action' which by 1968 formed the justification for ETA's military actions. The aim was to ignite a popular insurrection by catalysing and encouraging the full force of state repression to fall randomly and brutally over the entire Basque population. As the violence escalated, popular reaction would become more revolutionary. The structure of ETA would be protected from the repression and the organization would prepare militarily for a *coup d'état* and politically for a take-over of power. Propaganda to educate the masses in the proper understanding of events would be a necessary feature of the process. (ETA currently continues to follow a version of this strategy.)

The second innovation – *el pueblo trabajador vasco* – became a key notion in the renovated nationalist vocabulary. (In Spanish a distinction is made between *trabajador*, worker, and *obrero*, which usually means industrial unskilled wage worker.) For ETA, this notion underlined a fundamental subjective and objective element of the Basque condition. Because *el pueblo trabajador vasco* – to which most Basques belonged by definition – had been culturally nurtured in the virtue of labour and egalitarianism and politically and economically oppressed by Francoism and capitalism, its subjective values and objective interests led inevitably to socialism. Socialism was part of 'the essential Basque substance'.

However, the 'colonialist model' did not fit comfortably with the economic conditions of Basque life. As K. R. Minogue has remarked (1969: 138), 'Marxism horizontally divided the world into exploiters and exploited; nationalism vertically cut it into many distinct nationalities.' In the Basque case, where the majority of the urban proletariat was non-Basque and capital largely in Basque hands, the two creeds intersected disastrously.

Indeed, popular grievances againt immigrants were given political shape by the resurgence of nationalist feeling during the mid-1960s when immigration was at its height. For many young radical nationalists of the 1960s and 1970s, the immigrants were a direct enemy. They were part of a conscious plan by Madrid to wreck Basque society.[5] One of the most ardent advocates of this view was Txillardegi, a founder of ETA and himself of immigrant origins.

> Deprived of Basque political and cultural institutions, the Basque people as such are condemned to disappear submerged by this enormous mass of 20,000 foreigners a year who objectively are at the service of cultural genocide. With modesty and respect for those immigrants who deserve it, we say 'objectively' because most immigrants do not realise that they have come to a FOREIGN, OCCUPIED country. The immense majority of these 20,000 immigrants say, 'we are in Spain'. And be very careful if you try to insinuate the contrary. (Txillardegi, 1973: 9, emphasis in text)

The disastrous effect which immigrants had on the Basque language was allegedly proven in 1973 by a Basque linguist, Larresoro, who showed mathematically in a frequently-cited study that in a population in which 25% were Basque-speakers and the rest *erdaldunes* (lit. half-language, used to mean Spanish speaker), 99.6% of all conversations would be conducted in Spanish. If 50% were Basque speakers, still only 4.5% of conversations would be in Euskera.[6] The political conclusion was self-evident. 'The degree of patriotic irresponsibility and the genocidal efficiency of one simple *erdaldun* (Spanish speaker) is demonstrated with figures in a way that does not permit doubts' (Txillardegi, 1973: 12).

Certainly one crucial factor behind the renewed groundswell of nationalist sentiment was hostility towards immigrants. Although some nationalist leaders tried hard to separate the two, on the local level the two sentiments fed on each other.

The new hybrid of Basque socialist nationalists, therefore, either had to limit their socialism to Basques only, which grossly diluted any claims to socialist purity; or to extend their nationalism to everyone who lived in the Basque country, which seriously undermined all nationalist arguments based on ethnic distinctiveness and logically led to a doctrine of regionalism rather than nationalism. The efforts to bridge this contradiction sparked off waves

of successive divisions in ETA and over the years filled the Basque political scene with a potpourri of political initials; ETA 6, MC, ESB, LAIA, HASI, ETA 5, HB, etc. etc. Each new political group formed possessed its own special mixture of socialism to nationalism and its own programmatic means for achieving its ideological aims.

Abertzales and españolistas: the renovation of Sabino de Arana

On first impression contemporary Basque nationalist doctrine and the ideology of Sabino de Arana are radically different on a wide range of issues. Early Basque nationalism was arch-conservative and deeply religious. Contemporary nationalism is socialist and secular. Sabino de Arana was concerned with purity of race. Modern nationalists argue for the protection and redemption of the Basque language and culture. Yet the elements which articulate the modern nationalist arguments remain faithful to the primitive Sabino de Arana. They are subordinated to the same covert political functions through which one section of Basque society, self-defined as 'Basque', is differentiated, consolidated and mobilized in moral contrast to other competing sections of society whose claims to full 'Basque' status and, hence, to Basque resources are rejected as illicit. If the nationalist creed is interpreted literally, its effects inside the Basque country become unintelligible.

Like the ideology of Arana, the modern nationalist ideology is built upon two interlocked sets of symbols. One set underlines the fundamental opposition between Euskadi and Spain and provides the legitimacy for an *external* nationalism directed against Madrid. The elements in this set remain the same as in early nationalism: Basque history, *fueros* and the concept of original Basque sovereignty. The essence of the proposition they serve is that the Basques have and have always had an inalienable right to self-determination. Its economic corollary is that the Basque country is entitled to exclusive control over and benefit from its own economic resources. At its core this proposition does not concern Basque independence and statehood. It concerns the right to determine the manner in which political and economic resources are distributed between the Basque country and Madrid. Statehood is just one of numerous possible arrangements.

The second set of symbols underlines the fundamental opposition between 'Basques' and 'anti-Basques' and supports arguments for a differential access to resources inside the Basque country. This cleavage between 'Basques' and 'anti-Basques' must be distinguished from that which separates Basques in general from immigrants. Although a severe divide does separate the Basque and immigrant population, in political terms this is not the *operationally* important cleavage. The *internal* function of the Basque nationalist ideology seeks to transfer total power over the economic and social resources inside the Basque territory, which is occupied by people of many political orientations, to only one political community. Previously this 'Basque' community was defined by a set of symbols derived from Euskera, Basque customs, Basque character and Catholicism. Now it is defined by a renovated set of symbols derived from Euskera, Basque culture and Basque socialism.

However, in contrast to early Basque nationalism when these arguments were accepted by only a minority of the population, now the idea that the Basques form a distinct nationality with sole rights to determine their political and economic destiny is profoundly acknowledged by nationalists and non-nationalists alike. Because of the excessive, brutish centralism of the Franco period and the repression inflicted upon the Basque country, the vast majority of the Basque population are Basque nationalists in the external sense. Moreover, they not only believe in the concept of Basque nationhood, but also place high value on Euskera, Basque culture, and profess to one version or other of socialism.

But a principal function of Euskera, culture, socialism and home rule as symbols is to delineate and defend an exclusive 'Basque' solidarity inside the Basque country. Therefore, the broad consensus on the nationalist message – understood literally – imposed an unwanted alliance on Basque nationalists. Consequently, the political instrumentality of the symbols articulating the message was forced to become overt, manifest and aggressive. In order to retain exclusive ownership over the symbols of national legitimacy, Basque nationalism has proceeded in two ways. The first has been to redefine the symbols.

Take the case of Euskera. For the modern Basque nationalists Euskera and Basque culture in Euskera are building stones of Basque nationhood. The regeneration of Euskera is now regarded as an urgent task for all patriots. These are ideas with which all nationalists and the majority of Basque non-nationalists would unquestionably agree. For non-nationalists the political conclusion is that, because of its linguistic past and present, the Basque country should become a fully bilingual society in which Euskera would be favoured. This conclusion formed a basic nationalist demand from 1914 to 1971 or so. By 1968 many non-nationalists – who previously had shown little real concern with the language and, thereby, had amply demonstrated their 'anti-Basque', *españolista* attitudes – had adopted the cause. But by then the nationalists had begun to reprogramme the symbol.

Basically Euskera acquired two new, highly abstract and ambiguous components. The first is implicit in the proposition that to work for Euskera in the various ways available – financial contributions to Basque cultural institutions, organizing *ikastolas*, learning the language or even speaking the language – is not sufficient. One must *love* the language. The required love means an exclusive moral binding to the cause of Euskera. A leading Basque historian and influential member of the PNV discussed Euskera in the following terms:

Euskera is the lifeblood that ties us together into a family. It is the language which makes the family possible. And it is the family which cherishes and gives nourishment to our beloved language. Neither our *pueblo* nor our language can survive without the other. Those of us who do not speak the language – like myself – are like children who were deformed from birth. It is only through Euskera that a Basque can achieve his full human potential... There are many in our country who are *euskaldunes* [Basque speakers] but who act in ways that make them traitors to our *pueblo*. Their concern with Euskera is simple opportunism. Their motives are not to protect it. But these are problems which all families face. In your country [i.e. Norway] you have had your Quisling so you understand these things.

When asked what these *euskaldunes* had actually done, the respondent after an initial moment of bewilderment replied, 'Well, they have joined political groups that are always hostile to us.' (He was referring to left-wing non-nationalist groups.) To all nationalists this answer is self-evident. Sufficient love for Euskera means political loyalty to nationalism.

The second, related element is implicit in the proposition that language moulds thought. Euskera shapes a Basque mode of thought. Spanish shapes a distinct Spanish mode of thought. What is at stake here is not Euskera, but Basque thought regarded as the quintessence of Basqueness. A Basque with a Spanish-speaking mind is defective – at best a half-Basque. Luis Maria Múgica Urdangarin, a member of the Academy of the Basque Language, states the argument in the following terms:

A clear correlation exists between national and idiomatic identity. Identity does not mean exclusiveness. A person from Bilbao who does not know Euskera is a victim of the secular situation of diglossia of our *pueblo*. We consider him Basque, but the coordinates of his 'Basque' personality are not as integral as those of the Basque speaker... In the Basque conceptual world communion with the national community is realized through the language. The Basque is self-defined as he who 'speaks Euskera'. The traditional 'euskaldun' would not suspect that he could be a 'member of the Basque community' without sharing with his compatriots their maximum national value, the language. Although the non-Basque speaking *euskotar* [member of the Basque race] is considered Basque, his claim to 'integrality' in the traditional community of our pueblo is anthropologically amputated and impoverished.

('Identidad nacional e idiomatica', *Punto y Hora*, 23–29 June 1977, p. 33)

On one level this formulation shows a certain political flexibility. All those who speak Basque are Basque. All those who learn Basque become Basque. But the formulation does not operate politically on this level. Instead, a simple political conclusion is revealed. If language moulds thought, then for the Basque people to regain their full historic personality, the Basque language must be the *only* language of the Basque country. Bilingualism is not sufficient. It subversively prolongs the cultural distortions that have deformed the Basque mentality.

Thus, the true Basque, regardless of linguistic abilities, is the person, inspired by love for Euskera, who defends the demand for a monolingual Basque country. The vast majority of non-nationalists – again regardless of linguistic abilities – cannot endorse this proposition and, therefore, are unable to fulfil this new requirement for membership in the 'Basque' community.

Another means that has been employed in order to preserve the discriminatory power of the symbols of Basque national legitimacy has been physical exclusion from contact.

Basque nationalist culture is the Basque equivalent of what T. Nairn (1977) terms the 'tartan monster' in reference to Scotland. It is seen as an continuity of 'Basque original culture' and is conducted solely in Euskera.[7]

During the period of my fieldwork no non-nationalist party argued for a cultural plurality that reflected both the Basque urban and rural traditions as well as the ethnic diversity of the Basque country. Because of the weight of nationalism, Basque 'nationalist' culture had gained general acceptance as the only Basque 'national' culture. For example, in an internal document presented to the Communist Party of Euskadi in October 1978, the idea of cultural plurality and 'the coexistence of two communities' in the Basque country is forcefully rejected. Although of rural origins, the Basque cultural patrimony in Euskera, it argues, must be regarded as the base or host culture of Basque society. Those who live in this society, if they are to be considered 'Basque', must integrate into this culture. This formulation is indistinguishable from those advocated by nationalist groups.

Therefore, because of the overwhelming consensus even on the strictest nationalist criteria, Basque culture as a symbol of national differentiation had lost its power to distinguish between the two political camps inside the Basque country. Since political differentiation could not be established on the level of cultural performance or political demands concerning culture (the demand for monolingualism is an exception), nationalist possession over Basque culture was maintained by physically excluding non-nationalists from manifestations of the culture. The political instrumentality of culture as a symbol conveying exclusive legitimacy was no longer covertly hidden under shifting layers of emotional academic and intellectual argument. It was forced to become explicit.

For example, during the cultural renaissance of the 1960s a demand grew for contemporary fiction in Euskera. In response a publishing house, Gero (The Future), was established which specialized in the works of young Basque writers and poets. The initial reaction to Gero was highly enthusiastic as measured by the enormous numbers of books sold. For a brief period, Gero was lauded as a fine example of the Basque struggle to recover the fullness of their culture. However, it was soon discovered in nationalist circles that Gero was run by a group of young Basques several of whom sympathized with the Basque Communist Party. Within a year another publishing company, Lur (The Earth), was founded. Lur was run by nationalists and published only nationalist writers. In addition a boycott of Gero was launched. Nationalists staunchly refused to publish their books with or buy their books from Gero. Starved of authors and sales, Gero went bankrupt. Until the economic crisis of the late 1970s, when all book sales plummeted, Lur flourished.

This period also witnessed a blossoming of young Basque folk-singers and folk-groups, again received with great popular enthusiasm and support. One of the best groups was called 'Oskorri'. 'Oskorri' attempted with considerable musical talent to popularize old Basque songs which members of the group travelled throughout the Basque country to collect. The lead singer of 'Oskorri' was, however, a sympathizer of the Movimiento Comunista, an *españolista* offshoot of ETA. 'Oskorri's main competitor was another group called 'Ozkarbi', which was also endowed with considerable musical skill and composed entirely of radical nationalists. 'Ozkarbi', along with all other nationalist singers and groups, adopted a stringent policy of never performing on the same stage as 'Oskorri'. Nor would 'Ozkarbi' accept invitations to perform from people or organizations who were suspected of *españolista* affiliations. Such affiliations were easy to discern. If an individual or organization invited 'Oskorri' to perform, then, by definition he, she or it was *españolista*. 'Oskorri', like Gero, was boycotted. This boycott was frequently marked by violence. During one concert by 'Oskorri' in commemoration of the death of the famous Basque poet, Gabriel Aresti, a demonstration of radical nationalists made the performance inaudible through high-spirited chanting of slogans such as, *españolistas, kanpora*! (*españolistas* out), *social imperialistas*!, etc. and raucous renditions of nationalist songs. Several bewildered spectators were pelted with insults and refuse as they left the auditorium. On another occasion during a performance by 'Oskorri' in the French Basque country, Basque exiles standing furtively at the back of the hall broke out in cheers when an ETA militant mounted the stage and bashed the wife of the lead singer on the nose.[8]

Similarly in the late 1960s and early 1970s the *ikastolas* were transformed into political battlegrounds. Although most people connected to the *ikastolas* were nationalists, many of the teachers were affiliated to the various communist parties. While the conflicts which ripped through these schools are complicated and reflected a whole range of political issues, in general they followed a set pattern. The nationalists, usually successfully, strove to oust the non-nationalist teachers.

Contemporary nationalism has added a new symbol to the Basque cause:

socialism. Even certain leaders of the PNV have publicly declared themselves socialists, albeit of the non-Marxist kind. 'In Euskadi the national question is the primary social question and the social question is above all a national question' (from a report of Iñaki Aldekoa, general secretary of ESB (Basque Socialist Convergence) for the party programme, 1977). To a significant degree Basque advocacy of socialism, a secularly just order, is a substitution for the pre-war Basque advocacy of Catholicism, a divinely just order, as a symbol of the superiority of the Basque social and moral world. Certainly the structure of Arana's arguments concerning religion and contemporary nationalist arguments – despite the diversity of the latter – is the same.

The fundamental opposition remains between the Basque country and Spain on one level and Basque socialism and Spanish socialism on another. Whereas Arana insisted that only through separation from Spain and things Spanish, i.e. nationalism, could true Catholic sentiment be restored, nationalists now declare that only through nationalism can Basque socialism be instituted. Basque socialism is *socialismo abertzale*, the socialism of true liberation. The other socialism is *socialismo estatalista* (statist socialism), *socialismo surcursalista* (literally – branch office socialism) and *social imperialismo*, the socialism of reaction that supports the state against the *pueblos naturales*. As importantly, this false socialism is constructed upon the mass of immigrants in the Basque country who, even if through no fault of their own, carry the ideology of Spain. In the Basque country the expressed socialism of left-wing nationalists and non-nationalists never forms a basis for alliance making. The banners of Basque socialism are, 'Gora Euskadi Askatuta!, Gora Euskadi Batua!, Gora Euskadi Euskalduna!, Gora Euskadi Sozialista!' (Long live free Euskadi, Long live reunified Euskadi, Long live Basque-speaking Euskadi, Long live socialist Euskadi).[9]

Euskera, Basque culture and socialism are buttresses of the overarching concept of 'Basque'. The ascription of Basque status is never determined by Basque descent or knowledge of Euskera, although preferably they should coincide. One of Basque nationalism's most revered martyrs, Juan Parades Manot, who allegedly cried, 'Gora Euskadi Askatuta!' (Long live free Euskadi) as he was executed by Franco's police, was an immigrant who spoke no Euskera. Conversely, the former general secretary of the Communist Party of Euskadi, Roberto Lertxundi, is a Basque speaker from the Basque rural area. For political purposes a person is not born Basque. To be Basque is a political option. For the PNV, a Basque is, 'all those who have integrated into our *pueblo* and conform with its identity' (PNV document 1977, 'El partido nacionalista vasco hoy', p. 11). For the radical nationalists, Basques are, 'all those who live and work in Euskadi and make the national problem their own'. During a performance of Basque folk-singers I attended in 1975, an enormous banner decorating the stage declared, 'Nor da euskaldun? Euskera eta zazpi probintzi batean maite dituna!' – Who is Basque? Those who love Euskera and the seven provinces in one (a reference to the ETA slogan). In short, the only true Basque continues to be the Basque nationalist.

In conclusion, the definition of 'Basque identity' and 'the national problem' like the definition of the *pueblo vasco* has become two-tiered. Each tier corresponds to a different level of political competition. One definition presents the various elements of Basqueness literally. A Basque is someone who fights for the Basque language and culture, the restoration of the Basque historic personality, Basque autonomy and so forth. This definition is used in an *external* nationalism to present a united front to Madrid. But in the other definition these elements become subordinated to the political functions required to maintain an exclusive nationalist community inside the Basque country. A Basque is one who publicly and consistently performs according to the prescriptions, legitimized by the ambiguous, shifting symbols of Basqueness, that are necessary to protect this nationalist community, and who extends total loyalty to the community. *El pueblo vasco* who confronts Madrid has a very different composition from *el pueblo vasco* who lays exclusive claim to legitimacy inside Euskadi.

Paradise partly regained – Basque autonomy

The speech delivered by Arias Navarro, Spain's last prime minister of the Franco period, on 12 February 1974 prompted the rapid return of party politics to Spanish political life. Arias promised liberalization and reform. In response the entire Spanish opposition was galvanized behind the slogans *ruptura democratíca* and *unidad* in order to ensure that no continuity of the crumbling regime – even in a liberalized version – would be possible. In the belief that a new, democratic Spain, untarnished by Francoism, was just a matter of political will and theoretical analysis, the opposition in every significant Spanish region coalesced into unitary organizations. The only exception was in the Basque country.

The historic and intricate events that marked Basque politics from 1974 to 1980, the date of the referendum which approved a Basque autonomy statute, go well beyond the limits of this monograph. But the underlying, crucial dimension was the battle over access to Basque national legitimacy. Because the Basque non-nationalists had enthusiastically joined the nationalists in the common struggle against Madrid and the Spanish right, they assumed that their claims to full Basque status inside Euskadi would be automatically co-validated by the Basque nationalists. By the logic of the internal dimension of nationalist ideology, this co-validation could never occur.

After twenty-five years of near dormancy the PNV reemerged with vigour in early 1975, when competitive party politics again became the mainstream of political activity. The PNV was abundantly financed and the top echelons of the party leadership were well staffed. Historical figures like Manuel de Irujo and Ajuriaguerra gave the party the image of solid, experienced continuity. Younger leaders like Javier Arzalluz, whose background typically coupled a Carlist family with a Jesuit education, provided the image of urbane modernity. Importantly, the party still dominated the Basque government-in-exile, the president of which was the PNV leader, Leizaola. Although the PNV had little organized grass-roots support inside the Basque country, sentimental attachment to the party had remained strong. Politically the PNV defined itself as Christian Democratic, with heavy populist modifications, and sought the most ample autonomy possible for the Basque country. In contrast to the intransigent nationalist groups that dominated the nationalist movement under Franco, the PNV's platform did not mention the right of Basque self-determination, 'reunification of Euskadi' or Basque independence.

Almost immediately the PNV started to organize the ebullient and massive nationalist fervour that the radical nationalists had rekindled but which, characteristically, they had been unable to capture politically. Within a year of its reappearance, the PNV was regarded as the most powerful political force on the Basque scene. In the wake of the PNV's resurgence the whole range of the party's organizations – *batzokis* (local branches), women's organizations, peasant associations, youth groups, cultural groups, etc. – reemerged and blossomed. The full infrastructure of the Basque nationalist community was resurrected, extended and consolidated.

As in the rest of Spain, the idea of unity, *batasuna*, dominated Basque political rhetoric. However, the nationalists, both the PNV and the *abertzales de izquierda* (left-wing patriots), assumed that their overriding political position was unassailable. Alliances with the non-nationalists – specifically the Basque socialists of the Partido Socialista de Euskadi (PSE, the new name for the Basque branch of the PSOE) and the Basque communists of the Partido Comunista de Euskadi (PCE) – would implicitly extend 'national' respectability to the *españolistas*. The nationalists refused to breach the boundary. It has been argued that when the ideological symbols that signalled this boundary of national legitimacy, for example, Euskera, were threatened with absorption by the non-nationalists, the symbols were simply redefined. Similarly on the political level, the redefining of a minimum, unitary platform occurred constantly during the long, arduous and always unsuccessful negotiations over Basque unity. The intense debates over Navarra, '*soberanía originaria*' and *conciertos económicos* are cases in point.[10]

However, the Basque socialists and communists were also convinced of the political invulnerability of the PNV. Therefore, the PSE and PCE made increasing concessions to nationalism in order to format an alliance and, thereby, gain Basque 'national' credentials. In contrast to the tightly knit moral community bound to personal interaction, a common political loyalty and shared social codes upon which the nationalists rested, the non-nationalists depended on a sociologically fragmented, defensive and politically incoherent social base which shared no ideology, identity or political ambitions in common. In contrast to the ideological and social solidarity which automatically allied the radical and moderate nationalists against any *españolista* threat, the Basque socialists and communists were incapable of sustained joint action of any sort.

The build-up to the first general elections of the new Spanish democracy, celebrated on 15 June 1977, littered the Basque country with political propaganda and euphoria as more than fourteen political parties competed for an electoral following. The most intransigent wing of Basque nationalism insisted – true to form – on abstention. In any case it was a foregone conclusion that the PNV would emerge as the absolute victor. Hence it came as a staggering surprise that after the votes from all four Basque provinces had been counted, the PSE (PSOE) stood as the single largest party in the Basque country.

The election results reemphasized the triangular nature of Basque politics. With seven parliamentary seats, the right had been displaced by the PNV to some extent in Vizcaya and Guipúzcoa, but had reaffirmed its impressive, outspoken following in Alava and Navarra. With ten seats, the nationalists were predominant in the smaller towns, rural areas and middle-class neighbourhoods of the industrial cities in Vizcaya and Guipúzcoa. To a major extent the vote for the socialists was, among other things, a rejection of Basque nationalism, although not the notion of Basque autonomy. Its sociological core was the immigrant working class in all four Basque provinces.

On the internal level the election results had little effect. The socialists had gained votes. The PNV retained real social power. This point was continuously underlined during the ceremony that marked the public presentation of the newly elected Basque parliamentarians.

The ceremony was held in Guernica. The thousands of spectators who attended were festooned with *ikurriñas* (Basque national flags) and badges demanding a Basque university, insisting that Navarra *is* Euskadi, etc. Nationalist songs like *Euzko Gudariak Gara* (We are the Basque soldiers) and *Gora Euskadi* with its references to *Jaungoikua eta Lagi-zara* (God and Old Laws) were sung with ever-increasing gusto. No socialist red flags were waved nor renditions of the *Internationale* sung. Socialist supporters were notable only by their absence. The procession that led the sombre parliamentarians from Mass to stand in homage under the venerable oak tree of Guernica was headed by PNV deputies who formed a type of august bodyguard around this sacred symbol of Basque liberties and democracy. Socialist deputies were kept at a distance. The first speech of the day was given by the PNV deputy, Manuel de Irujo, who declared, 'We come with the best will in the world. Our hearts and arms are open to all those whose love begins and ends in Euskadi.' The victorious socialists were among the last speakers of the day.

But on the external level in the relations between the Basque country and Madrid, the election results were potentially devastating. Because of its electoral strength, the PSE could present itself on an equal footing as an *interlocutor* (mediator) between the Basques and the central government. However, a basic premise of Basque nationalism was that because the Basque 'national' community had exclusive claim to 'national' legitimacy, only the political representatives of this community could negotiate an acceptable distribution of political and economic resources between the Spanish centre and the Basque people. For the PNV, the Basque socialists of the PSE could never form part of this community regardless of their electoral implantation in Euskadi.[11] At immediate stake were (1) the type of autonomy the Basque country would eventually enjoy and (2) control over the channels through which power and resources flowed between the Basque country and Madrid.

By late 1977 negotiations for Basque autonomy had officially commenced. A Basque General Council was set up. The composition of this council was proportional to the 1977 election results. Its sole purpose was to negotiate a Basque home rule statute. Following the example already adopted in Catalonia, the socialists proposed that the president of the Basque General Council should be the president of the Basque government-in-exile, PNV leader Jesús María Leizaola. The PSE argued that although the Basque government was no longer representative of Basque political opinion – several of its constituent parties has ceased to exist – Leizaola would bring to the new body an historical legality and continuity.

The proposal was rejected out of hand by the PNV, who insisted that until the Basques regained their autonomy, the Basque government and the new Basque council were not comparable bodies. The PNV argued that since it was nationalist, the presidency and all important portfolios in the new council should go to the party by national right. 'The socialists of Euskadi, who are required to continually revalidate their Basque character, should submit to a secondary role' (PNV spokesman, *Punto y Hora*, 16–22 Feb. 1978).

Not surprisingly, this nationalist assumption was not shared by the socialists who then put up Ramon Rubial for the presidency of the Basque council. Rubial was from an immigrant family and had been born in an industrial area outside Bilbao. He had spent many years in prison after the war, worked clandestinely for the PSOE during the Franco period and at the time of his nomination to the presidency of the Basque Council was a mechanic in a small industrial workshop, a socialist senator from Vizcaya and the president of the PSOE. Partly to gain the PNV's acceptance of Rubial, the socialists made two further concessions to nationalism. First, the PSE renounced one of its seats on the Basque council in favour of an independent sympathetic to the PNV. Second, the socialists gave reluctant support to the nationalists' demand for *conciertos económicos*, i.e. Basque fiscal autonomy. The PSE had previously supported a block grant system because it feared that economic autonomy in Spain's wealthy regions would aggravate Spain's already extreme regional imbalances.

These concessions were welcomed. But Rubial was not. The PNV proposed Juan Ajuriaguerra, a PNV deputy from Vizcaya. Ajuriaguerra had been born in a middle-class area of Bilbao, entered the PNV in 1929, spent many years in prison after the war and had worked full-time for the PNV during the Franco era.

Neither candidate could count on sufficient votes to gain a majority. The ruling party of Adolfo Saurez, the UCD, held the balance. The political manoeuvres on both sides were complex, but the fundamental arguments were straightforward. For the socialists, Rubial should have the presidency since the PSE was the largest party in the Basque country. For the nationalists, Rubial could never be regarded as a representative for the Basque people since he was not only a socialist, but also president of a 'statist' and, therefore, 'anti-Basque' party – the PSOE. Moreover, as was repeatedly stressed, Rubial did not even speak Euskera. On television and in the press Rubial frequently stated that he lamented the fact that he did not speak Euskera. He never stated that very few of the nationalist representatives on the Basque council spoke Euskera either. However, as damaging, the PNV alleged a secret pact between the socialists and the UCD as final proof of the anti-Basque intentions behind Rubial's candidature.

In early February 1978 Rubial was belatedly elected president of the Basque General Council. The deciding vote was a blank ballot cast by a member of the UCD. When the results were announced, various nationalist deputies rose to their feet chanting, 'Españolistak kanpora! Españolistak kanpora!' (*Españolistas* out!). The PNV immediately claimed that Rubial had been imposed by Madrid. The radical nationalist press acrimoniously compared the election of Rubial, with the alleged connivance of the UCD, to the relations between China and Pinochet in Chile and the Nazi–Soviet pact.

Rubial's inaugural address was essentially nationalist in content. Among other things, he emphasized the need for a full restoration of the Basque foral regime and the incorporation into Euskadi 'of our sister region', Navarra. He declared that he wished to be considered the 'president of all Basques' and ended his speech with a fervent cry of 'Gora Euskadi Askatuta!' (Long live free Euskadi). In response the PNV declared that Leizaola, still exiled in France, was 'president of all Basques'. Nationalist recognition and

Table 6 *Constitutional Referendum, December 1978* (*as percentage of electoral census*)

Yes	35
No	11
Blank	3
Void	1
Abstention	50

collaboration were withdrawn from the Basque General Council as well as its bewildered president. Effectively boycotted by the PNV, the Basque council was moribund. Although the debate concerning Basque autonomy raged, negotiations were halted.

The new Spanish constitution represented a broad compromise between the government and the major opposition parties. However, in the parliamentary discussions over the constitution the PNV had presented a long list of amendments none of which had gained parliamentary approval. The PNV's major demand was that the constitution should explicitly recognize Euskadi as a nation endowed with 'original sovereignty'. The amnesty for political prisoners, recognition of the *ikurriña* (Basque flag) and official status for Euskera had all been granted. Despite a full and ferocious mobilization of the Basque community on the streets of Euskadi, the government did not accept the right to 'original sovereignty'. Article 2 of the constitution states, 'The Constitution is founded in the indissolvable unity of the Spanish nation, the shared and indivisible *patria* of all Spaniards, and recognizes and guarantees the right to autonomy of all its constituent nationalities and regions and the solidarity between them.'

In the constitutional referendum held on 6 December 1978, the non-nationalists, with the exception of the extreme right, argued that the constitution was a fairly liberal document, would consolidate Spain's fragile democracy and urged approval. The nationalists argued that the constitution was a requiem for Basque historic rights and, therefore, insisted on abstention. As usual ETA *militar* demonstrated its disapproval by a new campaign of assassinations. In the rest of Spain the constitution gained an overwhelming support. The results of the referendum in the Basque country are shown in Table 6.

The nationalist press added the number of abstentions, blanks and no votes and concluded that 64% of the Basque electorate had rejected the constitution. Regardless of the validity of such calculations, the political conclusion was unequivocal. The Basque nationalist community and, by inference, Euskadi was not bound by the Spanish constitution.

During this period the PNV used its representation in the parliamentary institutions of the new Spanish democracy as a sounding board for nationalist demands. However, its real political battle – both against Madrid and the Basque socialists – was waged from the streets of the Basque country. The PNV staged numerous acts to demonstrate to the government and the PSE that the nationalists *were* Euskadi. Any mediation between Madrid and Euskadi – especially if concerned with Basque autonomy – could be effective only if it took place under the auspices of the PNV. These demonstrations of nationalist strength and purpose were very impressive indeed. In contrast to other European conservative parties, the PNV is capable of quickly mobilizing hundreds of thousands of its well-disciplined rank and file supporters – well-dressed men and women, peasants, urbanites, youth and children – in acts of ritual solidarity. These mobilizations are accompanied by innumerable groups of folk-dancers – usually children – and musicians dressed in national costume, and are protected by long files of PNV ertzaiñas (police), tall, solid Basques dressed in dark trousers, *kaikus* (a collarless, woollen jacket) and black berets, who accept no interference.

Meanwhile, the *abertzales de izquierda* (the radical nationalists) mounted their own campaigns. Marches and demonstrations were organized to demand *Euskadi batua* (reunification of the French and Spanish Basque provinces), the incorporation of Navarra into Euskadi, amnesty for ETA militants who were again filling Spanish jails, and independence. ETA *militar* declared war on the state and its adherents in order to liberate the oppressed Basque people.

Unlike previous campaigns, these 'national' mobilizations were no longer seconded by the left-wing non-nationalists. Instead the socialists and communists continued in vain to seek an accommodation with the PNV within the formal political institutions. A fundamental weakness in the non-nationalist position was the inability of either the socialist or communist leadership to view the Basque political situation in other than nationalist terms. The non-nationalists assumed that power in Euskadi resided where the nationalist premise said it should reside, namely in the nationalist community. Therefore, rather than concentrate on constructing a solid electoral base by expressing the interests and aspirations of the large sectors of the Basque population that were not integrated into this community, the Basque socialists expended most of their political energies and capital attempting to build a bridge *to* the nationalist community. They assumed that a political dialogue with nationalism was at heart just a matter of speaking the same language and having the same concerns. Because of their nationalist preoccupations, neither the socialists nor the communists gave serious priority to the other issues under which the fabric of Basque society was slowly disintegrating.

By 1978–79 the Basque economy showed signs of impending collapse. Basque iron and steel and shipbuilding, the propulsion industries of the

Basque economy, were facing bankruptcy. Closures of small family industries were endemic. Under the constant threat of ETA's 'revolutionary taxation' many industrialists took both their money and families out of the Basque country and the Basque economy experienced little new investment of any sort. By 1980 unemployment had skyrocketed to around 20%. In addition the general level of violence in the Basque country imposed intolerable strains on large sections of the population. Death threats to prominent non-nationalists were widespread and assassinations frequent. Schools were often closed because of bomb scares. Many people feared going to the old city centres for the traditional stroll and round of drinks. These areas were frequently converted into battlegrounds in the ongoing confrontations between stone-hurling, often tipsy, radical nationalist youngsters and the police who responded with tear gas and bullets. Moreover, among the immigrant communities, who were the worst affected by the economic recession, alarm was growing that Basque autonomy would relegate them into second-class citizenship. The left-wing non-nationalists never took up the issue of the immigrants in a serious manner. In part they feared that to do so would reinforce their 'anti-Basque' image in nationalist eyes.

The results of nationalist action and non-nationalist impotence were clearly reflected in the general election results of March 1979 and the municipal election the following month. The socialists and the UCD vote crumbled – the non-nationalists lost some 300,000 votes – and the level of abstention increased accordingly. The PNV became firmly entrenched as the major Basque party. But the most unexpected result of this election was the ascendancy of the most intransigent stream of Basque nationalism represented by Herri Batasuna (HB, Popular Unity). Henri Batasuna rejects parliamentary democracy for what it calls popular democracy based on peoples' assemblies. It demands Basque independence, a socialist state, monolingualism, and gives tacit support to the armed struggle, and in turn is supported by ETA *militar*. (See Table 7 for election results.) In the cities HB gained considerable support from unemployed immigrant youth.[12]

With its political supremacy electorally affirmed, the PNV was at last in the position to move on the issue of the Basque autonomy. The PNV insisted that a satisfactory Basque autonomy statute had to be granted immediately if ETA's armed violence were to cease. This argument linking the cessation of ETA's attacks to the government's acceptance of PNV demands had been used on many previous occasions, for example in the campaigns over the Basque national flag and Euskera. For reasons that are unclear – ETA's violence had never stopped in the past – the governing party, the UCD, acquiesced. The Basque General Council was bypassed and the PNV as sole representative of *el pueblo vasco* rapidly concluded a Basque autonomy statute with the central government in July 1979. The exclusion of all other

Table 7 *Comparative election results in Euskadi*[a] (%)

Parties	General election 15 July 1977	General election 1 Mar. 1979	Municipal election 3 Apr. 1979	Basque parliament 9 Mar. 1980
PNV	29	27	36	37
HB	4	14	16	16
PSE	28	18	15	14
EE	6	8	6	10
UCD	16	16	10	8
AP	7	3	—	5
PCE	4	5	4	4
Others	6	9	13	6
Abstention	23[b]	34	37	40

Notes:
[a] Results from Navarra not included.
[b] This 23% includes the active abstention of the intransigent nationalists.
PNV (Partido Nacionalista Vasco)
HB (Herri Batasuna)
PSE (Partido Socialista de Euskadi)
EE (Euskadiko Ezkerri)
UCD (Unión Centro Democrático)
AP (Alianza Popular)
PCE (Partido Comunista de Euskadi)

Basque political parties from the negotiations was explained by the PNV as lamentable, but necessary since the urgency of the situation had not allowed sufficient time for multi-party discussions to take place. The loud and bitter protests of the Basque socialists were powerless against the *fait accompli*.

The Basque autonomy statute gives 'Alava, Guipúzcoa and Vizcaya, as well as Navarra, the right to form part of the Autonomous Community of the Basque Country.' The powers devolved to this autonomous community include exclusive authority over matters relating to the Basque electoral regime, public administration, social security, education, culture, the public economic sector, economic planning, sanitation, financial institutions, transport, public works and agriculture. In addition the Basque country is granted an autonomous parliament, judiciary, police force and treasury. The Basque parliament is 'integrated by an equal number of representatives from each historic Territory elected by free, direct and secret universal suffrage'.

But not secession

A referendum in February 1980 gave the Basque statute massive approval. The only political forces opposed were the Spanish right – because it denied the intrinsic unity of Spain – and the intransigent nationalists of Herri Batasuna – because the statute was a fraudulent betrayal of the Basque peoples' aspirations to independence.

The elections to the Basque parliament celebrated on 9 March 1980 confirmed the political hegemony of Basque nationalism and the collapse of its opponents. Of the 60 parliamentary seats, the nationalists gained 42. Of these, 11 were won by HB which boycotted the Basque parliament just as resolutely as it boycotted the Madrid one.

Since the establishment of a Basque autonomous government, to a large extent the vision structured by Sabino de Arana has come to its logical conclusion. On the external level the Basque country now enjoys a very generous autonomy. Moreover, the PNV has two potent instruments at hand which would enable it to extract further concessions from Madrid. It has recourse to extra-parliamentary political activities which the nature of its social base and populist ideology encourages. But, as importantly, the moderate PNV and the intransigent ETA dedicated to armed violence are both representatives of the Basque nationalist community, as the electoral support for HB demonstrates. The PNV has consistently impressed upon Madrid that if nationalist demands as peacefully pursued by the PNV are not met, then the nationalist community will give its support to ETA's violent methods of obtaining these demands. On the internal level, the power conceded to the Basque country by Madrid has been used to reward the Basque nationalist community. The two main protagonists of Basque industrialization have been politically vanquished. All important public political bodies and all institutions with public functions – chambers of commerce, health organization, cultural bodies, educational institutions, economic planning commissions, etc. – are under direct nationalist control. The Basque nationalist monopoly of political power has been used to establish differential access to economic resources. In the worsening economic crisis, access to industrial subsidies, academic grants, cultural subsidies and, very importantly, jobs in both the private and public sectors are increasingly reserved for nationalists only. These scarce resources are 'Basque' by national right. Many Basque non-nationalists are beginning to fear that this structural inequality of access to public resources may eventually generate tensions in the Spanish Basque country similar to those experienced in Northern Ireland – with equally tragic consequences.

Part 2

Inside the moral community: the village of Elgeta, Guipúzcoa

Introduction

Basque nationalism was a response to two interrelated and powerful integrative forces. Basque industrialization economically integrated the Basque country from within. State centralization enforced political conformity from Madrid. In Basque nationalism these two forces relate to different levels of competitive struggle. With regard to Basque industrialization, Basque nationalism involves a dispute over the distribution of economic and political resources inside the Basque country. In this context Basque nationalism created a Basque nationalist community out of those social sectors which were peripheral to the main thrust of Basque industrialization. The ideology of nationalism endowed this community with exclusive 'national' legitimacy and thus with exclusive rights to claim Basque resources. The aspect of Basque nationalism I have termed *internal* nationalism concerns a competitive battle between the Basque nationalist community and other social and political forces inside the Basque country.

With regard to state centralization, Basque nationalism involves a dispute over the distribution of economic and political resources between the Basque country as a whole and the state centre. In this context Basque nationalism created a Basque nation out of those social sectors opposed to Madrid's excessive centralization. This aspect of Basque nationalism I have termed *external* nationalism.

Until the civil war the social and political composition of the Basque nationalist community and the Basque nation was the same. In contemporary nationalism the composition of the Basque nationalist community and the Basque nation have become increasingly divergent. Although the large majority of the population of the Basque country acknowledge the existence of a Basque nation and declare themselves to be members of it, only those who give total political loyalty to the Basque nationalist community inside the Basque country have their claims to Basque status fully recognized.

In this competitive struggle Basque nationalism has utilized Basque culture as two-tiered political symbols which on one hand separate and legitimate the Basque nation opposed to Madrid and on the other the Basque nationalist community as an exclusive grouping inside the Basque country.

For urban nationalists the chief value of Basque culture resides in its ability to produce these symbols of ethnic and ethical differentiation, mobilization and solidarity. The ambiguous and shifting content of the symbols serves to absorb the contradictions between the two levels on which Basque nationalism operates. Underlying much of this analysis has been the notion of the Basque nation conceived of as a moral community.

So far this analysis has been largely confined to the urban context because it was here that the Basque nation first emerged. But in recent years the heartland of nationalism has moved away from the great urban areas. Now the stronghold of unchallenged nationalist support is located in the towns and villages which have only recently been captured by industrialization. Whereas the big cities still provide the bulk of the nationalist leadership, the newly industrialized areas now provide the Basque nation with the most loyal of her common citizens.

As Bilbao is the symbol of the Basque industrial world, I have chosen the village of Elgeta to represent this new heartland of nationalism. In the analysis of Elgeta, I shall take my argument a critical step further. Again the notion of a moral community is fundamental.

Culture must be viewed as existing on two overlapping levels. The first level comprises the visible surface elements of culture: dress, folklore, language, etc. These are the elements that nationalists in general elevate into the symbols of their cause. However, the second level is culture in a deeper, hidden sense. Here culture can be defined, in Geertz' terms (1975), as a set of shared meanings, as a series of cognitive categories embedded in the mind of the members of a culture through which experience is ordered and acted upon. Although by no means necessarily unique to a given culture, the whole set of meanings tends to be understood in the same way by members of that culture and parts of the set tend to be interpreted differently by members of other cultures. Importantly, it is this set of meanings and cognitive categories which shape the assumptions of the members of a culture as to what constitutes morally acceptable and legitimate social life (Heiberg, 1975).

Now for urban nationalists the first, visible level of culture as expressed through the nationalist ideology has been used to generate Basque ethnic identity, delimit the boundaries of the nationalist community and provide moral backing for the political hegemony of this community inside the Basque country. However, I shall suggest that in the local community of Elgeta it is fundamentally culture in its deeper sense – as a set of shared meanings – that has been the principal driving force guiding the actions of the members of this community and the political pattern they have achieved. In Elgeta it is the moral values and assumptions derived from this 'deep' culture that define the boundaries of the moral community, the *pueblo*, and legitimate the *pueblo*'s claims to political hegemony in the village. I shall further suggest that the politically instrumentalized cultural language of urban nationalists is, at least to some extent, a structural transformation of the embedded cultural meanings that operate in Elgeta. The same moral assumptions, discriminations and judgements are intrinsic in both.

Finally, although this section is a village study based on participant observation, I have decided not to use the standard ethnographic present. The period of my fieldwork in the village corresponded to a unique political period – the two years prior to the reestablishment of democratic institutions in Spain. As mentioned before, this period was marked by an accelerating, often violent, confrontation between large sectors of the Basque population and the remnants of the Franco regime as well as a growing polarization within the Basque population itself. Despite the village's relative isolation from the mainstream of Basque politics, these broader events intruded forcefully into village life. Since then Elgeta has changed in relation to the radical change in Spain's political system. However, I shall try to show that the underlying processes through which village life was organized and the moral categories by which the villagers were judged and classified and around which they mobilized were not just circumstantial.

8

Social organization in Elgeta

Elgeta is a small, recently industrialized village situated at an altitude of 473 m on a low mountain range that separates the provinces of Guipúzcoa and Vizcaya. The western municipal boundaries of Elgeta are contiguous with the provincial boundaries of Vizcaya, but the village is under the administration of Guipúzcoa. The villagers see themselves as *guipúzcoanos* and their history and traditions as closely tied to the rest of the province.

The compact, urbanized village nucleus presents a sharp contrast to the dispersed farmsteads dotting the surrounding countryside. But both the village centre and the farmsteads are hemmed in by forests of low quality pine which expand each year in size as the farms are progressively abandoned and pines planted on land once used for animal pasturage and crops.

The central plaza of the village is a crossroads which connects Elgeta on all four sides to the outside world. To the north with pine forests on both sides, a curving, pot-holed road descends down to the town of Eibar 9 km away. Eibar is heavily industrialized, has 38,206 inhabitants (1973) and historically has been a major centre for socialism in the Basque provinces. The town has had a significant influence on both Elgeta's economic and political development. To the south 10 km away along another curving road also through pine forests is the town of Mondragon (pop. 23,050 in 1973). Mondragon is famous in the Basque provinces for its industrial cooperatives and in recent years for its ardent nationalist activity. To the east Elgeta overlooks an intensely cultivated valley which leads to Vergara (pop. 15,813 in 1973), yet another industrial town which has played an important role in Basque political life. Finally, to the west through more pine forests is yet another winding road which leads down to Elorrio 9 km away and then links into the main road to Bilbao, 45 km distant.

In many respects the inhabitants of Elgeta have been relatively secluded until recent years. The emergence of Elgeta from its largely rural past into its industrial present began in earnest only in the late 1950s. One farmer who now works in an Elgeta shotgun factory expressed the villagers' former seclusion: 'When all you know is the farm – you only talk to your animals, your wife, your children and sometimes other *baserritarak*. But when you work in a factory, the world opens. Industry is more communicative.'

The village plaza is not merely the intersection of four roads. It is also a focal point of village life. Facing on to the plaza is the most dominant building in the village, the beige, three-storied town hall. Less imposingly the plaza is also fronted by the Provincial Savings Bank, some modern apartment buildings, the Sociedad Intxorta, a billiards and games parlour, the doctor's surgery which is open for one hour each morning, and the Ostatu and Panaderokua bars which are open from early morning to late at night. The village itself is mainly composed of two streets, the *calle* San Roque and *calle* San Salvador, both of which lead into the main plaza from opposing directions.

Directly behind the town hall is a small formal garden planted with low shrubs which separates it from the parish church. Except for the older buildings immediately surrounding the town hall and the church, the rest of the village is composed generally of slightly shabby, postwar three to five-story buildings. In spite of its luxuriant green, rural environment, Elgeta is not a beautiful village. The dominant colour of its buildings is a grayish-beige dulled by the black smoke that rises constantly out of the chimneys of the main furniture factory. It is a colour broken only in the summer by the ubiquitous pots of pink and red geraniums that fill every windowsill.

The three new factories located just outside the village arches on the Elorrio road have a crisp, modern look to them. The other factories, scattered throughout the village, look run-down and their architecture betrays their origins – small workshops started in garages or the back rooms of farmhouses to which bit by bit new additions were built as the workshop prospered. Elgeta reflects in miniature the urban neglect and lack of planning that has physically blighted Basque city life.

Population

In 1974 in Elgeta the population of the village was just under 1,200 inhabitants. Until 1974 Elgeta experienced a steady population growth. The one exception to this general trend corresponds to the period of the civil war and the years immediately following. Elgeta was part of the northern front for seven months. During this time many families left the village. Some fled to the safety of areas taken by the Franco forces. Many more were evacuated to areas still held by the Republic.

Until 1950 population growth was mainly due to births and in-marriage. Although some immigrant workers settled briefly in Elgeta during the Second Republic, most of them left during the war. Exact figures are not available, but the village consensus is that before the early 1960s there was never more than a slow trickle of immigrants into the village.

This situation changed in the 1960s. The nearby towns of Eibar and Ermua demarcated a particularly fast-growing industrial area. The burgeoning industrial activity in neighbouring towns spilled over onto Elgeta. With the spillage came the first real influx of non-Basque immigrants into the village. The problem posed by these immigrants was widely regarded by the Elgeta Basques as the single most important problem the village had to face.

Most villagers estimated the number of non-Basque immigrants in the range of 20% to 30% of the village population. The actual figure in 1974 appeared to be 17%, or 202 individuals, the majority of whom came from the northeastern part of Spain: Burgos, Léon, Santander, Galicia. However, 20% of the village population consisted of Basque immigrants. These Basque immigrants did not form a separate category in the perception of the native villagers. Indeed many denied that there had been any significant inflow of Basques.

Of the total population of Elgeta 940 individuals (1970 census) lived in the urban nucleus and 285 in the surrounding rural areas.

Village economy

During the previous fifteen years there had been a strong movement of people away from agriculture and into industry. Many of the farmsteads around Elgeta had been abandoned. Within the municipal boundaries there were sixty-eight farmsteads. Of these, forty-six were still occupied although in only thirty-one cases was at least some of the income of the resident domestic unit derived from agricultural exploitation. However, there were probably not more than eleven farmsteads in which household income was derived solely from agriculture. In the remaining twenty cases the income of the domestic unit was derived mainly from industrial or commercial sources, supplemented by income from agriculture (mainly dairy farming and horticulture).

In 1960 49% of the active population worked in agriculture, 42% in industry and 9% in commerce. The figures for 1970 were 16% in agriculture, 71% in industry and 13% in commerce. There is ample evidence to show that this trend has continued.

Industry in Elgeta consisted of 15 different enterprises which gave employment to 333 individuals. The two furniture factories produced solely bedroom units, or *dormitorios*. The products of both factories were more or less identical. In addition there were three factories producing almost identical models of shotguns, five workshops producing shotgun parts, two enterprises producing dyes, one factory producing machine tools, a polishing workshop and a carpenter. Only three of these businesses employed more than twenty workers. Most were family owned and run.

The commercial sector was divided into two categories – services and shops. The first sector included the village doctor, the priests, the secretary of the town hall, the bank employee, a seamstress, telephonist and those employed in transport. The shops included two meat shops, one fish shop, three animal feed shops, five grocery shops, two dry goods shops, one furniture shop, three general goods shops cum hairdressers, a tobacco shop and seven bars. Again the vast majority were family-owned and run, and in total provided work for thirty-seven people.

Communication with the outside world was provided by private cars (approximately one car to every six inhabitants), a twice daily bus service to Eibar and six times daily to Vergara, thirty-eight telephones in a newly automated village telephone system, newspapers of which some eighty were sold daily, and radios which were a fixture in every household.

Health services were dispensed by the village doctor. There were no nurses, chemists or health clinics in the village. The nearest veterinary surgeon was in Vergara.

Village entertainment was furnished by the annual village *fiestas* and the seven bars and four recreational and gastronomic societies. The bars were open to everyone. The societies were private clubs. Except for the *Sociedad* Ozkarbi which was open to both sexes, membership in the other societies was restricted to men only. Immigrants were rarely admitted.

Educational facilities consisted of an *ikastola* and a state school. Both schools had kindergartens for children of three to six years of age, and neither provided education above the fifth year of primary school. In order to obtain secondary education the village youth went to Vergara or Eibar. In general the village Basques sent their children to the *ikastola* and the immigrants to the state school.

Almost without exception the native-born villagers spoke Euskera and used it as their daily language. The majority of the Basques not born in the village also spoke the language. Of the immigrant community only two individuals had some fluency in the language. For most immigrants, Euskera was totally unintelligible.

Social and moral stratification

Visible signs betraying the presence of a clearly defined social hierarchy or an economic élite were notably absent in Elgeta. For instance, a man's mode of dress would probably indicate whether he was a farmer or an industrial worker. However, it would be much more difficult to gauge whether he was a landed or tenant farmer, or an administrative worker rather than a manual one. It was thought proper that clothing should be neat, clean, modest and subdued and, above all, practical. And almost all people were in fact dressed accordingly. Nor could a person's relative social ranking be judged from his or her residential address. No one section of the village was regarded as more fashionable than others. Most villagers, be they factory owners or semi-skilled labourers, lived in similarly equipped three or four-bedroom flats. These flats were generally immaculately tidy with an infrequently used parlour furnished with a sofa, two matching plastic covered armchairs, a small bookcase, some floor lamps and, perhaps, a record player. The kitchen, which during the winter was often the only heated room, was normally spotless and equipped with modern appliances such as a refrigerator, cooker, coffee grinder and so forth. While women were pleased to show visitors around their homes, protocol demanded they inject a note of modesty by saying something like, 'Let me show you around – although God knows, there *isn't* much to see!'

The villagers did not perceive the acquisition of consumer goods as a necessary aid to social status. Material ostentation in any form was frowned upon. Those who were tempted to indulge in material display were censured by only thinly concealed ridicule. Material consumption in village ideology was regulated by considerations of frugality and practicality. There was no overt emphasis on economic competition. Material consumption *per se* did not give prestige. Criticism fell on those who dropped below village norms and those who attempted to rise above them. In village ideology wealth was seen as desirable, but its acquisition was morally suspect.

The villagers placed great emphasis on uniformity of social behaviour and status. They liked to see themselves as responsible, sober and equal individuals. The ideas that village Basques held concerning social stratification were indicative of the fundamental values they felt should govern correct village social relations. Without question the most profound distinction made was between Basques, native or not, and non-Basques. This was the division between '*los de aqui*' (those from here) and '*los de fuera*' (those from outside), between *euskaldunes* (those who speak Basque) and *erdeldunes* (those who speak unclearly – lit. half-language), between *Vascos* (Basques) and *Castellanos* (Spaniards). However, other social distinctions were also made. Except by one or two newly politicised Elgeta youths, these social distinctions were never conceived of in class terms. Both the well-off and the less prosperous energetically denied that any definable class structure existed.

The division between Basques and Spaniards was the only social division in the village viewed as hierarchial. The Basques saw themselves as socially superior to the Spaniards. In Elgeta there were no high-ranking Spaniards except the village doctor. The other social distinctions were viewed in terms of moral categories arranged in a series of concentric circles with the morally élite forming the centre and the morally contemptible the periphery.

Elgeta's stratification system was based on morality and honour rather than economic or political position. But honour in the usual Mediterranean sense was not involved. Control over the sexuality of women was not a concern nor was honour a commodity for which individuals could compete. Honour did not give precedence; it gave acceptance. The degree of honour an individual was publically granted related to that individual's adherence to village norms. The village system of moral stratification was a system that enforced group conformity.

Most villagers when asked about social distinctions in Elgeta quickly and proudly emphasized, 'Here we are *all* workers!' Work and self-improvement through work were the only legitimate sources of social prestige, acceptability and promotion. To describe a person as hard working was to confer respectability. While other criteria were also fundamental, work – or rather being seen to work – was an essential requirement for membership into the moral community.

The poor

Few justifiable economic or structural reasons were recognized for someone to be poor and unable to make ends meet. Implicit in the villagers' attitudes was the idea that opportunities existed for everyone to provide themselves and their families with a reasonable living and steadily improve their position in life through conscientious endeavour.

In Elgeta open criticism within the Basque community directed at other Basques was rare. But there was at least one notable exception. Those Basques who had fallen below the standard levels of sobriety and prudent economic management were targets for ridicule and contempt. These individuals elicited little pity or sympathy, although they were treated leniently and never with malice. The Basques in this category were not viewed as people who had fallen on adverse circumstances. They were judged as people who had not been able to organize their lives properly. They were described as people with little intelligence (*poca cabeza*) as demonstrated by their inability to budget. They were seen as *vagos* (vagrants), misfits, indolents who disliked work and spongers who often became drunk and made public spectacles of themselves. A shopkeeper described one such family:

> Whenever you see that woman, her clothes are filthy and she never combs her hair. It just sticks out all over. Her children are just as bad. But, you know, they are not poor. Her husband has some sort of job in Vergara. But every time he gets his hands on it, he buys wine for everyone in the bar. And the woman comes in here and buys nothing but cheese, york ham and chocolates. Imagine the fortune you have to spend to fill your belly with york ham! Then she tells everyone that her husband doesn't earn enough money for her to feed her family properly. Its a disgrace.

This family was a large one. There were six children several of whom were mentally retarded. According to a local doctor, this was due to Rh incompatibility. The father was an unskilled worker, rumoured to drink a lot. The mother when she spoke to her neighbours did so in a very soft, slightly stammering voice. The grandmother was constantly seen walking the streets of Elgeta in a soiled grey coat talking to herself.

The people who fell into this category probably numbered only two or three families. When not providing material for village mirth, they were ignored.

The rich

The picture was much more complicated at the other end of the economic spectrum. While the lower stratum of the village Basques were seen as irresponsible and amoral, the upper economic stratum always risked being dismissed as immoral. The villagers' attitudes concerning the economic élite were ambivalent and contradictory. Members of this élite trod a very precarious margin between being regarded as accepted community members and being condemned and isolated. Economic, political or social élites of any sort fitted uneasily into the villagers' view of what constituted a just, moral order.

No titled member of the nobility had ever lived in the village. Although many villagers were hesitant to so designate them, the village industrialists i.e. the owners of the larger Elgeta factories, all of whom were village-born Basques, constituted an upper echelon of village society. But this upper sector was seen purely in economic terms. Both ordinary villagers and the industrialists denied fervently that any social superiority accrued to them.

The number of people classed as industrialists were few and included the owners of the largest shotgun factory, Zabala Hermanos, the owners of Tornillos Elcoro and the Erostarbe family who owned Modelo, the largest furniture factory. These families did not form a distinct group with social barriers that removed them from the rest of the villagers. The normative rules applied to these industrialists were the same as those applicable to all. They were expected to follow the same norms of modesty, sobriety, egalitarianism and prudent domestic management. Even though a distinction was made between the *patronos* (owners) and their employees inside the factory, outside working hours the *patronos* and their workers were expected to and did interact as equals. They drank in the bars and dined together in the *Sociedades*. Nor was the *patrono* permitted to pay more (or less) than his exact proportion of expenses on these occasions. As the industrialists were expected to behave as the social equals of other village members, they were also expected to do the same amount of work. In general the industrialists entered their factories at 7.30 in the morning and finished at 6.00 in the afternoon. In many respects the lifestyle of the industrialists was indistinguishable from that of their fellow villagers. Most of them insisted that they too were just workers – like everyone else.

People frequently noted that the factory owners in Elgeta had achieved their position through hard work and skilled management and continued to merit their position by their persisting efforts. The industrialists' claim to equal moral and social status was also supported by the villagers' detailed knowledge of their family histories. In all cases the industrialists or their families were born into medium or small farmsteads. They were men from poor rural backgrounds made good.

However, many villagers expressed a dislike for the rich. This attitude was an ingrained part of village ideology. 'To be rich, you have to steal', summed up the widely-held notion that somehow rich people were rich by illegitimate means. Although Elgeta's industrialists publicly stressed that they were by work, by birth and by behaviour part of the community, for most of the villagers they were subject to latent suspicion. This suspicion was activated and reinforced whenever the behaviour of one of them was perceived to go against the interests or moral norms of the village. If the behaviour of one industrialist infringed village norms, the industrialists as a category were condemned. 'What can you expect! *Los amos* are always like that.' The only industrialist protected from such suspicion was José Mari Elcoro, the owner of Tornillos Elcoro. Elcoro was a member of the PNV (the Basque Nationalist Party), a keen supporter of the *ikastola* in Eibar and the only Elgeta industrialist who had a conspicuous lack of business acumen.

The terms *industrialistas*, *pudientes*, *rico-ricos*, *amos*, *patronos* – all terms used to refer to these people – are negative in connotation. In village eyes these terms also implied a certain type of behaviour. The director and co-owner of Modelo was described to me by one of the workers in Dormicoop, the furniture cooperative, in the following manner.

> There [in Modelo] the *amos* decide everything. They tell you what to do – *they* give the orders – and you have to keep silent and work like a donkey. All this so that they get rich and you stay poor. They think they own people. They're just like the priests. No, they're worse than the priests.

Another worker in Zabala Hermanos listed the industrialists as the most negative aspect of village life.

> The worst thing about Elgeta is the *ricos*. The former mayor [one of the owners of Zabala Hermanos] made a factory here and then made another in Zaldivar. What sort of mayor is that? They make their fortunes here, but spend it outside the village so that we get nothing. If there is money here and the biggest industrialists go elsewhere, where will we ever get the pesetas? If there are 4 pesetas, they must be put into our *pueblo* – *not* into another!

There were also other aspects of the industrialists' behaviour which laid them open to suspicion. In spite of their assurances that they were part of the community, their economic activities extended outward into wider economic and social realms. The relations established in this wider world were outside the view of the villagers and, hence, beyond their control. To many villagers the outside world was an inherently dubious and potentially hostile place. It was the place where police informers, state authorities, the CIA, Francoists and Guerilleros de Cristo Rey (a right-wing terrorist group) worked and conspired. The villagers extended trust and confidence, crucial ingredients for membership in the moral community, only to those whose lives were entirely visible and, thus, controllable. This was not the case with the industrialists.

In short, Elgeta's economic élite, by virtue of their industry, sobriety and origins from humble, rural stock, were part of the moral community. Simultaneously they were seen as people who gave orders without receiving them in equal measure, whose economic superiority might become translated into social superiority and whose wider social contacts were potentially dangerous and subversive. All these factors placed the economic élite, regardless of their many virtues, in a morally peripheral position.

The professionals

Formerly the upper sector of village society was composed of two distinct élites. One élite was based on wealth (the rich farmers). The other was composed of the village professionals, the *señores de carrera* (gentlemen of education), and included the village teachers, priests, pharmacist, doctor and secretary of the town hall. Because of their education they were assigned notably more respect and social prestige than the wealthy farmers who were usually illiterate. It was to these cultured individuals that, as the Basques say, 'we took off our berets'. The village professionals, none of whom were from Elgeta, were viewed as the benevolent representatives of the powerful urban world outside the village. In addition to their professional tasks, the *señores de carrera* would be called upon to offer advice and mediation on all matters related to this world: court cases, tax problems, educational problems, money matters and so forth. Although education, *kulturua*, still gives more prestige than mere wealth, the village professionals no longer enjoyed élite status. In the main two factors were responsible.

First, the village professionals no longer had a monopoly on education. The vast majority of the villagers had become literate and fluent Spanish speakers. Most of the generation who had grown up in the post civil war period had received some specialized training in addition to primary education. Second and more importantly, since the civil war the outside world was no longer viewed as even possessing benevolent representatives. It was seen as dominated by a regime totally opposed to all village interests and the village professionals were its officially approved appointees. They were regarded as neither knowing nor caring about Elgeta. The villagers constantly pointed out properties of the professionals' behaviour that breached village norms. Although some were respected for their competence and professional skills, the warmth and authority previously bestowed on the professionals had been withdrawn. The village professionals did not participate in complex, reciprocal personal relationships with other villagers.

The case of the doctor, Don C., was illustrative. Don C. was in his late fifties in 1974 and was undoubtedly the most fashionably dressed man in the village. With a neatly trimmed moustache and well-groomed grey hair, he was generally dressed in an expensive white shirt, grey cashmere V-necked sweater, tweed jacket, sharply creased flannel trousers and spruce leather loafers. His wife was the only woman in Elgeta with a fur coat. Some five years previously on a prominent site overlooking the Vergara valley, Don C. at great expense built a futuristic villa which the villagers felt added little to the architectural unity of Elgeta. However, Don C. had not been always so prosperous.

The doctor came to Elgeta from Burgos sometime around 1950 with only a bicycle and some shabby clothes. He spoke no Euskera and, indeed, never learned the language. He opened a surgery for one hour daily in which he treated patients on social security for which he was paid a set salary by the state. In addition, over the years he developed a thriving private practice in Elgeta and in Vergara. In Elgeta at the time the medical services consisted of Don C. and a *practicante* who also received an income from the state for his services. The *practicante*'s livelihood was derived from giving people injections – a form of medication much esteemed locally – which the doctor had prescribed for them. After some time the doctor stopped prescribing injections altogether. In this manner Don C. effectively cut off all business from the *practicante* who in the end was forced to leave the village through lack of work. However, the law stated that every village must have a *practicante* and, since the doctor argued that he was doing the *practicante*'s work, he began to collect both his own and the *practicante*'s salary. However, he still refused to prescribe injections. The villagers felt that this was in order to spare him the extra effort which could be more profitably invested in his private practice in Vergara.

But there were other aspects of the doctor's behaviour which also brought him into disrepute. Because of the system of social security in Spain, if a social security doctor makes out a prescription, then that medicine could be purchased for a minimal fee. It had long been village custom for the doctor to fill out prescriptions for aspirins, bandages or whatever else a villager thought was needed. Don C. stuck to the letter of the law and refused to do this. As one of his discontented patients, a 65-year-old Basque farmer's wife, said: 'We have always considered the mentality of the Castillian as more dictatorial. The *pueblo* has little respect or affection for Don C. Rather than do you a favour like one ought to, Don C. always refers to the law and this is resented. Their laws have never been our laws.'

The oldest daughter of Don C. was considered to take after her father. She had few friends in the village nor did she apparently seek them. The son, on the other hand, went to the bars with other village youths, danced enthusiastically during the fiestas and smoked cigarettes clandestinely with the rest of the young people of the village.

The villagers extended similar resentment, although for different specific reasons, to the state teachers. The state school was housed in a long, two-story whitewashed building. One half of the building contained the two classrooms which comprised the school. In the other half the lower floor was abandoned and the windows broken. The upper floor served as flats. After the civil war a long succession of Falangist teachers took up duties in Elgeta. Few were Basque, none knew the language and many were openly hostile to Basque culture, which they regarded as inferior. Many villagers felt that these teachers harmed the village considerably. One person who was educated by these teachers said,

> They tried to make the children anti-Basque, to turn them against their own traditions. We learned to sing 'Cara al Sol' (the Falangist anthem). We read Primo de Rivera and were told that the Basques during the war were separatists and against God. They are better now – more subtle – but it's the same sausage.

The teachers saw their stay in the village as temporary, a stepping stone to more prestigious postings in larger towns. The turnover rate was high and the average stay only a couple of years. Like the doctor, priests and the secretary of the town hall, the teachers did not join in village life except in their specific professional capacity. They were treated formally as befitted their role, but multistrand, personal links were rarely established to other villagers. They were not invited to weddings, baptisms or to the long line of frequently held dinners.

El pueblo

Lying at the heart of the community was the notion of *el pueblo*. *El pueblo* was the final arbitrator and protector of village norms, values and morality in all spheres. It is with reference to the *pueblo* that the moral categories that underpinned the stratification system of Elgeta formed a coherent pattern.

There are two definitions of *el pueblo*. The dictionary would define it as a 'town, village, settlement, nation, population, populace, common people, working class'. This is essentially a neutral definition. But at the core of the term as it is most frequently used in political, social or emotive discourse is a moral notion. In this context the *pueblo* is a subjective moral community. It is subjective in that the moral definition of the *pueblo* related to the self-image that the villagers possessed.

However, the *pueblo* was also an objective reality on two levels. First, the members of the *pueblo* – those individuals who considered themselves and, more importantly, were considered by others as members – defined and defended the regulating moral codes and behavioural norms of the *pueblo* and in turn submitted their behaviour to these codes. Moreover, those individuals whose claims to membership in the *pueblo* were not co-validated nevertheless recognized the *pueblo*'s moral leadership. In short, the *pueblo*'s moral image and codes corresponded to the moral image and codes of the village as a whole. Second, the *pueblo* was not only seen as a moral community, it was politically explicit. Through a specific process which will be examined in a subsequent chapter, the *pueblo* had become a political alignment and interest group. During the mid-seventies it became the main source of political power in the village and, therefore, on a political level as well as a moral one demanded obedience.

In Elgeta there was close to total unanimity on the boundaries of the *pueblo*. Although the *pueblo* was closed to all those whose behaviour or social and political behaviour went counter to its moral dictates, its boundaries were not rigid. They were floating. The pool of individuals included changed according to context. For example, a man who in the evenings helped prepare a village cultural event – say a performance of Basque singers – was part of the *pueblo* 'who defends Basque culture'. However, this same man who was also married to a Spanish woman was not part of the *pueblo* because '*el pueblo* sticks to its own'.

As the boundaries of the *pueblo* were not fixed, its moral content also changed over time. Previously Catholicism had been a fundamental aspect of village values. Agnostics and atheists were the antithesis of the Basque. Religion was now becoming increasingly marginal in village values. However, certain ideas concerning political sentiment were gaining ascendancy as defining criteria of inclusion. With the onslaught of nationalist sentiment and politics in the village, politics and morality to a large extent fused. To be, say, communist was evil since communists were believed to be authoritarian, not honourable, non-Basque and have their interests centred in Madrid if not Moscow.

The list of moral values that defined the *pueblo* were few in number; but the behavioural prescriptions they generated were long and covered most aspects of village lives. On one level the *pueblo* was non-authoritarian and egalitarian, honourable, prudent and modest, hard-working, submitted the interests of the individual to the interests of the group, and Basque. When these values were expanded and made programmatic, the village behavioural prescriptions became defined. It was this set of values which determined the limits of acceptable behaviour.

The values listed above generated the norms of behaviour governing exchange and reciprocity, which had to be strictly balanced, the distribution and maintenance of political power and authority, the modes in which social behaviour had to be expressed, the acceptable forms for the accumulation of wealth and social prestige. They also generated the norm that *pueblo* members should have their social sights within the village and work for its commonweal. To be Basque meant to speak Basque. Unless a person in Elgeta spoke the language, he could never have complete status as a Basque.

With the growth of nationalism in the village, the idea of 'to be Basque' also began to carry a political load. Although knowledge of the language remained an essential precondition, it was no longer sufficient. The behavioural prescriptions generated from 'Basqueness' became increasingly specific and extended. In the ideology of the *pueblo* a Basque now became someone who also defended Basque culture and was nationalist in sentiment. This implied, among other things, attendance at Basque cultural events and political sympathy or affiliation in Basque nationalist parties. Because behaviour was phrased in moral terms, it became obligatory.

The sum of moral values and behavioural prescriptions defined the *pueblo* in terms of an ideal model. Although the moral code, and the behavioural norms generated by it, was precise and extensive, the majority of the Elgeta Basques conformed to and carried out its strictures. This part of the population – egalitarian in their dealings, honourable in word and deeds (which meant adhering to the rest of the moral values), hard working both for individual and village benefit and who were Basque by language and sentiment – formed the *pueblo* of Elgeta.

While the *pueblo* consisted at its core of individuals who were *seen* to comply with all its moral, political and social norms, the village as a whole was perceived as a series of concentric circles with this group at its midpoint. Outside the inner core was the circle formed by those who fulfilled some of the criteria for inclusion, but not all. In this circle were some of the industrialists who, as discussed previously, were morally suspect because of their economic position and wider social ties, among other aspects. It also included those with some personal idiosyncracy (e.g. a drinking problem) or political faults (e.g. were absent from cultural events) and those Basques who were recent arrivals to the village. These people were included in the *pueblo* in some contexts, but were excluded from the more sensitive aspects of village life (which usually meant politics) in which total trust was deemed a crucial factor. Effective inclusion in the *pueblo* terminated here since the categories of people not included in these two circles were viewed more in negative than in positive terms.

Outside the two circles which comprised the *pueblo*, seen as a moral community, lay the category of individuals who were marginal to the *pueblo*, but needed and to some extent respected by it. In this category were the village professionals (*señores de carrera*), the state teachers, doctor and priests. They were isolated from the mainstream of *pueblo* life, but still linked to it via their specific, formal role relationships. Unless these people meddled in village affairs (as was the case with the secretary of the town hall), moral judgement was largely suspended. They were assessed mainly in terms of their professional competence. Although disliked and often ignored, these people were tolerated.

The fourth group of individuals was composed of people who were by no means part of the *pueblo*. They were understood as its enemies and, therefore, anti-Basque. In this grouping were the former political bosses and *jauntxoak* of the village, known police informers (suspected or real was irrelevant), Francoists and anyone who was suspected of having confidential links to such people. Most of them were Basques, but morally they were seen almost entirely in negative terms. Politically they manipulated in obscure, illegitimate ways activating ties to outside political powers. They worked only for their own interests and against the interests of the village. They tried to exercise control through recourse to physical and economic coercion. They were beyond the limits of what constituted moral human beings. However, these people were recognized as individuals. Their personal histories were known in detail and occasionally positive aspects about their family records might be mentioned.

The final circle did not consist of individuals at all. It comprised an ethnic group – the immigrants. The Basques in general acknowledged that immigrant labour had been essential to the industrialization of Elgeta from which considerable benefits had been derived. However, morally the immigrants were the exact opposite of the Basques, reflecting the moral virtues of the *pueblo* in reverse. They were dictatorial, dishonest, braggarts, lazy and out only for their own interests. Being Spanish, they were by definition anti-Basque. They spoke Spanish and were against Basque culture which they mocked. They reflected both the culture and political attitudes of Francoism. The village Basques knew little about the immigrants as individuals. Their names, places of origin, the foods they ate, social habits, problems and ambitions were of little interest. Many Basques did not recognize individual immigrants by sight even after many years of coresidence.

Both these latter two categories were regarded as dangerous since they contained the enemies of the *pueblo* and potential police informers. Not only were such people immoral, but in a sense this immorality could be contagious through contact.

Chivatos

The village Basques firmly believed that many police informers, *chivatos*, lived in Elgeta. During my stay two lists of village informers were drawn up. On one list thirty-three people were named of whom twenty-eight were immigrants and five were Basques. It was implied that in due time these people would be dealt with by ETA. No one seemed sure what criteria had been used to establish the lists. Obviously no one expected to catch an informer red-handed giving information to the police. The immigrants, especially the more aggressive young ones, were believed to be informers because they sympathized with the police politically and their main concern was with money. The police allegedly paid well. Another sign that a specific immigrant was a police informer was if he attempted to become overly friendly with the more politically active Basques.

The Basque informers were characterized as people whose only ambition was money. Anyone who was seen to have money, the source of which was obscure and who appeared to slight work, was immediately considered a possible *chivato*. However, *chivatos* could sometimes be discovered from their personal characteristics. They could be people who were too friendly and encroached into other people's affairs. On the other hand, they could be highly introverted, sitting alone in bars apparently without friends. ('When you are up to no good, you don't want companions.') They could be Basques who did not send their children to the *ikastola* and did not attend village events. In short, potential police informers were understood as people who one way or another broke village norms and, by so doing, revealed themselves as anti-Basque. One obvious sign of an informer was someone who associated with the police – or with other informers.

Clearly the notion of police informers functioned as a powerful mechanism to ensure compliance with village norms. I could never substantiate whether there were in fact paid police informers in Elgeta. The villagers were unable to produce convincing evidence against any given individual. In one case the only evidence offered was that the suspected individual, a Basque, had been seen driving in a car with Madrid licence plates. My impression was that their actual numbers were vastly exaggerated. The parallels between accusations of *chivatazo* (informing) and witchcraft accusations in other parts of the world were very striking.

However, like most Basque villages, Elgeta had undergone a very specific experience during the prior forty years. Police informers had existed and the political sentiments of the villagers were never trusted by the Franco regime, a fact for which the villagers had been punished. It was the villagers' personal experiences which provided the final moral back-up for their beliefs.

For instance, while I was living in Elgeta during 1975, one local man was arrested and tortured. During his stay in the police station, he was brutally beaten (one eardrum was shattered, the other became seriously infected). He was hung by his arms for three nights with his feet barely reaching the floor and was repeatedly submerged in a bathtub filled with human excrement and vomit until he lost consciousness. He was then revived and the torture continued. After his release, he fled to France.

Distancing, isolation and exclusion

The village Basques avoided open conflict whenever possible. Direct confrontation and acts of personal violence were rare. The village employed only one mechanism of social sanction. This mechanism was based on avoidance and the creation and maintenance of social distance. It existed in three forms which constituted a continuum. It ranged from momentary distancing through isolation to ostracism which was irreversible. It was this mechanism of avoidance, applied as a social sanction, that physically created and maintained the boundaries between the different categories of people in the village's moral universe.

The form of avoidance varied with the category of people and breach of norms involved. *Pueblo* members rarely discussed each other in negative terms. Gossip and idle speculation were regarded as frivolous and risky. When *pueblo* members infringed village norms, they were met with, for lack of a better term, momentary distancing. Usually the specific infraction was never mentioned. There was no open airing of grievances. Instead the wayward individual found that his relationships to other *pueblo* members had become cooler, more formal. The offence was usually minor, for instance, failure to honour a debt or pay one's share in a drinking round. The distancing ceased when the offender rectified his misdeed.

However, if an individual persisted in breaking village norms or committed acts (such as marriage to a Spaniard) that put his/her status as a full *pueblo* member in doubt, the distancing hardened and the trust bestowed on the individual was partly withdrawn. In such an event the individual found himself relegated to the second ranks of *pueblo* membership. Although such an individual could continue to participate in a wide range of non-political activities – for example, organizing charitable events of behalf of the village elderly – he was barred from the more sensitive, political areas of *pueblo* life, for example, the planning of a public lecture on 'the labour movement in Euskadi'.

Further out from the moral centre was a third category of people composed of the professionals and those people whose constant and serious infringement of village norms had led to their isolation from all *pueblo* activities. For this category of people isolation was more or less a permanent state of affairs. These individuals were greeted only perfunctorily and addressed formally with little personal warmth. They were largely cut off from any personal relations with *pueblo* members. Since they were not trustworthy, association with them could be dangerous and was regarded as suspicious.

Isolation was applied to those individuals who were judged mainly in morally negative terms, but who were regarded as possessing at least some morally redeeming features. Because isolation did not preclude all contact with the *pueblo*, in rare cases it was a reversible state. The case of Javier A. is illustrative.

Javier A. was a member of the *pueblo* who worked in a shop in a nearby town. Unknown to his friends, Javier had managed to save a substantial amount of money. In 1973 Javier lost his job when the shop he worked in closed down. Instead of searching for new employment, Javier used his enforced leisure to travel – he visited Andalucia, France and Germany – and buy items he had always wanted but never felt he had the time to enjoy. Javier bought, among other things, an expensive stereo system. Javier's leisure lasted almost one year. After a few months Javier noticed that he was frequently not invited to go with his friends on weekend trips to the mountains. He was especially surprised when he realised that no one had told him about plans being made for the village *fiestas* to be held in the summer. Slowly Javier realised that he no longer had privileged access to any information about the activities of his former friends and acquaintances. What Javier did not realise was that these former friends had begun to suspect that Javier's leisurely lifestyle probably had only one explanation – Javier was suspected of being a police informer. Because Javier was isolated, the rumours that circulated freely within the *pueblo* concerning his informing were never shared with Javier himself. Javier's timid enquiries as to the reasons behind the changed attitude of his former friends were met with frosty evasion. As the year wore on and Javier continued to enjoy his luxuries, the diagnosis that he was a police informer seemed to be confirmed. However, some of Javier's old friends could not fully accept that Javier was capable of betraying the *pueblo* so completely. One of these people confided to Javier in a furtive meeting why he had become an outcast. Javier was horrified. He immediately produced his bankbook to show the money he had saved over the previous years. Within one week Javier had found a new job. After one more year Javier had been finally readmitted to the *pueblo*. Except for Javier's furtive friend, no one ever mentioned Javier's debatable career as a police informer to Javier himself.

While isolation was sometimes reversible, ostracism was not. No voluntary association with ostracized persons was tolerated. Since they possessed no morally positive features at all, redemption was not possible.

The effectiveness of this mechanism of sanction, based on progressively more permanent and severe avoidance, was due partly to two factors. Firstly, the idea that informers existed, that trust could not be extended lightly, was an idea that pervaded village social life. Life was inherently unsafe. To a certain extent a cloud of mistrust covered all village inhabitants. Accusations and suspicions were rarely specifically detailed.

For example, when a man in a nearby village was detained by the police, many in Elgeta felt that a police informer had been involved. There seemed to be no concrete evidence that this had been the case. It was just felt that this usually *was* the case. Commenting on the matter to me, one woman in her late forties whispered cryptically as we were walking to her house for lunch:

Here we all go around together without anyone trusting in the others. We are always talking about the *Castellanos* – but it's the Basques as well. Before there was a woman who was in our *cuadrilla* – she used to play cards with us. Everyone was always talking. But when there were *bestsolaris* [Basque oral poets] in the fronton, or the Basque festivals – well, she – ah! nothing. She never cared. Very quickly you notice these types of people and you know who is who.

Some days later it was heard that thc young man arrested had been severely beaten in the police station. A friend of this man confided:

Probably there are some people here who are laughing [about the torture]. Sometimes you are talking in total confidence and they turn out to be... well, you know. Here it is not what you say, but what you do. At any rate in Elgeta there are people of all types – and you never know.

Secondly, the effectiveness of this sanction was also due to its devastating social results. One of Elgeta's bars was owned and managed by a Galician who married a Basque woman from a nearby village. Although he gave generously to all village affairs to raise money for the *ikastola* or other village causes and tried to be affable with all, he was believed to be a police informer. When Civil Guards came to the village, they often frequented his bar, the only 'modern' bar in Elgeta. Moreover, he was thought to be related to a Civil Guard stationed in Mondragon. The bar was resolutely boycotted especially by the village youth who tended to be the most militant defenders of the *pueblo*. His family was also isolated from village affairs. In the presence of any member of this family, political talk died and rapid, undisguised glances expressing the need for caution were given to those around. Moreover, people who consistently patronized the bar became suspected persons.

When I first came to Elgeta, I used to write up field notes in this bar because it was the only one in the village that was quiet – and empty. One afternoon a woman came in to see me and I began to inquire about the rumours that the police had gone on strike. The police control at the village entrance that morning had been staffed by soldiers rather than the customary Civil Guards. She immediately shot me a glance which I had long since learned to regard as a sign for instantaneous silence. I broke off mid-sentence and was rushed out to the street where I was then told about the danger I had put myself in. I didn't return to the bar for several weeks. When I finally did, the owner's wife brought me a coffee and said, 'I know what they have told you... It isn't true, you know. Really, it has never been true.'

Economically the bar was viable. It was patronized mainly by immigrants and people passing through the village.

Cuadrillas

Outside the domestic realm of the family, the principal unit in the public and private social life of the villagers was the *cuadrilla*. A *cuadrilla* is a group of individuals (usually from eight to twenty) who tend to be of similar age, marital status, sex and who share a similar lifestyle. The element that is given primary importance in defining a *cuadrilla* is that all its members are bound by a common way of thinking. It was often stressed that only within the *cuadrilla* grouping could conversation be free and casual since one knew all attitudes were shared. Notably, uniformity of economic levels was not a factor in determining *cuadrilla* membership. Within a *cuadrilla* the son of a factory owner and the son of a manual worker existed on equal footing. This was frequently cited as further proof of the egalitarian nature of village life.

A *cuadrilla* was not the same as a group of friends. Although co-members of a *cuadrilla* would consider themselves friends, these friendships were weak and could easily be broken by change of marital status, political attitudes or changes of working hours. Moreover, the villagers perceived relations based on friendship and those based on common *cuadrilla* membership as distinct. Friendship implied a close, dyadic relation whereas *cuadrilla* relations were multipersonal. To Basques in general and to the villagers in particular friendship was a much more serious affair, rarely achieved and never given or received half-heartedly.

The surest sign of a *cuadrilla* was found in its most frequent and typical activity – the drinking of *chiquitos* or *potes*, two names for small glasses of wine costing 3 to 5 pesetas. Every midday before lunch and every evening after work at 6.30 or 7 o'clock, the *cuadrillas* of young people, older men, teenagers accumulated in the bars and, on warm days, in the streets. The *cuadrillas* were clearly demarcated. Members of a *cuadrilla* stood in a semi-circle talking to each other and exchanging greetings with passers-by. Normally the *cuadrillas* drank small glasses of wine, an activity called *chiquiteando* or *poteando*. When everyone in the *cuadrilla* had finished his drink, the group moved into the street and on to another bar where another round of *chiquitos* was ordered and consumed. The *chiquiteo* was completed when all the bars in Elgeta (with the exception of the 'modern' bar) had been visited. An empty bar at the hour of the *chiquiteo* in any Basque village was an infallible sign that the proprietor was under suspicion of being an informer.

Usually each bar was crowded with people exchanging news and telling jokes. Although the *cuadrilla* moved from bar to bar as a discrete grouping, inside the bars conversation occurred across *cuadrilla* barriers. *Cuadrillas* making the rounds of the bars during the *chiquiteo* provided the means for a continuous and daily communication between villagers.

Not only was *cuadrilla* membership fixed, but so was the place and time in which the *cuadrilla* met. Several *cuadrillas* of men in their forties and fifties could be seen meeting daily at 7 o'clock at the *Sociedad* Intxorta. If you needed to talk to Antxon Albistegui about ordering timber, he could be found any afternoon with his *cuadrilla* in the Bar Ostatu playing mus, a card game. Most of the village youth joined their *cuadrillas* at set hours at the *Sociedad* Ozkarbi.

A person could be a member of several *cuadrillas* although rarely more than three. However, these *cuadrillas* were always functionally distinct. For most people one's daily *cuadrilla* was the *cuadrilla* with which one enjoyed the daily round of bars. The other *cuadrillas* of which an individual might be a member related to special interests. For example, a man might have one daily *cuadrilla*, another with which he went fishing – his 'fishing *cuadrilla*' – and still another based on membership in a clandestine political party or shared political sentiments, his political *cuadrilla*. Political *cuadrillas* were the main vehicle for political organization and activity in the village and, thus, played a fundamental role in village political life.

Cuadrillas had clearly definable life cycles. The origins of most *cuadrillas* came from childhood. The village of Elgeta was roughly divided into two sections each of which corresponded to one of the main streets in the village, San Roque and San Salvador. During childhood the main criterion for the formation of a *cuadrilla* was residence. Basque village children were loosely organized into two *cuadrillas* each of which consisted of the children who lived together in one of these two streets. Although the rivalries between these two *cuadrillas* were often fierce and were expressed in competition at games or sporting events, the *cuadrillas* of young children were permeable and unstable. When people were around fifteen or sixteen years old, residence ceased to be the main criterion for inclusion into a *cuadrilla*. The original *cuadrilla*, based on residence, was reshuffled and new, smaller, more uniform and more discrete *cuadrillas* were precipitated out. Place of work, school, general attitudes to life and political sentiment became, in combination, the determining factors for inclusion. It was during this period that the *cuadrilla* formed could last as a definable grouping of individuals for the lifetime of its members.

However, for the *cuadrillas* formed at this period to survive, it was essential that its members had the same daily timetable. *Cuadrillas* did not possess non-participatory members. A *cuadrilla* was maintained through the shared activities of its members. If an individual moved away from Elgeta, changed jobs or schools, usually his or her ties to the *cuadrilla* weakened and eventually broke, although warm personal relations would remain.

An important stage in the life cycle of a *cuadrilla* was initiated with the marriage of its members. Upon marriage a person was not excluded from the *cuadrilla*, but a married member of a *cuadrilla* in which the majority were unmarried excluded himself. Marriage meant obligations on one's time which conflicted with adherence to the *cuadrilla* schedule. Although a specific *cuadrilla* was a discrete and definable unit, most *cuadrillas* were informally linked with other *cuadrillas* which were similar in composition and general outlook. Therefore, as the members of these linked *cuadrillas* married, a new *cuadrilla* of young married people was generated. With time the pre-marriage *cuadrilla* might be replicated with some minor adjustments in membership, but considerable adjustments on the routine pursued.

Another factor which took its toll on *cuadrilla* membership was changes in attitudes of its members. If one individual began to deviate from the hitherto shared moral, political and social views of the group, expulsion of the non-conformist was almost assured. This related directly to the fact that trust, based on shared values and adherence to similar norms of behaviour, was the crucial ingredient binding co-members. A rupture in attitudes led to a rupture in the trust extended.

In the context of the fear, anxiety and hostility generated by the broader political situation, the trust necessary to feel safe could only be enjoyed with those who shared the same moral and political views. These views were constantly controlled and reinforced through the *cuadrilla*'s daily round of social activities. Like Elgeta's system of moral stratification, the *cuadrillas* also served as a mechanism for conformity and control

The *cuadrillas* in the village were closed, exclusive social units. Gaining entry into a *cuadrilla* once it had solidified was very difficult. The most important element for late membership was gaining the confidence of existing members. And trust was not a commodity bestowed lightly.

Most *cuadrillas* consisted exclusively of men. However, women could also form *cuadrillas*; these tended to be more unstable and less active. Ramona Basauri, for example, a woman in her fifties with two grown sons, belonged to a *cuadrilla* composed of married women who were linked through kinship or affinity or through the *cuadrilla* relationships of their husbands. These women saw each other as a *cuadrilla* on Saturdays and Sundays in a local bar where they drank tea, ate cakes and played cards with staggering determination. Moreover, women who worked together in the same factory might form a *cuadrilla*. Such was the case of the girls who worked in the Modelo furniture factory who assembled for joint meals on special occasions.

While *cuadrillas* composed of older, married women could last many years, *cuadrillas* of young unmarried girls were short-lived. When these young women started to have *novios* (fiancés), they tended to leave their *cuadrillas* and attach themselves to the *cuadrillas* of their boyfriends. Women linked to men's *cuadrillas* via their relationships to male members were not members in their own right. A woman's link to this *cuadrilla* was dependent upon the continuation of her relationship with the man.

The functions of *cuadrillas* in village life were in the main three. First, they tended to provide the framework for the entirety of the social life of the villagers. After the evening meal a person would again rejoin his *cuadrilla* to decide on joint activities. This could range from going to the movies, attending the fiestas in a nearby village, hearing Basque singers, planning the forthcoming performance of *bertsolaris* in Elgeta's fronton or just simply settling down to a game of cards. Or it could involve more ambitious plans – weekend trips to Navarra or a visit to a well-known restaurant in a coastal village. In all these activities it was implicit that all *cuadrilla* members would participate unless special circumstances prohibited it.

The most frequent activity of a *cuadrilla*, regardless of whether it was a *cuadrilla* of women or a special interest *cuadrilla*, was eating together. Most Basques approach good food with an attention and sensuality most Spaniards reserve only for women. The Elgeta Basques were no exception. Dinners were always held for a specific reason and reasons were never lacking. It could be to celebrate the chestnut season or mushroom season or the fact that Elgeta's *pelota* team was about to play in the championships, or had won the championships, or had lost the championships, or someone had just had a birthday or was about to go on a trip or just come back or simply because it was Saturday night.

The second function of the *cuadrillas* was as an organization for mutual aid. If a *cuadrilla* member needed a loan, medical help, legal advice, a house to live in, a job, etc., the first people whose advice and help he called on were other *cuadrilla* members. The *cuadrilla* as a whole was expected to mobilize to solve its individual members' problems.

Cuadrillas, either singly or together with other *cuadrillas*, were mobilized for a range of tasks. Hence, the third function of *cuadrillas* in the village was as the organizing units for village social and cultural events. The most active *cuadrillas* in this respect were those composed of young unmarried people. These *cuadrillas* were responsible for the organization of the Basque fiestas, cultural conferences, performances of Basque singers, the *ikastola* and so forth. But other types of *cuadrillas* were also active. In fact political life in the village, both official and unofficial, depended on and took place within the confines of *cuadrilla* organization. The *cuadrillas* provided the means by which communication, coordination and decision in the political domain was achieved. This aspect will be discussed more fully further on.

It is also worth noting that most *cuadrillas* expressed the aspiration of having a private place for meeting and sharing meals. As one person said, 'A *cuadrilla* without a place to meet in private is like a family without a home to live in.' This desire furnished the main inspiration behind the establishment of Elgeta's four *sociedades* which were private social clubs. The membership of the *sociedades* was usually composed of a founder *cuadrilla* in addition to *cuadrillas* linked to the founder *cuadrilla* together with persons who were related through kinship or affinity to the members of these *cuadrillas*. The *sociedad* was viewed as a type of extended *cuadrilla* and it endowed *cuadrillas* with jointly-held property.

In general the only means of entry into the mainstream of village life was through *cuadrilla* membership. Easy, casual social relationships, like easy, casual hospitality, did not exist. *Cuadrilla* membership was also necessary in order to link into the main communication networks of the village. Since casual social relations were rare, generalized gossip and transmission of information were not features of village life. But inside a *cuadrilla* the exchange of information was continuous. The links between *cuadrillas* corresponded to the networks along which communication flowed within the village. The nature and degree of information exchanged between the members of one *cuadrilla* and another depended on the degree of confidence established between the two *cuadrillas*. This had one crucial effect on political process. Since no *cuadrilla* could have direct links with a *cuadrilla* in a different moral category than itself – because of the rule of guilt by association – information did not flow over moral boundaries. The networks of communication in Elgeta stopped at the moral boundaries that divided the villagers. The manoeuvres and manipulations of the *pueblo* were not known by those outside it – and *vice versa*.

Finally, it should be mentioned that exchange within a *cuadrilla* was determined by adherence to a strict rule of immediate and balanced reciprocity. No one was permitted to pay more or less than his exact share. *Cada uno, el suyo* (to each and from each, his own) and *berdin–berdin* (equals–equals) was again the rule. During each round of drinks in the *chiquiteo*, a different member of the *cuadrilla* paid. It was not looked on kindly if a person who was not paying for the round suddenly decided to order expensive French cognac. Moreover, anyone who attempted to pay more than his share also met with disapproval. Overt economic generosity was interpreted as crossing the grain of egalitarianism and as a bid for *cuadrilla* leadership. As such, it was stoutly obstructed.

The strictness with which accounts were kept was at times astonishing. To illustrate, I once went with a *cuadrilla* to see a movie in Eibar. There were six of us and two cars were used to make the trip. When we arrived in Eibar, we headed for the nearest bar and had a glass of wine. The six glasses of wine cost 30 pesetas which I paid. Entering another bar, we had one more glass of wine each and some fried squid (total cost 95 pesetas). We finally went to the movies and one person paid 480 pesetas for the six tickets. At the end of the evening we returned to Elgeta and the privacy of the *Sociedad* Ozkarbi. As the last event of the evening, one person produced a piece of paper and made a list of everyone's names and what each had paid. The average cost of the evening's activities was calculated and compared with the sum paid by each person. The owners of the two cars had their costs for the 20 km trip calculated at 75 pesetas for petrol and 20 pesetas for car depreciation. I energetically offered to invite the *cuadrilla* to the round of wine I had bought and was noisily turned down. Hence, everyone paid the exact equivalent of one-sixth of the cost of the wine, squid, tickets, petrol and car depreciation. Unlike in other parts of Spain where the animated struggle to pay the bill – and thus make a bid for precedence – is a symbolic part of group relationships, in Elgeta as in most Basque villages accounts were settled in an orderly way, each paying up immediately and equally.

The principle of strict symmetrical reciprocity was reflected in the authority structure of the *cuadrillas*. On one level there was none. No decisions, no matter how insignificant, affecting the *cuadrilla* as a whole could be taken except by total consensus. The achievement of consensus was often a time-consuming process. Life in *cuadrillas* could be very slow moving indeed. On many occasions I stood in the middle of a village street with a *cuadrilla* for up to ten minutes because some people in the group had expressed a preference to visit one bar while others wished to visit a different one. It was self-evident to everyone that both bars would be eventually visited in any case. However, no one person felt he/she had the authority to make the decision single-handedly. On these occasions no explicit decision was ever taken. Slowly the *cuadrilla* just seemed to gravitate to one of the bars.

However, one individual sometimes did function as an informal leader of a *cuadrilla*. His dominant position within a *cuadrilla* was usually related to the respect and prestige that he commanded in the wider village society. Publicly this person was considered as the *cuadrilla*'s central figure and the *cuadrilla* was often known by his name. However, inside the *cuadrilla* the dominant position of this individual was never explicitly acknowledged and by no means was it reflected in the nature of economic transactions. His role was limited to the subtle coordination of group consensus. However, within these boundaries the informal leader of a *cuadrilla* could exert notable influence on the attitudes and activities of the *cuadrilla* as a whole.

The relationships established between individuals within a *cuadrilla* were often depicted as a model for what was regarded as the ideal form of moral, acceptable social relations. They were egalitarian, personalized and multi-stranded based on shared attitudes, mutual respect and trust. They were also closed to outsiders. Most people in Elgeta belonged to one *cuadrilla* or another. A person who was not part of a *cuadrilla* relationship was regarded as untrustworthy since his actions were not subject to the constant control exercised by a group.

Immigrants

However, social organization based on *cuadrillas* was only applicable to village Basques. Life in Elgeta viewed from the eyes of the immigrants presented a radically different picture. As mentioned previously, the distinction between *los de aquí* and *los de fuera* formed the fundamental division in the village social universe. While the Basques regarded themselves as a community tied together by adherence to shared behavioural prescriptions and moral codes and had mechanisms to organize for common political and economic interests, the immigrants were a collectivity with no sense of either a common identity or shared values – only a coinciding fate. They were outsiders, regardless of length of residency in the village. The Basques of Elgeta, the village owners, were viewed as bewildering and as encompassing an alien culture which was neither understood nor seen as particularly alluring. Most immigrants perceived themselves as still belonging to their village of origin and expressed the desire to return or at least to leave Elgeta for some larger Basque town.

Most immigrants arrived in Elgeta as young, single men. Those who managed to establish themselves with a job usually married quite quickly although almost never to Basque girls from the village.

For the young men especially, life in Elgeta was problematic and lonely. In general they lodged with an immigrant or, less often, a Basque family. For those who did not receive full board in addition to lodging, lunch was taken in the Bar Martinchu or at the Bar Panaderokua. Basque workers also ate in these bars, but the tables were rarely ethnically mixed. Evenings were filled by the perpetual quest for something to do. None of the immigrants were members of the village *sociedades* which in addition to the bars supplied the only form of local entertainment. Usually most drifted off in twos and threes to nearby towns to see a movie or go to a disco. During the infrequent village dances, these immigrant men could easily be singled out. While the Basques were neatly united in their *cuadrillas* both sitting and dancing as a group, the immigrants wandered the premises singly or in pairs asking young women to dance. If the woman asked was a Basque, the answer was usually an unequivocal no. As a whole the immigrants' participation in village life was minimal.

The loose and shifting social groups formed by immigrants were generated by the principles of kinship, shared employment, residence (either with reference to Elgeta or, more importantly, village of origin) and dyadic friendship. Whereas the bigger towns had been target areas for chain immigration, this was not the case in Elgeta. Most immigrants came to the village because they were unable to find jobs in other Basque towns.

The first immigrants in the postwar period came around 1960 and entered in more significant numbers from 1963 onward during the period when Elgeta was expanding industrially. Although they were referred to as *maketos*, a pejorative term, the initial reaction of the Basques was neutral – they were neither disliked nor liked – they were simply an unavoidable addition. The village needed unskilled labour and was unable to supply it. Most of the young Basques in Elgeta had schooling and some specialized trade. Thus, they were unwilling to accept the unskilled and generally low-paid employment available in the growing village factories. In contrast, the immigrants tended to have no special qualifications and they accepted the jobs available.

As the number of immigrants arriving in Elgeta increased, the attitudes of their hosts changed from neutrality to hostility. In part this was due to the sheer size of the influx. However, the full reasons behind this hostility were complex and reflected not only factors traceable to the civil war, but also changes within the village and political currents outside the village that filtered in. When I completed my fieldwork in August 1976, the separation between the two ethnic groups was complete and the barriers were hardening. Many Basques said that for the first time a hard-core hatred towards the immigrants was developing.

There were many elements in village life that served to maintain the barriers that separated the two groups and none that integrated them into one community. The closed, independent Basque family was one such factor. Informal visiting between neighbours was rare and no particular hospitality was extended to either Basque or non-Basque newcomers. Moreover, the Church had also aided in the stiffening of barriers. Mass was celebrated at different hours in Spanish and in Euskera with the non-Basques attending the former services and the Basques the latter. The church made few initiatives to break through the separations dividing its flock although the village priests were acutely aware of the problem.

The schools also reinforced the separation of Basques from Spaniards. The immigrants sent their children to the *escuela nacional*, the state school, whereas the vast majority of the Basques sent their children to the *ikastola*, the private, Basque language school.

As discussed before, social life in Elgeta was centred on the *cuadrillas* which were closed and the *sociedades* which were private and to which non-Basques were refused entry. Since social contact between Basques and non-Basques was avoided, intermarriage between the groups was rare. In the village there were only three cases of such marriages. Marriage with a non-Basque was regarded as marriage with an inferior, and a Basque who contracted such a marriage was viewed with contempt.

The Basque language was, of course, an extremely powerful barrier preventing integration. Few non-Basques spoke or understood Euskera, whereas for the village Basques Euskera was their daily language. The problem of language raised sensitive issues on both sides. Because of Elgeta's relative isolation from the currents of nationalism, most villagers had not been mobilized into an aggressive awareness of their ethnicity and instead felt slightly awkward in their Basqueness. Basqueness was equated with being *baserritarak* (peasants) and *aldeano* (rustic) – the opposite of the sophistication required to be a proper citizen of an urban world. Hence, the culture of the immigrants was accepted in an ambivalent manner. On the one hand, in spite of their lack of formal education, the immigrants spoke Spanish, a valuable skill. On the other, the immigrants often belittled the language of their hosts. In any serious conflict with the immigrants the Basques assumed that they would be at a disadvantage. The police and courts were regarded as inherently 'anti-Basque'. One *baserritar*, recounting an incident in which he felt that his honour had been severely affronted, concluded bitterly, 'With this regime the Basques have always been repressed. They [immigrants] can say anything and all you can do is keep quiet and walk away.'

Although the Basques argued that it was they who had to assimilate to these outsiders – in any social encounter with non-Basques, the Basque speaks in Spanish – even on those few occasions when immigrants attempted to learn Euskera, their motives for doing so were not found acceptable. For instance, on one occasion the two *andereños* (teachers) at the *ikastola* decided that in their free time they would give classes in Euskera to the immigrants. The classes were free. About thirty immigrants, mainly women, signed up. Immediately many village Basques expressed their opposition to the classes. The parents of the *ikastola* children claimed that they had not paid the *andereños* so that they should teach *maketos*. Others exclaimed that the only reason the immigrants attended was because the classes were free of charge. One woman who was especially active in village affairs told me: 'Yes, one or two of them attend the Basque classes. But they're not doing it because they love *our* language – love *our* pueblo. No! They just think that they'll get something out of it. You can't do anything with people of their mentality.' The classes were dropped through the public protest of the *pueblo* less than six weeks after initiation.

However, the public bravado the immigrants may have levelled at Basque culture in the past had for the most part ceased due to a confluence of factors. First, Basque nationalist sentiment had slowly reemerged in Elgeta. The village Basques now actively stressed their culture and, reversing the previous situation, often refused to speak to immigrants in Spanish. Although Basque culture was viewed as impenetrable, most immigrants expressed a desire for their children to learn Euskera. This positive valuation of Euskera was also related to another factor. The immigrants were well aware that the political and economic ownership of Elgeta lay in the hands of Basques. They believed that Basques would always have first priority in housing, employment and the social benefits that accrued to village membership. The immigrants had no representation in either the official or unofficial centres of political and economic power in the village which could affect the distribution of these resources in their favour. Since the immigrants lacked useful networks of influential friends and relatives to help and be helped by, they saw their continued residency and prosperity in the village as dependent on the goodwill of Basques. Since this good will was not anchored in a web of social relations, the immigrants felt that it could be arbitrarily withdrawn if any offence was given.

In response to this situation, most immigrants vehemently denied that any conflict between Basques and Spaniards existed. They publicly stressed the village ideal of harmony. The immigrants also forcefully repeated the reigning ideology of the *pueblo*. 'Here we are all friends. Its like a family to me and we're all equal, all friends.'

The following case is indicative of the intricate fabric of ethnic relations in Elgeta.

When Patxi Basauri, a young man extremely active in *pueblo* affairs and an increasingly ardent nationalist, was elected mayor in 1976, one of his first acts was to request that people in the village tell him the problems which they felt needed to be solved. The *ikastola* and the *escuela nacional* were asked to participate in this endeavour. A committee from the *ikastola* wrote explaining that it was becoming increasingly difficult to maintain the school up to sufficient standards because of lack of teachers and money. The *ayuntamiento* (village council) then called a meeting of all the parents of children in the state school and asked them to elect a committee that could analyse and suggest solutions to the problem facing the school. Although the vast majority of the parents of the state school children were Spanish, the elected committee was composed primarily of Basque parents. The Spaniards felt that no one would listen to them anyway. In the state school the main problems were the lack of teachers – both of those presently employed were leaving at the end of the year – and lack of funds. Because the problems faced by both schools were similar, it was thought that the only solution was to combine the two schools.

To this end the representatives from the *ikastola*, state school and the *ayuntamiento* held a series of meetings. The main issue under debate was whether this new united school should be public, private, in Euskera or bilingual. It was quickly decided, with only one dissenting vote (cast by the only immigrant attending these meetings), that the new school would be a public *ikastola* in which all teachers would be Basque-speakers and all classes given in Euskera. It was argued that in this way all children in Elgeta could receive a proper education in the village until the age of nine. More importantly, if all village children studied together in Euskera, then assimilation of the non-Basque children would be an automatic result.

Many immigrant parents reacted with horror. Although they wanted their children to learn Euskera, they did not want them to learn *in* Euskera. Also, many parents doubted that the state authorities would ever permit such a school to be supported from public funds. Hence, they feared that, instead of providing their children with a free education, the new school would charge heavy fees. But, more bitterly, many immigrants felt that they were being used by the Basques who wanted to create one private *ikastola* for the benefits of Basques only. However, little of the anxieties of the Spanish community reached the ears of the Basque planners.

The first step toward uniting the schools was an attempt to have the children from both the *ikastola* and the state school play together during recreation periods. The two schools were located side by side, separated only by a low concrete wall. The children, some of whom are barely four years old, stayed strictly to their own side of this wall. Many Basque children learned early that immigrants were to be rigidly avoided. Any *ikastola* children caught crossing this cement ethnic barrier were immediately reported by other children to the teachers. This was the situation that the first stage of the scheme was meant to correct.

The weather was sunny and hot, but during the first two days of mixed recreation the children still refused to cross the concrete wall. They continued as usual to play each in their own ethnic groups. Finally, in order to set an example, a young, socially minded female teacher from the *ikastola* and a young, socially minded male teacher from the state school started to play football together, to the amazement of the children. Cautiously some of the older boys followed suit and slowly the little children joined in the first mixed football game the village had ever seen. The reaction of many of the Basque parents was prompt and harsh. Many complained that their children were returning home singing Spanish songs. 'Have I spent all these years working and sacrificing to send my children to the *ikastola* so that they can learn Spanish? Forget their own customs? The day they [immigrant children] sing in Euskera – but that will never happen!', explained one mother at an emergency meeting of Basque parents called to discuss the situation. The young *andereño* was accused of having an affair with the state school teacher, although it was doubtful that many parents actually believed this. To make matters worse, several Basque parents alleged that their children had become ill from standing neglected in the sun while the teachers were directing their attentions solely to the immigrant children. The situation was finally saved by a spell of bad weather that forced the children to stay indoors. When they emerged after one week onto the rain-drenched playing fields, the recreation periods were as segregated as ever. The plan to unite the two schools was also dropped. As the young mayor said, 'There was no other choice. The *pueblo* was against it.'

One bewildered architect of the plan for mixed recreation said at a subsequent meeting of the Asociación de Padres de Familia (The Parents Association), 'It was a good idea, but some parents adopted very radical positions. We live in a village of 1,200 people. All of us know each other and we live in two opposing parts. It poisons everything.'

Played out upon the background of total antagonism between the Basque *pueblo* and the Spanish state which the immigrants are envisaged as reflecting, the Basques perceived the immigrants as inherently different types of beings. The *castellanos* came to be regarded as the root cause of most of the village's difficulties from the lack of proper school and true community spirit to the 'Castellianization' of the village.

Although living side by side in Elgeta, the two groups, Basques and non-Basques, rarely meet except through formal and impersonal contacts at their places of employment. As more immigrants entered the village and nationalist sentiments became more actively widespread among the Basques, the barriers separating the two groups became insurmountable. The decline in Elgeta's population since 1977 is almost entirely due to immigrants leaving Elgeta to start new lives in other Basque communities, or to return to their place of origin.

9

Morality manifested: village politics, 1872–1936

Moral codes and values are deeply rooted in and largely inseparable from the social personality of a society's members. I suggest, and it is a central suggestion of this monograph, that these codes and values, a part of culture, are among the principal organizing agents in a social collectivity. They are essential to the definition of morally acceptable, understandable and, thus, legitimate social life. Because they are part of a collective conscience, moral codes exert a constant pressure on social formations to conform to their precepts – to the extent external circumstances permit.

Elgeta's concentric system of social organization has been described (Chapter 8) with reference to a set of moral categories which the villagers felt defined proper human beings. While some of the content of the categories – *chivatos*, anti-Basque, etc. – was a specific response to the situation which prevailed at the time of my fieldwork, I believe the system itself was a variation of a structural pattern through which the villagers have traditionally sought to conduct their affairs.

The main theme of this chapter is the circumstances in which the moral categories held by the villagers became manifested in political life. I shall suggest that the circumstances involved were those which opened choice. Within this context I shall also try to show why, when the villagers finally were able to exercise choice, overwhelmingly they chose Basque nationalism.

Rural ideology

While *Vascos* and *inmigrantes* form the deepest cleavage in Elgeta's social universe, the opposition between *kaletarak* (those from the street) and *baserritarak* (those from the farms i.e. peasants) refers to an essential division among Basques. It denotes the distinction between urban and rural life. Many farmsteads are now abandoned. Of those still functioning few will remain viable for more than ten years. Yet young people who had never worked on the farmsteads, older people who have recently abandoned them and those few peasants who still devoted their time solely to agricultural endeavours felt that somehow the farmstead symbolized the real values of human life.

Traditionally the basis of economic, social and political life in the rural sector was the autonomous farmstead, or *baserria*, occupied by an active married couple, their unmarried children, the unmarried siblings of the current heir and his or her semi-retired parents. All farmsteads were named. The domestic group was known by the name of the farmstead on which it resided. Although the family name of those residing on the farmstead could change and land could be bought and sold, the farmstead itself was seen as immutable. These named farmsteads provided the fixed coordinates for the social map of the village. (See W. Douglass, 1969, for further discussion.)

Historically the participation of most *baserritarak* in a market economy was minimal and consisted largely of selling milk and excess garden produce to nearby towns. Otherwise, the resident domestic group consumed what they produced.

Economic differences between farmsteads were acknowledged. The wealth of any given farmstead was calculated in the number of cows owned. In farmsteads lying at lower altitudes, wealth was calculated in *fanegos* (c. 45 kg) of wheat. Nevertheless, the reigning ideology insisted that, despite economic discrepancies, all farmsteads were socially and politically the equal of all others. The only exceptions were those farmsteads that had been allowed to deteriorate below the point of viability because of mismanagement and slovenliness.

The farmsteads were loosely linked by ties of voluntary association into neighbourhood groupings called *auzoak* (*auzoa*: singular). *Auzoak* were measured by the number of farmsteads within their boundaries and marked the outer limits of economic cooperation between farmsteads. Relations between *baserritarak* in one *auzoa* were socially reinforced by mutual attendance at weddings, funerals, baptisms and a series of ritual exchanges. Furthermore, each *auzoa* had its own chapel and patron saint. Between neighbours there were no politics. People helped each other when help was needed and on the level of the *auzoa* worked for the common interest.

The ideology of equality was well reflected in the forms of cooperation which existed between the *baserriak*. The forms of cooperation practised were generally of two types. One type was connected to periods in the agricultural year and the other to joint projects of the *auzoa*, or *auzolan* (neighbourhood work).

Until recently the agricultural methods employed on the farmsteads, for example, the *laya* (a two-pronged tool used to turn over soil) and sickle, meant that the farmsteads at peak points of the agricultural cycle, especially planting and harvesting, had to recruit outside labour. A system of day labourers never developed in Elgeta. Therefore, at these periods a group of neighbouring farmsteads – generally three to six in number – would combine their labour resources and unite. Less frequently, individuals related by kinship and friendship would also be mobilized. The exchange of labour and services in these cooperative endeavours was calculated on the basis of strictly balanced reciprocity. Ten men working the land of one farmstead for one day meant that the recipient *baserri* was obliged to contribute the equivalent of ten days labour on the other, specified farmsteads. If a *baserritar* lent out a pair of oxen for one day, this was regarded as the equivalent of three days labour. The sequence of *baserriak* worked cooperatively was determined by geography. In Elgeta because of the steeply sloping land, the cooperating group of *baserritarak* would begin by planting, or harvesting, the farmsteads located in the low lying areas and then work up to those on higher ground.

Relationships within these cooperating groups were viewed as more enduring and intimate than non co-resident kin relations, or as one elderly *baserritar* described them, 'Even if they aren't relatives, they are treated like relatives – or better!' Refusal to reciprocate at these exchanges was unthinkable. The only sanction employed against an offender was the withdrawal of further cooperation – or avoidance.

In the second form of cooperation, *auzolan*, which dealt with the shared tasks of the *auzoa* – mainly road building and the upkeep of chapels – all farmsteads that belonged to a specific *auzoa* would be mobilized. Road building was also the greatest single cause of conflict among neighbouring farmsteads. The sum that each farmstead was to pay was impossible to calculate exactly. The farmsteads that would eventually use the road were of differing sizes, had different needs for the road, were closer or further from other roads and so forth. The majority of court cases in Elgeta dealt with conflicts of this sort. However, the basic principle of cooperation remained the same. Each person was to contribute exactly his share – no more, no less.

In addition to these two forms of wider, more institutionalized, cooperation between farmsteads, there existed also a constant exchange of minor goods and services. Neighbours would borrow sugar, salt and other items for domestic consumption as well as oxen and farm tools. Although here too reciprocity was expected, the duration of the exchange cycle for these items would depend on the state of personal relations between the farmsteads involved. If relations were good, the debt was not immediately repaid. If relations were strained, repayment was immediate and often goods and services extended would be compensated by money. A village saying goes, 'Some feel the debt, others do not.'

Political authority in the village was vested in the village council, freely elected by and responsible to the *baserritarak*. The village council also provided a forum in which disputes, complaints and ideas could be discussed by all adult villagers.

Rural life in Elgeta reflected a life in which all relationships were stable and personalized; where all men were equal and could be equally judged according to a specific set of values because all men believed in them. People moved in a world of serious, religious, just, moral and knowable human beings tied together in a series of balanced, personal relationships. Work, an inherent ability of all men, gave merit and prestige and was the basic source of honour. For honourable men, the spoken word was like a legal document. There was little need for recourse to an outside, alien bureaucracy to formalize treaties between individuals. Above all, since each *baserritar* paid his own way, rural life represented the ideal in which each person by virtue of being a *baserritar* was a respected, independent member of the wider community. It was a society in which politically and socially equal individuals arrived at wider decisions by means of consensus, in which withdrawal of cooperation was the only means of social sanction. This was the shared ideological framework in which social life was acted out.

Rural reality

While Elgeta's *baserritarak* argued that this was the manner in which people perceived the ties and values governing rural society, they were also quick to point out that on the ground life was never quite so egalitarian or harmonious. Although ideology was imposed upon reality, the two coexisted uncomfortably.

To begin with, in 1900 of the 109 farmsteads in Elgeta 25% were owner-occupied and 75% were worked by tenant farmers. It was only in the 1960s that the majority of farmsteads still functioning were owned by those who worked them. Although most tenants did own some small parcels of land, most were impoverished. The family diet was based on corn, broad beans, chestnuts, pulses and pork fat. Wheat was cultivated, but most of the crop went to pay the landlord, the barber and the priests. Bread was made out of rye or corn meal, regarded as inferior cereals. Oil and sugar were rare in the family diet, since few had money to purchase such items. Indeed, few handled much cash at all. For most families shoes were a luxury and leather shoes unknown. The one or two pairs of shoes owned by a family would usually be worn only to attend Church. Family members would share the shoes by attending Mass in rotation.

Most *baserritarak* stated that a major cause of poverty on the farmsteads was overpopulation. Seven to nine children was not uncommon. The supply of labour was abundant; but land was acutely scarce. Although means of birth control and abortion were known, to practise either was condemned by the Church. If measures to prevent conception were employed, it had to be confessed to the priests who in turn warned the offenders that they had placed themselves in a state of moral danger. While the Basques were profoundly religious, simultaneously they had a keen awareness of the worldly attributes of the clergy. One farmer in his late seventies reminisced:

> Here it was the priests who gave the orders. Before if a family had nine children whom they couldn't support – everyone was hungry – and the tenth died in childbirth, the priest and the doctor would bring the bereaved family an orphan to care for. They would say, 'God wanted you to have a child – and now you have one to make up for your loss.' The priest and the doctor simply brought the child to the house. Most people didn't want the child, but they had no choice. Before there were a lot of illegitimate babies so there were a lot of orphans. For the priests to have children was like a factory – many children, many baptisms, many burials. Since you had to pay for all this, for the priests it meant a lot of money. The priests would deny this, but many *baserritarak* saw it this way – having babies was a business for the priests to earn money.

In Elgeta the various means of draining excess labour away from the farms were not regarded as sufficient. Some people found employment in road construction and related, public endeavours. Some children were given for adoption to childless families. Others went into service with richer farmers or in the cities. Many young men abandoned the village entirely and migrated to the cities or to the Americas.

The landowners, in turn, were of two distinct types. The majority of the farmsteads were the property of four families all of whom were titled and none of whom lived in the village. These families had large landholdings throughout the Basque provinces. One of these families, Arteaga de Ayala, owned over twenty-five farmsteads in the village. These families rarely, if ever, came to Elgeta. Their interests were overseen by professional administrators who occasionally did live in Elgeta, but who more often lived in Vergara or Elorrio. The contacts between the administrators and the tenant farmers were minimal and usually consisted of biennial visits to collect rent.

The tenants knew very little about the absentee landlords besides their names and, frequently, not even that. To the villagers these were rich, powerful people who lived in Vergara or San Sebastian or Madrid (no one was ever really sure) and had titles. When asked about their political affiliation most *baserritarak* whose memory goes back to the early 1900s insisted they were Carlists. One informant in reply to my inevitable question about the politics of the landlords finally said in exasperation, 'You don't have to repeat that question all the time! In those times to be rich and to be Carlist were the same thing. All rich people were Carlists. All Carlists were rich!'

In spite of adamantly held local opinion, however, it is likely that these absentee landlords, unlike the local landowners, were not Carlists, but liberals. Most of the *baserriak* that, for instance, Arteaga de Ayala owned in Elgeta were acquired shortly after the Second Carlist War. Arteaga de Ayala had lent a considerable sum of money to the *ayuntamiento* during the Carlist War. Because the *ayuntamiento* went bankrupt in the process of the war, he was compensated with land instead of money. In contrast, most Carlists who lent money to the *ayuntamientos* were never compensated. Certainly in the first twenty years of the 1900s Elgeta contained an unexpected number of liberal voters. Most of these liberals were tenant farmers on the farmsteads of the absentee landlords.

The annual rent tenants paid was calculated in fixed quantities of *fanegas* (45 kg) of wheat and was proportional to the size of the farmstead. The amount of wheat paid did not vary with the success of the harvest. In general rent took almost the entire wheat crop. When the harvest fell below that required for rent, payments in wheat were supplemented with other food crops – usually pulses or corn.

From around 1910 onwards the industries in the towns near Elgeta, especially Eibar, began to expand rapidly. With this expansion the absentee landlords began to sell off their land holdings since investment in industry was more profitable than investment in agriculture. The land was generally bought by the tenants at prices considered reasonable. In fact it was only the tenants who were serious potential buyers, since all ready capital tended to go into industry rather than agriculture. The tenants borrowed money from family members and the wealthier Elgeta farmers at interest and usually took years to repay. One farmer told me that his father bought his *baserria* in 1910 and took forty years to repay his debts. From this period onward the absentee landlords steadily unloaded their economic interests in Elgeta until in 1975 there were only seven farmsteads still owned by this group.

The absentee landlords intruded only minimally into the daily life of the village and had little interest in Elgeta besides collecting their rents and on occasion collecting votes. The villagers in turn paid them little heed.

The second type of landowner had a far greater impact on village affairs. These were the local landowners who participated in every aspect of village life. The majority of these landowners were probably only slightly more prosperous than their tenant counterparts. But there were five landowning families who were considered the *caciques* or *jauntxoak* of the village. Not all wealthy farmers were regarded as *jauntxoak*; only those who actively transformed their control over economic resources into political power through economic coercion. The widely used term *jauntxo* is itself indicative. The term is composed of the word *jauna*, which is the equivalent of the Spanish word *Don*, plus the diminutive *-txo*. The respected personalities of the village – the doctor, priests, teachers, i.e. educated people – were referred to as *jauna*. The rich local landowners on the other hand were generally called *jauntxo*. The term was derogatory. To the villagers these were people who claimed the right to be *jauna*, but to whom respect and, hence, the title of respect was denied. They were perceived as individuals who attempted to dominate others and, thus, broke the rules governing acceptable social exchange. In a sense the *jauntxoak* occupied the same position later filled by Elgeta's industrialists.

The *jauntxoak* and wealthy farmers in general did not display a lifestyle that was conspicuously different from other *baserritarak*. Their farmsteads were more solidly built, better maintained and usually had a fine pair of draught oxen in addition to other livestock. But the *jauntxoak* did own considerably more land – usually from 30 to 80 hectares – upon which were several other farmsteads, in general from one to five, run by tenant farmers. The *jauntxoak*, like most of Elgeta's farmers, were uneducated, illiterate, spoke only Euskera and dressed in a style indistinguishable from other farmers.

The sources of power of the *jauntxoak* were in the main two. One was the network of debt relations which they could establish with the more impoverished *baserritarak*. The other was the network of personal connections which these people had with local and non-local political and religious authorities.

The creditor–debtor relations established were generally of three types. First, as mentioned previously, most of the *baserritarak* of Elgeta were poor and participated only marginally in a monetary economy. Since they had little, if any, cash, there were many occasions such as marriage, inheritance settlements, road building and, most importantly, after 1910 the purchase of land, which forced the *baserritarak* to seek loans. As a rule only the *jauntxoak* had surplus capital to utilize in lending. The loans were called *hipotecas*. Generally in return for a *hipoteca*, the borrower would put up some land, usually mountain land, as security. Failing land, the borrower would pledge a specific term of services. The loan carried an interest of 4% annually which was paid each year as long as the debt was outstanding. Repayment of capital could either be on fixed terms, say five years, or more commonly on indefinite terms. Both the lending of money and the terms of its repayment were always officially notarized. The vast majority of small farmsteads had *hipotecas* held on indefinite terms. If the capital was repayable on indefinite terms, then the lender had the right – rarely exercised – to foreclose at short notice.

While the debt remained outstanding, the bonds created between creditor and debtor enabled the former to mobilize the latter for labour during harvest time, for general services and for political support during elections. It was understood that after each favour granted – labour, services or votes – the outstanding debt was reduced. It must be stressed that these were not patron–client relationships. These creditor–debtor relations were never seen as permanent nor, from the debtor's viewpoint, even desirable. Their continued existence was dependent on the initial debt remaining unpaid. Furthermore, the rights which the *jauntxo* had to repayment of the loan were explicitly stated in the notarized, legal contract. The additional favours from debtor to creditor were extended because (1) they reduced the outstanding debt, and (2) they avoided the threat of foreclosure.

The links established between a *jauntxo* and those indebted to him were not utilized by the latter for other purposes, for example in dispute mediation or political protection. Nor did debtors attempt to cement the loyalties of creditors through pseudo-kinship. For instance, it was regarded as appropriate that godparents were chosen from close friends or immediate kin. In Elgeta I found no case of a godparent who came from a significantly higher economic stratum than the parents. Most *baserritarak* infinitely preferred to avoid unbalanced relationships altogether.

A second form of debt relationship was that between tenant and landlord. Most *jauntxoak* owned from one to five farmsteads which were rented out to tenants on the basis of a fixed annual rent and on inheritable contracts. Frequently, crops fell below that which was required for payment of rent and the maintenance of the resident domestic group. Usually in these cases the landlord would forego full payment of rent. Again the implicit relation of debt would be translated into favours by the tenant to the landlord – most often in the form of services and votes. Although by tradition tenancy contracts were inheritable, in fact the landlord was able to evict his tenants when he wished to.

Third, the most short-term form of unbalanced relations that the *jauntxoak* or indeed all wealthy farmers established took place in the context of the *auzoa* cooperation units. Ordinarily in any one *auzoa* it was only the wealthy farmers who had ploughs and oxen. These were freely lent to neighbours in accordance with the rules of *auzoa* amity. Moreover, the wealthy farmers were the only ones with sufficient land to rent out parcels of land for the most part at low rents. Hence, faced with a precarious economic position, most *baserritarak* felt forced to enter these unequal exchanges with the *jauntxoak*. Again the *jauntxoak* would translate these economic disparities into political favours.

It must be emphasized that these unequal relationships created by economic indebtedness were annulled the moment the debt was repaid. The *jauntxoak* constantly had to recreate these ties if they were to maintain their political supremacy within the village which in pragmatic terms meant control of the elected *ayuntamiento*. The need for the *jauntxoak* to maintain and preferably expand the pool of individuals indebted to them explains why the *jauntxoak* only very rarely demanded full repayment of outstanding debts or evicted their tenants. One *baserritar* who purchased his farmstead in 1921 with money loaned from a *jauntxo*, who was also the previous owner, reported:

If it had been up to Arana [the *jauntxo*], I would never have repaid the loan at all. Arana said to me, 'Well, the 4% interest you have to pay because that's the law. But the rest – well, times are difficult and you have better ways of spending the money than giving it to someone who doesn't need it.' I knew what he was up to. Every time there was an election, Arana would come to see me – 'to have a friendly conversation', he'd say. And every time I would always agree that the candidate that Arana supported was certainly the candidate I supported. What else could I say?

One day I thought, 'This debt is too much for me'. So I borrowed money from some relatives in Vergara and Bilbao. I went to Arana with the full amount I owed. Arana at first refused to accept it. 'Why don't you buy that nice piece of mountain land that's up for sale?' he said. 'You know you need it.' But I insisted. I never had a 'friendly' conversation with Arana again.

Similar cases of individuals raising money from sources outside the village in order to terminate debtor relations with individuals inside the village were frequent. The *jauntxoak* and in general all the wealthier farmers in Elgeta were Carlists.

In Elgeta there was no acceptance of subordination and in all these unequal relationships the etiquette of equality had to be exactly observed. The requests of a *jauntxo* for services or votes were rarely explicit. Rather people would enter casual discussions which roamed over most areas of village interest. Finally the discussion would turn to politics directly. The tenant or debtor would 'voluntarily' agree that the candidate of the *jauntxo* was probably the man to vote for. In spite of the casual appearance, a vote had been promised, and that promise was binding. Failure to keep it resulted in loss of honour and in life becoming notably more difficult. Yet the social form gave the impression that all agreements reached, all favours exchanged, occurred between equal neighbours in accordance with the rules of amity, free will and mutual respect.

However, despite their economic predominance, the *jauntxoak* were neither perceived as nor did they perceive themselves as forming a social élite. In spite of occasional intrusions into the courts to settle disputes, the property markets of Eibar and political circles of Vergara, their world was confined to Elgeta. They participated as equals in village social life. With the rest of the villagers, they would agree that the only social élite in Elgeta were the priests who, with their refined manners, sheltered lives and general air of social piety, were the ones who truly formed a class apart.

Carlists, liberals and peasants

The Second Carlist War (1872–76) marks the outer limits of the villagers' memory of their own history. At the time political control over the *ayuntamiento* was firmly in the hands of the more powerful local *baserritarak* who were Carlists and the absentee landlords who were liberals. These two groups had distinct interests in the *ayuntamiento*. For the local landowners political control meant control over municipal policies of taxation, budget expenditures and public works. The absentee landlords on the other hand had little interest in these local matters. For them it was political access to the Provincial Assembly that was important. According to the *fueros* then still in force, representatives to the Provincial Assembly were elected by the *ayuntamientos* from among their own number. Usually it was the *alcalde* (the mayor) who was so elected. During the 1860s and 1870s the *acalde* of Elgeta's municipal council was usually a liberal who was either a tenant of one of the absentee landlords or a propertied farmer (who may well have had Carlist sympathies) with substantial debts to these landlords.

The priests constituted another fundamental point in the axis that delimited the village's power élite. Despite the villagers' awareness of their worldly corruption, the priests were also ordained, had the power of absolution and performed the miracle of transforming wine and bread into the blood and body of Christ. The priests for their part enjoyed a close, mutually supportive relation with the *jauntxoak*. The *jauntxoak* were ardent Carlists and Carlism meant, among other things, defending the supremacy of the Catholic Church in defiance of liberal impiety. Furthermore, the *jauntxoak* were a profitable source of income for the priests, markedly worse off after the sale of church lands in the first half of the 19th century.

Defence of the *fueros* was supposed to be the main reason for the galvanization of the Basque peasantry to the Carlist cause. However, from the municipal records it is clear that few *baserritarak* in Elgeta knew much about the *fueros*. For them the Carlist War concerned a defence of the Church about which they did care and the reinstatement of common lands and the reduction of taxes about which they cared a lot. Most villagers were not very interested in politics, feeling that it was mainly a concern of priests and landlords. A *baserritar* usually voted the way his landlord did.

In July 1873 when the Carlist forces took control of Elgeta, the *alcalde*, José Maria Irarraga, a liberal, was forced to step down. A new *ayuntamiento* composed solely of Carlists was constituted. Throughout the remaining three years of the Carlist War, the *ayuntamiento* expended considerable effort in raising money for the cause. Taxes were raised, municipal lands sold, loans sought and public expenditure in other fields drastically cut. The village council also expropriated a portion of the wheat, corn, and bean crop to send to the Carlist troops.

Although most poorer farmers were apolitical or liberal voters, all between the ages of eighteen and forty were liable to conscription into the Carlist ranks. Few wanted to fight. The municipal archives record innumerable accounts of men attempting to avoid military service. However, economic pressure exerted by the *jauntxoak*, coupled to moral pressure from the priests, coaxed most to join.

In 1876 the Carlists lost the war. Elgeta was bankrupt and faced large war debts. The *ayuntamiento* sold most of the remaining municipal lands which were bought either by the few local Carlists who still had money or by the absentee landlords. Additional loans from the absentee landlords were also sought. Arteaga de Ayala lent 80,000 reales at 6% interest. These creditors were compensated during the later parts of the 1880s and early 1890s with the remnants of the municipal lands. Moreover, in 1876 the *fueros* were abolished and the village council was placed under the dictates of the central Spanish constitution.

The Carlist War and its aftermath resulted in several significant changes in the village. First, the economic differentials between wealthy and poor farmers (both tenant and small landholders) increased. The tenants had lost both livestock and the possibility of grazing on the now non-existent municipal lands. Several of the more fervent village Carlists had lost small fortunes because of their support for Carlism. Unlike the more powerful absentee landlords whose claims to compensation were backed by the new liberal regime, the local Carlists were never repaid. Hence, the economic penetration of the absentee landowners was expanded and consolidated. Because of this economic polarization, creditor–debtor relationships between the wealthy and the poor were markedly extended. Most *baserritarak* were in desperate need of extra land and loans.

The political situation in the village altered as well. With the abolition of the *fueros*, election to the provincial assemblies and the Madrid Cortes was no longer indirect, based on the *ayuntamientos*. These elections became direct and, hence, the interests of the absentee landowners in the village *ayuntamiento* diminished. Therefore, the *ayuntamiento*, elected by the villagers, remained until 1923 almost the exclusive preserve of the local Carlists. In 1910, of the fifty-six farmers who owned their farmsteads, forty-six were Carlists and the rest, usually the poorer ones, were either independents or liberals.

The political monopoly exercised by the Carlists was maintained by a combination of factors. First was the direct translation of hierarchical economic relations into votes. Second, only the wealthier farmers had the spare time to dedicate to political organization. Third, the position of the Carlists was also anchored in two fundamental supports which enabled them to link into the wider political world. One was the support of the priests and, therefore, that of the provincial ecclesiastical authorities. The other was the support of the secretary of the *ayuntamiento*, a post usually filled by a Basque born outside the village.

The role of the secretary has been crucial in village politics. The Carlists, along with most other *baserritarak*, were usually illiterate, often spoke Spanish poorly and had only a rudimentary knowledge of legal procedures and state bureaucracies. The secretary, however, was a political professional with a specialized education (*carrera de secretario*) which gave him experience in the official political and legal system. Backed by his personal contacts in the state bureaucracy and his literacy, the secretary was in many ways an independent political power in the village. He enabled the village *jauntxoak* and Carlists to function in the outside political world and, therefore, it was also he who often manipulated and provided leadership for the *jauntxoak*.

However, the Carlists never translated their political hold over Elgeta into participation in the broader political arena. The village Carlists were never integrated by a formal party structure. They worked entirely on the basis of informal, local *cuadrilla* organization. Therefore, in the elections for representatives to the provincial and Madrid parliaments, the absentee landowners once again came into their own. In these elections, however, the rate of abstention was extremely high – less than 50% of those eligible voted – and until 1918, of those who did vote, their votes were cast solidly behind the candidates backed by a large part of the Basque commercial bourgeoisie. These elections for the most part were run for and by outside interests largely unconnected to the village. With the elections themselves blatantly corrupt and the issues unrelated to local concerns, most villagers voted only if they were economically obliged to do so.

However, the forces that had already transformed much of the Basque country were approaching Elgeta. These forces of change would eventually result in a complete political inversion of village life.

The opening of choice: industrialization

With the First World War Eibar became a major centre for armament production. With the expansion of the Eibar arms industry, the tidal waves of industrial boom also flowed over Elgeta. The spread of industrialization brought relief to many villagers from the poverty that had been the mainstay of rural life. In the rapidly swelling nearby urban populations the Elgeta *baserritarak* found lucrative outlets for their dairy and garden products. Eibar's industries offered alternative employment to those whose labour was unwanted on the farmsteads.

From Elgeta several people went to Eibar to gain a technical training and returned to install small workshops in their farmsteads with money from savings or borrowed from relatives. These *tallers* employed a maximum of three to four workers, although there was one exception, and produced components for the Eibar arms industry. In the 1930s the two major village

factories, Modelo and Zabala Hermanos, started operations. Throughout, industrial production in the village remained fairly undiversified – in the main bedroom furniture and shotgun components.

The process of industrialization in Elgeta had two immediate and far-reaching social effects. One was a specific structural inversion in the Basque family. The other was the introduction of urban culture.

The system of inheritance practised among the rural population of Elgeta is central to understanding the effect of industrialization on the family unit. Throughout the Basque provinces the farmsteads are inherited by only one heir. Subdivision through multiple inheritance is thought economically suicidal. In Elgeta the person usually chosen to inherit was the eldest son. The term *mayorazgo* referred to the heir. In rural society the *mayorazgo* was publically more eminent that his siblings since only he was ensured of becoming a *baserritar*. From 1910, when educational opportunities became available in the Elgeta area, the younger, dispossessed sons were generally compensated with an education in which some useful trade was learned. For the vast majority of these younger sons, farming in Elgeta had ceased to be a possibility for gaining a livelihood. Traditionally, then, it was only the eldest son who enjoyed the prestige of being a full community member since only he would eventually participate fully in the village through his control over a farmstead. His unmarried brothers and sisters were viewed as social minors who upon ascendancy to adulthood and specifically marriage would leave the *baserri* and usually the village as well. It was these younger brothers, compensated for their fate by education and literacy, who fell into industrial endeavours.

Since eldest sons inherited the farms, they also stayed on them. None of the initiators of Elgeta's industries were eldest sons. Nor were any of them from the families of the richer *baserritarak*, although for different reasons. Almost without exception the founders of the village workshops were younger sons from poor farmsteads who left the farms early in life and went to Eibar for an education either in a technical school or as an apprentice. After completing their education, they returned to Elgeta with some savings and experience. They either set up workshops or, failing that, went to work in one of the village factories.

Although the factories and workshops prospered, the farms did not. Moreover, the younger sons became the vehicle for new values, such as money and urban refinement, and the reinforcement of others, such as literacy. By their ability to exploit the new economic niche opened by industrialization – an industrialization that was in part paid for by the decapitalization of the countryside – Elgeta's ascending industrial entrepreneurs reversed the relations that had hitherto governed the roles of younger and eldest sons. It was the eldest sons, tied to the *baserriak*, often illiterate and speaking only Euskera, who came to be became regarded as disadvantaged, culturally stigmatised and unsuitable as marriage partners. The prestige linked to the farmstead dwindled in favour of the economic and social benefits derived from urban work and living. This process, launched in the first decades of this century, has continued to date.

While industrialization had subversive effects on family structure, it had equally subversive effects on Euskera and rural culture.

One of the major barriers the villagers saw in obtaining urban success was their lack of fluency in Spanish. Spanish was the language of *kalea* (the street), culture and literacy. Euskera was equated with the farmstead, rusticity and cows, items not yet made fashionable by nationalist sentiment. For men of ambition, Spanish was essential since all aspects of business and industry, even though solely in Basque ownership, were conducted in Spanish. For women, fluency in the language implied the possibility of entry into the social life of the nearby towns with the connected possibility of marriage to an urbanite. Such a marriage brought status as well as a comfortable lifestyle and was regarded as vastly preferable to the common drudgery of being a farmer's wife. Both men and women made considerable efforts to master this symbol of urban belonging. Often in the afternoons after the midday meal groups of women would stroll along the village roads practising Spanish and roaring with laughter at their frequent errors. The men approached the language more shyly. Usually in the company of individuals speaking Spanish, they would be silent, fearing embarrassment.

Although Basque domestic life continued in Euskera, in the public domain Elgeta became culturally polarized with the rural *baserriak* managed in Euskera facing the urban flats and factories managed in Spanish. However, it must be stressed that the opposition was not between Basque culture and Spanish culture. This argument of urban Basque nationalists did not reflect the view of the rural population. Instead it was the opposition between Basque rural culture and Basque urban culture – the former being steadily abandoned and the latter gaining in precedence. The remnants of rural culture and the beginnings of urban culture coexisted in the village. At times they mixed, at times clashed; but each was built up from a distinct base.

While rural culture was autochthonous to the village, urban culture was alien, emanating from the big cities and far-reaching in scale. It involved, among other things, knowledge of specific bureaucratic and institutional formations, technical skills, literacy, money and political parties.

But the transition from rural to urban was by no means complete. Typically most of the new village urbanites felt distinctly ill at ease in the cities. Not only were the social codes of the cities different, but the class system in San Sebastian or Bilbao slotted the villagers into its lowest ranks. While in Elgeta they were people of *la calle* – and often regarded as a type of locally raised intelligentsia – in the cities the village urbanites were still peasants.

The opportunities opened up by industrialization during the first three decades of the century affected the various sectors of the village population in different ways. With the tremendous profitability of urban investment the absentee landlords began to change over into purely industrial interests and started to sell their landholdings in Elgeta. This land was usually purchased by their increasingly prosperous tenants. In addition, the younger sons of the *jauntxoak* and wealthier farmers, also disinherited from their farms, went to the cities and with the capital given them as compensation, the *dote*, invested in urban property. Investment capital was also raised by the sale of land which again tended to be bought by tenant farmers. Simultaneously several of Elgeta's wealthy farmers, while remaining illiterate and temporarily on the farmsteads, also invested in urban enterprises. Usually these urban investments signalled the first step in a process whereby most of the younger sons of the wealthy landowners in addition to some of the landowners themselves would abandon the village entirely in order to live in the cities.

Very critically, the spread of industrialization was concomitant with the spread of educational opportunities. During my period in Elgeta, many villagers insisted, 'Elgeta has always been very revolutionary!' They were specifically referring to the new attitudes that emerged – attitudes that challenged traditional hierarchies – as people acquired education. As contacts with nearby urban centres increased, many villagers began to equate their inability to take full control over their lives with their illiteracy and lack of education. Pressure mounted on the *ayuntamiento* to improve the quality of education available in the village. One farmer, in his late eighties, stated, 'The priests didn't want to teach the poor because then the poor would know as much as the priests did. Also when everyone was ignorant, no one could dispute what the *jauntxoak* said and that's how they wanted it to remain.' Many of the older villagers argued that the rebellion started when a socially committed order of friars took over the Church school in 1901. The education they provided was judged extremely good. Although most children attended only during the slack winter months, nonetheless people learned to read, write and to gain knowledge about the world outside the village. Popular pressure on the *ayuntamiento* finally resulted in the establishment of a state school at the end of the First World War.

As important as the improvements in village schools, was the founding of the *Escuela de Armería* (The Armament School) by the socialists in Eibar. Many villages, Elgeta included, paid a fixed sum to enable village members to attend the school free. Most of the poorer landowners and tenant farmers, unable to compensate dispossessed sons with capital, sent them instead to the *Escuela de Armería* to learn a trade. It was these people who provided the seeds from which Elgeta's industry grew.

The role of the village professionals, *los señores de carrera*, was also crucial. As mentioned previously, *los señores de carrera* were a parallel élite opposed in the villagers' minds to the economic and political élite of the landowners. While the landowners imposed subordination, the professionals provided a model for liberation. Respected and admired by *jauntxoak* and tenants alike, the professionals were physical proof that through education alone, one could become a full and independent human being. These professionals – the doctor, chemist and teachers, most of whom were Basques from small rural villages – actively sided with the villagers in their demands for educational improvements.

In summary, the first thirty years of the 1900s saw fundamental changes in the village. Industrialization began to penetrate the village and brought with it relative prosperity. Patterns of land tenure changed. Landlords – both absentee and local – began to sell land and the tenant farmers began to buy it. The benefits of industrialization also included opportunities for younger sons to gain technical skills which they frequently used to open workshops in Elgeta itself. The urbanization of the village commenced. Moreover, in Elgeta the poorer villagers began to acquire two new basic skills: Spanish and literacy. However, as a whole education was a means of compensating those who would not inherit the farmsteads. Hence, those in the 'privileged' position of *mayorazgos* (farm inheritors) tended to remain illiterate and monolingual, while the landless became literate and Hispanicized.

From about 1910 onwards the links established between the urban centres and the newly emerging village urbanites provided channels for new political doctrines and the sentiments to enter into the village. Eibar until the civil war was one of the key centres in the Basque provinces for socialism, ardent republicanism and the more recent ideology of Basque nationalism. In contrast Vergara remained largely the domain of Carlists. While the new Elgeta urbanites looked to Eibar for their economic and political inspiration, the land *mayorazgos* and *jauntxoak* looked to Vergara.

Choosing Basque nationalism (*1918–31*)

The changes accompanying industrialization took time to make a noticeable impact on village political life. The *ayuntamiento* continued to be controlled by the Carlists. With every election the local landlords went from house to house collecting votes from those indebted to them. However, the mechanisms of control exercised by Elgeta's traditional hierarchy had already been severely eroded by the growing economic independence of the villagers. All that was required for the final rupture was time and appropriate circumstances.

The period from 1923 to 1930 corresponded to the Primo de Rivera dictatorship. Elections to the village council were suspended, like all other elections, and the *ayuntamiento* was appointed directly from San Sebastian. However, few villagers described these years as politically repressive. Instead they functioned as a gestation period for a new political correlation.

The social transformation of the village was expressed in new political currents. Several of the budding Elgeta industrialists, like the five Erostarbe brothers, founders of the furniture factory, the Zabala brothers, founders of the shotgun factor, some shopkeepers, many of the skilled factory workers and two or three *baserritarak* adopted republican or socialist sympathies often because of their association with Eibar. For many of the emerging village capitalists socialism and republicanism were the political creeds of educated urbanites and, therefore, served as symbols of their newfound urban identity. Many farmers dismissed these recent converts by saying, as in one example, 'Those who left the *pueblo* upon their return always felt that they knew more than the rest. They thought now that they were socialists, they were more cultured [*culto*].' With reference to Eibar and its subversive effects, one Carlist *concejal* is quoted in the municipal archives as saying, 'If you took my advice, money should be spent building a high wall around Elgeta to protect it from these reds and anarchists!'

The ideology that was to dominate the village throughout the Second Republic began to make its modest appearance in 1916. Until the end of the 1910s Basque nationalism in Guipúzcoa was largely confined to the big cities. Although a political force in Eibar and to a lesser extent Vergara, the PNV had made few inroads into the rural areas. In part this was due to the system of local *caciquismo*. There was simply no way in which the PNV could openly mobilize an active clientele. But as importantly, failure to attract a rural audience was due to its 'Basque' ideology. In Elgeta farmers regarded their very Basqueness and lack of Spanish as handicaps not only in advancing themselves economically, but also in defending themselves from urban official bureaucracies staffed by Basques, but run in Spanish.

However, after the myth of the noble *baserritarak* had performed its mobilizing function in the cities, the clarion call of the PNV in the 1920s became that the land should belong to those who worked it. Many arrangements, from the extension of credit facilities to expropriation schemes, were proposed to enable tenants to purchase their farmsteads.

Despite its illegality during the Primo de Rivera years, the PNV mobilized considerable support in the rural areas by setting up mutual insurance schemes, consumer cooperatives and stressing the need for increased expenditure on public works such as road building and education. All these activities were publicised through public meetings and mobile libraries complete with educational and legal pamphlets. The PNV strongly attacked the socialists on the issue of religion and attacked the Carlists for their role in maintaining rural oppression. Both assaults found a fertile response among Elgeta's farmers.

The first official recruit to the PNV ranks from Elgeta was Daniel Tellería, a bricklayer, general handyman and shopkeeper. Tellería was also a member of the governing board of the Church school and was extremely active in agitating for better schools and roads. Tellería came into frequent contact with large numbers of the villagers through his work and used these occasions to spread his political views. In the process he mobilized a group of some fifteen villagers, several kin and others already in *cuadrilla* relations, into a political *cuadrilla*.

The PNV's initial social base in the village consisted of those *baserritarak* who had recently purchased their farmsteads, small landowners and those who had abandoned their farms for life in the urban nucleus, as was the case of Tellería himself. Indicative of this trend was the political affiliation of the village's forty largest taxpayers (*mayor contribuyentes*) in 1912 compared to 1923. (It should be noted that these lists, which were drawn up to establish who had the right to vote for representatives to the Senate, were not necessarily representative of the wealthiest individuals in the village. The most wealthy tended to be the most powerful and, thus, usually avoided paying their share of taxes.) In 1912 these 40 individuals consisted of 38 Carlists, 1 liberal who was the only local landowner rather than tenant of that persuasion, and 1 sympathizer of the PNV, a landowner whose brother was a PNV member in San Sebastian. In contrast, by 1923 these 40 *mayor contribuyentes* consisted of only 27 Carlists, 1 independent who owned a mill and wholesale business, and 12 PNV sympathizers. Of these 12, 10 were *baserritarak* who had bought their farms since 1912, 1 previously had been a Carlist and another owned a workshop in Elgeta. Nationalism quickly spread also to Elgeta's industrial artisans and growing urban population. The village Carlists scorned the nationalists as 'sons of the reds' and the few village socialists called them 'sons of the Vatican'.

While the PNV's social programme found favour among Elgeta's farmers, its cultural activities mobilized the youth. Performances of Basque singers, *bertsolaris*, rural sports, folk-dancing together with conferences on cultural themes, organized by the PNV, became the chief form of village amusement. Very importantly, nationalism was also fun.

The Second Republic

The Second Republic was declared on 14 April 1931. With the restoration of political liberties, political parties became extremely active through the Basque provinces. After seven years of gestation, the politicization of Elgeta was rapid. By the time of the first elections of 1931, the vast majority of adult men had affiliated into political parties. Like the broader political scene, the political coordinates of the village were triangular. They consisted of the Carlists, an informal alliance of republicans and socialists, and Basque nationalists. In 1931 their respective force in Elgeta was approximately 350 supporters of the PNV, 45 Carlists, 40 socialists, 25 republicans and 1 member of the Communist Party.

The Carlist support was organized by the Carlist *cuadrilla*. This *cuadrilla* consisted of four important landowners: Juan Arana, Juan José Aranceta, Patxi Albistegui, Cesario Eguren and his son, Casimiro. In addition, Patxi Aranzabel, who was the *concejal* in charge of public works in Elgeta, was also part of the *cuadrilla* as were the Elcoro brothers, the owners of Elgeta's first factory, Tornillos Elcoro. Arana, Aranceta and Albistegui each had more than seventy hectares of land and large networks of debtor–creditor relations. Cesario Eguren had been mayor of Elgeta for many years and had developed important contacts with ecclesiastical and state authorities. Aranzabel had been in the *ayuntamiento* during the 1920s. His considerable influence was due to his forceful, reassuring personality and his position as head of municipal public works, a position he used generously as a patronage resource. The Elcoros were fervent Carlists principally because they were fervent Catholics.

The Elgeta Carlists, unlike other political groupings, organized their activities solely through traditional patterns based on personal, informal links. No official Carlist organization was ever established in the village. The Carlists never held open meetings, public rallies or conferences. Their links to the wider Carlist political apparatus also operated informally.

The main support for the Carlists came from the richer farmers and *mayorazgos*. During the Second Republic the Carlist cause attracted very few young people. Most village Carlists were over forty years old. During election time the Carlists continued very much as they had previously. Votes were bought and those in debtor relations 'influenced'.

The village republicans and socialists on the other hand became formally organized immediately. A *Centro Republicano* which was tied to the *Casa del Pueblo* in Eibar opened in 1931. The *centro* functioned as a meeting place for the village socialists/republicans and was always well equipped with the latest political tracts. As mentioned previously, there were some sixty-five individuals in Elgeta with republican or socialist sympathies. The vast majority were urban residents and young – very few were above thirty years of age. Occupationally, the majority were part of Elgeta's emerging industrial sector.

In 1932 the village nationalists opened a *batzoki*, a local branch of the PNV. The internal organization of the *batzoki* is noteworthy. All *batzoki* members formed a general assembly which was the ultimate authority. Elected officers, who could not succeed themselves in office, had only administrative duties and no power of decision. No policy of the PNV executive in San Sebastian would be implemented by the *batzoki* until it gained majority approval by the *batzoki* members. A local branch of the

PNV's agricultural organization, the Euzko Nekazarien Bazkuna (Basque Agricultural Association) and a local branch of the nationalists' trade union, the Solidaridad de Trabajadores Vascos, opened the same year. By 1933 more than 300 villagers were members of one or more of these Basque nationalist organizations.

The increased prosperity of the previous twenty years had helped to break the political links between many villagers and the Carlists by severing the economic ties between them. This is one factor which explains why the villagers were able to exercise political choice. The 'social programme' of the PNV which many *baserritarak* credit for enabling them to purchase land was a major reason why many villagers chose Basque nationalism. But additionally, there was a strong attraction for the ideology of Basque nationalism – at least for the ideology as understood in Elgeta.

The villagers themselves say that they sympathised immediately with the PNV because the party articulated politically that which they had always felt to be the case morally. Or, as one early PNV supporter told me, 'What the PNV thought was right and what it wanted for Euzkadi was the same as what we thought was right and what we wanted for Elgeta.' Many villagers found three ideological aspects of the PNV's platform particularly appealing. First, the PNV attacked the Madrid government not only because it was corrupt and impotent, but also because it represented rule by outsiders who were unresponsive to local interests. Second, the PNV attacked the hold of the rural *jauntxoak* over the peasantry because rule from above was as repugnant as rule from outside. Third, the PNV was the only party that defended *real* Basque values: the dignity of work, religion, honesty, egalitarianism and individual autonomy.

Importantly, however, the Elgeta nationalists did not relate these ideological points to a wider Basque 'national' context. Instead they were modified to fit local concerns. Indicative of this localist interpretation of the nationalist message was the agitated reply of a PNV supporter to one of my questions. The question concerned whether my informant preferred rule by Basques in San Sebastian to rule by Spaniards in Madrid.

> *Coño*! Haven't you heard anything I've been saying? In those days we were fighting *against* Basques in San Sebastian. Where do you think the people who would come here at election times to help the *jauntxos* influence votes lived? They didn't live in Madrid and they weren't Spaniards. The *jauntxoak* controlled Elgeta because people in the provincial government helped them control Elgeta. That's what the PNV was fighting against also. We joined the PNV because it defended the right of the *pueblo* to rule itself.

For Elgeta nationalists the primary focus of political loyalty remained in the *pueblo* of Elgeta. Loyalty to the wider concept of the *pueblo* of Euzkadi was not regarded as conflicting with or superseding loyalty to Elgeta. It merely seemed very remote.

The local concept of the *pueblo* pre-dated the entry of nationalism into Elgeta. But the force behind the concept had been confined to a moral drive to make individual behaviour conform to local norms. One of the chief effects of Basque nationalism in the village was the transformation of the *pueblo* into an operational entity that could be mobilized for concrete aims. Nationalism was seen and used primarily as an organizational vehicle on the local – rather than 'national' – level. The main aim the village nationalists themselves had in mind was the dismantling of the political monopoly of the Carlists which rested on unequal economic exchanges.

For example, the political bonds formed by common affiliation to nationalism replaced those of *auzoa* relationships in the formation of cooperating units during the agricultural cycle whenever the *auzoa* relationships involved unequal exchange. Rather than borrow, say, oxen from a Carlist who lived in the next farmstead, a peasant would now borrow them from another PNV member who might live in a distant *auzoa*. Money to pay debts or compensate disinherited siblings would likewise be raised through the *batzoki* (the local PNV branch) rather than through local wealthy landowners. The records in Vergara show that economic transactions, i.e. loans, between the wealthy Carlists of Elgeta and the small landholders and tenants had almost ceased by 1933 despite the sharp increase in land purchases during this period.

In Bilbao, Basque nationalists perceived themselves trapped between the Basque industrial oligarchy and the Spanish immigrant workers – two forces which the nationalist ideology depicted as immoral and anti-Basque. The nationalist *pueblo* in Elgeta equally saw itself caught between two morally negative poles. On the one hand were the Carlists who were Basques, rural and religious; but also manipulative, secretive and hierarchical. On the other were the socialists and republicans who were Basques and egalitarian; but urban and atheist. Although the Basque nationalists saw their principal political opponents as the Carlist *jauntxoak*, a major point of conflict – religion – effectively inhibited cooperation between the nationalists and socialists. The only instances of violence during this period took place between the socialists and Basque nationalists. However, neither people nor property suffered injury; except for the occasion when the socialists attempted to burn down one of the village churches (the hermitage of San Roque) in 1934.

The presence of Elgeta's *señores de carrera* inside party ranks added intellectual weight in any ideological or political confrontation. The opinion of one professional could only be effectively counteracted by the opinion of another. Those professionals resident in Elgeta during the Second Republic had differing political sympathies. The doctor tended toward Carlism, the chemist, a Basque from Bermeo, was nationalist. (When the Franco forces entered Elgeta during the civil war, the chemist was accused of poisoning the water and sent to jail.) Both state teachers had republican sympathies. Two of the village priests (the parish priest and a coadjunct) were Basque nationalists. The third priest, a coadjunct, was a fanatical Carlist. These individuals were expected to articulate political debate. The following case is illustrative.

One of the state teachers was a man aged fifty-five (in 1931) who was born outside the Basque provinces. The state school had few pupils at the time since most of the Basques sent their children to the Church school. Only the republicans and socialists sent their children to the *nacional*. In 1932 this teacher wrote an article in one of the major newspapers defending the theory of evolution. The combined republican forces of Elgeta were very proud of him. He soon became the leader of the socialists/republicans in the village. The teacher received a very strong reprimand from the Church. However, although the teacher's arguments were certainly sinful, this was not sufficient to prove in village eyes that they were also wrong. Therefore, the village nationalists recruited *gente culta* (cultured people) – doctors, lawyers, engineers – from Vergara to give lectures in Elgeta demonstrating in great scientific detail that the theory of man's descent from monkeys was nonsense. Many nationalists wanted to fire the teacher, but typically no actual showdown ever occurred.

The role of the village priests was also important both as active participants and as focal points of debate. Don Felipe, the parish priest and ardent nationalist, wrote articles in Euskera for various magazines and, hence, gained considerable influence on village opinion. The priests as a whole were vehemently opposed to the socialists accusing them of, among other things, sexual immorality. The socialists were equally forceful in their counter-attack. One village socialist described them: 'The priests at that time lived extremely well. They said mass, went to funerals, took walks in the countryside and took siestas. If they came to a *baserri* to give benediction for the land, the *baserritar* had always to give them a chicken or some eggs.' The nationalists' attitudes to the priests were ambivalent. As one nationalist told me when I was pressing him on the subject, 'I don't really like to talk about or criticise the priests. In the end the priests are always right even when they are totally wrong.'

Elections

Surrounded by a barrage of political rallies and meetings, the municipal elections, held every two years during the Republic, were very passionate affairs. The *ayuntamiento* consisted of nine elected *concejales* who among them elected the major from their number. Voting was theoretically by secret ballot. Each party drew up an electoral list of six candidates and each voter had four votes. When it came to electioneering, the village Basques, like other Spanish citizens, were adept strategists.

These elections put into relief the personalized nature of the political groupings in the village all of which operated through *cuadrillas*. Each party would attempt to achieve what was called a *cupo*. A *cupo* consisted of distributing the votes in such a manner that all six candidates on the electoral list would be elected. In the required calculations, it was crucial to know exactly who would vote for the party's list. Each person who promised a vote for a specific list was instructed exactly how to distribute his four votes among the six candidates. The risk was that, with all votes equally distributed among a certain number of candidates, any unexpected abstentions or defections could mean that candidates who otherwise would have been safely elected were not elected.

Although all ballot papers were supposed to be exactly similar, in fact each party had papers printed up by different printers. A party's ballot papers could then be recognized because of the cautiously pre-planned irregularities – slightly different quality paper, different shades of white and so forth. This was necessary to ensure that each person who had promised a vote delivered it despite pressures from political competitors.

The Carlists, lacking youthful affiliates and a formal structure, confined their electoral activities to influencing votes. The nationalists and socialists littered the village plaza and bars with *ikurriñas* (Basque national flags), red banners and political propaganda of all sorts. While the elections were hard-fought, they were non-violent. The *trucos* (tricks), although strictly illegal, were a respected part of the election process.

On the day of the election each party set up a table in the election hall. The proceedings were presided over by the municipal judge. When a person entered to vote, usually with a ballot collected beforehand, the judge would loudly announce, 'So and so is about to vote!' All the parties would then reply, 'conforme!' (Agreed). If one person was not agreed, the ballot would be placed under the voting urn. If any irregularities were discovered in the ballot, these ballots also would be placed under the urn. In fact, since all ballot papers were irregular, only those persons suspected of changing their votes would be called into account by the betrayed party. When the polls closed at 4 o'clock, the party representatives would discuss whether or not these questionable votes should be accepted. Since everyone knew for whom these 'secret' votes had been cast, the trick was to find some sort of argument by which the votes of one's opponents would be discounted, but one's own included. The debates usually lasted well into the night.

From the first municipal elections in 1931 to the last one in 1936, the PNV never lost its political hegemony. In 1931 the newly elected village council consisted of two Carlists, one of whom was Felipe Elcoro. A member of the

Carlist *cuadrilla*, Elcoro was elected *alcalde* and remained *alcalde* throughout the Republic. Four were Basque nationalists and three republican/socialist. In subsequent village councils, in spite of shifting personnel, all had the same political composition. Since no one party had an absolute majority and an alliance between the Carlists and republicans over anything was an utter impossibility, the Basque nationalists, located at the pivotal point of the triangle, took full control over the *ayuntamiento*.

In the provincial and state elections the majority of the villagers supported the Basque nationalist candidate.

In summary, during its first period, Basque nationalism, aided by urbanization and the increased prosperity in the village, succeeded in breaking down the hierarchical relations that had hitherto existed in the village and that prevented villagers from exercising political choice. The PNV provided credit facilities and legal aid which enabled many *baserritarak* to buy their farmsteads. The PNV also provided the villagers with the technical means, e.g. oxen, farm equipment, which further eroded their reliance on the wealthy landowners. Basque nationalism gave the villagers the organizational means by which they could contest the political hegemony of these landowners. In concrete results this meant that by 1931 the village council was firmly in control of Basque nationalists, an ideology supported by the great majority of the villagers. It was also these villagers who felt themselves to be the *pueblo*, a moral community. Basque nationalism, although imported from the urban areas, was not imposed on the village. The *batzoki* was organized by the villagers and was totally autonomous within the wider party structure.

It is questionable to what degree the village nationalists supported the idea of independence – statehood – for Euzkadi. Most informants replied that they did want Basque independence, but few appeared particularly interested one way or the other. However, the symbols upon which the Basque nationalist argument is constructed are ambiguous. Arguably, the grass-roots strength of Basque nationalism during the Second Republic – as well as in the 1980s – relates more to the ability of the Basque nationalist message to be understood and to be used to organize and mobilize on various levels rather than to widespread and explicit agreement on the overarching goals of the Basque nationalist doctrine. Although the various levels of understanding and mobilization imply attachment to different political loyalties, these loyalties – because they possessed the same moral content – were viewed as reinforcing rather than conflicting with each other.

10

Hierarchy reimposed

Civil war

Civil war erupted on 18 July 1936. The villagers had little information about events and few realised how serious General Franco's insurgency was. After one month the Carlist *Requetés* (militias) from Navarra invaded Guipúzcoa. One column quickly overran Irun on the French border. Another column attacked Tolosa. In Elgeta rumours started to circulate about executions of PNV sympathizers carried out by the Navarrese.

During the first few months of the war with rumours thick and hard news sparse, people listened to their radios and waited. Work continued as normal on the farmsteads and in the factories. The village Carlists gave immediate support to Franco. Within the PNV ranks people were initially ambivalent. The Basque nationalists found both the Carlists and the republicans disagreeable allies.

The village Carlists held many secret meetings which, of course, became public knowledge the morning after. Publically they agitated for Franco and maintained close contact with Navarra. Clandestinely they began to distribute some light arms.

The loyalties of the socialists and the republicans were also never in doubt. They waited for orders and arms to come from the *Casa del Pueblo* in Eibar. The orders came, but the arms did not.

Similarly the PNV held meetings and was in touch with local PNV headquarters in Vergara. Initial doubts were dispelled by a radio communiqué. Euzkadi was to fight with the Republic. The Basque nationalist youth in the village were particularly anxious. The forces of General Mola, supported by *Requeté* militias, were advancing on Vergara. The loyalist youth of Elgeta and Vergara had been haphazardly organized into militias and were attempting to resist the onslaught. They lacked both arms and training and were steadily being pressed back.

By September General Mola had established the front in Vergara and the town was placed under Carlist control. Many people fled and headed towards Elgeta in carts, wagons and on foot loaded down with their removable possessions.

The Carlists of Elgeta were exceedingly nervous. Reports that Carlists were executing loyalists were mounting. Many village Carlists feared reprisals against them. However, at this stage of the war, the rules governing moral, personal relations between villagers still took precedence over political divisions. For instance, one day government orders arrived to arrest two village Carlist leaders. The orders were reluctantly carried out by the local PNV who placed the Carlists under a lax house arrest. Because of their increasing fears of reprisals, the two Carlists begged the PNV to help them escape to Vergara. The PNV complied with the request. The village Basque nationalists knew the men personally and did not want them harmed. The two were released and found lodging with a Carlist family in Vergara. However, the older of the two began to assist the Mola forces. He took small search parties into the mountains near Elgeta in order to acquaint them with the terrain. On one such reconnaissance mission he was caught by a socialist patrol. The Carlist was taken first to Eibar, where he was detained for two days, and then to a village 8 km away where he was executed. The Basque nationalists in Elgeta were appalled and disgusted by the execution.

By the end of September both the village republicans and the nationalists had started to receive some small arms, mainly pistols, shotguns and some repeating rifles. Under instructions from their respective headquarters, both groups had begun organizing themselves into militias. Although separately organized, the relationship between the two groups was good and they collaborated whenever needed. In Elgeta everyone more or less stayed put except for some twenty young men who volunteered to fight at the front.

The front came to Elgeta on 4 October 1936. At 8 o'clock in the morning the people of Elgeta, looking into the Vergara valley, watched as the *Requetés* set up cannons for an attack. Many of the villagers heard the first shots fired while they were attending Mass. After Mass people saw the National (Franco) red and yellow flag waving over one of the farmhouses in the Vergara valley. The assembled forces of the *Requetés* had begun a slow push up the Vergara valley towards Elgeta. The villagers were terrified. Everyone believed the stories of executions by the *Requetés*. Few villagers had arms with which to defend themselves. Frightened and bewildered, many villagers reacted by hanging large, white flags from the windows and balconies of their houses. The Basque forces, popularly called *gudaris*, were enraged at this gesture of surrender. People were commanded to remove the flags immediately.

Also on the morning of 4 October a PNV company from Vizcaya, Companía Erratia, came to Elgeta. Supported by the militias of Eibar, Vergara and Elgeta, the Companía Erratia commenced the counterattack at

5 o'clock in the afternoon. In the face of the attack, the insurgent troops divided. Some retreated down the hill to Vergara; but others surged up the mountain of Assensio directly overlooking Elgeta. Although there were many injured and dead in the attack, no one from Elgeta died. People regarded the retreat of the *Requetés* as a great victory. The bars and streets were filled with Basques wildly singing 'Euzko gudariak gara' (We are the Basque soldiers). On 4 October also arms – machine guns and rifles – finally arrived. People settled down and resumed work on the farmsteads.

But the front that was to last seven months had been established. The *Reguetés* were firmly entrenched on Mt. Assensio opposing the *gudaris* who were dug in on Mt. Intxorta. Elgeta was located directly beneath and between the two.

The villagers never lacked food. The farmstead provided the basis of self-sufficiency. Although food was rationed, supplies arrived from Bilbao and the rations were sufficient. But a perpetual stream of people flowed in from the big cities to the village trying to buy foodstuffs – eggs, milk, beans. Since the farmsteads were in full view of the Franco forces on Mt. Assensio and under constant fire, most work had to be done under the cover of fog, a frequent occurrence in Elgeta, or else at night. Most farmsteads between Vergara and the village nucleus were evacuated by order of the government. Taking their animals and farm tools people went to Elorrio and Bilbao. Many came to stay on the farms of Elgeta. Most industries, except for Tornillos Elcoro, closed down. The schools closed and the priests were recruited into the militias.

On 7 October the autonomous government of Euzkadi was proclaimed and José Antonio Aguirre was inaugurated as president. In Elgeta there were no celebrations, but a Mass was said. The front itself was stable. Armaments were improved with the arrival of cannons. The trenches were always manned and the soldiers rarely left the mountains. In spite of the constant exchanges of gunfire, few people died.

By November almost no young men remained in the village. All of them had joined the *gudaris*. Many families had refugees living with them. There were about fifty in all, among them entire families. The refugees lived off food distribution which they received free and the products of the farms, for which they were expected to pay or work.

Although the military and civilian leaders had forbidden the practice, soldiers frequently came from the front to the farms to demand food. Few *baserritarak* had means of self-defence and, therefore, they gave reluctantly. On 30 November news came to the village that several Elgeta youths had died during the fascist attack on Villareal in Alava.

During December the front was further reinforced. On the front there were four to five battalions, two of which were in the trenches and the rest held in reserve. The battalions were rotated every month or so and consisted of PNV, UGT (socialist) and CNT (anarchist) battalions.

On Christmas eve the two sides agreed to a two days' cease-fire. For these two days the guns were silent. The *gudaris* and fascists (as by now all the Franco troops were called) exchanged newspapers, wine, bread and cigarettes. Then the shooting started again. Christmas itself was not celebrated. People sent bread and special Christmas food to the young men stationed in their battalions. For most it was a depressing time.

Elgeta remained tense, but calm. Life was modified to fit the war. Social activities had largely ceased. People retreated into the privacy of their farmsteads. They did not go to the bars except hurriedly, almost secretly, to exchange news. Few people went to the political centres and no political meetings were held. If someone had a problem, for instance a cow that had been sold but not paid for, he bypassed the *ayuntamiento* and went directly to the Basque government, which offered help and support. Although the Carlist *alcalde*, Felipe Elcoro, remained in the village for the duration of the war, the *ayuntamiento* itself ceased to function.

There were several fascists (all Carlists by then were also called fascists) living in the village. Among them were the mayor, Felipe Elcoro, one *concejal* and several Carlist families. Because of the rumours of fascist atrocities, several fled to Vergara in fear of retaliation. However, village values remained intact. There were no violent incidents nor were there any detentions. The idea of personal violence remained repellent to the village Basques. The 'fascists' were simply ignored and ostracized.

On the front the situation continued much the same. Neither side could launch an attack since neither side had sufficient forces and, being winter, the weather was bad. However, rumours began that the fascists were preparing for an all-out attack. On the front cannons were beginning to be used and cannon attacks were occasionally directed on Elgeta from Vergara. But little damage was done and no one hurt. The people of the village had adapted. To them it was the front that was under attack, not the village.

During February more battalions came to the front from Bilbao. Rumours of an imminent attack became more prevalent and people began to worry. Along with rumours of attack came rumours of the barbarities committed by the Moors, the Moroccan soldiers fighting on the Franco side.

At the beginning of March after the winter snow had melted approximately 300 cannons were brought to Vergara. At the end of March an order came from the Basque government to evacuate Elgeta. In Durango the bombing had started and throughout the region aerial attacks were frequent. Elgeta remained quiet, but the evacuation to Vizcaya started. Women, children and, especially, livestock were taken to places of greater safety.

On the front the Basque forces had fifteen cannons. In order to resist an all-out attack, they waited for aeroplanes to arrive. The planes never came.

People started to panic. They feared aerial bombing, the Moors, and executions. Many villagers had heard that when the fascists entered a village, they brought with them a blacklist of those in the village who would be executed. Largely because of the rumours of rape, most of the remaining women were evacuated. Many men remained behind to work on the farms and provide some infrastructure for the coordination of the war. The local leaders of the PNV, socialists and republicans had left for areas of greater safety.

In March also the Moors arrived in Vergara. The fascist forces in random reconnaissance attacks started to test the defences of Elgeta.

The attack started on Tuesday 20 April in the early afternoon. There were nine aerial bombing raids by Heinkel bombers. Three civilians in Elgeta and numerous *gudaris* in the nearby trenches died. The church and many other buildings were destroyed. Despite heavy bombing, the front remained intact. By nightfall the bombing had stopped. The *gudaris* came down from their trenches into Elgeta. Many of them with *txistu* (a type of flute) and drums started to play Basque songs, especially 'Euzko Gudariak gara', over and over again. The front remained and it had been a victory of resistance. Throughout the village soldiers, *baserritarak* and women were overwhelmed with exhilaration.

The next day, Wednesday, Elgeta was covered by a thick fog. No planes could fly and the remaining livestock was evacuated.

On Thursday at around 8 o'clock in the morning a general attack was launched. Most of the 300 cannons in Vergara and more planes were used in intensive bombing. In one field just outside the village arches more than ninety bombs exploded. The noise of the explosions was deafening. The manoeuvres of the enemy were hidden behind the dense air thickened by smoke and dust. The Franco forces did not attempt to make a direct assault on the front line trenches on the summit of Mt. Intxorta. Instead, the bombing of Elgeta provided camouflage for an attack on a mountain behind Intxorta. The mountain was defended by an anarchist battalion who retreated immediately towards Bilbao. The Basque forces were surrounded. The *gudaris* fled their trenches on Mt. Intxorta. The front after seven months had broken. The attack by the Franco forces was led by the Moors. In Elgeta hysteria erupted. The remaining villagers desperately tried to hide or escape.

After gaining control of Intxorta, the Moors descended upon the farms lying at the base of the mountain. They entered one farmhouse and killed a PNV *concejal*. In the neighbouring farm, the Moors entered with hand grenades and killed the *baserritar* and some *gudaris* whom they found hiding. The Moors also went to one *baserri* on the fringe of the village nucleus and attempted to rape a 14-year-old girl (who now runs the village tobacco shop).

The father tried to defend his young daughter and was shot. He died instantly. The daughter ran to her father and put her arms around him in a futile attempt to protect him. The Moors fired again, shattering both the father's head and the daughter's hand. The daughter managed to escape to Vergara where she was put in a military hospital. Most of her fingers were amputated. The girl's mother was found hiding in the stables. The Moors first raped and then shot her through the back and shoulders. On most farms the Moors stole what they could and destroyed much of what they could not steal.

Elgeta had fallen. Upon his arrival in Elgeta one National officer was overheard telling a village Carlist who was overjoyed by the victory, '*Si hay alquien aquí par eliminar, ahora es el momento propicio para hacerlo*' (If there is someone here to eliminate, now is the proper time to do it). But by then most people had left the village. Those who remained, mainly the old, had to present themselves at the *ayuntamiento*. Political repression was to become a grim and routine way of life.

Upon the fall of Elgeta the majority of villagers were dispersed. Most young unmarried men were fighting. Koldo Aguirre, for example, the eldest son on the farmstead of Pagasta, was in a PNV battalion, Zugarieta, fighting near Durango. He was taken prisoner on 24 April 1937 and was sent to a concentration camp near Vitoria in the province of Alava where he stayed several months. From this camp he was conscripted into the Franco forces and made to serve in the National military stationed in Logroño. After he finished his term of service, Koldo expected to return to his *baserria* in Elgeta. Instead, he was conscripted again. This time he served with the infantry near Burgos. In all he served thirty-eight months in Franco's army. Looking back at his experiences in the war, Koldo said:

> Three times I was *quinto* [conscript]. Fighting for the PNV was not bad. I believed in what we were fighting for. But fighting for the fascists – well, that was different. I would have preferred to stay in the concentration camp. Every time we had to fire on the Republican troops, I always fired to miss. But I was very nervous. If an officer thought that you were not really fighting, he could shoot you then and there. People like me were very demoralized. Although we Basques were very Catholic and, I guess, conservative, the fascists always called us *rojos separatistas*. They ridiculed us. I still feel bitter about that. We were separatists, yes – but *rojos*, never.

Most married *baserritarak* had been evacuated shortly after their families. Felipa Elcoro (no relation to the mayor, Felipe Elcoro) had gone to live on a farm in Ceberío, a small village near Bilbao, in early March 1937. Modesto Elcoro, her husband, had stayed in Elgeta along with his elderly mother to work on his *baserri*. When the fall of Elgeta seemed certain, Modesto with seven other young men from the village (all PNV members) went with their livestock to Deusto near Bilbao. The field where the livestock was kept was near an airfield. A week after Modesto's arrival a bombing attack killed twenty-one cows and one boy. The group then took their cows to Santurce further to the west. As the front approached Ceberío, Felipa decided to join her husband in Santurce. They lived with a group of families in a makeshift refugee camp.

On 29 June with the fall of Bilbao, Modesto returned home on foot to Elgeta with his cows; Felipa returned a day later. On their return to the village, the family had to present themselves before the *Junta de Guerra Carlista* which was then the governing body of the village. The *Junta* demanded that the family give two cows to be distributed to the people who lost their cows in the Deusto bombing. It also demanded that Modesto work without pay on the reconstruction of Elgeta. General Franco had decreed that reconstruction work was to be carried out by the *contrarios*. Modesto's mother, who had remained on the *baserri* throughout, already worked on reconstruction as punishment for her family escaping Elgeta. Economically the family was broke, as were most villagers. They possessed only money issued by the Basque government, now worthless.

In September after a difficult delivery, Felipa gave birth to her first child. Some months afterwards Modesto's *quinto* was called up for mobilization into the fascist army. Since he was a farmer and sole support of his family, Modesto went to the military barracks to protest his mobilization. He expected to return to Elgeta that evening. Instead, he was ordered to San Sebastian where he did guard duty in the jails in which several young men from the village were imprisoned. From San Sebastian Modesto was sent to fight in Teruel near Valencia where he remained until the end of the war.

When Felipa gave birth to her second child, Modesto received leave to return temporarily to Elgeta. Whilst there, he was denounced as a PNV militant and a subversive. The official in charge of Modesto's case was a friend of a friend. At his trial the charges were dropped through lack of evidence and Modesto was sent back to Teruel. During his trial, however, Modesto inadvertently discovered who had denounced him. It was a village Carlist.

Aftermath of war

When the war ended in March 1939, church bells rang all day in Elgeta. A long pealing of bells accompanied every fascist victory. The final victory saw a great celebration in the village with a special Mass, a *romería* and a banquet. Liberation day was celebrated in Elgeta every year until 1969. It was a public holiday marked by street dancing, *pruebas de bueyes* (a type of bovine endurance test) and a *romería* to offer thanks to Elgeta's patron saint. Most people attended because they were afraid not to. Although they disliked what they saw as collaboration it was felt that very little was needed for a *denuncia*.

From the end of the civil war until 1945 a Basque resistance was organized clandestinely in Elgeta. Elgeta was particularly convenient for this purpose since no *guardia civiles* were stationed there. The meetings were held in the mountains and people would assemble in one of the village bars for a joint meal cum political meeting. Money was collected for those in jail, news was exchanged and the latest directives of the Basque government in exile discussed. When the Allied troops had reached Hendaye on the French border, Radio Euzkadi broadcast that the invasion of the Basque country was just days away. In the village a suppressed euphoria erupted. The Basque resistance in the village prepared to help the invasion although no one had any arms. Several of the village Carlists discussed fleeing to Madrid. People plotted, planned revenge on the hated local authorities, waited and speculated until it was obvious that no liberators would come.

With the Republican defeat every aspect of village life changed drastically. The village *jauntxoak*, the political bosses whose economic and political power had crumbled during the prior decades, were reimposed as Elgeta's power élite. They were the victors and, thus, the reapers of the spoils. But the source of power of this reestablished élite no longer depended on the careful nurturing of individual relations within the village. Their power was now backed by the new military regime. And it was absolute. Elgeta's new rulers were under no obligation to enter into reciprocal relation with the ruled.

On 17 May 1937 the *Junta de Guerra Carlista* was replaced by the first official *ayuntamiento* of the Franco period. Bartolo Elcoro, the younger brother of the former mayor, Felipe Elcoro, was appointed mayor by the military government of Guipúzcoa. Under Bartolo Elcoro were four *concejales*. These *concejales* were Francisco Albistequi, a Carlist and one of Elgeta's richest landowners, Juan Francisco Aranzabal, another Carlist landowner who remained in charge of public works, Juan José Aranceta, another Carlist landowner and uncle of Francisco Albistequi, and Francisco Elorriaga, another Carlist landowner. With the exception of Elorriaga, all these appointees to the new municipal council belonged to the Carlist *cuadrilla* of which Casimiro Eguren and Juan Arana were also outstanding members. They all spoke Euskera considerably better than Spanish. Francisco Albistequi spoke no Spanish at all.

Reinforcing this power élite were the *jefe local de movimiento*, the secretary of the *ayuntamiento* and the new parish priest.

The *jefe local de movimiento* was the local head of the FETS and JONS, Spain's only political party. The job of the *jefe local* was to provide the government with political reports on the villagers. All candidates to the municipal council were vetted by the civil governor on the basis of the political reports of the *jefe local*. In addition these reports were used to evaluate applications for a certificate of good conduct – a document required in order to obtain a passport, driving licence, permission to open a shop or construct a building, access to certain social benefits, employment in the public sector, a permit to carry a shotgun for hunting purposes and so forth. In short, the *jefe local* exercised tremendous power over the daily lives of the villagers. Casimiro Eguren held the post for ten years. He was followed in office by Bartolo Elcoro upon his retirement as mayor.

After the war the secretary of the *ayuntamiento* was Don Hilarion Dolara, a Basque from a small village in Guipúzcoa and a sympathizer of the Falange.

While the main coordinates of power centred on Bartolo Elcoro, the mayor, and Dolara, the secretary, informally supported by the local Carlist *cuadrilla* and formally by the official state apparatus on the local, provincial and national level, this new political arrangement was spiritually sanctioned by the new parish priest, Don José. Don José was a Carlist sympathizer and open supporter of the new regime. His sermons stressed the value of law and order and respect for political authority. In addition to Don José, Elgeta had the services of two more priests. Don Leocadio was a Carlist and Don Juan never appeared to express political preference of any sort.

Finally one other person was widely regarded as forming part of Elgeta's new ruling class. Juan Erostarbe, the owner of the Modelo furniture factory, was the richest industrialist in Elgeta. After Franco's victory Erostarbe gave up his socialist sympathies and became an ardent Falangist. Although not part of the Carlist *cuadrilla*, Erostarbe was a brother-in-law to the Elcoro brothers, Felipe and Bartolo, and succeeded the latter as *jefe local de movimiento*.

The new political institutions of Elgeta were, of course, anchored in Franco's constitutional changes, in particular, the Ley de Bases de Regimen Local de 17 Julio, 1945. This law established a municipal regime based on the 'organic representation' of the 'natural entities of social life'. These natural entities were the family, municipality and vertical trade unions. The *ayuntamiento* was, according to the new law, to be composed of the *alcalde* (mayor) and, in the case of Elgeta, six *concejales* divided into three *tercios* (thirds) corresponding to the three different spheres of organic representation. The family was represented by individuals elected by the heads of households, the vertical trade unions by individuals elected by the unions. The municipality was represented by individuals elected from among the economic, cultural and professional entities in the village.

The various laws which covered municipal organization were extremely complicated. With the possible exception of the secretary of the *ayuntamiento*, it would seem that no one in Elgeta actually knew who could vote or not vote in the various *tercios*, who could be candidates or what prior formalities had to be satisfied. Most villagers' attitude to the *ayuntamiento* was simply to boycott it.

With minor variations in organization and personnel, this political structure controlled village political life for the next twenty-five years. Those with privileged access could use their power freely with only scant reference to Franco's comprehensive laws. The villagers' constant fears of *denuncias* were sufficient to prevent any accusations of wrongdoing.

The villagers saw this political system as operating as an integrated whole. The following incident was reported by Luis Aguirre.

Before and after the war the priests gave the orders around here. And after the war they had declared that the *baserritarak* could do no work on Sundays except for things like feeding the cows – things that had to be done. Of course, this rule didn't apply to the workers in the factory. Juanito Erostarbe saw to that. The *amos* liked that the workers worked 7 days a week. And what the *amos* liked – the priests liked. But a system of mutual cooperation between the *baserritarak* continued after the war. Especially during harvest time there was no other way. Usually there were from 10 to 20 of us, also women, all working together. But unlike before the war when we also worked with the Carlists if they happened to live nearby, after the war we only worked with people we trusted – we worked with kin.

It was very important to have the timing right when we were harvesting. If we did it wrong, some fields would be reached when it was too late and the crop would rot. So – I think it was in the autumn of 1943 – there were 18 of us working. One Sunday we decided we had to bring in the wheat crop in one field and stack it before the wheat became over ripe.

We all got our tools and I had my harvester. We were going to a field near the cemetery. As I approached the field, I saw the municipal guard. I asked him, 'What are you doing here? Watching to see if anyone is trying to bring in the wheat?, The guard said, 'What me? no, no! I'm just looking around – I don't care about the harvesting.' So I went on. What a devil! Did he think I believed him – that fascist? Well I met a friend and told him about the guard. Then my friend went to talk to him and was told, 'What you do with your harvesting is your affair.'

So we all started to work – all 18 of us. When we had cut all the wheat and it was lying spread on the ground, the guard came rushing up. 'Stop!' he shouted, 'Stop!' And who was with him? Bartolo, the mayor. 'Stop that harvester – don't you know that you can't take in wheat on a Sunday?!' We all explained that, if that were the case, the guard should have told us – at any rate we couldn't stop now. If the rain came before the wheat was stacked, it would rot – the whole harvest ruined. Everyone was extremely angry. We were all shouting at the guard – especially the women.

Don José [the parish priest], when he heard all this made a formal *denuncia* against the 18 of us. Bartolo fined us 100 pts. each. The fine was made for 'threatening a municipal authority'. I was so angry that I went to see the Civil Governor. I didn't think he would see me, but he did. So I protested, 'This never happens to people who work in the factories. They are forced to work on Sundays!' The governor was smiling. In that office he was the *amo* of God. He said he understood, but the laws had to be obeyed and we would have to pay the fines. 100 pts. was a lot of money then. We were all poor. But priests are priests, Sundays are Sundays and fascists will always be fascists.

In the immediate postwar years public life in the village was shaped by the prohibitions of Euskera, requisitions, the reconstruction of the village and the dread of *denuncias*.

The prohibition on the public use of Euskera could not be enforced since many people spoke no other language. However, salutations in Euskera were effectively prohibited. Instead of saying *agur* or *gabon*, the villagers had to say *adiós* or *buenas noches*. All villagers with Basque first names had to register themselves with Spanish 'Christian' names. Especially resented was the fact that no Euskera could be used in any religious ceremonies.

But the requisitioning of farm produce was the most unpopular aspect of the new regime. Immediately after the takeover of Elgeta, all PNV sympathizers were punished by having two cows taken away. Juan Arana of the farmstead Arroaz and Casimiro Eguren were responsible for ensuring that these expropriations were carried out. The cows were meant to be redistributed to those families particularly hard hit by the war. However, many cows ended up in the stables of the farmstead Arroaz.

The *baserritarak* had to register their annual production with the *ayuntamiento*. The figures given would be checked by members of the Carlist *cuadrilla* who made frequent visits to the farmsteads. From this annual production a certain amount in kilos was allotted to each person in the household. The remainder had to be sold to the *ayuntamiento* at fixed prices roughly one half of market value. The proportion that went to the *ayuntamiento* was referred to as a *cupo*. For Luis Aguirre's farm, this amounted in an average year to 450 kg of wheat, 600 kg of potatoes, 350 kg of pulses and 5 kg of pork fat per pig. On Modesto Elcoro's farm, in 1943 the figures were 5 litres of milk per day, 250 kg of wheat, 400 kg of potatoes, 75 kg of pulses and 5 kg of pork fat per pig. The *cupo* constituted from one-third to half the annual production.

There is considerable dispute among the *baserritarak* over the destiny of the expropriated produce. But it would appear that from one-sixth to one-half was redistributed to the village through the rationing system. In Elgeta all food was rationed and goods purchased with ration coupons were considerably below market prices although higher than the prices given to the farmers. However, all my informants agreed that at least one half of the produce was sold directly onto the black market by Bartolo Elcoro, the mayor, who pocketed the proceeds. Generally at the end of the year most families went short of food and were hungry.

The punishment levied on those *baserritarak* who attempted to avoid paying their *cupos* was severe. One farmer, who was caught selling 10 litres of undeclared milk at 1.25 pesetas a litre, was fined 3,000 pesetas, a sum equivalent to the market price of three cows. In 1944 a group of twenty-five *baserritarak* protested and tried to withhold a portion of their produce. The mayor, backed by the provincial governor, retaliated by taking away their ration coupons. The protesters were therefore obliged to buy a range of needed items at prices four times higher than the ration price. In fact, the requisition system seems to have turned many of the local Carlists against the new government as well as against Elgeta's mayor.

At the end of the war Elgeta was declared part of the devastated regions. In 1940 an office was set up to direct the reconstruction of the village. This office was staffed by architects and engineers who lived in nearby towns and four local villagers under the charge of Francisco Aranzabal, the *concejal* responsible for public works. The municipal records do not mention the quantity of money allocated to or spent on the reconstruction of Elgeta. Many villagers insisted that a large percentage of these funds was siphoned off before reaching Elgeta and another portion was pocketed by Aranzabal, the *concejal* in charge. Nonetheless, the village was cleaned up, the town hall and church rebuilt and a series of apartment buildings constructed. The manual work was done by the *contrarios* – the losers of the war – who were not paid for their labour.

After the war village social life became totally private. The casual lending of sugar, salt, bread, oil and so forth ceased. The cooperating groups of *baserritarak* were no longer based on *auzo* (neighbourhood) relations. Instead they consisted of relatives and people tied by *cuadrilla* relations. The members of any one cooperating group were often dispersed throughout the entire municipality. The *cuadrillas* themselves became impermeable, and were seen as the only circle of individuals outside the immediate family within which there was no need to fear *chivatos* (police informers) and *denuncias*. The moral consensus of the village had been shattered.

Public politics no longer existed. All political activity – both official and clandestine – was organized behind the protective shield of the closed *cuadrillas*. Political conflict was never expressed openly. But it was manifested in disputes which on the surface were not directly political. The following incident is indicative. It began as a dispute over a farm road. The year was 1949 and the worst aspects of the war's aftermath were over. Food was ample and the requisitioning had stopped.

Bartolo Elcoro, the *alcalde*, wanted a road, linking a farmstead to the main street, removed so that some gardens could be built. Most *concejales* were opposed as, indeed, were most villagers. The road was essential to the economy of the farmstead involved. Bartolo proceeded regardless. The road was duly covered with trees and flower beds. However, undeterred, the farmer continued to use what had formerly been his road, trampling the rose bushes and tree seedlings in the process. Bartolo fined him 100 pesetas for trespassing. Since the matter had nothing directly to do with politics, some villagers saw an ideal opportunity to attack the mayor. Bartolo's popularity had steadily dwindled, even among members of the Carlist *cuadrilla*. The farmer was persuaded not to pay the fine. Instead, he took his case to court. At the preliminary hearing Bartolo, who had no legal right to remove the road, testified that there had never been a road there to begin with. To his astonishment, all the *concejales* whom Bartolo had called upon to testify on his behalf declared that there had indeed been a road.

A trial was set for San Sebastian. Since it was quite obvious that Bartolo would lose the case, the civil governor of Guipúzcoa dismissed him from his post as *alcalde* and appointed him *jefe local de movimiento* instead. The governor then sent a list of names to the *concejales* from which they were to elect Bartolo's successor. All the names on the list – drawn up, of course, by the *jefe local* (i.e. Bartolo) – were found unacceptable since they consisted of those who had been most active in the requisitioning. The various candidates for mayor were never officially rejected because they were politically undesirable. A non-political excuse was always found. The candidate was too old, too inexperienced, or, in one case, it was claimed that he had just died.

The *concejales* composed their own list of more moderate Carlists. After three months of haggling Francisco Elorriaga, who previously had been a *concejal*, was elected mayor, a post he held for the next twenty years. Elorriaga was considered a great improvement on the hated, authoritarian Bartolo. Although he was a Carlist and fervently anti-PNV, Elorriaga was regarded as more 'Basque'. Although wealthy he had not been viewed previously as a *jauntxo*. Moreover, Elorriaga was a *danzari* (dancer), a skill which brought him a certain popularity.

The personnel in power had changed somewhat. But the coordinates of power – the *alcalde* and secretary of the *ayuntamiento* supported spiritually by the parish priest, economically by the *jauntxoak* and politically by the *jefe local* – remained unaltered. Although these individuals were culturally Basque from rural stock, their sources and exercise of power broke all the village's moral ideas as to what constituted moral behaviour. They were judged illegitimate and rejected as anti-Basque.

However, as certain moral ideas and informal organizational mechanisms – coupled to wider economic and social changes – had eroded this illicit hierarchy previously they were to do so again.

11

Hierarchy dismantled

I have described Basque nationalism as founded on an ideology which views the social universe inside the Basque country as morally divided. This divide separates *abertzales* (patriots) or true Basques, defined as those who publicly and continually adhere to the political prescriptions contained within the symbols upon which the ideology is constructed, from *españolistas* or anti-Basques, defined as those whose behaviour (e.g. loyalties) breaches these prescriptions. This moral divide was reinforced by the creation – encouraged by the Basque ideology itself – of parallel institutions which gave the community of true Basques a largely self-contained social infrastructure. With the victory of Basque nationalism this infrastructure, although it remains exclusive, has, to a significant extent, been fused with the official institutions of the autonomous Basque country.

A similar process occurred in Elgeta. The moral system of Elgeta also saw the social universe in terms of a moral divide. Only those individuals who publicly adhered to local moral prescriptions were granted full membership in the moral community, the *pueblo*. Whereas the political prescriptions of the Basque nationalist community demand mobilization against the forces that threaten the community, equally the moral prescriptions of the *pueblo* led to a similar mobilization. Changes in the wider political and economic environment imposed on Elgeta official institutions that the *pueblo* judged illegitimate. In response the *pueblo* created a full set of parallel institutions that were sealed off and opposed to their official counterparts.

Questions immediately arise concerning the relationship between the moral self-image of the nationalist community and of the *pueblo* of Elgeta – the moral self-image of both tends to be the same – and concerning the relationship between the parallel institutional infrastructure of both. Arguably, parts of the nationalist mythology were absorbed by the *pueblo* and certainly the initial guidelines behind Elgeta's parallel institutions came from outside the village. But I suggest that, whereas the political prescriptions of Basque nationalism have operated to produce a 'national' collectivity and endow this collectivity with a new culture and traditions, the moral prescriptions of the *pueblo* of Elgeta operated to maintain a collectivity and the pre-existing moral traditions of that collectivity. In this chapter I shall try to show that, while the moral logic and political mobilization derived from nationalism reinterpret the moral logic and political mobilization derived from locally held beliefs, in time, place and fundamental inspiration the two must be seen as independent – but mutually reaffirming – processes.

It is through this reinterpretation and reaffirmation that the urban élites of the Basque nation have been able to attract and cement the loyalties of their semi-urban grass-roots followers.

The parallel institutions of Elgeta

The institutional changes generated by the industrialization of the village on the one hand and the onslaught of the Franco regime on the other transformed vast areas of village life. In the economic sphere, autonomous farmsteads were replaced by factories where the conditions of work were established by central decree of the employer. In the political sphere, a freely elected *ayuntamiento* was cancelled in favour of one imposed from San Sebastian. In the ceremonial sphere, the village *fiestas*, previously organized by the villagers themselves, were placed into the organizing hands of this new municipal council. The state school was the ward of the Madrid Ministry of Education, who hired the teachers and set the curriculum. The village bars were no longer regarded as the *foci* of village social life. Exposed directly to the vigilance of hostile public authorities, the bars belonged to a public space in which open and free discussion had become impossible. The social unity of the village was further disrupted by the influx of non-Basque immigrants holding different customs and often conflicting world views. Finally, news was officially distributed through a strictly censored press and mass media which few villagers regarded as either reliable or believable.

All these items – the new factories, *ayuntamiento*, patronal fiestas, bars, state school, immigrants – were viewed as linked to an external, public, illegitimate world governed by physical and economic forces and relationships which were explicitly hierarchical. They were perceived as going counter to the interests of the *pueblo* and were dismissed as anti-Basque.

In response, with customary values as points of reference and prime movers, parallel institutions were slowly created by and for the *pueblo* to cover all realms of village activity. These parallel institutions were tightly held within the domain of the *pueblo* where adherence to the dominant moral code determined inclusion. In the economic sphere, cooperatives were established to compete with the factories. In the political sphere, an Asociación de Padres de Familia (Parents' Association) was founded to act as an alternative *ayuntamiento*. Later the *ayuntamiento* itself was reconquered. In the educational realm, the *ikastola* became the school of the *pueblo* and the state school was marginalized. Socially, *sociedades* became the meeting places of the *pueblo* instead of the public bars. The immigrants were cut off from village life. In the realm of ceremonial, Basque fiestas were organized and the patronal fiestas relegated to secondary importance. Finally information was transmitted through informal networks of individuals bound in trust which provided an alternative to the state-controlled mass media.

All these parallel institutions were devised by and remained exclusive to the *pueblo*. All benefits, therefore, were also held within the *pueblo*. Relationships in this parallel structure were personalized and viewed as occurring between moral, equal individuals united in trust and common goals. In fact large areas of the operation of this parallel structure were governed by trust rather than contract. Each of these 'popular' institutions had an explicitly egalitarian form of organization. Authority emanated from below and mechanisms existed, for example circulation of office, which ensured that power could not accumulate in specific persons. Again in all these institutions, the structure was such that individual competition was minimized. To gain personal benefits an individual had to work for the common interest. Created in conformity with the moral ideas of the *pueblo*, this parallel, 'popular' structure was regarded as legitimate and Basque.

Until the consolidation of Basque nationalism which occurred in Elgeta simultaneously with the death of General Franco and Spain's transition to a democratic system, the village was composed of two parts, the *pueblo* and the *anti-pueblo*. Each had its own institutional structures.

Access to these institutions corresponded to the moral stratification of the village described previously. It must be stressed that these parallel organizations were also alternative means for distributing social, economic and political benefits.

The world of bars – the world of sociedades

During the time of my fieldwork, there were three *sociedades* in the village. These *sociedades* were private clubs. Entrance was restricted solely to members and their invited guests. The exclusiveness of the *sociedades* was symbolized by the key to the front door that each member proudly owned. The doors to the *sociedades* were always locked. The doors of the bars were always open. Each of the *sociedades* had been established by a *cuadrilla*. Gastronomic and recreation *sociedades* have a long tradition in the Basque country; but their establishment in Elgeta was a postwar phenomenon and linked back to the political and social atmosphere in the village after the war.

The first *sociedad* was the Mendi-mendian which opened in 1952. The founding *cuadrilla* consisted of seven men, all of whom had been active in nationalist and socialist politics before the civil war. After the war they continued as a tight-knit group sharing *chiquitos* (small glasses of wine) and occasional meals. Because of their constant fear of *denuncias*, these people felt insecure and exposed in the streets and bars of the village. A *cuadrilla* member described the situation:

In *la calle* you couldn't talk about anything. If you talked about politics, a *chivato* [police informer] might turn you in. If you talked about the factory, an *amo* might get to know about it and say if you didn't like your job, you could leave it. That was not the life for men.

Sociedades in nearby towns had already been established by *cuadrillas* and this group followed suit. Premises were found and first rented. Several other men tied to this *cuadrilla* by kinship joined the *sociedad*. The premises were finally purchased for 10,000 pesetas. Each member became an equal stockholder.

According to Spanish law, all organizations of any sort had to draw up statutes and apply to the provincial authorities for legalization. Failure to do so could lead to arrest. But, as the frequent saying goes, the law gets obeyed – but not fulfilled. The *sociedad* members applied to the government to form a musical society. The authorities extended legal status. The club's musical activities were limited to raucous singing after dinners and hiring the occasional accordionist for feast days.

The main activity of the *Sociedad* Mendi-mendian was conversation in addition to eating, drinking and card playing protected from the prying eyes of hostile non-Basques and vigilant womenfolk. Both food and drink were provided at prices below those in the bars. The *sociedad* bar was run by the members and the food cooked by the *cuadrillas*.

In its two well-decorated and meticulously neat rooms, the *sociedad* had in 1976 thirty-four members – all men, all Basques and most between forty and sixty-five years of age. There had been several applications for membership from non-Basques, but these were turned down. With the *Castellanos*, it was thought, everyone would have to speak in Spanish instead of Euskera, and besides, '*Castellanos* can never be trusted. You can see that they are different from us and against us', said one member to the nodded approval of those listening. The members frequently referred to their *sociedad* in friendship or kinship terms. The word *alkartasuna* (union of friends) and the phrase, 'It's like a family in its home!' were common.

The organization of the *sociedad* was egalitarian. The members liked to stress that all members had equal rights and obligations. The entrance fee was 5,000 pesetas, in return for which the new member became a co-owner of all *sociedad* property. All members formed a general assembly, the supreme governing organ. During its annual meeting, the general assembly decided on all major business. All decisions required a majority vote, but almost all decisions were passed unanimously. Applications for membership required an 85% favourable vote. The general assembly also elected officers for their two-year terms. The functions of these officers were administrative. Any matters of greater importance than ordering more wine or paying the electricity bills were referred back to the general assembly. Officers were rotated with every election and no individual could succeed himself in office.

Daily management was based on trust. Members went to the bar, took what they wanted and signed a note stating what they had consumed. Bills were paid once monthly. Controls against infringement of this system were non-existent. Yet, in the *sociedad's* history there had been only one case of someone breaking the society rules. One member was discovered to be eating and drinking far more than he was signing for. The other members began to watch the culprit, noting what he consumed and then comparing their lists with the list of the offender. This continued for some months with no one, typically, confronting the member with his misdeeds. Finally, when the offender showed no signs of relenting, the other members presented him with proof of his cheating. He accepted without protestations of innocence, was expelled from the *sociedad* and refused permission to enter.

The *Sociedad* Intxorta, established in 1971, presented a similar picture. Previously the *sociedad* premises was a bar. This bar was the meeting place of one *cuadrilla* with twenty-two members who every Saturday and Sunday night took over the back room for shared meals and card playing. The owner of the bar, also a member of the *cuadrilla*, planned to shut down the bar and suggested to the *cuadrilla* that they turn it into a *sociedad*. 'In these days, a *cuadrilla* needs a house', stated the landlord. None of the *cuadrilla* members wanted to join the Mendi-mendian even though most would have been accepted. For one, it was too small to absorb all twenty-two of them; but, more importantly, none of the *cuadrilla* wanted to be subjected to a vetting process. Eventually this *cuadrilla*, along with parts of other *cuadrillas* (forty-five people in all) bought the premises, drew up statutes, submitted them to the provincial governor, and the *Sociedad* Intxorta was founded.

The *Sociedad* Intxorta was less openly political than the Mendi-mendian. For most members the prime reason for the *sociedad* was love of good conversation and good food consumed in the privacy of the *cuadrilla*.

The *sociedad* had sixty-two members, all men and mostly in their forties and fifties. Unlike all other *sociedades* in Elgeta, the Intxorta also had two members who were immigrants. They entered when the *sociedad* was first formed. Both had been resident in the village for many years. However, these two members only occasionally came to the *sociedad* and almost never ate there. Most Basque members felt that it was a mistake to admit them. As one said, 'Here we are like a family. We all know each other and our ways of behaving are the same. But with them, well... but, I guess they are members now.' Certainly no other non-Basques have been admitted. But some have applied. The doctor, Don C., applied and was refused, a fact the members were rather proud of.

While these two *sociedades* absorbed the older men of the *pueblo*, the Ozkarbi was the *sociedad* of the Basque youth. It was also by far the largest and most influential in village activities. It has 220 members, informally organized into 16 *cuadrillas* and formally organized into one of 5 sections – cultural, mountaineering, fishing and hunting, *pelota* and dancing. Of the Ozkarbi's members 50% were less than sixteen years old (in spite of the *sociedad's* rules that limited memberships to those 18 or over), and few were over forty. Members were both male and female. Only the Ozkarbi of the three village *sociedades* offered cultural as well as recreational activities. Over the years since its legalization in 1965, the *Sociedad* Ozkarbi took over the organization of most of the village's social events: from the Basque fiestas to conferences on Basque autonomy statutes to *pelota* matches to hunting dog competitions and card-playing championships.

The *sociedad* was started by a special interest *cuadrilla*. No immigrants were members and none had ever applied.

Like the other two *sociedades*, relationships among the members of the *Sociedad* Ozkarbi were warm and multistranded. Again the *sociedad* was viewed as uniting its members into a family and as providing a second home. Outsiders, when permitted into the *sociedad*, were treated with the hospitality deemed befitting a guest, but not the intimacy normal between members.

Because of the presence of the five sections into which the *Sociedad* Ozkarbi was organized, its structure was slightly more complicated than the previous two; but the principle remained exactly the same. Members had equal status. Decisions were reached by consensus. Officers had only administrative and not executive powers. The system of signing was exactly the same as in the other *sociedades*. There had been only one case of an individual cheating. One person took some wine and noted it on the paper of another member. The deception was quickly discovered and the culprit suspected. However, he was never directly approached. He finally confessed voluntarily and was suspended for one week to *kalea* (the street). (The term *kalea* is not only seen in opposition to *baserria*; but also in opposition to *etxea*, the house or domestic sphere.)

While the bars were still the scene of the lively, ambulatory *chiquiteo*, the main parts of Basque social life occurred behind the locked doors of the *sociedades*. Here was where joint meals were enjoyed, conversations pursued in earnest, accounts settled among *cuadrilla* members and so forth. The *sociedades* also provided the premises for the constant meetings through which the entire parallel structure of the village was organized.

In the *sociedades* four elements stood out. (1) The *cuadrilla*, a group of individuals bonded by common ideology, acted as organizing agents. (2) Relationships within the *sociedad*, a type of extended *cuadrilla*, were viewed in terms of pseudo-kinship and the *sociedad* itself seen as a type of home. (3) The *sociedades* possessed an explicitly non-hierarchical structure. (4) The *sociedades* were exclusive.

With modifications these same four factors underlay all the institutions of the moral community.

The world of capitalism – the world of the cooperative

There were two factories producing almost identical bedroom furniture in Elgeta. The larger, Modelo, was owned by the Erostarbe family. The other, Dormicoop, was a cooperative. The origins of Dormicoop can be traced to a labour dispute in Modelo.

The conflict started in 1958 and concerned general working conditions as well as wages. A group of seven workers, who formed a *cuadrilla*, were particularly rancorous. They criticized bitterly the behaviour of the owners and especially the owners' sons who helped in the management. Said one, 'They were dictators who refused to treat their workers as one ought to. We were like dogs – no friendship, nothing. If a person went to a friend's funeral during working hours, he got 300 pts. docked from his wages. There everyone worked 8 hours and no more.'

In January 1959 the seven left Modelo. Although most of them had a skill, many spoke Spanish badly, could not read fluently and had no experience in administration. Nevertheless, they decided to set up their own bedroom furniture factory. Each of the seven contributed 25,000 pesetas for the purchase of machinery, and one local farmer lent the group 50,000 pesetas. In 1960 they 'bought' 100 square metres of land upon which to build a proper workshop. Each member had valued his share in the new enterprise at 100,000 pesetas. José, who owned the land and also worked in Modelo, decided to join in. He contributed the land as his share. It was decided that each should receive equal wages and all decisions be taken by consensus.

Esteban was the first director and at the heart of the new factory. He worked extremely hard, had a good business head and the enterprise went well. A conflict soon developed, however, because Esteban argued that he should receive a bonus for being the director. All eight members called a meeting. They decided unanimously to refuse Esteban's request and to reduce him to the status of an ordinary worker. Esteban left shortly afterwards.

The business quickly started to go sour. No cost study was ever done. No one knew how much the furniture cost to produce. The price set was simply that of the competition. The quality of the furniture was reduced to save money and many clients were lost. There was no production control and endless faults were found in the products. Moreover, in spite of the appointment of a new director, a Basque from another town, most workers came and left when they felt like it and did only jobs they found interesting. Moreover, the new director was largely boycotted because he was an outsider – and because he was the director. Yet everyone agreed that some form of administration was needed.

Partly because of the by now chronic economic difficulties, and partly because the idea seemed appealing, it was finally decided to form a cooperative. The idea was copied from the Mondragon industrial cooperatives. The Caja Laboral Popular in Mondragon advised the workers on how to establish a cooperative, more people were brought into the venture and finally a young man from Elgeta, who had previously helped found the *Sociedad* Ozkarbi and eventually became the village mayor, was asked to take on the administration. The new director brought in a management company to study the factory's problems and train an administrative staff. Dormicoop was formed and began to prosper. The original founders still occasionally grumbled about the fact that the administrative staff, all relative newcomers, received a higher salary.

In 1975 Dormicoop had forty worker/owners. All were Basques from Elgeta except three, of whom two were Basques from Vergara and one a Spanish girl. Most were former Modelo workers.

To become a shareholder in Dormicoop a person first had to obtain employment. Then he/she had to pay a minimum of 50,000 pesetas for a *cartilla*. On this sum the *socio*, or member, received 6% interest annually unless the cooperative lost money in which case interest payment was reduced. The salaries within the cooperative were paid on a 1:3 ratio for the lowest to the highest paid. The capital invested played little role in the distribution of profits. Profits were supposed to be distributed according to effort and sweat expended, not prior wealth. The profits of Dormicoop were distributed in the following manner. A 10% minimum was put into a social fund (in 1976 this money went to the *ikastola*, *Sociedad* Ozkarbi and the *Asociación de Padres de Familia* in order to 'work for the *pueblo*'); 15% was set aside for reinvestment, and the remainder distributed among the *socios*. Dormicoop was successful. In fact at the time it was the only factory in the village that looked to the future optimistically.

The members of Dormicoop described their factory in terms similar to those used to describe the *sociedades*. An older worker told me,

> It is ours. It is a home and we live here. It is better because we know that there will be no tricks and that everyone is united to work for our common benefit. If you work for a capitalist, everything goes to him and you get left with nothing. A cooperative is a friendship.

Most workers do not receive higher wages than they did in Modelo. Notably, the ultimate authority was a general assembly where each worker had equal voice and vote. Whereas decisions required a majority vote, again few were passed without near unanimity. The officers after their terms of office were not entitled to reelection.

The vast majority of the members of the cooperative belonged to the *sociedades*, sent their children to the *ikastola*, supported the *Asociación de Padres de Familia* and later the candidature of their young director for mayor of the village.

A particular feature of the industrial structure of the village should be mentioned here. As noted previously, although the industrial sector of Elgeta consisted of fifteen different – mostly small-scale – enterprises, the production of these enterprises was relatively undiversified. Five workshops produced shotgun parts, two factories produced identical bedroom furniture and so forth. This economic structure was economically viable only because it was partly removed from competitive market conditions. The relationship between Elgeta's industrial firms and their markets was personalized. Most of Elgeta's workshops sold their entire production to one factory. Usually the owner of the workshop was formerly employed in the factory to which he sold his product. Prices and production quotas were set through the personal relationship between the workshop owner and his former boss. For the large factories this meant that the supply of component parts was guaranteed. Moreover, if the factory changed its supply requirements, the workshop would switch its entire production to satisfy this new demand. Although the price set by the workshop suppliers was usually above market prices, this was compensated by the fact that the factory owner no longer carried the social cost – for example, social security payments – of his former employee nor the fixed capital costs of vertically integrating within the factory production processes that were technically linked. For the workshop owners this arrangement meant that their entire production had an ensured market at a profitable price.

But the value of the system was viewed more in social than economic terms. The income of the workshop owners was not significantly different from the income of employed skilled labour. The proliferation of workshops in Elgeta reflected the value placed on social equality; a value seen as incompatible with the status of employee. The case of Julio B. was typical. When Julio first arrived in Elgeta from Vergara, he went to work in the factory of Zabala Hmnos which manufactured shotguns. Although Julio's relation with his employers was friendly, he felt increasingly dissatisfied with his work. 'When you spend eight hours a day taking orders from someone, it is difficult to hold your head up when you meet that person in the street or in a bar.' Therefore, Julio decided to open his own workshop to produce the only thing he knew how to make – the same shotgun component he made at Zabala Hmnos. Zabala guaranteed to buy all of Julio's production and extended him credit in order to purchase the necessary plant. Julio opened his workshop in 1968 with four workers. Zabala in turn dismantled the part of his production line previously under Julio's charge. Two years later, one of Julio's employees, Ramon, who had been responsible for polishing, started up his own workshop. The only service that Ramon's workshop provided was polishing the shotgun components manufactured by Julio B.

The escuela nacional – the ikastola

Perhaps most illustrative of the separation of the 'moral' institutions from their official counterparts was the cleavage between the state school and the *ikastola*. The *ikastola* was the emotive heart of the entire parallel structure. Confronting a moral and ethnic task, the *ikastola* attempted to form moral and ethnic children and, thus, ensure moral and ethnic continuity. There could be acceptable excuses for not working in the cooperative or not belonging to a *sociedad*; but there were no acceptable excuses for not participating, one way or another, in the constant round of activities (raffles, lotteries, cultural performances, etc.) designed to raise funds for the *ikastola*. Whereas support for the *ikastola* was a constant theme in village activities, one could live for quite some time among Elgeta's Basques and not be aware that the state school even existed.

The state school had approximately sixty pupils from grades 1 to 5 of primary education, and two teachers. Both teachers and 70% of the pupils were non-Basques. The Basque children came from the poorest Basque families or from families who were entirely rural. The teachers had the appropriate degree in education and the required certificate of good political conduct. The teaching methods were traditional. The children sat in long, disciplined rows absorbing most of their education by rote. Teaching was solely in Spanish.

The *ikastola* was on the other side of the concrete wall in a fine building with majestic views over the Vergara Valley. It had fifty-nine pupils ranging from kindergarten to the fifth year of primary education. All the pupils, like the two *andereños* (teachers), were Basque. The *ikastola* was a private school and charged a modest tuition fee. In contrast to the state school, the children in the *ikastola* studied in informal groups sitting around tables. Teaching in the *ikastola* was in Euskera.

The *ikastola* was the school of the *pueblo* and the *pueblo* sent their children to the school. No children whose parents were classed among the morally suspect – industrialists, professionals, immigrants, *jauntxoak* – attended. The large majority of the children came from urbanized families. Their fathers tended to be semi-skilled or skilled factory workers.

The idea of establishing an *ikastola* was also an imported idea. In certain respects the *ikastola* was an exception among the *pueblo*'s parallel institutions. Initially it received little support from the *pueblo*.

In the late 1950s a young, socially committed priest, Don Joaquin, arrived to take up duties in Elgeta. Don Joaquin was typical of the young priests from rural backgrounds who had strong sympathies with Basque nationalism. He quickly organized a small group of village youth around him. When the premises of the former Church school in the village became vacant, Don Joaquin suggested that an *ikastola* be established to open in the autumn term.

The argument that the children would benefit from an education in their maternal language and that being Basques they *ought* to be educated in Euskera was greeted with scepticism. To village Basques, most of whom spoke Euskera much more fluently than Spanish, Euskera was still the language of the *baserriak* and illiteracy. They feared that teaching in Euskera would be counter-productive. Many were also suspicious of the new teaching methods proposed. In order to smooth village opinion, Don Joaquin invited the Harami Community, a Basque order of nuns, to come to Elgeta to teach. In the autumn the *ikastola* opened. Two nuns and a local Basque woman were employed as teachers. The nuns were quickly replaced by lay teachers. Most parents reacted to the new school by sending their daughters to the *ikastola* and their sons, for whom a proper education was judged more important, to the state school. In all eighty pupils attended. Unlike in the larger Basque towns where the *ikastolas* particularly mobilized the youth, in Elgeta the youth were apathetic towards the new school. The parish priest, Don José, was officially president of the *ikastola*. Don José, a fervent moralist, took his job seriously and made life impossible for the *andereños* (teachers). He insisted that it was sinful to go to dances, that the catechism had to be given first priority, and he pried unsparingly into the lives of all connected with the *ikastola*. Don Joaquin finally convinced the ageing priest to hand over the presidency to him. Don Joaquin in turn immediately handed over the school to the parents and school's supporters who formed themselves into a governing general assembly.

The *ikastola* was launched, but the villagers continued largely uninterested. At the frequently-held parents' meetings, convened by the *andereños*, few bothered to attend. Some parents sent their children to the *ikastola* because of the prestige to be obtained from a private school. A very few thought that the teaching methods were in fact better than those employed by the state school. Even fewer still believed that their children ought to be taught in Euskera. Most sent their children simply because it was connected to the Church.

With the slow diffusion from nearby urban centres of nationalist sentiment into Elgeta in the early 1970s, attitudes to the *ikastola* gradually altered. This change was spearheaded by the village youth. The change in attitude towards the *ikastola* was part of a much wider reevaluation of the idea of Basqueness in general and the value of Euskera in particular. Propelled also by the hidden resentments and bitterness of thirty-five years of Francoist rule,

Euskera became redefined as dignified, valid and noble in the villagers' eyes, while Spanish was denigrated. These new ideas were made all the more desirable and acceptable by their urban origins. Spanish became the stigmatized language, Euskera the language of cultural and political modernity. In Elgeta the key to cultural revindication was found in the *ikastola*.

Many of the village youth, working through their *cuadrillas* and mobilizing linked *cuadrillas*, started to work for the school. By 1975, of the eight members of the governing assembly, four were young people who were also members of the *Sociedad* Ozkarbi. Faced with the chronic economic problems of the *ikastola*, these young people began to organize an endless array of fund-raising activities. Raffles, Basque cultural festivals, dances, lotteries, petitions for donations from shops and businesses and so forth became common local events. These activities were tied to the overarching idea of 'defending Basque culture', by ethnic logic a fundamental obligation of a 'Basque', and quickly took on political overtones. Attendance at and support for these events became a means of separating the sheep from the goats. Those who did not publicly support these events were not regarded as truly 'Basque' and, therefore, part of the moral community. Conversely, those who had claims to inclusion had to make a public statement of support.

The following is a description of the *ikastola* given to me by a parent while she was working as a volunteer at the school one Saturday morning. It is notably similar to the description of the cooperative.

> This is our school. The *pueblo* built it and the *pueblo* supports it. Since no one gave it to us, no one can tell us what to do. What have outsiders ever known about the problems our Basque children face? Here we are like a family. Everyone discusses and decides things together – like one ought to.

During my time in Elgeta the state school was largely neglected. In spite of its financial needs and perennial shortage of teachers, it had been entirely relegated to the unresponsive hands of Madrid. To many the state school symbolized former times when the organization of village institutions was under total command of those insensitive, if not hostile, to village interests.

No immigrants attended the *ikastola*. For the immigrants the *ikastola* represented 'Basque' Elgeta from which they were structurally excluded. One resentful Spanish woman summed up her view,

> First we are told that we have to learn Basque. Everything here is in Basque and that's all you ever hear. So they set up Basque classes and so we are happy to go. Then we are told that we only go to the Basque classes because we have nothing else to do and the teachers shouldn't waste their time. So they stop the Basque classes. Now they say we should send our children to the *ikastola* so they can integrate. For God's sake, what are we to think?

Fiestas patronales – Fiestas Vascas

Elgeta traditionally celebrated two main village fiestas. *La Feria Mayor* (Azoka Nagusi Eguna), held on the first Sunday in July, centred around livestock and displays of rural sports. The patronal fiestas were held in August on the day of San Roque, patron saint of Elgeta. While the *Feria Mayor* disappeared largely because of the declining importance of agriculture, the reasons for the decline of the patronal fiestas were of a different nature.

The manner in which these fiestas came to be organized and controlled resulted in creating popular resentment against the fiestas. Prior to the Franco years the village council would ensure that the appropriate accordionists were hired and that the local guard was present to maintain a minimum of order. Otherwise the fiestas were arranged by the villagers themselves. During the Franco period the fiestas became formally organized by the *ayuntamiento* who planned all events and printed programmes, needless to say, in Spanish. Many traditional Basque instruments, such as the *txistu*, a type of flute, were prohibited as signs of separatism. Thus the fiestas were seen as belonging to the domain of *la gente que manda* (those who gave the orders). Organized from above, they were no longer regarded as popular affairs and were attended with little enthusiasm.

During my time in Elgeta even though the *Feria Mayor* had disappeared, the patronal fiestas were poorly attended, exhibitions of rural sports non-existent and a 'theatrical' folkloric tradition absent in the village, Basque folklore flourished. In Elgeta nationalism existed as a cultural phenomenon first and a political one only afterwards. Whereas the *ikastola* formed the emotive heart of the parallel structures, the cultural revival served, among other things, to define them as 'Basque'.

The development of the cultural renaissance and the emergence of a 'popular' political élite in the village were linked. In both processes the village youth were the key element. However, similar to the initial inspiration behind the formation of the *ikastola*, cooperative and *sociedades*, the initial force behind the cultural revival was also from outside the village.

During the summers in early 1960s a group of five to six Basque seminary students used to come to Elgeta to work on the *baserriak* in return for board and lodging. These seminarists were politically engaged nationalists. Together with Don Joaquin they instilled into some of the village youth an awareness of Basque folklore which they argued was the essence of the Basque way of life and on the verge of extinction. Under the patronage of Don Joaquin, a group of twenty-four young people, both boys and girls, formed the village's first ever dance group which they called Ozkarbi.

Although it was illegal to do so, in 1963 Ozkarbi, mobilizing many of Elgeta's youthful *cuadrillas*, organized the first Fiestas Vascas. The date was the first Sunday of July which previously had been the *Feria Mayor*. It was a modest affair with only some *bertsolaris* (spontaneous oral poets) and performances of dance groups from a few nearby towns. It proved an overwhelming success. Everyone enjoyed themselves. Older people were deeply moved since many had not heard the instruments played or seen the dances performed since before the civil war. With abundant energy and many hours spent in organization, the following year the second Fiestas Vascas were given. The programme was ambitious and advance publicity was circulated throughout neighbouring towns.

This time, however, the fiestas were expressly prohibited by the civil governor, since legal authorizations for the various events had not been granted. On the day of the fiestas many outsiders, who had already made their way to Elgeta, turned back upon seeing Civil Guards massed around the plaza. The organizers were ordered to take down all posters and cancel all events. The *alcalde* called the president of the dance group, Patxi Basauri, to his office and made him accept full responsibility for whatever might happen in the street. Don Joaquin, also present at this meeting, replied, 'Lo que pasa contigo es que faltas un par de huevos!', a remark that made him the hero of the day.

The idea equating the village authorities, backed by law, organizing the patronal fiestas in opposition to the *pueblo*, persecuted by law, organizing the fiestas vascas had been fixed.

In 1965 the dance group transformed itself into the Sociedad Ozkarbi. After one year of petitioning, the civil governor granted legal status. Ozkarbi fought its final battle for the right to organize *all* cultural activities in Elgeta the same year. In 1965 the *Sociedad* Ozkarbi organized a boycott of the officially sponsored patronal fiestas. No one attended either the *pelota* games, usually a village passion, or the *berbena* (street dance) that followed. After this show of strength the *sociedad* went to the *alcalde* and requested permission to organize the patronal fiestas as well as the Fiestas Vascas. Both permission and money to do so were granted. However, the enthusiasm of the *sociedad* members was limited to the fiestas vascas.

During the subsequent years the activities organized by Ozkarbi increased in frequency and began to take on explicit ideological overtones. A literacy campaign for those who wanted to learn to read Euskera was started. A library was begun. Alternative 'spiritual exercises' on themes such as man's inhumanity to man, and women's rights were offered to compete with the spiritual exercises given by the Church. Conferences on all subjects from premarital sex to Basque traditional rights became monthly occasions. In addition, the *Sociedad* Ozkarbi coordinated the constant fund-raising activities for the *ikastola*.

After 1970 the fiestas vascas, with a vastly increased budget supplied by donations from the *pueblo*, were extended to a full week and included a

Basque cultural week among the more usual festivities. In 1975 the fiestas vascas included: (1) the theatre group EGI BILLA performing the play *Mugausleak*; (2) a series of conferences on Basque journalism, education in the *ikastolas*, *bertsolarismo*, *fueros*, *conciertos económicos* and the foral charter; (3) 23 different dance groups comprising a total of approximately 700 dancers and (4) Basque folk singers. In addition there were *pelota* games, donkey racing, special events for children, *sokamutura*, *txaranga* bands, *berbenas* and an endless array of group meals. The organization was handled entirely by the *cuadrillas* linked to the *Sociedad* Ozkarbi. The fiestas of 1976 were equally elaborate, but with the death of General Franco they had become openly political. Outlawed Basque flags were waved, *Eusko Gudariak gara* (We are the Basque Soldiers), a nationalist song long prohibited, was sung constantly, everyone had their hands raised in the V sign made famous with the execution of Txiki, a member of ETA, and the shout 'Gora Euzkadi Askatuta!' (Long live free Euskadi) was the battle cry of the week.

During these fiestas vast hordes of outsiders converged on the village. The fiestas provided one of the very few occasions when calculations of strict reciprocity in exchanges were brushed aside. The entire fiestas were conducted in Euskera. These were not village fiestas. They were fiestas of the *pueblo*. Although they could observe fiesta activities, immigrants and anti-Basques were structurally excluded from deeper participation. Active participation was the exclusive right of the *pueblo*; but, according to the *pueblo*'s values, the moral obligation of all villagers. 'The Basque works for the common benefit.' Organized by and with reference to the *pueblo*, in turn the fiestas symbolically underlined the *pueblo*'s public claim to cultural, in its widest sense, dominance in the village.

So far we have seen that in opposition to a social order regarded as illegitimate, the *pueblo* of Elgeta, via its basic social unit, the *cuadrilla*, created another, parallel order. The *ikastola* was the school of the *pueblo*, the cooperative its factory, the *sociedades* the centres of its social life and the FIESTAS VASCAS its means of cultural affirmation. These new institutions, regarded as moral, legitimate and Basque, were also closed. Francoists, suspected police informers, industrialists, the poor, professionals, and immigrants were barred from participation. The moral institutions and their official counterparts were in direct competition because they represented different, incompatible, means for distributing social, economic and political benefits. The outcome of the struggle for precedence between the *pueblo* and its perceived enemies and competitors depended largely on the result of the political confrontation.

The reconquest of political power

By the mid-1960s the personnel of political power had changed in correspondence with the general shift of the village economy away from agricultural and into industrial endeavours. Political control had moved from the Carlist *cuadrilla* whose power rested on landownership to a group of important industrialists and their supporters, a group known collectively as the *cuadrilla de los industrialistas*. Its central figure was Juanito Erostarbe, the director of Modelo, who had paved the way for his political dominance during his time as *jefe local de movimiento*. Working in close alliance with Erostarbe was the secretary of the *ayuntamiento*, a Basque from Vergara who reportedly had many influential contacts throughout the hierarchy of the provincial government. In supporting ranks were the trade union delegate (*delegado sindical*), Pedro Igartua, who worked in the Savings Bank, and the new *jefe local de movimiento*. This *jefe local* was an immigrant who worked for Erostarbe and was popularly known as the *alcalde de Burgos* after his city or origin. Although Elorriaga continued as the village *alcalde*, he and his *concejales* were regarded as strictly subordinated to the political dictates of the *cuadrilla*.

However, the political configuration imposed on the village after the war was becoming increasingly unstable. The discrepancy between the growing economic prosperity and educational sophistication of the villagers and their complete lack of political representation was unsustainable.

The elections of 1967

The counter-attack was launched in 1966. In this year a group of some twenty people began to meet clandestinely in the back room of the *Sociedad* Ozkarbi. These people – all Basques – had organized themselves into an *Asociación de Padres de Familia*. The vast majority were urbanites who worked in Dormicoop or owned small industrial workshops. Except for two individuals, they had received specialized education in the nearby towns. They referred to themselves as the *fuerzas vivas del pueblo*. The purpose of their meetings was to reclaim the *ayuntamiento* for the *pueblo*. They planned to participate actively and indeed win the forthcoming municipal elections.

In the elections of 1967, three seats on the municipal council – one from each *tercio* – were up for election. The *fuerzas vivas* prepared candidates to contest each seat. In the *tercio de cabezas de familia* (heads of households), the group chose Luis Mari Irazabal to be its candidate. Luis Mari was not considered ideal. But it was thought that his candidature would pass the censorship of the provincial civil governor. Next the *Ley de Regimen Local* was studied in detail and the services of friends and relatives in other villages were requested to advise upon procedure. When all official rules had been satisfied and the appropriate application forms completed, Luis Mari presented himself to the secretary of the *ayuntamiento*. Totally unaware of these behind-the-scenes manoeuvres, the secretary was taken completely by surprise. The *cuadrilla de los industrialistas* had also presented a candidate whose election was considered a mere formality. Fearing a contest between the two would emphasize how unpopular the *cuadrilla* actually was, their candidate was immediately withdrawn. Luis Mari Irazabal became a *concejal* unopposed.

The voting in the *tercio de sindicatos*, the vertical trade union, was the most complicated part of the municipal elections and particularly vulnerable to manipulation from all sides. In Elgeta the trade union had two sectors. One sector represented the industrial workers and the other agricultural workers (*labradores*). In the industrial sector each enterprise employing over a certain number of workers had to have at least one *enlace sindical* (shop steward). During elections these *enlaces sindicales* elected *compromisarios*. The *compromisarios* were the individuals who had the right to vote in the *tercio de sindicatos*.

In the rural sector the Comision de Labradores consisted of one appointed representative for every twenty farmsteads. During elections some of these representatives were appointed as *compromisarios* by the official trade union. In all Elgeta had twelve *compromisarios* who on a simple majority vote elected the *concejal* for the *tercio de sindicatos* from a list of candidates approved by the civil governor. Previously no vote had ever taken place since never more than one candidate was ever presented.

The secretary of the Comision de Labradores was also the trade union delegate in Elgeta, Pedro Igartua. His candidate was one of Elgeta's Carlist landowners. The *fuerzas vivas* presented Maximo Aranceta, a more modest landowner. The process of 'influencing' the twelve *compromisarios* was then set in action. Influencing consisted of persuading the *compromisario* that he was part of the *pueblo* and, therefore, owed his loyalty to it. The sanction backing this argument was the implied threat that those *compromisarios* who voted against the popular candidate would be ostracized from the community.

On election day, Pedro Igartua, realising that the majority of *compromisarios* had been influenced against his candidate, refused to distribute the ballot papers to the *compromisarios* representing the Comision de Labradores. Instead he filled out the papers himself. The presiding election officer, who had also been 'influenced', refused to accept Igartua's ballot papers. Igartua was told that the law required that voting be done in person and at the election table proper. Acutely embarrassed, Igartua withdrew his candidate and Maximo Aranceta became *concejal* unopposed.

The right to vote in the *tercio* of entities went, in practice, to the five *concejales* who had one vote each. The *concejal de entidades* was decided on a majority vote among *concejales* from a previously approved list of candidates. This *tercio* presented the *fuerzas vivas* with no problems. Two of the five *concejales* were their newly elected representatives. One of the remaining three *concejales* was 'influenced' and the group's candidate, Alejandro Aranceta, entered – again unopposed.

The election of 1967 resulted in total victory. The former apathy with which all official matters had been treated vanished. Although the *fuerzas vivas del pueblo* were initially few in number, by 1971 the large majority of villagers had given them explicit support. Interest in the affairs of the *ayuntamiento* became intense.

Just before the elections of 1971, when the remaining three *concejales* were up for re-election, an incident occurred which resulted in the resignation of Luis Mari Irazabal. The secretary of the *ayuntamiento* without proper consultation had authorized José Mari Elcoro, Elgeta's only industrialist who was a staunch Basque nationalist, to construct windows in his warehouse. Legally construction changes of this sort required an official permit. Luis Mari said until such official permission was granted the windows, which had already been opened, would have to be bricked in again. He insisted it was matter of principle. José Mari Elcoro argued that, since he planned extensive construction on his warehouse, it hardly seemed practical to solicit still another permit for such a trivial detail. But Luis Mari remained firm and threatened to resign his post as *concejal* if the windows were not bricked up. The *fuerzas vivas* while applauding Luis Mari's stand for democracy and against corruption, felt that a more important issue could have been chosen for a showdown. Moreover, they wondered why Luis Mari, usually a reasonable man, should have become so fanatical over the issue. However, Luis Mari was not to be moved. When he realised that the windows would remain open, he simply stopped attending meetings of the *ayuntamiento* and was, therefore, automatically expelled. What few people knew at the time was that Luis Mari had been 'influenced'.

Elections of 1971

So for the municipal elections of 1971 the group had to manage the election of four candidates: two for *cabezas de familia* (one of which would replace Luis Mari), one for *sindicatos* and one for *entidades*.

Although planning for the election was still limited to the group who met in the Sociedad Ozkarbi, village anticipation was fierce. The *fuerzas vivas* knew that the *jauntxoak* would not present a candidate for the *tercio de cabezas de familia*, the only semi-democratic aspect of the procedure. But they wanted to use the election to provide a show of popular support. Therefore, instead of nominating only one candidate, the group nominated Tour. Three of these candidates were supported by the group. One was not.

The election for this *tercio* was the only case of a popular vote in Elgeta since the war; 83% of the electorate voted; the 17% that did not vote were in the main immigrants; 92% of the votes cast went to the group's three 'real' candidates.

In the election for the *concejal* to represent the trade union, the *cuadrilla de los industrialistas* attacked with full force. The result was illustrative of political processes in the village.

Don Joaquin had obtained the official list of *compromisarios* from the *Casa Sindical* (Trade Union House) in Vergara. The group drew up its list of candidates. Patxi Basauri, the president of the Sociedad Ozkarbi and director of the Dormicoop furniture cooperative, headed the list. His candidature was rejected by the Civil Governor. It was assumed that the *jefe local* and Juanito Erostarbe had exercised their influence with the provincial authorities. However, the group's other candidates were approved and the slow work of influencing began. After some weeks seven *compromisarios* had promised their votes.

Juanito Erostarbe was in a difficult position. Without at least one representative in the *ayuntamiento* his entire economic future in Elgeta would be jeopardized. Official permits for building repairs, expansion and so forth would become difficult, if not impossible, to obtain. Juanito presented Gregorio Romanelli, an immigrant who was a tenant in a house Erostarbe owned, as his candidate.

Two days before the election, two *compromisarios* who had promised their votes to the *fuerzas vivas* were suddenly removed from the list. Erostarbe and Igartua, using their contacts within the official *sindicato*, were believed to be responsible for this change. Election day itself was dramatic, bitter and confused. Juanito Erostarbe presented himself as a *compromisario*. The presiding official told him that he did not have the right to vote. The vote belonged to Juanito's brother who was not present. One *compromisario* simply refused to vote at all. He declared loudly to all present, 'If I vote for one candidate, no one will speak to me. If I vote for the other, I lose my job.' Julio Ugalde and the former *concejal*, Luis Mari Irazabal, both of whom had promised their votes to the group, switched at the last moment and voted for Gregorio Romanelli. Ugalde had a small workshop that supplied Modelo with wooden crates. Luis Mari had a small workshop the output of which was also totally dependent on Modelo. Both had been threatened with economic retaliation. Romanelli became Elgeta's first and only non-Basque *concejal*. However, his term in office was short. Romanelli's life in the *ayuntamiento* was made intolerable. He soon stopped attending council meetings and was, therefore, automatically expelled.

Since only the *alcalde* and Gregorio Romanelli were not hand picked by the *fuerzas vivas*, the group's candidate in the *tercio de entidades*, Roman Zabala, the owner of a feed shop, was elected unopposed.

The transformation of the *ayuntamiento* seemed complete in 1976 when Patxi Basauri, a leading personality behind all of Elgeta's parallel, moral institutions, was elected – again unopposed – as the village's first 'popular' mayor. Patxi's victory was cemented some days later when Juanito Erostarbe approached Patxi in the street to congratulate him. The news of the incident spread like wildfire throughout the furniture cooperative, the *ikastola* and the *sociedades*. Wine, cognac and coffee flowed in abundance with Patxi on this occasion footing most of the bill. The vast majority of the young people in Elgeta's moral community celebrated joyously until 3 o'clock in the morning in the Sociedad Ozkarbi.

In conclusion, village politics during the process of reconquering the *ayuntamiento* had been transformed into an open confrontation between two factions. The faction of the *fuerzas vivas del pueblo* backed its strategy with social sanctions and operated by mobilizing the village *cuadrillas* within the infrastructure of Elgeta's parallel institutions. The faction of the *cuadrilla de los industrialistas* backed its strategy with economic sanctions and operated by mobilizing it outside contacts in the official institutions of the state.

After the reconquest of the *ayuntamiento* the political influence of the industrialists in village affairs was reduced to the secretary of the *ayuntamiento*. This last vestige of power was steadily eroded through Spain's constitutional changes during the period 1976 to 1980.

With political power restored to the moral community, the parallel organizations which arose, often on the margins of legality, either replaced the official organizations in the village or absorbed them. Most of the members of the *ayuntamiento* were previously members of the Asociación de Padres de Familia, the state school was neglected and rapidly fell into decay, although many immigrant children still attended it. All public funds were directed to the *ikastola*. Indeed, the two schools were eventually merged into one Basque language school. The cooperative was the only factory that prospered. The Modelo furniture factory was unable to get the necessary permits to carry out rebuilding and some years later closed down. The patronal fiestas became moribund and the Basque fiestas were the highlight of the year. Although these institutions were the only ones functioning in the village, they remained exclusive. They were the property of the moral community. The perceived enemies of this community were not permitted access. And many immigrants as well as morally suspect Basques simply left the village.

The political loyalty of the moral community – the reemergence of Basque nationalism

In the preceding discussion little reference was made to Basque nationalism because the process was at no time conducted in terms of it. (This conclusion was adamantly reaffirmed by my informants when I returned to Elgeta in 1985). The *pueblo*'s pre-existing moral ideology, rather than Basque nationalism, provided the mobilizing drive behind the reconquering of political power in Elgeta. The villagers who had grown up under Franco felt sympathy towards Basque nationalism, but gave little active support. During the Burgos trials of 1970, for instance, when large parts of the Basque provinces were in violent uproar, Elgeta remained relatively unmoved. Although the folk cultural revival in Elgeta had served to instill a renewed awareness of and pride in Basque identity, 'Basqueness' was viewed as a matter of cultural content and not as a basis for political claims. In part this lack of concern was due to the relative isolation of Elgeta from the industrial pulse of the Basque country.

Until 1974/75 Basque nationalist politics were a strictly clandestine affair conducted through protected personal networks which in general did not extend into the village. Moreover, because of the weight of repression in Elgeta – the constant fear of *denuncias*, police informers, the *jefe local de movimiento* as well as the ubiquitous police controls monitoring all traffic in and out of the village – the villagers shut themselves off not only from the anti-Basque world, but also regarded any political involvement in the outside world with extreme caution and suspicion. A favoured expression was, 'Everything different is political. Everything political is dangerous.' Although the arrival of Spanish immigrants ethnically polarized the village into 'them' and 'us', this polarization was not expressed in Basque nationalist terms.

During most of the Franco period Basque nationalism was mainly confined to the older generation who had fought in the civil war and whose sentimental attachments to the PNV remained strong. But their nationalism was only voiced behind the safely locked doors of the *sociedades*. It was never used, covertly or overtly, as an organizational vehicle in the public sphere. The *fuerzas vivas del pueblo* who were responsible for initiating most of the cultural and political changes that occurred in the village were guided mainly by local loyalties and concerns. They did not see themselves as part of the wider Basque movement, a movement they had neither much information about nor contact with.

Elgeta had provided a small but steady flow of recruits to ETA; among them the young man mentioned previously who was tortured. However, the political activities of these individuals took place outside of the village. Most villagers were unaware of the *etarras* (members of ETA) in their midst until they were either arrested or had sought unexpected refuge in France. Although the *pueblo* regarded ETA with considerable admiration, the nature of its cause and creed was rarely commented upon.

Despite this apparent apathy, during the Franco period the *pueblo* of Elgeta had constructed almost the complete infrastructure for nationalism.

The exclusive, morally differentiated parallel organizations of the village – the *ikastola*, the cooperative, the Basque fiestas, the *sociedades* – were replicas of the institutions set up to serve the cause of the Basque nationalist community. Furthermore, the fundamental division in Elgeta – the moral *pueblo* on one hand and the immoral world of anti-Basques consisting of immigrants and suspect Basques on the other – mirrored the fundamental cleavage, that of *abertzales* and *españolistas*, generated by the logic of Basque nationalist ideology. Finally the political aim of the *pueblo* to exercise exclusive control over the village's economic, social and cultural resources mirrored the driving ambition of Basque nationalism with regard to the Basque country as a whole.

However, although the private institutions, moral vision and political purpose of the *pueblo* of Elgeta were analogous to those of the Basque nationalist community, the *pueblo* was not a microcosm of the nationalist community. The *pueblo* conducted its affairs with reference to its local, moral imperatives. The nationalist community operated with reference to 'national' political imperatives.

Critically, the integration of the *pueblo* of Elgeta into the Basque nationalist community occurred in 1975 when urban nationalist politics energetically emerged from clandestinity. Except for those older villagers who remained loyal to the PNV, the *pueblo* entered the ranks of radical nationalism – *abertzalismo de izquierda* (left-wing patriotism). The *pueblo* was captured for radical nationalism through its parallel institutions, the coordinates of *pueblo* life.

During the Franco period the institutions of the nationalist community had been reestablished in the main by the nationalists inspired by ETA. The political message that permeated these institutions – the *ikastola* movement, the Mondragon cooperatives, the cultural revival, etc. – was that of radical nationalism. The factors that inhibited the penetration of radical nationalism into Elgeta disappeared the moment the nationalist creed could be transmitted publicly. Furthermore, the intense competition for a political following that accompanied the reintroduction of party politics in 1974–75 compelled the radical nationalists to consolidate their social constituency.

The initial carrier of the radical doctrine into the village was a group of some ten village youths who were fifteen to twenty years of age during the seventies. Although they lived in Elgeta, these youths had either gone to school to taken jobs in nearby industrial towns during the period 1973–75, and had been caught up by the youthful, nationalist rebellion against the enemies of the Basque nation. The nationalism this group imbibed in the towns was quickly transferred to the *sociedades* of Elgeta – in particular the *Sociedad* Ozkarbi.

Facilitated by the total absence of other competing political creeds, most of the *cuadrillas* inside the *Sociedad* Ozkarbi – representing the most active sections of the village youth – were swept into the tide of radical nationalism. In turn these *cuadrillas* injected their radicalism into the village as a whole through their role as organizers of Elgeta's cultural events. The Basque singers, *bertsolaris*, and theatre groups invited to Elgeta were inevitably *abertzales de izquierda* whose political vision provided the content for their performances. In addition, numerous conferences designed to inform the villagers about historical and political issues of current interest were also staffed by outside 'experts' who transmitted only the radical nationalist position.

The *pueblo*'s main economic institution – the furniture cooperative – and the 'reconquered' *ayuntamiento* also served to attach the *pueblo* solidly to the radical wing of the Basque nationalist community.

As mentioned previously, Dormicoop, the furniture cooperative, had been established under the guidance of the industrial cooperatives in Mondragon. Moreover, the Mondragon cooperatives continued to provide a full range of marketing, research, financial and social welfare services upon which Dormicoop depended. The Mondragon cooperatives had always looked to Basque nationalism for their political inspiration and ideological cohesion. Whereas the Mondragon cooperatives had openly propounded their cooperativist philosophy to the *socios* (members) of Dormicoop, by 1975 the nationalist view of the cooperative movement was absorbed rapidly into the ideas the *pueblo* held concerning Dormicoop. Cooperativism was the Basque national mode of production. Many of Dormicoop's worker/owners moved readily into the radical nationalist political parties and trade unions that were strongly represented in Mondragon.

The integration of Elgeta's parallel organizations into their wider radical nationalist counterparts also occurred in the reconquered *ayuntamiento*. After Franco's death a 'movement of Basque mayors' gained momentum. The purpose of this movement was to demand that King Juan Carlos restore the Basque *fueros*. The leading figure of the 'movement of Basque mayors' was the mayor of Vergara, José Luis Elcoro, a son of Elgeta's former mayor, Bartolo Elcoro. The movement was based in Guipúzcoa and received its main support from the mayors of the smaller towns and villages. Most of the mayors involved had been elected to their posts during the Franco regime through processes similar to those which resulted in the election of Patxi Basauri in Elgeta. The mainspring of the movement was radical nationalism.

Although he initially knew little about the *fueros* or why, how, by whom or when they were abolished, Elgeta's 'popular' mayor, Patxi Basauri, zestfully joined the movement in early 1976. The *pueblo* greeted this initiative with great admiration and pride. Even though the movement eventually petered out in failure, its impact on the political attitudes of the *pueblo* was considerable. Elgeta's *ayuntamiento* and the *pueblo* that had brought it to power became mainstream participants in the confrontational politics that characterized the Basque political scene at the time. Often accompanied with impressive nationalist ceremonial, the *pueblo* of Elgeta mobilized in support of the manoeuvres of the Basque mayors in pursuit of the restoration of the Basque *fueros*, the legalization of the Basque flag and language, the concession of total amnesty and so forth. As the movement of the Basque mayors became increasingly entrenched within the radical camp, the radical sympathies of the *pueblo* of Elgeta were reinforced and consolidated.

Few members of the *pueblo* saw their swift conversion to radical nationalism as representing a real shift in political attitudes. Instead Basque nationalism was viewed as co-validating the moral categories underpinning the *pueblo* by giving these categories a fuller and more complete meaning. The political prescriptions and vision of 'Basqueness' supplemented rather than replaced the pre-existing moral prescriptions and world view of the *pueblo*. The moral claims of the Basque nationalist community to political, cultural and economic hegemony inside the Basque country reinforced the claims of the *pueblo* to a similar hegemony inside Elgeta. Membership in the nationalist community on the 'national' level and in the *pueblo* on the local level was determined by a continual obedience to the moral/political imperatives that would make this hegemony possible.

Postscript

Research for this monograph finished in 1980. The democratic Spain of today is radically different from the authoritarian Spain I knew well during the late 1960s and 1970s. As a member of both the European Economic Community and NATO, the country has regained her place in Europe's mainstream. The extravagant centralization of the Franco years has been replaced by a comprehensive devolution of political power to Spain's regions. The Spanish state has become an *estado de los autonomías*. Reflecting these major political achievements, the principle problems the country now faces tend to be economic – Spain has Europe's highest rate of unemployment – not political. But there is at least one exception: the Basque country.

The Basque country now has its own police force, schools and, critically, is the only region in Spain empowered to raise its own taxes. Since the first elections to the autonomous Basque parliament in 1980, Basque nationalists have gained majority control over all political institutions – local, provincial and national – of the Basque country. In 1984, the PNV gained control of the Basque government, the three provincial governments and 85 % of all local authorities, including those of the three provincial capitals. In addition, Basque nationalists dominate, among other things, the trade unions, employers' organizations, chambers of commerce, cooperatives, provincial savings banks (the *cajas de ahorros*) and, very importantly, the public administration. Even the Basque bishops and Bilbao's famous football club, Athlétic de Bilbao, move within the nationalist orbit. In short, for most purposes Basque nationalism has won its battles both with Madrid and with its Basque non-nationalist opposition. Although Basque socialists still receive votes – and frequently many of them – the cultural, social and political hegemony of the Basque nationalist community is now uncontestable.

On my visits to the Basque country I keep expecting to see change. Certainly the progressive economic decline of the area is starkly visible. Moreover, although the unyielding cleavage between *españolistas* and *abertzales* remains, the boundary is maintained with less tension. The competition is over. But otherwise, the region's political patterns and attitudes seem essentially unaltered although at times they are manifested in a novel manner.

Despite eleven years of democracy and eight years of home rule, the majority of Basque voters still do not accept the legitimacy of the Spanish state, although most reluctantly concede its legality. Despite the resounding economic crisis of the Basque country which has rendered many industrial areas into wastelands, created an unemployment toll of 24%, fed urban crime and made the area into a seedbed for drug abuse, political debate focuses on issues of a different sort. The position of Navarra and Euskadi Norte, *derechos históricos*, *fueros*, the right to self-determination, positive discrimination in favour of Euskera and so forth continue to command prime attention. Another issue is ETA whose violence still disfigures Basque political life and has shattered the moral cohesion of the Basque nationalist community.

Since Spain's first democratic elections of 1977, ETA has killed over 500 civilians and members of the security forces. Recently ETA has been seriously weakened by the coordinated efforts of the Spanish and French security forces which has led to massive arrests of ETA militants, including key ETA leaders, in France and the dismantling of ETA commando groups in Spain. But the organization retains its power of reproduction. As very imperfectly measured by votes given to Herri Batasuna (HB), ETA's political wing, some 14% to 17% of the electorate extend at least tacit support to ETA. The sociological core of ETA's support has moved in two directions. On one hand there has been a major shift toward the most *euskaldun* rural areas. On the other, ETA is receiving increasing support from the least integrated and economically most vulnerable sectors of the immigrant population. The *abertzales de izquierda* continue to use millenarian rhetoric, combining elements of permanent negation and utopian nationalism, and nationalist culture, now enlivened with the raucous sounds of heavy metal rock, as the spearhead of their appeal to youth.

The *abertzales de izquierda*, with ETA at its centre, claim that during these last eleven years nothing really has changed. The Basque people, surrounded by anti-Basque enemies and traitors, remain oppressed. The Spanish police continue to be an army of occupation bringing torture and brutality upon a subject Basque nation.

There is ample evidence that the Spanish police use unacceptably brutal methods of interrogation. This fact bolsters the legitimacy of ETA's violence in the eyes of its supporters. But the violence of ETA cannot be understood primarily as a reaction to either the violence of the previous Franco regime or the current Spanish police.

Stated very briefly and inexactly, ETA is a charismatic organization. The relationship between ETA and its members is not institutionalized. Rather it is governed by symbolic and ritual behaviour required for the group's maintenance. The source of charisma is 'The Cause', understood more as revealed truth than as a rational argument. Whereas, in a religious organization, the relation between the believer and the divine is mediated by, for instance, saints, in ETA it is mediated by martyrs, those who have suffered or died for 'The Cause'. Their portraits are ubiquitously displayed on city walls. During interviews with ETA's sympathizers, photographs of violated bodies are reverently shown as an inevitable preface to the presentation of 'The Cause'. Indeed, inside ETA life is lived through the refraction of death's images.

Despite endless ideological disputes and fragmentation, the independence of a reunited Euskadi and armed struggle have persevered, since ETA's inception, as the dogmatic pillars defining ETA as an organization and underpinning its mission. But ultimately armed struggle is not a means to an end. The twenty years ETA has dedicated to armed struggle have not brought the goal of independence any closer. Rather ETA's violence – car bombings, kidnappings, assassinations of military officers, informers and ETA defectors – is an imperative ritual serving the crucial functions of group solidarity and maintenance.

On one level, violence is a sacrificial sacrament of blood through which 'The Cause', source of charisma and ETA's legitimacy, is given substance. In a sense violence gives intimacy and reality to a cause which is basically remote and intangible. On another level, violence is a ritual of self-affirmation and the solidarity of the radical nationalist community, the *abertzales de izquierda*. Whereas the defence of Euskera, original Basque sovereignty, Basque culture and so forth, serve as symbols defining the Basque nationalist community as a whole, defence of the armed struggle is a symbol defining *abertzales de izquierda* as a distinctive branch within this community.

Although their political ascendence is assured for the foreseeable future, the nationalists have managed the transition from opposition to government with only limited success. Not surprisingly, the PNV has used the vast public resources under its control to favour the nationalist community. For instance, the *ikastolas*, which remain institutions for nationalist socialization, are now fully supported by government subsidies. The autonomous Basque television channel broadcasts almost entirely in Euskera despite the fact that only 25% of the resident population is Basque speaking.

However, the Basque government has been incapable of formulating coherent policies to deal with the urgent economic and social problems crippling the area. A standard nationalist response is to lay blame for failure on the doorstep of Madrid arguing that insufficient resources have been transferred to the Basque country to make satisfactory corrective measures possible. And, indeed, Madrid's socialist politicians often tend to view the

Basque nationalists as unreliable crypto-separatists and thus have attempted to limit the powers of self-government granted in the Basque home rule statute.

Finally, in 1986 the PNV suffered a major split out of which a new nationalist party, Eusko Alkartasuna (Basque Solidarity) whose electoral weight challenges that of the PNV, emerged. The core of the dispute was the rivalry between the two most powerful leaders of Basque nationalism, Mr Xabier Arzalluz, head of the PNV, and Mr Carlos Garaikoetxea, the first president of the Basque government. Both men come from Carlist families, have church backgrounds – Mr Arzalluz is a former Jesuit priest – and have been educated as lawyers.

In Elgeta the consolidation of the moral community has also been achieved. The municipal council is run solely by nationalists of various political shades. Public monuments have been erected to the village martyrs. The state school has been closed. The *ikastola* has replaced it. The Modelo furniture plant has also closed and Dormicoop has opened a new, modern plant. *Cuadrillas* remain the social and political coordinators of village life. Many immigrants and former *jauntxoak* have left the village. Basque nationalist culture has become village culture although now Spanish rock and roll also can be heard in the bars.

The greatest problem the village currently faces is unemployment which has particularly affected the youth. Between 1984 and 1986 Elgeta lost some 100 jobs in the industrial sector. The villagers no longer believe that they can solve the problem through their own resources. Consequently, they look to the Basque government to bring forth solutions. No solutions have been forthcoming and the crisis has only deepened. Therefore, a certain disillusionment has grown. One of the village's former *fuerzas vivas* said to me in 1986: 'Before we had answers to our problems. They were self-government, *conciertos económicos*, the restoration of our Basque culture. All that has been achieved. We have achieved power. Now our problems seem to have no answers at all and what we have achieved doesn't seem that important.'

The village youth respond to their situation in a range of ways. The majority are passive showing little interest in either politics or, to their parents' astonishment, education. Many leave school early and many leave the village entirely. Some join Herri Batasuna or ETA.

Most villagers are afraid of both HB and ETA. They are also afraid to voice public opposition. Many argue that they feel caught between ETA, which is anti-democratic and whose aims and actions they do not understand, and the Spanish state and, especially, the security forces which remain anti-Basque. ETA sympathizers are still included in the *pueblo* of Elgeta. But the moral unity of the *pueblo* is now decomposed.

Conclusion: Ethnic nationalists and patron–clients in southern Europe

Despite the wide diversity of theories that offer explanations of the emergence of ethnic nationalism, most have two points in common. First, the factors inducing nationalism are located in the deep structural changes that have accompanied the process of modernization, the economic part of which is industrialization, the political one, state centralization. Second, the theories are compelling. In the areas affected by the complex package of factors described, those groups which possess the diverse raw materials for a nationalist movement should be expected, more often than not, to generate the leadership and mass support for such a movement. In other words, in the modern world mass based ethnic nationalist movements should be relatively commonplace.

From a brief survey of Mediterranean Europe two self-evident, but contradictory, conclusions can be drawn. First, nationalism has been overwhelmingly the most powerful political force to have operated in the area during the last 150 years or so. Indeed, almost all the states that open onto the Mediterranean are creations to a greater or lesser extent of a recent nationalist drive. Spain is not really an exception. Spain as a nation, in contrast to Spain as a state, had little reality before the mid nineteenth century.

Second, nationalism has been a feeble force. Despite the weight of the nationalist ideology in modern political thought, nationalism has produced very few nation-states in the strict sense of the word. Portugal is perhaps the only exception. Most Mediterranean states are composed of a rich mosaic of culturally different peoples each of whom, according to the nationalist premise, has the right to a separate state or – in the case of German and Slovene speakers in Italy, for example – the right to insist on a readjustment of present political frontiers. Although the intelligentsias of Europe's ethnic minorities – and potential ethnic minorities – frequently press one sort or other of nationalist claim, they rarely receive the loyal mass support needed to make these claims politically threatening to current nation-state arrangements. Indeed, most political boundaries seem relatively secure – at least for the time being. Strong ethnically based drives against these boundaries, as in the case of the Basques or Ulster Catholics, are exceptions, not the rule.

I have tried to show in the Basque case that nationalism has been a very effective instrument in the intense competition for scarce economic and political resources. The same beneficial spin-offs have also accrued to the Scots, Corsicans and Catalans, for instance. If what some defenders of centralism would view as predatory group aggrandizement is such a powerful form of competitive battle, then the relative rarity of strong ethnic nationalist movements in contemporary Europe becomes even more bewildering.

Therefore, explanations of modern ethnic nationalism have to address themselves not only to why these political movements emerge, but just as importantly to why – assuming the necessary political, economic and cultural ingredients are present – ethnic nationalism tends not to emerge.

Obviously to understand the rarity – or negative cases – of ethnic nationalism many factors have to be considered. The role of war, regional policies, economic change, ethnic relations and the size of the cultural unit involved are just some of them. But here I should like to concentrate on only two factors. The first concerns the nature of the state.

The state in the Mediterranean

A major characteristic of the pre-modern world was that the number of written languages were few. In the western part of this world these languages were, by and large, limited to Latin, Greek and Arabic. It was through these languages that the state conducted its business. A major movement over the last 400 years or so has been the transformation of local vernaculars to literary languages and the elevation of many of these to state languages. This movement was part of the process by which the modern world order of nation-states was built. In short, languages with some claim to universality have been replaced by languages that are locally specific as the linguistic medium in which modern states govern their citizens and run their affairs.

On the institutional level, however, it is frequently assumed that a reverse process has occurred. The movement of history, it is often claimed, has entailed the replacement of local political vernaculars with political and institutional norms of a more universal nature. Between states there is considerable overlap in the content of, for instance, their constitutions. Within states the assumption underlying official constitutions, statutes, policies and regulations is that they consist of rights, obligations and rules that are equally applicable to all citizens under the state's jurisdiction. On an official, formal level this replacement has to a large extent occurred. The special exemptions, privileges and local legislative bodies which made most of pre-modern Europe – as well as most of the rest of the world – into mosaics of autonomous localities have been abolished and replaced by unified centralized states. However, I shall suggest that on the unofficial, informal level, the level on which things actually happen, this replacement has not taken place to the same extent. Real power is still exercised to an important degree through the vernacular idiom of local values, structures and particularities. This, I believe, is a salient feature of many states in Mediterranean Europe.

As Stein Rokkan (1982) has pointed out, the great paradox of European development is that the strongest and most durable state systems emerged at the periphery of the old Roman Empire. The Mediterranean heartlands remained fragmented. This heartland was densely studded with cities linked in a broad trade belt. When the unifying mantle of the Roman Empire collapsed, the area was left with a patchwork of intensely possessive and competitive city–states and principalities which made it impossible to single out any one centre as superior to all others. There was no geographic core around which a territorially based state system, commanding the resources of a periphery, could emerge.

However, while this whole area was politically fragmented, on one level it was culturally – nationally – unified. Latin and Greek not only remained the languages of élite communication, they were also the languages of religion. The parallel of this on the other side of the Mediterranean was the fragmentary effects of segmentary kinship organization on the political level and the unifying effects of Islam and Arabic on the cultural one.

In contrast, in the periphery of this city-studded territory, state centres could be built up under much less competition. Because of two developments these emerging state systems could imprint a national culture onto their inhabitants from an early stage. The first development was the Gutenberg press, the essential technology of political propaganda and, therefore, of nation-building. The second was the Reformation which untied the peripheral areas from Roman cultural uniformity and began to bind élite and religious communication to a particular vernacular. The combined effects of both developments was a strengthening of the cultural distinctiveness of the emerging state systems. Each possessed its own priesthood and intelligentsia who were confined to a given vernacular and who in turn instilled a sense of national distinctiveness onto the population at large. In this context the devastating effects of the Counter-Reformation on southern Europe, which set the area still further behind, should be noted.

Equally notable was the failure of 19th-century liberalism in southern Europe. The central vision of liberalism was the construction of a political and economic framework for a modern bourgeois society. Although liberalism was part of the ideological foundation of the nationalist cause in Spain, Italy, Greece and so forth, in none of these areas was it able to overcome deep pre-existing social and regional cleavages and rivalries.

That most Mediterranean nation–states emerged late with only a very brief experience of nation-building or state-building has had several crucial consequences. The central point is that within these states differing and conflicting modes of political legitimation and representation continued to coexist.

The following six features are characteristic, at least to some extent, of most southern European states.

First, although these newly consolidated states, modelling themselves on their northern European neighbours, adopted democratic institutions and took on the full range of modern state functions and obligations, they were and often are incapable of fulfilling their constitutional and statutory obligations. The main reason is that the bureaucracy of the state emerged ineffective and inefficient. In many respects the shortcomings of the *ancien régime* were never corrected. Although the state is capable of making decisions, laws and short-term plans, it lacks the mechanism for implementing its decisions and plans. An impartial, responsive and technically competent bureaucratic apparatus which smoothly links the state to the local level and the citizens is missing.

Second, these states do not appear as modern states in a Weberian sense. Arguably no states operate as modern states in a Weberian sense, but the difference between say, Sweden and Italy is qualitative, not quantitative. Frequently the state is viewed both by those who staff it and those governed by it as an 'institution for the allocation of spoils', a phrase used by Weber to describe the pre-bureaucratic state. The notions of 'civil service' and 'citizenship' have never been translated into practice in a real way. State functionaries tend to regard their positions in terms of a personalized exercise of authority and not in terms of an obligatory extension of service to or the implementation of the rights of individual citizens.

Third, the state clearly reflects the particularistic, personalized social structures from which it arose. These states are often staffed by a high proportion of individuals from rural and pre-industrial backgrounds who remain carriers of traditional values and are tied to traditional political and social obligations. Indeed, traditional social relations and values have been superimposed onto and have often subordinated normative state rules. The relationship between normative, but often inoperative, state procedures and informal, but often traditionally sanctioned, procedures depends on a complex interplay between the two.

Critically, the apparatus of these states is interwoven with thick, intricate networks of patron–client relationships. These are the networks upon which individuals depend, through a chain of patronage, in order to exercise many of their claims on the state, be they claims to social benefits, economic credits or, very importantly, jobs. Conversely, these networks – rather than the formal institutions of the state – tie the individual, through a chain of clientelism, into the state centre.

Fourth, local loyalties, identities and power structures have remained strong. The state has been incapable of usurping the power of local notables. Moreover, while the state claims a monopoly of the legitimate use of physical force within its territory, it is frequently unable to enforce this claim. ETA in Spain and the *mafia* in Sicily are two examples.

Fifth, important resource controllers within the public administration (or, in fact, government) often have a personal following outside the state upon which they rely to maintain their position within the state. Therefore, decisions made regarding the allocation of resources frequently relate more to the need of maintaining this clientele support group, either through rewards or controls, than to considerations of a general concern.

Finally, the state is unable to reform itself, to transform itself in accordance with the changing requirements of its citizenry. The reasons are three-fold. First, it is unable to reform itself for the same reason it is unable to implement policy; a disinterested, competent apparatus of administration is absent. Individuals tend to be recruited into the state primarily on the basis of ethnic, political or personal loyalties. Consideration of professional merit is often secondary. Second, state functionaries whose jobs, chances for promotion and privileges depend on an ongoing system of patronage and administrative inefficiency constitute a potent obstacle to change. Third, the very nature of the state militates against corporate action by outside forces aimed at its reform. Since patron–client networks, which channel the flow of favours and benefits, are anchored in hierarchical relations between individuals, individuals tend to perceive and pursue their interests in terms of the vertical linkages that are open to them. If sufficiently pervasive, such networks tend to reinforce a fragmentation of the population. Moreover, public dissension can be diffused by extending the chains of patronage and the consequent flow of benefits to include potentially disruptive groups. In short, the state's deficiencies are self-perpetuating.

However, the state is not static. The political realities with which it contends are subject to change. The balance between clientelism and informal, personalized procedures on the one hand and technical professionalism/legal bureaucratic authority on the other varies in accordance with changes in social, political and economic conditions.

I suggest that this type of defectively institutionalized state is related to regionalist or ethnic nationalist movements on two levels.

First, a notable feature of ethnic nationalism in southern Europe is that the nationalist option is more commonly adopted by, and is more politically intractable among, economically advanced groups than among groups suffering the effects of relative underdevelopment. And the reason relates in part to the nature of the state. For those groups who possess a claim to a differentiated culture and whose economic interests are founded in sophisticated industrial or commercial activities, this heavy, immovable state structure presents a serious obstacle. This type of state requires the sacrifice of economic rationality to personal political considerations. Modern economic activity requires a modern efficient and effective state. It requires a state that is capable of carrying out the appropriate economic plans and is able to reform itself.

In order to protect their economic interests there are four options open to these relatively advantaged groups, three of which require one form or other of nationalist legitimation. First, they can simply withdraw from the state and disclaim all obligation and responsibility to it. This has been the option adopted by Basque nationalism. Second, they can attempt to modernize the state from behind the protective barrier of ample political autonomy. This has been the strategy of Catalan nationalism. Third, they can insist on monopoly control over, or at least privileged access to, the state despite competing claims for representation from other groups. Here Greek Cypriots come to mind. The fourth option, illustrated by northern Italy, does not entail nationalism. This option involves an implicit treaty of mutual non-interference between a social sector and the state.

To explain the second level on which the state is related to nationalism, the concept of regional brokers must be introduced. Here we return to the personalized nature of Mediterranean states. A regional broker is that person or group of people who form a nodal point or synapse in the chain of patron–client relations between a region and the central state apparatus. Examples of individuals or groups who operate as regional brokers are numerous in anthropological literature. Anton Blok describes the role of the *mafioso* in Sicily as 'predicated on his ability to acquire and maintain control over the paths linking the local infrastructure of the village to the superstructure of the larger society' (1974: 7). A similar role has frequently been attributed to local Christian Democratic politicians in other parts of Italy. E. Kofman (1980) suggests that the clans in Corsica traditionally mediated between the local population and the French authorities. The system of *caciquismo* in Spain has received considerable attention (Pitt-Rivers 1954, Romero-Maura 1977). John Campbell (1964) has described the intricate web of power brokerage between transhumant Sarakatsani shepherds and the Greek bureaucracy. In short, regional or, in the case of the Sarakatsani, ethnic brokers are characteristic of most, if not all, Mediterranean states (see Davis 1977 for further discussion). Usually they represent a continuation of traditional power structures over which the state has not been able – or willing – to exert its authority.

Regional brokers are not the same as a regional élite although specific brokers may form part of such an élite. A regional élite possesses some degree of corporate identity and may or may not have direct access to the apparatus of the central state. The position of a regional élite depends on the political and economic structure of the region. The attitude of this élite to the central state may be one of either collaboration or confrontation. Regional brokers are political entrepreneurs who function between the two political domains. As Richard Adams has pointed out: 'His actual control over either sphere depends on his success in dealing with the other; his controls on one level of articulation provide a basis for controls on the other... He controls one domain only by virtue of having access to derivative power from a larger domain' (1970: 320–21). The attitude of the regional broker to the defective state is one of collusion. These brokers operate in the interstices of the state.

If regional brokers tie the individual into the state by forming a critical link in the personalized network through which material and political rewards are channeled, it follows that local political loyalties will be articulated with reference to these brokers. Therefore I suggest that it is only when this network of regional brokerage collapses – when it is no longer able and/or willing to deliver benefits to the individual from the state, or benefits from the individual to the state – that a regionalist or nationalist movement with widespread local support *can* emerge.[1]

Certainly this proposition seems to be supported by at least some evidence.

In Corsica one of the immediate effects of the French regional plan of 1957 was to undermine entirely in the eastern part of the island the *chefs de clan* whose position depended on their relation to a traditional rural society. Bypassed by imported French administrators and outside capital, the clans were unable to integrate into the new 'foreign' economic and political forces that were transforming Corsican society. Since the clans were no longer in a position to mediate profitably between the French bureaucracy and the clan's local constituents, the tie that linked, albeit indirectly, many Corsicans to the French state was also severed. Into this vacuum emerged a politically invigorated Corsican regional élite in confrontation, rather than collaboration, with the French state. However, in the Corsican hinterland where the regional plan had little effect, the role of the clans as brokers continued unchanged. W. Bertels (personal communication) has pointed out that the mayors (or *chefs de clan*) continue to control the distribution of social benefits, jobs and protection and 'therefore people vote for them. The inhabitants of the villages in the hinterland are not interested in an autonomous Corsican nation, for it is the French state – and on the local level the *chef de clan* as mediator between the state and the individual – that keeps them alive'.

In Sicily the short-lived separatist movement of 1944–45 can be traced to similar factors. The links of the large estate owners and the *mafiosi* to the Italian regime were ruptured by the fall of fascism and the installation of a new Italian administration. When it became clear that the Christian Democratic Party was willing to establish new ties of patronage to the Sicilian estate owners and their satellites, the separatist movement lost all momentum (Blok, 1974: 192–93).

The enthusiasm for Andalucian autonomy can also be related to the disintegration of the traditional system of power brokerage, *caciquismo*. The decline of *caciquismo* and the emergence of a popularly based autonomy movement occurred more or less simultaneously and, it is possible to argue, are causally related. Very broadly speaking, the position of the *cacique* was eroded through two fundamental changes. First, his economic power as employer of labour was undercut because of the introduction of modern agricultural methods which drastically reduced the need for seasonal labour. Second, because of the replacement of the authoritarian Franco regime with a new democratic government in 1976, the *caciques* no longer had assured access to power in the wider political system or control over local political institutions. Although Andalucian autonomy had been ardently espoused for some ten years by a group of intellectuals, the movement did not gain a significant popular foothold until 1978 or so when the ability of the *caciques* to serve either patrons or clients had collapsed.

Clearly a wide range of factors is crucial to understanding the three cases briefly described above. However, I suggest that in all three examples the disruption of traditional systems of power brokerage released people from vertical, individual linkages and, thereby, made them available for corporate forms of opposition. In other words, the breakdown of patronage was a necessary pre-condition for the emergence of a regionalist or nationalist movement. Arguably, in Corsica and Andalucia autonomist aspirations will diminish dramatically if an effective system of brokerage is reestablished.[2]

Patronage, ethnic nationalism and culture

In the introduction to the section on Elgeta I defined culture as existing on two interrelated levels. The first level comprised the visible, surfaced elements of culture. The second comprised culture as a shared set of meanings and cognitive categories. I have suggested elsewhere (Heiberg, 1975) that because of the cognitive embeddedness of cultures, there is no reason to assume that specific cultures are totally and immediately malleable. Moreover, specific cultural complexes have been formed and moulded by a lengthy historical process. Cultures seem to possess an inherent inertia. Almost inevitably a time lag exists between changes in the external economic and/or political environment surrounding a culture and an adaptive response stemming from that culture. Cultures also seem to impose restrictions on the types of change that they can absorb.

It is in this context that four characteristics of modernization become vitally important. (1) The imperatives of Western industrial economies have to a large extent replaced traditionally determined role relationships as the mechanism for structuring vast areas of social life. (2) From an historical viewpoint, the spread of industrialization has occurred with great rapidity. (3) Industrialization has been the only phenomenon in human history that has caused persuasive and almost global economic and cultural integration. The multi-ethnic empires of the past did not possess this ability. Except for the centres of these empires, people enjoyed considerable political, economic and certainly cultural autonomy. (4) This cultural integration has occurred because industrialization, radiating out from Western Europe, is a specific culture in its own right.

Inherent in the nature of modern industrialization is contained a specific concept of social order backed by a certain set of values such as individualism, work, literacy, impersonalized and general standards. It also entails special concepts of time and space, specific organizational norms based on bureaucracy and a new pattern of social stratification founded, theoretically, on achievement. In the areas to which it has spread, industrialization and modernization have imposed from above and without regard to the raw cultural material involved this specific cultural complex (Heiberg, 1975).

In other words, within a very brief span of time a multitude of different, culturally relative ways of ordering, thinking and doing things have been threatened with complete replacement by *one* way of ordering, thinking and doing things. It has frequently been argued that the nineteenth-century German nationalist ideal was born out of a protest against French intellectual universalism. Equally, but perhaps more compellingly, twentieth-century ethnic nationalisms can be viewed as an attempt to combat the uniformity, homogeneity and universalism implied in the culture of industrialization. Nationalism and its stress on the sovereignty of cultures attempt to create the conditions by which the forces of modernization can be regulated and shaped to fit pre-existing moral and cognitive orientations and attitudes. It is an attempt to make modernization appear acceptable and understandable. Folkloric elements such as dances, dress and even language act as symbols for other deeply hidden cultural elements which are much more difficult to display, justify and defend. Within the framework of the special characteristics of modernization, the fact of cultural diversity leads to the felt need for cultural sovereignty.

Let us return to the Basque material briefly. Initial Basque industrialization (1876–1900) occurred with a rapidity which many foreign observers in Bilbao at the time declared was probably unequalled in the European experience and it placed intolerable strains upon the entire social fabric of Bilbao. The social sectors which so intransigently turned to nationalism were those which formed part of pre-industrial Bilbao – shopkeepers, artisan producers and so forth. Their principal target was not Madrid, but the process of industrialization itself. The basic accusation was that through industrialization, the massive inflow of foreigners (i.e. Spanish immigrants) and the hierarchical economic and political relations enforced by the Basque oligarchy, Basque values had been inverted. Modern Basque life was judged illegitimate. It was simply anti-Basque. To justify this resentment the urban nationalists resorted to a mythical ideology based on rural symbols. In terms of factual information, the nationalist arguments concerning the nature of pre-industrial Basque society are demonstrably incorrect. However, if one examines the ideological guidelines of traditional Basque society, it can be understood why modern Basque life appeared an intolerable inversion of social codes and values. Culture on the level of language and 'pristine Basque dances' was not really the issue – few urban nationalists were Basque in this sense – but culture on the deeper level which determines the moral forms of social relations.

Ethnic nationalists or clients

However, as mentioned previously, Mediterranean Europe, despite the rapidity of modernization and ethnic diversity of the area, is not convulsed by nationalist activity. Italy is a good case in point. One reason is that ethnic nationalism has a very powerful competitor in the modern world. The competitor is patron–client relations of one version or another. The establishment of personal hierarchical networks is another means of avoiding and dealing with the universalism and disruptions of modernization. These networks are dependent on particularistic rewards and personal loyalty and contact. Like nationalism which attempts to administer modernization through culturally understandable norms, patronage and clientelism are also means by which the culturally alien drive behind modernization can be subverted to comply with local norms and perceptions. Like nationalism which can change its meaning and content in response to changes in circumstances, patron–client relationships have a similar flexibility. Neither are necessarily diminished by, although both have come to terms with, for instance, the rise of class action and consciousness. Moreover, both can be used for the achievement of individual goals. Clientelism, like nationalism, offers a potentially effective strategy in the competition over scarce economic and political resources. Finally, both are modes of social cohesion. Nationalism represents a vertical mode of cohesion among, theoretically at least, equals. Clientelism represents a vertical mode of cohesion among unequals.

Marcel Mauss, among others, has argued that exchange – people giving things to each other – is the fundamental integrative act of society. I suggest that in southern Europe we can distinguish between two different culturally preferred modes of exchange. For lack of better terms, these modes can be labelled (1) unbalanced, delayed exchange and (2) balanced, immediate exchange. In those societies in which the former is the preferred moral norm – and preferred moral norms are a part of deep culture – in local, individual exchange, permanent patron–client relations will tend to be generated as a logical consequence of the mode of exchange practised.

In unbalanced, delayed exchange there is a significant interval between the presentation of a gift or service and the reciprocal presentation of a counter-gift or service. The items exchanged tend to be unequal in kind and in value. Implicitly or explicitly, the delay in the exchange and the inequality of things exchanged establishes or consolidates ongoing creditor–debtor relations. These relations become part of permanent hierarchical networks, which on each level demand unbalanced, delayed exchange, when they are perceived as the means by which individual interests are best served. In such societies the cultural, political and economic challenges of modernization will tend to be handled through individual manipulation of these hierarchical relations. Such societies will tend to develop popularly supported regionalist or nationalist movements only under the two circumstances mentioned previously. One, if their economic base depends on a type of coherent, predictable political intervention which is well beyond the capacity of personalized hierarchies to satisfy. Two, if these personalized hierarchies collapse at the 'regional' level.

In those societies in which the second mode of exchange – balanced, immediate exchange – is the preferred moral norm regulating individual exchange, this form of personalized hierarchical relations, if they develop at all, will tend to be unstable, temporary and not perceived as legitimate. It is only these latter societies, under conditions which E. Gellner describes as 'the uneven spread of modernization', which have an inbuilt propensity for strong, mass ethnic nationalist movements.

These two modes of exchange should be viewed as ideal forms. They do not necessarily describe the actual form or the only form of exchange practised in a given society. Moreover, neither is necessarily stable over time. They describe the mode of exchange that individuals believe *ought* to be practised. On the local level the moral justification for unbalanced, delayed exchange is conceived in terms of the value of social harmony, amity, hospitality and the general obligations between neighbours, friends and kin. Insistence on balanced, immediate exchange implies the absence of or refusal to enter into a social relation. Although this unequal mode of exchange may co-exist with a popular ideology of egalitarianism – and on the local level it usually does – the pressure in the system supports hierarchy. This type of exchange on the local level, deemed as moral, forms a model for the flow of authority and power in the wider political system, deemed as legitimate. The apex of the network this form of exchange generates in any given society is also the point at which power and resources accumulate. That apex tends to be the state and state functionaries are often the pivotal figures.

Societies in which balanced, immediate exchange is the preferred norm are less frequent. Basque and Catalan society are two examples. The moral stress behind this form of exchange is the insistence that exchange should explicitly reflect the social equality of the individuals involved. Unbalanced exchange is perceived as an attempt to subordinate. In those societies in which the drive is toward balanced exchange, the logical moral conclusion, i.e. the culturally acceptable norm, is that political power ought to be evenly distributed. Centralized power is rarely judged legitimate.

Again, returning to the Basque material, in the historical section I attempted to show that Basque political and economic life has been nowhere near as egalitarian as the chief advocates of this ideology proclaim. But this is not the point. In the section on Elgeta I suggest that balanced, immediate exchange is the only form that is judged fitting, decent and desirable although realities have often made this form of exchange difficult to put into practice. This insistence upon social and political equality has had evident effects not only in Elgeta, but throughout Basque society as a whole. In the sixteenth century, because of popular agitation, all Basques were granted equal noble status in order to abolish the special status of the Basque aristocracy. Permanent patron–client relations have never been a feature of the area. Mechanisms to disperse political power and severely restrict the exercise of authority are common features of many Basque political, social and economic institutions. The industrial cooperatives at Mondragon, the internal organization of Basque nationalist parties as well as the entire parallel organizations of Elgeta and the Basque nationalist community are just a few examples. (See S. Ott, 1979, for discussion of exchange among French Basques.)

On the local level this emphasis on equality is striking especially to an observer familiar with other parts of Spain. For example, in Castile and Andalucia it is usual for individuals to use pseudo-kinship institutions, such as godparenthood, to consolidate unequal relations with other individuals. It is considered desirable and advantageous for a child to have a godparent who is of a higher status than the parents themselves. In the Basque country such explicit statements of inequality are very infrequent. For example, at a restaurant meal in the Basque country one rarely witnesses the ceremonial battle to pay the bill so common in the rest of Spain. The battle concerns a public claim for precedence, for social and political authority. The outcome of the battle is seldom in doubt. Although personal pride demands that everyone present their claim, the individual whose claim to precedence has already been established usually pays. The remaining diners willingly accept the status of social debtors. In the Basque country each participant pays exactly his or her share of the expenses. The often repeated phrases, *cada uno el suyo* (each his own) and *berdin–berdin* (equal–equal) represent unbreakable rules in these matters.

The argument in this concluding section can be roughly summarized as follows: most theories of ethnic nationalism rest their analysis on factors that tend to be applicable to most societies and/or ethnic groups. While some ethnic groups under the described conditions take up the nationalist option, the majority do not. Especially in the light of the weight of the nationalist ideal and the strategic advantages for group benefit this ideal offers, the question then becomes why most ethnic groups (or potential ethnic groups) are apparently immune to nationalism. Within the context of southern Europe I have suggested that ethnic nationalism and patron–client relations are alternative – although not necessarily mutually exclusive – strategies for dealing with certain fundamental political, economic and cultural problems. On one level the alternative adopted in any given case depends on political and economic factors relating to the state and on another to pre-existent cultural orientations of the society involved which become relevant because of the nature of modernization.

Notes

1 The Basques in history

1 The latter three provinces lie inside France and form approximately one-third of the modern *département* of Basse-Pyrénées.
2 The evidence for this theory was derived from the etymology of certain Basque words. For example, Guipúzcoa = gu-iz-puzhko-ak which can be taken to mean 'We whose language was interrupted.'
3 In a recent study among the Basques (D. F. Roberts, E. Coope, B. Kerr, 1976, 'Dermatoglyphic variation among Spanish Basques' in *Man*, vol. 2, no. 4), testing for dermatoglyphic variations showed homogeneity of patterns among Spanish Basques, local heterogeneity in the French Basques and significant differences between the French and Spanish Basques. In the measurement of blood group frequencies significant differences in the ABO and MN systems of the French and Spanish Basques were also apparent. None of the studies of physical anthropologists have provided any conclusive evidence in support of the various theories concerning the origins of the Basques.
4 The political position of Navarra in relation to the other Basque provinces has been an issue of intense debate among Basque politicians and ideologues. The nationalists hold that Navarra by nature is part of Euskadi and by history its very centre. Navarra, however, has followed a historical trajectory quite distinct from the other three Basque provinces.
5 The *Recopilación foral* of Guipúzcoa of 1583 has an entire section dedicated to regulations concerning the *parientes mayores*. Some examples: Chapter 41, Law 2: 'No council, villa or place may give presents or promises to any Pariente Mayor of other persons.' Law 3: 'The Parientes Mayores may not form bands, nor associations, nor assemblies, nor *allegamientos* of armed people against anyone.' Law 9: 'The Province from public and common funds may pursue the *Parientes Mayores* and their servants and allies for the misdeeds they have committed.' Law 11: 'Those *Parientes Mayores* who resist the execution of the mandates of the hermandad and the mayors must be punished.' Law 13: 'No *Pariente Mayor* may participate in the elections for public office in this province.'
6 Against this view, Garcia Venero (1969: 92–94) has argued that the *pase foral* signified that the kings of Castile conceded to the Basque *Juntas Generales* the right to act as consultative organs with the function of ratifying royal decrees and administrative practices. They were not regarded, according to Venero, as legal bodies with direct, autonomous legislative power.
7 The word for 'God' in Euskera is *jaungoiko* which literally means the *jaun* of the heights.

8 Data concerning land tenure during this period is extremely scarce. The census for Vizcaya and Guipúzcoa taken in 1704 puts the peasantry who owned land near 50%. Approximately 47% were tenant farmers and another 2% landless labourers. In Alava and Navarra the percentage of peasants who owned land was significantly lower. These figures represent, however, only the percentage of peasants who owned land and not the percentage of land that was worked by peasant landholders.

9 Although all Basques by birth were entitled to noble status, socially those who were noble 'by blood' were distinguished from those made noble 'by law'. The king of Castile used the argument that the Basques were entitled to noble status since they had never been invaded by the Muslims and their blood was not contaminated by either the Moors or the Jews. This argument was false, but, nonetheless, provided the excuse for the king to grant this privilege to the Basques while withholding it from the Castilians.

10 The *vecindad*, or *auzoa* in Euskera, was a fundamental political grouping in traditional Basque society. A *vecindad* was composed of various neighbouring farmsteads and in turn various *vecindades* were grouped into a municipality. Participation in public municipal affairs required the status of *vecino*, i.e. recognized membership in a specific, linked *vecindad*. Such status could normally only be obtained through birth or marriage into a farmstead of the *vecindad*. Thus all outsiders were barred from political intervention in municipal life.

11 Although all *Vizcaínos* were legally noble by birth, new ordinances were introduced which required this nobility to be proven officially. The process was complicated and costly. Hence, for many political purposes only those with titles of nobility granted by the kings of Castile and later Spain were considered sufficiently noble.

12 Basque fishermen were often found at the vanguard of the many popular uprisings that have afflicted the Basque country. And they have always been regarded as forming a society apart. Sharing entrepreneurial skills that have characterized so many Basque economic adventures, Basque fishermen have been ardent internationalists economically in spite of their intense political localism. By the fourteenth century whaling in the Atlantic was almost a Basque monopoly. As Julio Caro Baroja has pointed out (1971: 196) it was probably more than coincidence that the first voyage to circumnavigate the globe was begun by a Portuguese, Magellan, and successfully completed by a Basque, Elcano. Moreover, Basque seafarers played a decisive role in the reconquering of Sevilla and Granada from the Muslims.

13 The 1787 census gives the following figures concerning the number of individuals with *la condición de hijodalquía*, noble status.

Guipúzcoa
50,502 nobles out of a population of 119,128 (approx. 50%)
Vizcaya
54,250 114,863 (approx. 50%)
Alava
12,161 70,710 (approx. 25%)
Navarra
13,054 224,548 (approx. 6%)

14 The role of the Jesuits has been extremely important in the Basque country. Closely allied to the upper Basque bourgeoisie, the Jesuits nonetheless rejected the aristocratic vision of life common to the Spanish upper classes. Instead they emphasized the virtue of hard work and efficiency and gave their spiritual support

to many of the economic and technological reforms introduced into the Basque provinces.

2 The foundations of the modern Basque country

1 Prior to the nineteenth century the *villas* had been dominant in the provincial *junta* and *diputación* of Guipúzcoa. This changed, however, in the early nineteenth century when the *diputación* was reorganized. San Sebastian became just one more member in a body controlled by the rural notables. A similar situation had always existed in Vizcaya.

2 Pinedo has remarked (1974: 474) in reference to its peasant base and guerrilla nature that the Carlist Wars are the clearest example of a 'counter-revolutionary, revolutionary war'.

3 The most prolific mine – already exploited in Roman times – was in Somorrostros 10 km west of Bilbao. Of all the ore extracted between 1876 and 1891, 87% came from this mine.

4 In comparison, in 1864 France was producing around 1 million tons and Great Britain almost 5 million tons.

5 Table 8 *Extraction of iron ore in Bilbao mining industry* (*tons*)

	Total production	Export abroad
1870	201,875	
1876	400,000	350,000
1880	2,444,656	2,345,598
1885	3,836,572	3,295,982
1890	4,795,876	4,272,918
1895	4,621,291	4,037,057
1899	6,004,364	5,412,763
1900	5,229,922	4,632,502

Source: Solozabal, 1975: 87

6 Portilla (1977) estimates that of the total benefits obtained from ore export between 1878 and 1900, 53% went to the Bilbao bourgeoisie and 47% to foreign interests.

7 By 1914 336 km of railroads had been built in Vizcaya. This gave the province the highest density of railroads in Spain and among the highest in Europe.

8 The wages in the major steel factories were considerably higher than in the mines. Jobs in Altos Hornos in particular were subject to intense competition. This wage differential was one of the reasons why the steel workers, of whom a high proportion were Basques – unlike the miners – were less militant and often gave only very limited support to the strikes in the mining industry. Partly due to the shortage of labour, between 1885 and 1895 wage increases largely kept pace with increased prices. However, between 1895 and 1905 food prices increased around 37%, whereas wages rose by only some 5%.

3 History as myth

1 Prince Louis Lucien Bonaparte, who made various trips to the Basque country during the mid nineteenth century, estimated the number of Basque speakers at 800,000 of which 140,000 were French Basques. Ladislao de Velasco in 'Los Euskaros en Alava, Guipúzcoa and Vizcaya', Barcelona 1879, calculated the number of Basque-speakers at 471,000 of which 80,000 were French Basques. The total population during this period was approximately 876,000 of which 165,000 were French Basques.

2 *Linguae Vasconum Primitiae*, by Bernart Dechepara, was printed in France and could better be described as a pamphlet than a book. The second book was a translation of the New Testament published in 1571.

3 In 1888 Carlism underwent a split. On the one hand was the *Comunión* headed by Carlos VII and on the other was the Integrist Party led by Ramón Nocedal. The *integristas*, although theocratic, refused to accept the Carlist monarchy.

4 'Vizcay′tik Bizkai′ra' means 'from Vizcaya to Bizkaia'. Bizkaia, according to Azkue, was the Basque spelling and Vizcaya the Spanish.

5 It should be noted that Sabino de Arana's elder brother, Luis, exerted a critical influence. Arguably Basque nationalism originated first with Luis who believed that the prime struggle was not between liberals and Carlists, but between Vizcaya and Spain. Luis de Arana first formulated this thesis to his brother at Easter of 1882. Years later the nationalists began to commemorate this event at Aberri Eguna (National Day) now held annually on Easter Sunday.

6 The origin of the term *maketo* is not clear. Possibly it was taken from the French word, *métèque*. Alternatively it may derive from the Spanish word, *maco*, meaning a small bundle, usually containing clothes, which was standard equipment among many immigrants. In any case the term made its first appearance in Spanish political vocabulary during the Carlist Wars. It was then used by the Carlists to designate the liberals. For Arana a *maketo* was anyone from *Maketania* which consisted of the entire Iberian peninsula minus Portugal and the Basque country.

7 Arana was, of course, as much a product of Bilbao as the Basque industrialists. However, his rejection of industrialization led to a rejection of Bilbao. 'In Bilbao, today and ever since its foundation, live a handful of bad *bizkainos* who govern the *villa* by whim and maintain a continuous fight against the peasant, the *baserritar*, the native of the Anteiglesias and the only authentic Bizkayan ... The harm that Bilbao, terrible enemy of the Patria Bizkaya, has caused is incalculable ... Bilbao has always placed itself above the general interests of the Republic ... Poor Bizkaya, always sold by her own sons, always deceived' ('Mártires de la Patria', C. W., pp. 1281 and 1285).

8 Contemporary Basque nationalists have changed the spelling of this word to 'Euskadi'. The substitution of the 's' for the 'z' is supposed to represent a rejection of Arana's racism. Arana also invented the word *Euzkotar* (of the Basque race), to mean the Basque people. Whereas Euzkotar never gained popular acceptance, Euskadi has entered into official usage throughout Spain.

4 From the illuminated few to the Basque moral community

1 By his own admission Arana was well treated while in prison. Arana served another brief period in prison in 1902 after he had sent a telegram, which was

intercepted, to President Roosevelt congratulating him on 'the independence of the very noble Federation of Cuba over which you preside...'.

2 The evolution of foralism, or *fuerismo*, is complicated. In very brief terms, foralism can be divided into two periods. During the first period lasting up to 1876, foralism was spearheaded by the rural notables and contained several pre-nationalistic traits. For example, there was an insistence that education should be given in Euskera in order to prevent the penetration of teachers foreign to the Basque language and customs. However, after 1876 advocacy of foralism had largely shifted to the urban liberals. Foralism provided the political inspiration behind the nineteenth-century literary movement.

3 Ramon de la Sota y Llano was the only member of the oligarchy ever to join the nationalists. His financial interests were impressive and included Sota y Aznar Shipping, Euskalduna Shipbuilding, Polar Insurance, Sierra Menera, Setares and Alhamilla Mines, and Mediterranean Iron and Steel. He was also on the board of directors of the Banco de Bilbao, general secretary of the Bilbao Chamber of Commerce and Industry, president of Shipowners of Vizcaya. However, since his major holdings were in shipping, Sota was in a different position from other members of the oligarchy. He was much less dependent on state protectionism. Moreover, many of Sota's enterprises were technologically advanced and capable of competing on the international market.

4 Sabino de Arana won his seat with 4,545 votes. The distribution of votes in Bilbao is illustrative of the triangular configuration that was to dominate Basque politics. Most of the nationalist votes were obtained in the traditional middle-class *barrios*. In the working-class *barrios* the nationalists were defeated by the socialists and in the upper-class areas, they were defeated by the liberals and monarchists. A large share of the nationalist votes were not so much votes for the PNV as against Chávarri. Fusi (1975: 195) estimates that of the 2,300 votes that Arana received in Bilbao only some 300 were nationalist votes. The large number of votes polled in the rural areas give a deceptive picture of nationalist strength in the countryside. Integrists, Carlists and Catholic foralists also supported the nationalist candidates.

5 Partly this 'españolista' evolution was an attempt tactically to approach and emulate Catalanism. The Lliga Catalana had achieved an electoral triumph in 1901. The idea of collaboration between Spain's peripheral regionalisms became appealing to Arana and especially to the moderate nationalists. Furthermore, Arana viewed this change as a means of escaping governmental repression which had been specially severe during 1902. Arana maintained, however, his goal of an independent Euzkadi which, for complex reasons, he believed England would support and protect. However, the majority of nationalists were unaware of Arana's 'españolista evolution' and dismissed it as mere rumour-mongering.

6 The intransigent factions in the Basque movement have in general organized around a magazine (e.g. the *aberrianos*, magazine *Aberri*; the *Jagi-Jagi*, magazine *Jagi-Jagi*) which specialized in doctrinal positions.

7 Rural nationalism will be treated extensively in the section on Elgeta.

8 In Guipúzcoa industrialization not only came late (largely as subsidiary spill-over industry from Bilbao), but was characterized by small industrial concerns. Large industrial enterprises had little impact. Moreover, until the late 1950s Guipúzcoa experienced little Spanish immigration. Most labour needs were satisfied by a constant inflow of rural Basques. The most industrialized centre of Guipúzcoa

was Eibar which rapidly became a focal point for socialism in the province. However, most socialist militants – like the unskilled workers themselves – were Basque by origin and language. The first industrial expansion of Guipúzcoa took place between 1910 and 1917 – a period which exactly coincides with the initial expansion of nationalist sentiment (as reflected by electoral figures) in the province.

9 Engracio de Aranzadi reported that whereas the PNV in 1904 had 20 *batzokis* in Vizcaya and only 4 in Guipúzcoa, by 1908 Vizcaya had 37 local *batzokis* and Guipúzcoa 40 (Ereintza, 1935: 185–86). However, this is probably an optimistic view of nationalist strength, at any rate in Guipúzcoa. I investigated several of the villages in Guipúzcoa mentioned by Aranzadi – specifically Ataun, Oñate, Usurbil and in more detail Elgeta – and found that, while there was some sympathy for certain nationalist candidates and some attempts to implant a nationalist presence, in none of the villages were *batzokis* founded until 1915. In Elgeta a *batzoki* was not established until 1931.

10 Nationalist sentiment and ethnic identification have been notably strong among emigrant Basques. The Basque centres in the Americas served not only to preserve a sense of Basque culture, but also to maintain political and economic links to the Basque country. The emigrant Basque communities in the Americas played a critical role in the nationalist movement after the Spanish Civil War. For further discussion, see W. Douglass and J. Bilbao (1977), *Amerikanuak*: *Basques in the New World*, Reno, University of Nevada Press.

11 Ironically, Meabe, who came from an intensely Catholic, middle-class Bilbao family, was specifically requested by Arana to study socialist doctrine in order to combat it. Arana had a great personal affection for Meabe and his defection, it has been suggested, caused Arana to take the 'social question' more seriously.

12 In 1933 the SOV changed its name to Solidaridad de Trabajadores Vascos – Eusko Langille Alkartasuna, STV-ELA, the name it still uses.

13 The Navarrese defended a position demanding a separate autonomy for Navarra.

5 The moral community and its enemies

1 In *La Nueva Era*, Madrid, 1901 Unamuno wrote, 'In Bilbao the only firm fortress confronting the barbarians of local exclusiveness is socialism. Here the two poles are the so-called *bizkaitarrismo* on one side and socialism on the other.'

2 *La Lucha de Clases* ('El porqué del separatismo', 30 Sept. 1899) argued that the rise of Catalan and Basque nationalism was a direct consequence of the loss of Spain's colonies. Without this economic disaster separatism would have been reduced to 'a half dozen mad men dreaming of Andorran Republics, the great wall of China and a return to a pastoral existence.'

3 Usually Basque nationalist economic demands on the government were firmly backed by the Basque conservatives. Because of their economic power, the Basque conservatives exercised an increasingly influential voice within the various Madrid governments.

4 Because of its open criticism of the Republic, the PNV was approached in 1931 by General Orgaz requesting nationalist support for a military uprising against the Republic. During his meeting with Orgaz, Aguirre paraded 10–15,000 well-disciplined, uniformed *mendigoitzales* (Basque mountaineers) in front of the much impressed general.

5 Basque republicanism was a descendent of Basque liberalism. The republicans

increasingly viewed the *fueros* as democratic, liberal, republican institutions and by 1910 demands for Basque home rule were a persistent feature of the republican platform.

6 There is no evidence to support the frequent claim that a Basque statute was only granted to ensure Basque support for the Republic. However, because the Republican regime feared that the PNV could potentially become neutral in the conflict, the PNV was given the main portfolios in the provisional government. The composition of the Basque government reflected the 1936 election results:

President and Defence	(PNV) José Antonio Aguirre
Justice and Culture	(PNV) Jesús María Leizaola
Interior	(PNV) Telesforo Monzón
Treasury	(PNV) Heliodoro de la Torre
Agriculture	(ANV) Gonzalo Nárdiz
Commerce	(Republican Left) Ramon María Aldasoro
Labour	(PSOE) Juan de los Toyos
Social Services	(PSOE) Juan Garcia
Industry	(PSOE) Santiago Aznar
Public Works	(Communist Party of Euzkadi) Juan Astigarrabia

7 Although the human cost of the civil war in Euskadi is a highly contentious matter, the following figures from a nationalist source give one estimate. (Figures from Astillerra, 'La guerra en Euskadi'.)

Gudaris (soldiers) killed in combat	10,800
Gudaris killed by national planes	4,700
Civilians killed by national planes	10,500
Gudaris missing in combat	3,000
Gudaris injured in combat	17,500
Gudaris injured by bombing	12,500
Civilians injured by bombing	19,500
Basques imprisoned (civilians and military)	86,550
Basques killed in subsequent repression	21,780
Basques exiled	150–200,000

A special target of Franco's fury were the Basque nationalist clergy. During Lent 1937 all Basque nationalist priests were excommunicated. According to Beltza (1974: 321), 16 nationalist priests were executed, 273 imprisoned and 1,300 qualified as undesirable.

6 'España, una, libre y grande'

1 Official policy prohibited the *guardia civiles* from serving in their home areas.

2 Several studies on the subject of Basque – immigrant relations, based on written interviews, have suggested that, although the relations between the two groups may not be particularly good, they were at any rate adequate (Gaur, 1970). I would seriously question these findings because (a) of the extreme reluctance with which immigrants express their attitudes openly on this subject (b) of the reluctance of most people at the time to answer written questionnaires truthfully in any case and (c) these findings are at such radical odds with my daily experiences in the Basque country.

3 All the data on the socio-economic composition of Basque industrial areas show that Spanish immigrants are over represented in the category of unskilled workers. For example, the town of Vergara, Guipúzcoa, according to the 1970 census had a population of 15,184 of which 61.0% were born in the municipality, 20.4%

were Basque immigrants and 18.6% were Spanish immigrants. The socio-economic composition was as follows:

Table 9 *Socio-economic composition, Vergara, 1970 (%)*

Occupation	Vergara	Basque immigrants	Spanish immigrants
Agriculture	66.3	33.1	0.6
Unskilled workers	45.7	18.1	36.2
Skilled workers	61.5	20.1	18.3
White collar	62.6	20.4	17.0
Executive/proprietor	65.9	31.5	3.5
Total active population	55.2	20.2	24.7
Total inactive population	64.4	20.5	14.9

7 The moral community, from clandestinity to power

1 The car in which Txabi Echevarrieta was travelling was stopped by police directing traffic in an area under road repairs. Txabi became nervous, pulled out a gun and shot the policeman. In turn another policeman shot Txabi.

2 Needless to say, what ETA calls 'revolutionary taxation' is referred to by others as simple extortion. Several businessmen told me that they regularly paid more 'taxes' to ETA than to the central treasury. One person explained, 'Spain is corrupt and brutal, but at least the death sentence is not imposed for non-payment of taxes.' This aspect of ETA's economic activities is widely regarded as one factor seriously undermining the Basque economy.

3 In their many internal disputes the issue of Euskera was often converted into a bludgeon by ETA's Basque-speaking base against its Spanish-speaking leadership. Realizing the difficulties, the ETA leadership announced in *ZUTIK*, ETA's magazine, that 'Only in one case and with one aim can the provisional use of the languages of the oppressor be justified; to make possible the expulsion of the forces and administrative apparatus of genocide. The use of foreign languages is only legitimate for reasons of efficient resistance.' (*ZUTIK*, No. 23, 1965).

A more recent example occurred in July 1978 when one of the most radical nationalist parties, the ESB (Basque Socialist Convergence) split. The ESB was particularly emphatic on the need for the *reeuskaldunization* of Euskadi. Its party programme, for instance, stated that those party militants who do not speak Euskera are guilty of grave patriotic irresponsibility. However, the vast majority of the party's leaders were urbanite Spanish speakers. In the growing tensions between the base and the leadership, the linguistic ineptitude and hypocrisy of the leaders was the main argument used to oust the entire leadership and their Spanish-speaking supporters.

4 A variation of the 'colonialist model' is found in the argument – expressed with equal intensity by the moderates of the PNV and the radicals of ETA – that under Franco the Basque country was subjected to a highly detrimental and discriminatory process of Spanish exploitation 'because it was Basque'. This argument has three parts. First, Spain's regional policy was deliberately intended to undermine the Basque economy. Second, through policies in the public sector the Basque provinces were systematically drained of capital for the sole benefit of other parts of the country. The public funds that did return were used mainly to

support the oppressive Spanish administration in the Basque country. Third, Madrid nurtured a policy of massive immigration to the Basque country in order to annihilate the vestiges of Basque culture.

Without doubt, the Basque country suffered a net outflow of capital in the public sector, i.e. what was paid out in taxation and social security payments was greater than what was received in public investment, official credits and social benefits. But this fact does not constitute an argument. In the postwar period all of Europe's advanced regions have been subjected to a similar outflow in favour of their more depressed counterparts.

The relatively low levels of public investment during the period 1960–70 should be viewed more in terms of the redistributive functions of the state than any attempt by the state to deprive the Basque country of funds 'because it is Basque'.

However, the total flow of capital between the Basque country and the rest of Spain needs to be examined for the nationalist argument concerning 'decapitalization' to be placed in perspective. While the Basque country was a net contributor in the public sphere, it was also a net receiver in the private one. Available evidence suggests that the Basque region served as a strong pole of attraction for private investment capital from other parts of Spain. Indeed, a frequent argument expressed by Andalucian autonomists is that the Basque country and Catalonia have stripped Andalucia of its labour and capital resources.

5 This argument is reproduced uncritically in P. E. Mayo (1974), *The Roots of Identity*, Allen Lane, London. 'There has been a conscious attempt to dilute Basque culture by encouraging workers from other parts of Spain to seek work in Vizcaya and Guipúzcoa ...' (p. 111).

6 In the mathematical analysis of Larresoro no social or contextual factors that might influence linguistic choice are considered. He assumes that all Spanish-speakers are monolingual and all Basque-speakers are bilingual *and* communication is evenly distributed among all members of his statistical set. In one example, Larresoro takes five people and states that these five people can form twenty-six different groups. If one person (i.e. 20% of the five) is a Spanish-speaker – the rest bilingual – then conversation in fifteen of the twenty-six possible groups will be conducted in Spanish. In other words 20% of Spanish-speakers *desvasquizen* 58% of all conversation. A group with 60% Spanish speakers reduces to 3.8 'the communicative capacity of the Basque language'. Although Larresoro's arithmetic is correct, his sociolinguistic conclusions are highly questionable at best.

7 In 1980 ETA *militar* issued a warning stating that only singers who performed in Euskera would be tolerated in Euskadi.

8 The possible future effects of this nationalist cultural manipulation have been privately lamented by several leading Basque academicians. One important Basque cultural figure remarked while we were watching a group of young nationalists, 'They think they are protecting Euskera. They call it "renationalization". But they are destroying the language *and* the culture. These *abertzales* don't realize it yet. Those who do don't dare admit it. But, because of them, a hatred for the language is growing. When all this is over – when Euskadi is free – Euskera and our culture will be thrown away like so much repellent, poisoned meat.'

9 The statutes of several nationalist trade unions specifically bar workers who belong to non-nationalist political parties from membership. LAB and LAK are two examples.

10 Although Basque nationalism has always claimed Navarra to be part of Euskadi and Pamplona, the capital of Navarra, to be the capital of Euskadi, the issue did not receive much attention until December 1975. In December – in another futile attempt to create a unitary organization of the Basque opposition – the Asamblea Democratica de Euskadi (ADE) was formed. The main protagonist behind this organization was the Communist Party of Euskadi. The platform of the ADE demanded total amnesty for political prisoners, Basque autonomy, the right of Basque self-determination and so forth. The entire platform conformed roughly to that which the nationalists had stated would be an acceptable basis for unity. The issue over which the nationalists chose to justify their immediate condemnation of the Asamblea Democratica de Euskadi was Navarra. The ADE also demanded the immediate reinstatement of the Basque statute of 1936, in which Navarra was not included, and stated that, although it would be desirable for Navarra to form part of Euskadi, the decision would have to be made by the Navarrese themselves through a plebiscite. From this point on the debate concerning Navarra raged with accelerating ardour. The nationalists insisted, 'Navarra Euskadi da', (Navarra *is* Euskadi) and argued that to ask the Navarrese whether they were part of Euskadi or not was as nonsensical as asking a man whether he was male or female. This political position became not only part of the defining elements of the true 'Basque', but also incorporated into the nationalists' minimal platform for unity.

In Navarra itself the issue is complicated. First, the province is culturally divided between the Basque-speaking north and the Spanish-speaking south in which there is little sense of a Basque cultural identity. Second, in the Basque-speaking north Basque nationalism has always been weak. Instead right-wing parties who advocate a type of Navarrese nationalism which is more sympathetic to Spain than Euskadi are extremely influential.

11 PNV leaders immediately after the election issued statements aimed at discrediting the socialists' electoral victory. The most common argument used stated that the socialist vote was the immigrant vote and, hence, could not be considered either a conscientious or a useful vote. Certainly it was not the vote of the Basque people.

12 It is difficult to view the immigrant vote for the most intransigent and ethnically exclusive stream of Basque nationalism, Herri Batasuna, as representing support for the nationalist cause. Instead I would suggest that fundamentally this vote was a claim for Basque status. As discussed previously, the immigrants are socially fragmented and politically without a coherent expression or sense of power. They see their relation to Basque society in terms of an individual accommodation with Basques. Basque nationalists stress that to be 'Basque' requires the political option of Basque nationalism. In an economic situation in which the future for unskilled or semi-skilled youth is bleak indeed, the acquisition of Basque status is an essential precondition for any economic future at all. Arguably, the immigrant vote for HB also represented a blanket repudiation of present Basque society. HB is a type of permanent rejectionist party. It rejects parliamentary democracy, Basque autonomy, political plurality, the economic and social status quo, etc. It proposes millenarian solutions achieved by the purifying process of violence.

Conclusion

1 G. Joffé has pointed out (personal communication) that in the Moroccan nationalist movement against French occupation the traditional regional brokers

mobilized their clients in support of the nationalist cause and by so doing provided the Moroccan movement with a larger part of its social base.

2 Hugh Roberts (personal communication) has suggested that the Algerian government may be explicitly attempting to use patronage networks as one means to contain Kabyle opposition to its Arabization policy.

Bibliography

Newspapers and magazines

For period 1894–1936

La Lucha de Clases
Aberri
La Patria
El Correo Vasco
Bizkaitarra
Jagi-Jagi
Euzkadi
El Día
Euzkalduna

For period 1959–80

Euskaldunak
Enbata
Lan Deya
Zutik
Tierra Vasca
SAIOAK
Euskadi sozialista
Punto y Hora
Garaia
Zeruko Argia
Anaitasuna
Hautsi
Deia
Euzkadi Obrera

Archives

Archivo Municipal de Elgeta
Archivo Municipal de Eibar
Archivo Municipal de Elorrio
Archivo Municipal de Vergara
Archivo de la Exma. Diputación Provincial de Guipúzcoa
Archivo de la Exma. Diputación Provincial de Vizcaya
Archivo de Recuperación y Masonería, Salamanca
Archivo del Partido Nacionalista Vasco, Bayonne

Books and articles

Adams, R. (1970) 'Brokers and career mobility systems in the structure of complex societies', *Southwestern Journal of Anthropology*, 26.

Albaladejo, O. (1975) *La Crisis del Antigno Régimen en Guipuzcoa*, Madrid, Akal.

Anderson, B. (1983) *Imagined Communities*, London, Verso.

Angulo, José Maria de (1976) *La Abolición de los Fueros e Instituciones Vascongadas*, vol. 1, Aunamendi, originally published 1886.

Arana-Goiri, Sabino de, *Obras Completas*, Sabindiar-Batza, Bayona.
Arocena, Fausto (1964) *Guipúzcoa en la Historia*, Minotauro, Madrid.
Arpal Poblador, Jesús (1973) *Los Gargarza de Elgoibar*, San Sebastian.
(1977) 'Estructuras familiares y de parentesco en la sociedad estariental del País Vasco', *SAIOAK*, no. 1, San Sebastian.
Alzola y Mirondo, Pablo de (1902) 'La industria en Vizcaya', *Progreso Industrial de Vizcaya*, Bilbao.
Atkinson, William C. (1960) *A History of Spain and Portugal*, Penguin Books, London.
Azaola, José Miguel de (1972) *Vasconia y Su Destino, La Regionalización de Espana*, vol. 1, Revista de Occidente, Madrid.
Banco de Bilbao (1969, 1970, 1971, 1975, 1978) *Renta Nacional de Espana.*
Barandiaran, José Miguel de (1960) *El Mundo en la Mente Popular Vasca*, vol 5.1 and 4, Aunamendi, San Sebastian.
Barth, Fredrik (ed.) (1969) *Ethnic Groups and Boundaries*, Universitetsforlaget, Oslo.
Beltza (1974) *Nacionalismo Vasco (1076–1936)*, Ediciones Mugalde, Hendaye.
(1976) *Nacionalismo Vasco y Clases sociales*, Ediciones Mugalde, Hendaye.
(1978), *Del Carlismo al Nacionalismo Vasco*, Editorial Txertoa, San Sebastian.
Blok, A. (1974) *The Mafia of a Sicilian Village, 1860–1960*, Blackwell, Oxford.
Brenan, Gerald (1969) *The Spanish Labyrinth*, Cambridge University Press.
Bursain, Xabier de (1978) *Emakume, La Organización de la mujer en el nacionalismo vasco*, Revista de Estudios de Historia Social.
Campbell, J. (1964) *Honour, Family and Patronage*, Clarendon Press, Oxford.
(Campion) (1976) *Discursos Politicos y Literarios de Arturo Campion*, Editorial la Gran Enciclopedia Vasca, Bilbao.
Cano, Javier (1977) 'El derecho de Vizcaya en su historia', *Cultura Vasca*, vol. 1, Erein, San Sebastian.
Caro Baroja, Julio (1971) *Los Vascos*, Ediciones Istmo, Madrid.
(1974) *Introducción a La Historia Social e Economica del Pueblo Vasco*, Txertoa, San Sebastian.
(1975) *Los Pueblos de Espana*, Vols. 1 and 2, Ediciones Istmo, Madrid.
Carr, Raymond (1966) *Spain 1808–1939*, Clarendon Press, London.
Cillán Apalategui, Antonio (1975a) *La Foralidad Guipúzcoana*, Zarauz.
(1975b) *Sociologia electoral de Guipuzcoa (1900–36)*, Caja de Ahorros Municipal de San Sebastian.
Claveria, Carlos (1971) *Historia del Reino de Navarra*, Editorial Gomez, Pamplona.
Clissold, Stephen (1969) *Spain*, Thames and Hudson, London.
Cohen, A. (1969) *Custom and Politics in Urban Africa*, Routledge, London.
(1974) *Two-Dimensional Man*, Routledge, London.
Cohen, A. (ed.) (1974) *Urban Ethnicity*, ASA 12, Tavistock, London.
Collignon, R. (1984) 'Les Basques', *Mem. Soc. Anthrop.*, Paris, series 3.
Corcuera, J. (1977) 'Tradicionalismo y burguesía en la formación del nacionalismo vasco', *Materiales*, 5, Barcelona.
(1979) *Orígenes, Ideología y Organización del Nacionalismo Vasco, 1876–1904*, Siglo Veintiuno, Madrid.
Davis, J. (1977) *People of the Mediterranean*, Routledge and Kegan Paul, London.
Douglass, William (1969) *Death in Murelaga*, University of Washington Press.

(1971) 'Basque nationalism', in Oriol Pi-Sunyer (ed.), *The Limits of Integration: Ethnicity and Nationalism in Modern Europe*, Research Reports, no. 9, Dept. of Anthropology, University of Massachusetts.

Echevarria, Mario de, y Palacio, M. Alberto de (1894), *Higienización de Bilbao.*

Eisenstadt, S. N. and Lemarchand, R. (eds.) (1981) *Political Clientelism, Patronage and Development*, Sage, London.

Elorza, Antonio (1975) 'Sobre ideologias y organización del primer nacionalismo Vasco', in *La Crisis de fin de siglo: ideologia y literatura*, Ariel, Barcelona.

(1976) 'El tema rural en la evolución del nacionalismo vasco', in Delgado (ed.), *La Cuestion Agraria en la España Contemporanea*, EDICUSA, Madrid.

(1978) 'Sobre los orígenes literarios del nacionalismo', *SAIOAK*, no. 2, San Sebastian.

(1978) *Ideologias del Nacionalismo Vasco*, Txertoa, San Sebastian.

Erro Lascurain, Fernando (1976) *Introducción a la Problema Vasca*, vols. 1 and 2, Aunamendi, San Sebastian.

Escudero, M. (1976) *La Autonomia del País Vasco desde el Pasado al Futuro*, Txertoa, San Sebastian.

(1978) *Euskadi: Dos Comunidades*, Txertoa, San Sebastian.

Farias, Pedro (1975) *Breve Historía Constitucional de España*, Doncel, Madrid.

Fernandez Albaladejo, Pablo (1975) *La Crisis del Antiguo Regimen en Guipúzcoa 1766–1833*, Akal, Madrid.

(1977) 'Manuel de Larramendi: la particular historía de Guipúzcoa', *SAIOAK*, no. 1, San Sebastian.

Fusi, Juan Pablo (1975) *Politica Obrera en el País Vasco (1880–1923)*, Turner, Madrid.

(1979) *El Problema Vasco en La II Republica*, Turner, Madrid.

Gaile, G. L. (1980) 'The spread-backwash concept', *Regional Studies*, vol. 14, pp. 15–25.

Gallo, Max (1973) *Spain Under Franco*, George Allen and Unwin, London.

Gallop, Rodney (1948) *Los Vascos*, Castilla, Madrid.

Garcia Venero, Maximiano (1969) *Historía del Nacionalismo Vasco*, Editora Nacional, 3rd edn, Madrid.

Gaur (1969) *Asi está la Enseñanza Primaria*, San Sebastian.

(1970) *El Pueblo de Rentería en 1970*, Rentería.

(1971) *Euskera Gaur*, Zarantz.

Geertz, Clifford (1975) *The Interpretation of Cultures*, Hutchinson, London.

Geografía Histórica de la Lengua Vasca (Siglos VI al XIX) (1966), Aunamendi, San Sebastian.

Gellner, E. (1964) *Thought and Change*, London, Weidenfeld and Nicolson.

(1972) 'Scale and nation', paper prepared for participants in Burg Wartenstein Symposium, No. 55.

(1983) *Nations and Nationalism*, Blackwell, Oxford.

Gellner, E. and Waterbury, J. (eds.) (1977) *Patrons and Clients*, Duckworth, London.

Gerth, H. and Mills, C. W. (1948) *From Max Weber: Essays in Sociology*, Routledge and Kegan Paul, London.

Gorrono, Inaki (1975) *Experiencía cooperativa en el País Vasco*, Zugaza, Durango.

Goti Iturriago, G. L. (1962) 'Los Grupos sanguíneos de los vascos', *La Gran Enciclopedia Vasco I*, pp. 39–65.

Greenwood, Davydd J. (1977) 'Continuity in change: Spanish Basque ethnicity as a historical process', in Esman, M. (ed.) *Ethnic Conflict in the Western World*, Cornell University Press, Ithaca.

Hansen, Edward G. (1977) *Rural Catalonia under the Franco Regime*, Cambridge University Press.

Hechter, M. (1975) *Internal Colonialism*, Routledge, London.

Hechter, M. and Levi, M. (1979) 'The comparative analysis of ethno-regional movements', *Ethnic and Racial Studies*, vol. 2, no. 3, Routledge and Kegan Paul, London.

Heiberg, Marianne (1973) 'The Basque Jigsaw: A study of various aspects of Basque nationalism', Diploma dissertation, University of London.

(1975) 'Insiders/outsiders: Basque nationalism', *Arch. europ. sociol.*, 16, Paris.

(1984) 'Ethnic nationalists and patron-clients in Mediterranean Europe', in Boissevain, J. (ed.), *Ethnic Challenge: The Politics of Ethnicity in Europe*, Herodot, Gottingen.

Heiberg, M. and Escudero, M. (1977) 'Sabino de Arana: la logica del nacionalismo vasco', *Materiales*, 5, Barcelona.

Hermet, Guy (1974) *The Communists in Spain*, Saxon House, D. C. Heath Ltd, Lexington.

Hobsbawm, Eric (1977) 'Some reflections on "The Break-up of Britain"', *New Left Review*, Sept.–Oct.

Von Humboldt, Wilhelm Freicher (1975) *Los Vascos*, Auñamendi, San Sebastian.

Kedourie, Elie (1971) *Nationalism*, Hutchinson University Library, London.

Kofman, E. (1980) 'Differential modernization, social conflicts and ethnoregionalism in Corsica', paper presented to the Conference on Social Movements in Southern Europe, University College, London.

Laborda Martin, J. J. (1978) 'El arranque de un largo protagonismo: la recuperación comercial de Vizcaya a comíenzos del siglo XVIII', *SAIOAK*, no. 2, San Sebastian.

Larronde, Jean-Claude (1977) *El Nacionalismo Vasco: su origen y su ideología en la obra de Sabino Arana-Goiri*, Editorial Txertoa, San Sebastian.

Linz, Juan J. and Miguel, Armando de (1966) 'Within-nation differences and comparisons: the eight Spains', in Merritt and Rokkan (eds.), *Comparing Nations*, Yale University Press.

Loizos, P. (1972) 'The progress of Greek nationalism in Cyprus: 1878–1970', paper prepared for Anthropology Seminar, University of Sussex.

Martinez-Alier, J. (1971) *Labourers and Landowners in Southern Spain*, George Allen and Unwin, London.

Mendizabal, A. (1980) 'Influencia de la politica económica Española en el desarrollo industrial del País Vasco', University of Deusto, Ph.D. thesis.

Minogue, K. R. (1967) *Nationalism*, Methuen, London.

Monreal, Gregorio (1977) 'Las instituciones Vascas', *Cultura Vasca*, 1, Erein, San Sebastian.

Mukarovski, Hans G. (1972) 'El Vascuence y el Bereber', *Euskara*, 17, Bilbao.

Nairn, T. (1977) *The Break-up of Britain*, New Left Books, London.

Navajas Laporte, Alvaro (1975) *La Ordenación Consuetudinaria del Caserío en Guipúzcoa*, San Sebastian.
(1977) 'El derecho Guipúzcoana', *Cultura Vasca*, 1, Erein, San Sebastian.
Nunez, Luis C. (1977a) *Opresión y Defensa del Euskera*, Txertoa, San Sebastian.
(1977b) *Clases Sociales en Euskadi*, Txertoa, San Sebastian.
Orella, José Luis de (1977) 'Navarra y su Anexión a Castilla', *Cultura Vasca*, 1, Erein, San Sebastian.
(1977) 'Problematica y actualidad de las Guerras Carlistas', *Cultura Vasca*, 1, Erein, San Sebastian.
Ortzi (1975) *Historía de Euskadi: el nacionalismo vasco y ETA*, Ruedo Ibérico, Paris.
Otazu y Llana, Alfonso de (1973) *El 'Igualiterismo' Vasco: Mito y Realidad*, Txertoa, San Sebastian.
Ott, Sandra J. (1981) *The Circle of Mountains: A Basque Shepherding Community*, Oxford University Press.
Oyarzun, R. (1965) *Historía del Carlismo*, Madrid.
Payne, Stanley (1968) *Franco's Spain*, Routledge and Kegan Paul, London.
(1974) *El Nacionalismo Vasco: de sus origenes a la ETA*, Dopesa, Barcelona.
Perroux, F. (1955) 'Note sur la notion de la "pole de croissance"', *Cahiers de l'Institut de Science Appliqué*, 8.
Pinedo, Emiliano Fernández de (1974) *Credimento Economico y Transformaciónes Sociales del País Vasco 1100/1850*, Siglo Veintiuno Editores, Madrid.
(1977) 'El campesino parcelario Vasco en el feudalismo desarrollado (x. XV–XVIII)', *SAIOAK*, no. 1, San Sebastian.
Pitt-Rivers, Julian (1954) *The People of the Sierra*, Weidenfeld and Nicholson, London; Chicago, Chicago University Press, 1961.
(1977) *The Fate of Shechem, or The Politics of Sex*, Cambridge University Press.
(1965) 'Honour and social status', in J. G. Peristiany (ed.), *Honour and Shame. The Values of Mediterranean Society*, London, Weidenfeld and Nicolson.
Portilla, M. Gonzales (1977) 'Los orígenes de la sociedad capitalista en el País Vasco: transformaciónes económicas y sociales en Vizcaya', *SAIOAK*, no. 1.
Roberts, D. F., Pooper, E. and Kerr, B. (1976) 'Dermatoglyphic variation among Spanish Basques', *Man*, vol. 2, no. 4, December.
Rokkan, S. (ed.) (1982) *The Politics of Territorial Identity*, Sage, London.
Romero-Maura, J. (1977) '*Caciquismo* as a political system', in Gellner, E. and Waterbury, J. (eds.), *Patrons and Clients*, Duckworth, London.
Sanchez Carrion, José Maria (1972) *El Estado Actual del Vascuence en la Provincia de Navarra*, Disputación Foral de Navarra.
Sarrailh de Ihartz, Fernando (pseud.) (1973) *Vasconia*, 2nd edn., Ediciones Norbait, Buenos Aires.
Schneider, P., Schneider, J. and Hansen, E. (1972) 'Modernization and development: the role of regional elites and noncorporate groups in the European Mediterranean', *Comparative Studies in Society and History*, vol. 14.
Seton-Watson, H. (1977) *Nations and States*, Westview Press, Boulder, Colorado.
Siadeco (1979) *Conflicto Linguistico en Euskadi*, Euskaltzaindia, Bilbao.
Smith, A. D. (1981) *The Ethnic Revival*, Cambridge University Press.

Solozabal, Juan José (1975) *El Primer Nacionalismo Vasco*, Tucar Ediciones, Madrid.

Tejada, Francisco Elias de (1963) *El Señorio de Vizcaya*, Minotauro, Madrid.

Thomas, Hugh (1965) *The Spanish Civil War*, Penguin, London.

Trevor-Roper, H. R. (1956) *The European Witch Craze*, Harper and Row, New York.

Tuñon De Lara, M. (1975) *La España del Siglo XIX*, vols. 1 and 2, Editorial Laia, Barcelona.

Txillardegi (1973) *Proyecto de Manifeste Vasco*, Mugalde, Hendaye.

Ugalde, Martin de (1974) *Sintesis de La Historía del País Vasco*, Seminarios y Ediciones, Madrid.

Vicens Vives, Jaime (1970) *Approaches to the History of Spain*, University of California Press.

(1972) *Historía económica de Espana*, Barcelona.

Weber, Eugene (1976) *Peasants into Frenchmen*, Stanford University Press.

Xaho, Agustin (1976) *Viaje a Navarra durante la Insurrección de los Vascos*, trans. Xabier Mendiquren.

Zabala, Federico de (1971) *Historia del Pueblo Vasco*, Collección Auñamendi, vols. 1 and 2, San Sebastian.

(1977a) 'Fueros y conciertos económicos', *Cultura Vasca*, 1, Erein, San Sebastian.

(1977b) 'Personalidad politica de las Provincias Vascas en el Medievo', *Cultura Vasca*, 1, Erein, San Sebastian.

INDEX

Cambridge Studies in Social Anthropology

Editor: Jack Goody

1 The Political Organisation of Unyamwezi
R. G. ABRAHAMS

2 Buddhism and the Spirit Cults in North-East Thailand*
S. J. TAMBIAH

3 Kalahari Village Politics: An African Democracy
ADAM KUPER

4 The Rope of Moka: Big-Men and Ceremonial Exchange in Mount Hagen, New Guinea*
ANDREW STRATHERN

5 The Majangir: Ecology and Society of a Southwest Ethiopian People
JACK STAUDER

6 Buddhist Monk, Buddhist Layman: A Study of Urban Monastic Organisation in Central Thailand
JANE BUNNAG

7 Contexts of Kinship: An Essay in the Family Sociology of the Gonja of Northern Ghana
ESTHER N. GOODY

8 Marriage among a Matrilineal Elite: A Family Study of Ghanaian Civil Servants
CHRISTINE OPPONG

9 Elite Politics in Rural India: Political Stratification and Political Alliances in Western Maharashtra
ANTHONY T. CARTER

10 Women and Property in Morocco: Their Changing Relation to the Process of Social Stratification in the Middle Atlas
VANESSA MAHER

11 Rethinking Symbolism*
DAN SPERBER, translated by Alice L. Morton

12 Resources and Population: A Study of the Gurungs of Nepal
ALAN MACFARLANE

13 Mediterranean Family Structures
EDITED BY J. G. PERISTIANY

14 Spirits of Protest: Spirit-Mediums and the Articulation of Consensus among the Zezuru of Southern Rhodesia (Zimbabwe)
PETER FRY

15 World Conqueror and World Renouncer: A Study of Buddhism and Polity in Thailand against a Historical Background*
S. J. TAMBLAH

16 Outline of a Theory of Practice*
PIERRE BOURDIEU, translated by Richard Nice

17 Production and Reproduction: A Comparative Study of the Domestic Domain*
JACK GOODY

18 Perspectives in Marxist Anthropology*
MAURICE GODELIER, translated by Robert Brain

19 The Fate of Shechem, or the Politics of Sex: Essays in the Anthropology of the Mediterranean
JULIAN PITT-RIVERS
20 People of the Zongo: The Transformation of Ethnic Identities in Ghana
ENID SCHILDKROUT
21 Casting out Anger: Religion among the Taita of Kenya
GRACE HARRIS
22 Rituals of the Kandyan State
H. L. SENEVIRATNE
23 Australian Kin Classification
HAROLD W. SCHEFFLER
24 The Palm and the Pleiades: Initiation and Cosmology in Northwest Amazonia
STEPHEN HUGH-JONES
25 Nomads of Southern Siberia: The Pastoral Economies of Tuva
S. I. VAINSHTEIN, translated by Michael Colenso
26 From the Milk River: Spatial and Temporal Processes in Northwest Amazonia
CHRISTINE HUGH-JONES
27 Day of Shining Red: An Essay on Understanding Ritual
GILBERT LEWIS
28 Hunters, Pastoralists and Ranchers: Reindeer Economies and their Transformations
TIM INGOLD
29 The Wood-Carvers of Hong Kong: Craft Production in the World Capitalist Periphery
EUGENE COOPER
30 Minangkabau Social Formations: Indonesian Peasants and the World Economy
JOEL S. KAHN
31 Patrons and Partisans: A Study of Two Southern Italian Communes
CAROLINE WHITE
32 Muslim Society*
ERNEST GELLNER
33 Why Marry Her? Society and Symbolic Structures
LUC DE HEUSCH, translated by Janet Lloyd
34 Chinese Ritual and Politics
EMILY MARTIN AHERN
35 Parenthood and Social Reproduction: Fostering and Occupational Roles in West Africa
ESTHER N. GOODY
36 Dravidian Kinship
THOMAS R. TRAUTMANN
37 The Anthropological Circle: Symbol Function, History*
MARC AUGE, translated by Martin Thom
38 Rural Society in Southeast Asia
KATHLEEN GOUGH
39 The Fish-People: Linguistic Exogamy and Tukanoan Identity in Northwest Amazonia
JEAN E. JACKSON
40 Karl Marx Collective: Economy, Society and Religion in a Siberian Collective Farm*
CAROLINE HUMPHREY
41 Ecology and Exchange in the Andes
EDITED BY DAVID LEHMANN
42 Traders without Trade: Responses to Trade in two Dyula Communities
ROBERT LAUNAY
43 The Political Economy of West African Agriculture*
KEITH HART
44 Nomads and the Outside World
A. M. KHAZANOV, translated by Julia Crookenden
45 Actions, Norms and Representations: Foundations of Anthropological Inquiry*
LADISLAV HOLY AND MILAN STUCHLIK
46 Structural Models in Anthropology*
PER HAGE AND FRANK HARARY

47 Servants of the Goddess: The Priests of a South Indian Temple
C. J. FULLER
48 Oedipus and Job in West African Religion*
MEYER PORTES
49 The Buddhist Saints of the Forest and the Cult of Amulets: A Study in Charisma, Hagiography, Sectarianism, and Millennial Buddhism*
S. J. TAMBIAH
50 Kinship and Marriage: An Anthropological Perspective (available in paperback in the USA only)
ROBIN FOX
51 Individual and Society in Guiana: A Comparative Study of Amerindian Social Organization*
PETER RIVIERE
52 People and the State: An Anthropology of Planned Development*
A. F. ROBERTSON
53 Inequality among Brothers: Class and Kinship in South China
RUBIE S. WATSON
54 On Anthropological Knowledge*
DAN SPERBER
55 Tales of the Yanomami: Daily Life in the Venezuelan Forest*
JACQUES LIZOT, translated by Ernest Simon
56 The Making of Great Men: Male Domination and Power among the New Guinea Baruya*
MAURICE GODELIER, translated by Rupert Swyer
57 Age Class Systems: Social Institutions and Polities Based on Age*
BERNARDO BERNARDI, translated by David I. Kertzer
58 Strategies and Norms in a Changing Matrilineal Society: Descent, Succession and Inheritance among the Toka of Zambia
LADISLAV HOLY
59 Native Lords of Quito in the Age of the Incas: The Political Economy of North-Andean Chiefdoms
FRANK SALOMON
60 Culture and Class in Anthropology and History: A Newfoundland Illustration
GERALD SIDER
61 From Blessing to Violence: History and Ideology in the Circumcision Ritual of the Merina of Madagascar*
MAURICE BLOCH
62 The Huli Response to Illness
STEPHEN FRANKEL
63 Social Inequality in a Northern Portuguese Hamlet: Land, Late Marriage, and Bastardy, 1870–1978
BRIAN JUAN O'NEILL
64 Cosmologies in the Making: A Generative Approach to Cultural Variation in Inner New Guinea
FREDRIK BARTH
65 Kinship and Class in the West Indies: A Genealogical Study of Jamaica and Guyana
RAYMOND T. SMITH

* Available in paperback